WILD WILD EAST

Advance Praise for the Book

'A fascinating view into a subject many are familiar with but few really understand. Thakur takes us into an area poised to become more prominent as America cuts itself off from the world.'—**Aakar Patel, human rights and political activist, and author of, most recently, *After Messiah***

'At a time when immigration and job displacement dominate headlines, *Wild Wild East* takes readers deep inside the hidden machinery of the H-1B visa system and the shadow economy it fuels. Through years of immersive reporting, the author follows three unforgettable characters—an out-of-work Texas programmer, a tenacious IT veteran from Hyderabad and a young engineering graduate escaping an abusive home—as their lives collide with the murky world of "desi consultancies". What begins as the pursuit of a better future unspools into a gripping tale of scams, broken promises and impossible choices, rendered with the pace of a thriller and the intimacy of a novel. This is a moving, deeply human and empathetic portrait of a topic that is too often simplified and turned into fuel for demagoguery.'—**Akash Kapur, author of *Better to Have Gone: Love, Death, and the Quest for Utopia* and *India Becoming: A Portrait of Life in Modern India***

'This remarkable book combines autobiography, intensive real-life engagements and a rare interpretive voice to tell the story of a sad corner of the digital world, of skilled computer workers caught between semi-urban India and various nooks and crannies of the USA. This is a radical view of the world of labour visas that Trump has turned into a permanent purgatory.'—**Arjun Appadurai, anthropologist of globalisation and author of, most recently, *Failure***

'Before he became a journalist, Tanul Thakur nearly got trapped in the H-1B pipeline he once believed in. *Wild Wild East* is a gripping exposé of a shadow system that exploits ambition and fuels the global tech economy—one as relevant today as ever, especially in an era where American presidents promise reform but weaponise immigration. With a rare blend of lived experience and investigative rigour, Tanul gives us the untold story of a modern caste system: coded in visas, bound by silence.'—**Hansal Mehta, award-winning filmmaker (and an ex-IT professional)**

'Tanul Thakur's *Wild Wild East* is a brilliant and infuriating book. It reads like a novel. It hits with the force of a criminal chargesheet. It reveals a transcontinental fraud involving Indian staffing firms and American corporations and government agencies that seems to make everyone rich—everyone, that is, except for workers like the three brave characters at the centre of the story.'—**McKenzie Funk, staff reporter, *ProPublica*, and author of, most recently, *The Hank Show: How a House-Painting, Drug-Running DEA Informant Built the Machine That Rules Our Lives***

'Tanul Thakur has written a remarkable, deeply researched and gripping account—told through the life stories of those affected—of one of the most significant global movements of people in recent decades: the H-1B temporary visa programme, which has linked India and the United States, reshaped both economies, created winners and losers in both countries and stoked political controversy. Thakur exposes the systematic abuse of the programme by bad actors, and the resulting shattered dreams, while placing at the centre of his account a remarkable story of interpersonal solidarity across divides. This is a book that will educate readers about the seamier side of globalisation and make them think hard about what a just and effective approach to outsourcing and to immigration—beyond being for or against—may require.'—**Sanjay Reddy, Professor of Economics, The New School, New York**

A brilliant, heartfelt account. The perfect, timely book for understanding the encounter of two impostors—the American dream and the Indian gaming the system.'—**Siddhartha Deb, journalist, novelist and author of, most recently, *Twilight Prisoners: The Rise of the Hindu Right and the Decline of India***

WILD WILD EAST

Exiled Americans, Enslaved Indians and the Systemic Abuse of the H-1B Visa Programme

TANUL THAKUR

context

cntxt

Published by Context, an imprint of Westland Books, a division of Nasadiya Technologies Private Limited, in 2026

No. 269/2B, First Floor, 'Irai Arul', Vimalraj Street, Nethaji Nagar, Alapakkam Main Road, Maduravoyal, Chennai 600095

ISBN: 9789371970501

10 9 8 7 6 5 4 3 2 1

Typeset by Jojy Philip

Printed at Manipal Technologies Limited, Manipal

'There are two modes of invading private property. The first, by which the poor plunder the rich … sudden and violent; the second, by which the rich plunder the poor, slow and legal.'

—John Taylor, *An Inquiry Into the Principles and Policies of the Government of the United States* (1814)

'*Vasudhaiva Kutumbakam* [the whole world is one family].'

—*The Maha Upanishad*

Contents

Introduction

One evening in late 2010, I repeated a soul-sapping ritual in my dorm room: completing an application, uploading my resume, hoping my luck would revive. As an international student at an American university, I had to snag a job within three months of graduating. If not, I'd have to return home. I had five months left. My $40,000 loan was making me melt with stress, because over 400 applications had produced just one outcome: silence.

And then, my phone rang.

A recruiter on the line, an Indian woman. The clouds disappeared; a beam blazed. I had applied to this company through my college's career portal. Expecting a phone interview, I wore my Sincere Employee Voice and unloaded. But in less than five minutes, something else happened.

'We've selected you for a business analyst position. Your starting salary will be $60,000, and we'll sponsor you an H-1B visa.'

H-1B Visa.

My desperation, my dream. It'd allow me to work in the US, clear my loan and begin a blissful life. Her firm offered me everything. Still, it made no sense because she had asked nothing about me, my skills, my interests. Did she even realise I studied electrical engineering, not IT, making me unfit for the job? No, she didn't intend to hire but trap me. So I grilled her: 'Have you read my resume?' 'Do you know my major?' 'Do you have any electrical engineering jobs?'

'No problem, Tanul,' she droned on. 'We'll give you one-month training and place you at a Fortune 500 company.' She sounded indifferent, almost tired, as if mocking my naivety.

'Wait, sorry to cut you short. Are you from a desi consultancy?'

She hesitated. 'Yes.'

'Will you do me a favour?'

'Tell me.'

'Don't call me ever again.'

Desi consultancy: an IT body shop owned by a desi and almost exclusively hiring desis. A term that had entered my life, through my Indian friends, just a few months ago. I knew what such firms did, and I wanted nothing to do with them. I took a bus to the college's Career Center and complained about the company to an employee, convincing her to 'blacklist' it.

'What happened?'

'It's a long story, but this is a huge immigration scam. They exploit desperate foreign students.'

I had arrived in the US two years ago to escape my past. I had failed to score respectable marks in class XII. I had failed to secure impressive ranks in engineering entrance exams. I had failed. Like many Indians destined to worship engineering, I resembled a lobotomised mass: brain-dead, unconscious, indifferent. I'd drift with the herd, and do anything, to find success. Only one tag guaranteed respect, where what I did mattered less than where I was: America. I enrolled in a course in Manipal, which allowed me to transfer my credits to an American school after two years. I slogged through the semesters, scored decent grades and landed in an engineering wonderland, the University of Illinois at Urbana-Champaign (UIUC), whose alums had invented transistors, integrated circuits, light-emitting diodes, transforming our lives.

Over a dozen peers from Manipal, too, made it to the same school. Most of us had simple goals: a good job, a good salary, a good life. We cared little about bending the rules. We often 'collaborated' on weekly assignments, which demanded original work. Soon, we created more rules, such as partnering with a 'firang' (a foreigner), someone passionate about engineering, for tough lab courses.

In one semester, I chose a friend from Manipal. I didn't want to be a parasite; I wanted to learn. The course, however, defeated and embarrassed us, making me envy those with brilliant (firang) partners. Desperate for a better grade, I once copy-pasted a lab report from an Indian senior—without even skimming through it—and submitted it to the teaching assistant (TA). He called us after the class. I had described a circuit board with sixteen switches; the current machines had eight. 'Many Indian students have cheated this semester,' he told us. 'It hurts me, because I'm also from India.'

I wrote him a long apology. Another Manipal friend, enrolled under a different TA, had also got caught. After hearing about my remorse, he said, 'Thakur bhai, your English is amazing. Can I copy your email?' I shot him a blank stare; he didn't laugh.

Over time I reformed, choosing a specialisation that suited my interests, securing an internship at a firm in Colorado and converting it into a full-time job. Even in my new life, though, desi consultancies continued to tail me. They emailed me job openings, called me, chewed my head. But not all desis loathed them. Many Manipal folks now worked for them. One landed at my company as an 'experienced' IT consultant. A close friend had opened his own consultancy.

Yet I had not heard of this world in India—or my first year in the US. It must be the Indian diaspora's best-kept secret. As I kept reading about this knotty industry, my disgust morphed into intrigue, then fascination, then obsession. Because this America never featured in discussions or plans, movies or novels, dreams or desires. This America, swarming with desperate desis, never existed.

Who were these Indians, and what was this America?

Even though my firm treated me well, I turned restless and disenchanted. A nice salary didn't make me confident or contented or successful. My UIUC experience had de-lobotomised me, shaking me awake to the realisation that only one key would unlock freedom and success: passion. I had hidden a secret for long: a love for writing. So I wrote.

I tried a 'subversive' campus novel—you know, something like Chetan Bhagat but, erm, not Chetan Bhagat? It followed three college friends in India who transferred their credits to an American school. (Yeah, not autobiographical at all.) The climax featured my latest obsession: a desi consultancy. My restlessness intensified when I discovered another passion, narrative non-fiction, rivalling my interest in cinema. Maybe I could blend them both: novelistic writing and movies?

Two years into my job, I resigned, took a pay cut and raced to India to spark my love story: a job as a features writer at a film magazine. I wrote long profiles of professionals on the margins of fame, such as an Amitabh Bachchan 'duplicate' and a controversial Bhojpuri singer, examining identity, self-deception and misogyny in popular culture. Narrative non-fiction bewitched me, especially those books where journalists hid in the background, designing an addictive plot—marked by characters, scenes, dialogues—approximating a novel. A year later, I wished to try it myself. One day, the topic flashed through my mind, like a shadow that never left: desi consultancies.

Back then, I knew little about the H-1B programme, or its contentious political nature. I neither harboured ulterior motives nor strained to prove a point. Shunning ideological prisons, I sought to just follow a story where Indians completed a confounding loop: doing scams, getting scammed; perpetuating exploitation, enduring exploitation. Such a premise would let me investigate a slice of modern India: its morality, 'enslavement', identity. Desi consultants' despair disconcerted me, while desi consultancies' secrets fascinated me—few outsiders knew about them. All of it in America: how free was the land of the free?

But the results dwarfed my expectations. Turns out, desi consultancies weren't the only ones hiding secrets. So this book also incorporates those rabbit holes within rabbit holes. All along the way, though, I remembered my main goal: foregrounding normal people in an abnormal world. I yearned to be a movie camera: recording and relaying, revealing and receding. I didn't want to persuade but share.

I

DREAM

1

Virgil Bierschwale had the world in his fist. An IT contractor in Vegas, he had got a pay hike of 50 per cent. Annual salary, $140,400. He had bought two pieces of land—five acres each, one contained a rundown house, the other empty—near his hometown, Harper, in Texas. Now the next step, his last step: save enough, quit IT, trade stocks, country club, golf course, nineteenth hole. $100,000: one more project would set him free.

A retirement plan at forty-five. Vintage Virgil. Like most country boys in Harper, he had three options after school: stay on the ranch and become a rancher or find a job in the oil field or join the military. He had done all three—swept his whole world. But given a tiny lot, he dreamt of a high-rise that tickled the moon. So he found a new world, a new love: coding. Entering the IT industry in 1988, he travelled across the country, sleuthing out codes. Reverse engineering became his passion and prowess. His earnings soared: $25 an hour for the first six years, $50 in 1999 and now a new bump, $67.5. Nothing seemed impossible—not even retiring in his forties—because this Navy veteran, like his country, was exceptional: 'ten feet tall' and 'bulletproof'.

The Vegas project ended in early 2003, and he headed to Harper, where his girlfriend, Lisa, waited for him. He followed his decade-old routine: check career websites, search for jobs, drop his resume. Even a glance confirmed his presumption: that countless programming jobs paid over $45 per hour. He cast his net far and wide.

Virgil had cleared the raw land's mortgage and lived on the second property, hoping to soon pay the remaining amount. He spent the day job hunting and met with friends in the evening. Harper always had enough folks, enough pastimes, enough beer. Years and years passed, and the town remained unchanged: same old, good old. Ditto its people: after serving a few years in the military, they were all here, all the time.

But unlike Harper, something else had changed.

In the past, recruiters contacted him in a few weeks, and in less than a month—or two—he resumed his journey. This time, nothing. Not even emails of rejection. Days became weeks; weeks became months. His desperation leapt; his savings sank. Besides his long-standing dues—to the Internal Revenue Service (IRS) and his ex-wife for child support—the short-term payments worried him more: monthly mortgages for the house and the car. More weeks: nothing. One more month: nothing. Hundreds of applications: nothing.

What happened?

Was it just him? Had he been blackballed? But why, for what? Did he piss someone off? Was his name on a debarred list? He had been employed for the last fifteen years. This silence had to mean something; it had to speak.

Quick money meant a local gig. He approached grocery stores. To save the house, he needed $500 per week. For $10 an hour, he could work fifty hours a week. But the replies deflated him further: 'We can't pay that much', 'you won't stay when the times get better', 'you're overqualified'.

The unemployed Virgil turned into a new person: cynical, impatient, short-tempered. The days shrank; the nights lingered. Quarrels with Lisa flared into fights. He had to fix this. Somehow. So he camped out in front of the computer. Started applying from the morning and kept at it—search, upload, submit, repeat, repeat, repeat—till there was nothing left to apply, till he had nothing left.

Still no job.

No car, either. He couldn't afford the mortgage, and he still had bills to pay. He sold the raw land. With that $10,000, he paid the

IRS. He needed an extra $10,000 to save the second one. He hoped to convince the owner: some more time, and he'd arrange the cash. No point though. He had already decided. Virgil had planned a life in that house. He had made plans, many plans. But here he was, homeless in his own home.

Even Lisa left.

Six months. February 2003: a girlfriend, a house, a future. August 2003: a forty-five-year-old staying with his mother, unable to afford rent or food. He still applied daily. What else was left anyway? Every day, the same thought: plenty of jobs, all around the country. Jobs that paid well. Jobs that, in just a few months, would solve everything. Days and weeks dissolved, and the questions amplified: what if this was it? What if he got no more emails, no more phone calls, no more jobs? For how long would he wait? For how long could he wait? What if the night had forgotten to leave?

Naw, it would come back.

Maybe it was a phase. A numbers game—a dance of probability: the more job applications, the better—like how it was, like how it had been. So he applied and applied. On some days, hope swelled like ferocious waves. Just one company, one interview, one day. Just one chance: a flick of a match would swallow a thousand nights.

Over a year passed. Maybe his resume was the problem—something must be wrong after all—so he consulted his friends on the programmers' email list. They helped him rewrite the resume. Tried one version and applied, tried another and applied, tried one more and on and on. A nested loop of revisions and submissions, and still, nothing changed: as if he didn't exist.

After exhausting all his options, he was left with nothing but a question. A simple question. Just two words. Most punishments sprang from offences. But what if the punishment existed on its own: what would you do, where would you go? A question wailed by many before Virgil.

'Why me?'

2

P.K. Sreenivas, an IT worker, stood outside a Ganesh temple, in Chennai, at such an ungodly hour when even the gods were sleeping. At two-thirty in the night, the temple doors were shut. He mumbled a prayer and, twenty minutes later, reached the American consulate for the H-1B visa interview, a temporary work permit for the 'best and the brightest' foreign workers.

Hundreds of applicants had assembled outside the consulate. Hawkers sailed through the queue, hustling tea, cigarettes, snacks. Many hopefuls, like him, hailed from Hyderabad and worked in IT. Sreenivas had to nail this interview. Somehow. Only an American visa could wipe away the stains of his past life.

In 1992, at age eighteen, he had scored so low in class XII that he failed to meet the cut-off for engineering in his state. He became something he had not even considered: a BA graduate. Sreenivas switched to IT, via diplomas and certifications, and dreamt big: a multinational firm. The gatekeepers woke him up. 'How did you do IT with a BA background?' Satyam Computer's HR asked him. The pattern persisted. Every door locked; every knock unanswered. More than their words, their mannerisms deflated him. The way they looked at him, sized him up—as if he were 'some kind of a thief'.

His brother-in-law helped him find a job. It vanished in six months. The company's manufacturing unit shut, thanks to the upper management's corruption. He got a job in the Netherlands, but the firm withdrew the offer. An Indian software company had committed fraud, so the Dutch consulate was rejecting Indian applicants. But a 'divine coincidence' saved him next: an IT job at the Tirumala Tirupati Devasthanams (TTD), a trust managing an iconic temple. He enjoyed the work but ran into the same old problem—the big old problem. He met a manager whose eyes welled up explaining the pervasive corruption.

Sreenivas got a break in 1998: an IT body shop in the US offered him an H-1B visa. He received the documents during his TTD stint: the approved petition, the offer letter, the Labor Condition Application. This was it. A rare chance to step outside his shadow—to step inside the temple. The doors won't be locked forever.

So, in early 1999, this BA graduate stood among engineers for an H-1B visa. He entered the consulate, finished the formalities and awaited his turn. A recurring pattern: an applicant at the counter, a conversation and the visa officer handing out the 221(g) form, which meant rejection. One by one, all of them met the same fate. Only one reason explained it: the 'fake Hyderabad BTech racket'. Countless applicants with fraudulent degrees applying for H-1B visas. But he was different—he had cut no corners, done no fraud. When his turn came, he stood up and strode towards the counter. The visa officer asked no questions and gave him the 221(g) form. His passport's back page featured a new entry: 'AFU'.

AFU? Anti-Fraud Unit. Bizarre: rejected for years for not being an engineer, rejected that day for resembling an engineer—a dubious engineer—a young IT worker from Hyderabad. This was the India he wanted to escape, where someone else broke the rules, and he paid the fine.

The visa rejection made him hungry. Before the door banged shut on him, he hadn't looked at the world outside. But now his mind, body and soul ached for 'Dream America'. His wait ended soon because that world knocked again. The Y2K bug had heightened the demand for IT professionals in the US. Body shops, promising visas to desperate techies, conducted interviews in Hyderabad's hotels.

Sreenivas wore a white shirt, blue trousers, a patterned tie, and headed for interviews, holding resumes, certificates and a passport. He sat in a lobby or a conference hall and waited for his turn. The recruiters flipped the pages of his passport, noticed the AFU entry and rejected him for being rejected—or for being a BA graduate.

But he had a cheat code: caste (and its privilege of professional networks). Sreenivas accompanied his father—an ex-Andhra Pradesh government employee—to submit his resume to the Human Resource Development Institute (HRDI), a training centre for civil servants, for an IT contractor role. The employment screening took almost a year. He joined in late 1999.

Sreenivas finished his training in Lotus Notes R5. A friend's friend told him about its huge demand in Singapore. He contacted a travel agent, applied for leave and landed in the country. The set-up looked like Hyderabad: countless consultancies spread across different floors of a building. He carried a pile of resumes ('like a newspaper boy') and met company owners, all of them Indians, most of them Tamil and Telugu. He got only one client interview—that, too, resulted in rejection.

A few years later, a new manager at the Institute transferred Sreenivas from the IT department to make him his executive secretary. The very stereotype of a corrupt IAS officer, he came to the office in the afternoon and carried confidential files home. He cancelled existing agreements and hired professionals through a different contractor. It cost Sreenivas his job. His ex-colleague, Gopal, had already filed a lawsuit. Sreenivas joined him. The battle was so uphill that even their attorney dissuaded them.

'I want to see how judiciary works in India,' Sreenivas told him. 'I want justice.'

Wanting to sharpen his IT skills, he reached Ameerpet. It was a blizzard of billboards: a centre promising SAP[1] coaching here, one offering Java classes there. You name a software skill, especially one coveted in the US, and the training hub tossed classes for it. Students poured in from different parts of the country, including villages, carrying modest expectations: an entry-level job. Since many (private[2] and government) engineering colleges lacked qualified faculties,[3] it also functioned as an educational jugaad.

Most institutes followed a formulaic script: a receptionist dangling a 'free demo class' and a '24x7 lab'. The first session was great, 'like a movie trailer', the rest not so much. The coaching centres looked like two-bedrooms apartments: the living room became a reception and the bedrooms classrooms. Their instructors—often IT workers themselves—underscored rote learning, treating students like twelve-year-olds. Sreenivas enrolled in a SAP course; the patronising attitude annoyed him. The smell of America, though, wafted through the region. What did the USA stand for, ran the joke among students, 'United States of Ameerpet'.[4]

Besides training institutes, it contained offices of desi consultancies promising H-1B visas for a few lakh rupees. But not just in Ameerpet. A caste Hindu in Hyderabad knew someone in America. Or knew someone who knew someone. Or knew someone who knew someone who knew someone. Sreenivas had met all three types, countless times, over the last decade. Those men had all the answers, especially to his most desperate question: 'How can I go to America?' Simple: pay a few thousand dollars. The amounts changed with the years, from $4,000 to $5,000 to $6,000. It baffled him: why should he pay for a job?

So he continued to rot in India. Years passed, nothing changed.

In 2007, working as a system administrator for an IT company, he went to Bangalore to write the GMAT and TOEFL. Scored low, made it to an obscure school and travelled to Chennai for the visa interview. The visa officer asked him how he'd fund his education. He said his father, a farmer, would cover his tuition.

Rejected.

Not qualified under section 214(b) of the Immigration and Nationality Act.[5] The officer considered him a potential immigrant.

He wrote the GMAT again. An awful score once more. Carrying a new I-20 (a Department of Homeland Security document signed by an approved American school),[6] and keeping everything else unchanged, he re-entered the Chennai consulate.

'What's the difference between the last time and this time?' the visa officer asked.

'The I-20 is different.'

Rejected. 214(b), once more.

His phone rang one morning. A man named Vishnu Nidamarthi from an IT firm in New Jersey, 4M TechGroup, had received Sreenivas's resume. Did he have time for an interview? It lasted for around forty-five minutes. At the end of the call, Vishnu told him to attend another interview at the head office in Mumbai. The company was the IT division of a famous Indian bank; Sreenivas agreed. A few days after the second interview, he got an email. He had got the job. Edison, New Jersey, $55,000. He converted it in a blink: Rs 2 lakh per month, eight times his current salary.

When he reappeared at the American consulate for the interview, the first question stumped him: why are you coming again and again? He had done this so many times that he refused to spin an answer. He said, 'I need visa.'

The officer asked him about his failed attempts.

'I needed visa.'

'Who is the client?'

No client, he said, his company had an in-house network engineering job.

'Your visa is approved.'

Sreenivas collected the documents, rushed to the water cooler and swigged two glasses of water to calm himself down.

Finally, after twelve long years, America.

After a Recession-induced delay, 4M sent him the air ticket. Sreenivas travelled to Mumbai for his New Jersey flight. His goal was simple: earn in dollars, save in rupees and return to India after two years. He cleared the immigration check, boarded the plane and buckled his seat. As it glided on the tarmac, his heartbeat hopped and raced. Several feelings swirled inside: sorrow, of leaving his motherland, wife and child; excitement, of first-time international travel, a 10,000-mile journey and America; relief, of a new job, a new life, a new future.

His long turmoil—the sweat, the rejection, the corruption—was history. This BA graduate had fought, and won, against a predestined story. He had become an engineer—and not a regular engineer, but one working on an H-1B visa, the 'best and the brightest'.[7] Sreenivas had, finally, been chosen.

Two years: the promise he had made to his father, the promise he had made to himself. Just two years: then a flat in Jubilee Hills, enough cash to invest and the freedom to script his own life. For someone who had dreamt with his eyes open for the last twelve years, two more years were a blink.

3

Hitler Family.

Manu Mitra would coin that term later. The kid swallowed fear first. Once, late at night, his dad picked up a rod to whack his mom. Manu shouted; he backed off. Their fights turned more ugly, more scary, more … more. Another night, his father grabbed his mother's neck and slammed her face into the almirah. A crying Manu hit him, imploring him to stop.

They divorced. Manu was seven.

She transformed into a different mother. She'd bully him, insult him, beat him. Once, even burnt him because he couldn't memorise the multiplication table for nine and, scared by her, had begun to cry. Manu was a shy, silent kid. As if he had gulped down his parents' screams, as if he was rebelling against his own family. When acquaintances pulled his cheeks, he recoiled. He shunned eye contact during conversations. He sought friends but got taunts, so he shrank into a party of one.

Adulthood changed little. Bullies continued to hound him in college. He made few friends, but even with them, he barely hung out. Manu stood out from a distance: a tucked-in full-sleeved shirt, plain trousers, a pen in his shirt pocket. He perplexed his peers: 'Your dressing style is different. Is your father in the military?'

Manu's mother kept taunting and thrashing him. Visiting relatives were no different. His maternal grandfather, Nana, had hit his wife with an iron mug. Her head cracked and spilt blood. She left her husband after decades of marriage. His maternal uncle, Mamaji, also boiled with rage. One evening, his mother and Mamaji quarrelled about money. He grabbed her throat, saying, 'I will kill you.'

This was the family that had raised and ruined him. This was the family that he wanted to escape. The right time had come: 2008, the third year of engineering. Manu made a (cheeky) plan: he wouldn't just flee his tormentors but also make them pay for the ride.

Quite literally.

The plan was simple, tested and famous (especially in Hyderabad)[8]: America. The one place where the Hitler Family couldn't touch him. The one place where he would be on his own. The one place that would give him something eluding him for long: dignity.

But first, he needed to cross a hurdle: himself. Manu had always struggled with maths. He flunked the subject, more than once, in school. In college—P. Indra Reddy Memorial in Wanaparthy, Andhra Pradesh—he took private tuitions, pored over the previous years' question papers and memorised the textbooks' problem-solving methods. Maths mattered because he had to write the GRE to qualify for American universities.

Manu joined an educational consultancy, Vedi Global, to prepare for the exam, taking help for the entire process—from the application forms to the visa interview—paying around Rs 45,000. On the exam day, the verbal section flung tough words, and quant was, well, maths. After a four-hour-long ordeal, the result appeared on screen: 730. Verbal, 300 (sixth percentile); Quant, 430 (seventeenth percentile). His TOEFL score, 58 out of 120, failed to meet the requirements of most universities.

Vedi Global sent him a Statement of Purpose (SOP). Paraphrasing it, he finished his essay. American colleges needed confidential recommendation letters—written and sealed by the faculty—but the P. Indra Reddy professors instructed him to write letters on their behalf. Manu consulted Vedi Global's sample copies, wrote the letters and got them signed. The consultancy recommended four universities and told him to submit the documents.

Like most educational consultancies in Hyderabad, Vedi Global hijacked Manu's applications. It filled out his online forms, kept the log-in details confidential and couriered his application packets. Such consultancies virtually owned students' futures, pushing them to lower-ranked universities[9] to earn higher commissions.[10] This deception hid in plain sight. But some agents committed brazen fraud, preparing fraudulent bank statements, loan sanction papers[11] and college certificates.[12] Some misled and intimidated applicants—lied about the university's name, withheld its course structure and threatened to cancel admission if the student didn't pay the first semester's fees in advance.[13] The US federal law forbade financial affiliations with American consultancies, but no such rule existed for foreign brokers.[14]

Vedi Global forwarded him the results. 'Dear Mr Mitra,' read an email from Boston University, 'I'm sorry to inform you that your application has not been approved.' Two more rejections, from the University of Montana and North Dakota University. Only one school let him in: the University of Bridgeport.

Now the next hurdle: the education loan. A master's degree at Bridgeport, including tuition, food and dorm, amounted to $21,390 (then Rs 9.5 lakh) per year. His mother had stopped working; she had negligible savings. They approached a bank. A loan sanction letter needed a guarantor's signature. Only one person could help him.

He reached Hyderabad Central University. His father had sent him money, paid for his GRE and TOEFL fees. Manu visited him on a weekday; his PhD students worked in an adjoining lab. He informed his father about the Bridgeport admit, its costs and the loan requirement. Manu assured him that he'd only need to sign the letter, and Manu would do the rest.

His dad refused.

But why? It would allow him to study abroad, improve his skills, progress. Could he not even do this much?

No.

Manu screamed, smashing lab equipment and kicking a plastic dustbin. His father was a chain smoker; cigarette packets tumbled out. So did the students from the next room. They stood in a corner, enjoying the tamasha. His father didn't budge.

He got the loan by keeping his deceased Nana's property, a two-bedroom house owned by Mamaji, as collateral. The last step, the visa interview, was more daunting. Manu didn't have 'supplees'—'supplementary' papers (or backlogs)—but his GRE and TOEFL scores could destroy his chance. The University of Bridgeport wasn't prestigious either. Worse, the collateral belonged to Mamaji, not his parents.

But, like SOPs and recommendation letters, consulate interviews could also become plug-and-play models, with consultancies spoon-feeding applicants a set of answers. Vedi Global emailed him a four-page document that contained instructions to fill out the F-1 visa form—'among the three options, click on create a new application', 'later one more page opens up, click on I agree'—and answers to probable interview questions.

'Why USA,' read the first.

'Offers world's best education in _____ program. Flexible education system. Great opportunity to interact with the world's best faculty. First in the world to develop this integrated program of _____ (student specialization subjects). Latest courses offered in my field. Tremendous research opportunities.'

The next questions—'why not in India', 'why this particular university', 'how many universities you've applied'—simulated the interview's narrative, before settling on a vital question. 'How can you convince me you're not a prospective immigrant?'

'You have to emphasise that your specialisation has huge demand in India and you have to name some MNCs with good job prospects and salary at par with international standards.'

The document answered thorny questions, too: 'why do you've arrears in your degree', 'why are your scores low', 'why does your bank passbook reflect recent transactions'. The last one applied to Manu. A visa officer might ask for proof of 'liquid' funds—the loan covered only half of the fees; he had to prove he could self-finance the rest. Vedi Global proposed a solution: it would transfer Rs 20 lakh in his account a few days before the interview. He'd get the visa; the consultancy Rs 10,000.

Manu memorised the answers, consulted his friends for more questions and checked the *U.S. News & World Report's* website for information about Bridgeport. He had done everything; now everything else, in Indian theists' parlance, was 'in the hands of God'. So he followed the next step: praying at Chilkur Balaji, the 'Visa Temple'.

In 1983, according to a famous origin story,[15] a priest began circling the temple, as the nearby lakes had dried up. After eleven rounds, water emerged. He continued to walk, expressing gratitude, completing 108 rounds. A few engineers, learning about this divine connection, also made eleven rounds and secured US student visas. The temple's popularity exploded, uniting the two Indian obsessions.[16]

Manu reached the temple with his mother. She bought incense sticks, flowers, coconuts and prasad. He stood in the courtyard, his feet stung by the afternoon heat. Like every devotee, he had to circle the inner sanctum. Manu completed one quick round after the other. His mother, chanting mantras, ordered him to stop at regular intervals and do namaste. She gave him detailed instructions, sometimes got annoyed. Manu followed her commands, minimising conflict. She hadn't changed; the insults—and beatings—had not stopped. Two more months: if his plan succeeded, the Hitler Family would be history.

He took a train to Chennai for the visa interview. Besides Bridgeport, he had nothing else. The college placement cell charged Rs 3,000 for the campus interviews; his mother and Mamaji had refused to pay the amount. Even otherwise, his job prospects, relying on personal networks, looked dim.[17] At the most, a low-paying position, not more than Rs 15,000 per month. The college applications and exam fees had cost a lot. This failure would spit him back into the jungle.

On the day of the interview, he wore a blue suit, a white shirt and a blue tie. He had gotten a haircut, shaved his stubble and worn perfume. At the consulate, holding his files, Manu stood behind an applicant. He had applied multiple times with fake documents,[18] the visa officer said, and if he came here again, he'd 'go to jail'. Manu worried about his own documents, especially the Vedi Global fix. One tricky question, or a slight suspicion, could dismiss him, too.

'Next,' the officer called.

'Good morning, ma'am,' Manu said, placing the files to his right. Vedi Global's first instruction was easy to remember: greet the officer.

She didn't respond.

'Where does your father work?'

'He's a professor at Hyderabad Central University.'

Her accent confused him; he asked her to repeat some questions.

'Why did you apply to this university?'

He launched into a long answer, listing Bridgeport's ranks in different categories and—

'Give me a personal reason.'

'This was the only university that gave me I-20.'

She asked about his backlogs.

Manu had none.

'No backlogs?'

No backlogs.

'Sure?'

Sure.

She asked a few more questions. How much money did he have, did he plan to return to India? Her accent continued to bother him. Manu said, 'Sorry ma'am, can you repeat?' At the end of the interview, the officer let out an exhausted sigh. She placed his file on a stack, kept his passport and said, 'Next.' Now what? Did he get the visa? Should he ask for his passport?

The haze cleared some days later when his passport arrived by mail. One of its pages stood out. On the top left: 'VISA', to its right: 'United States of America'. A long trail had lit in the jungle. Manu would follow it and reach the University of Bridgeport.

II

DECEPTION

4

If Virgil could change anything, he would. But he couldn't unearth an answer if he didn't know the question. How could he assemble the missing pieces if the puzzle itself made no sense?

It eventually hit him. He had never been a college boy; he didn't have the damn degree. Maybe the rules had changed. Maybe the new gatekeepers, the HR departments, only valued frills and pomp. And if that was the game, then he'd play the hell out of it. He chose an online course, project management. It would polish his reverse engineering skills and launch him into the upper echelons of a company—like the Vegas project, which he had enjoyed and aced. He took courses from the University of Phoenix and Capella University.

One day, an employment agency contacted him. An Arizona-based insurance firm needed a full-time programmer. FoxPro and database; he re-entered his playground. First, a phone interview. Then, an offer letter: $72,000. Joy and relief—that it was all over. Twenty months of chasing darkness: wobbling, flailing, railing.

Seven months into the job, he got an email from a contracting firm, Primsoft Services. Virgil had worked for it before. Its manager, Leo, wanted him back. He liked Scottsdale and had no reason to move, except for one: a better-paying position near home. Primsoft, in Austin, paid $45 an hour. He accepted the offer and relocated. But Leo ran the company like a sweatshop. He accused an employee of loading malware into the machines. Virgil backed his colleague. Leo continued to blame them for silly reasons; they bickered a lot. Three months, enough drama: he quit.

The job market looked spirited, like the old times. Soon, an employment agency's call, an interview and an offer. After finishing the short project, he moved into an airstream travel trailer in Harper on a few acres of recently bought land. Returning from yearlong employment, he hoped to land another project soon. The twenty-month horror, however, still loomed on his mind. He needed a backup. His mentor nudged him to get a real estate licence. Virgil followed his advice.

He continued applying for jobs. But endless silence—once again. The same old routine: gaze at the monitor, scrutinise job boards and hunt. Fire as many shots as possible. Check email and phone. Sniff a sign: an unread email, a missed call. Anything that signalled the old life. Days and nights, weeks and months: nothing.

Damn. Again?

He frequented a café. Sat there all day, drank tea and waited for an outsider: a buyer asking for directions. Virgil struck a conversation, introduced himself and sparked an opening. He also scanned the properties on the local Board of Realtors' website. Sometimes he drove around, looking for a 'For Sale' sign. If he found one, he contacted the owner and pitched his services. But the real estate hustle tested patience and persistence: lucrative leads eluded him.

His other option, searching for contract positions, looked worse. A potential real estate deal at least made him meet customers, float conversations, envision possibilities. But the job hunt plunged him into the abyss once more.

He had already revised his resume over a hundred times. Submitted them all. He'd make a hundred more versions. If they, too, tanked, then a hundred more and on and on. This 'stubborn sonofabitch' would do anything but quit he would not. His realtor life provided momentary comfort: he sold three homes for $120,000 each, netting around $7,500.

But on the job front, nothing. Virgil fixed a few lawn mowers—for $35 an hour—but such assignments were rare. Now, a day stretched like a week, and a week, a month. His enthusiasm, his fight, sagged. By late 2006, he wanted to quit IT and sell properties. He sold a million-dollar ranch, earning $18,000. Enough for the next seven months. After that, nothing. So back to IT. But back where? Even though he had resumed college, his phone hadn't rung in the last one-and-a-half years. Harper turned out to be a disadvantage, too. A town so cocooned, so isolated, it resembled a forlorn island. But then, an idea lit his mind: if the world struggled to find him, maybe he could holler?

He'd create a website, where he'd upload his resume and discuss his unemployment. It would display his technical skills and differentiate him from others. He'd name it Keep Virgil At Work. After tinkering and tweaking for weeks, he launched it on 5 November 2007.[1] Black text, white background—no photos, no graphics. The hyperlinked bullet points on the home page read: 'Post a job', 'Why do we need this site', 'Who built this site', 'Help keep this site running', 'Employer guidelines' and 'Am I for protectionism'.

Virgil had still not cracked the puzzle, but parts of it emerged from a long, cold haze.

> Our country is facing some of the most serious problems it has ever faced:
>
> 1) We have large corporations sending our work overseas.
> 2) We have employers that don't understand what it means to be an employer (see Employer Guidelines).
> 3) We are seeing the tip of the iceberg with all the foreclosures that are getting some of the TOP CEO's sacked for losing so much money.
> 4) Our companies are saying they can't find qualified employees, yet at the same time our people are saying they have the qualifications to exceed at the job, but they can't get past the Human Resources department.

It ended with a plea.

> If you believe in the idea's discussed on these pages, then please help us to promote this site. Please list your jobs with us because

> we will do several things i.e., 1) we will fill your position and 2) we will help an individual to support their family by being employed and 3) most likely this person will be a vet because they gave everything that they have for your freedom, and they have the skills learned through on the job training that will complement your requirements.
>
> Call us, work with us, tell us what we can do to help you, but above all, support your friends and neighbors because they are the people that can help build your company into the company that you want it to be!

Virgil had no interest in writing or journalism. But he had a story—a story itching for a megaphone and an audience. He'd turn fifty next month, but his fight had just begun. A fight no longer personal. A fight to Keep America At Work.

5

Sreenivas ambled towards the baggage carousel, picked up his suitcases and exited Customs. A 4M colleague, Naman, had also taken the same flight. But no one came to receive them. Sreenivas called Vishnu from a phone booth.

'Wait, sending the office van.'

A blue Dodge Caravan arrived at the airport. They loaded their bags into the car; Sreenivas took the front seat. The sights on the highway bewitched him: gleaming metal, zipping wheels.

'You will also drive a car like this,' the driver Faizan, a Pakistani native, told him. 'It is just a matter of time.'

Around forty-five minutes later, he cut into a street named Iselin and stopped outside an apartment complex. Sreenivas and Naman lugged their bags to the second floor. In the living room, a 'Fat Belly Guy' (FBG) sat in front of a computer monitor.

'Why did you come to America?' FBG asked.

What?

Sreenivas checked the two bedrooms and returned to the living room.

'Why did you come to America?'

'Is there an Indian store here? I need to buy a calling card.'

FBG directed him to one. As soon as Sreenivas opened its door, a young Indian man at the counter asked, 'Why did you come to America?'

Why is everyone asking the same question?

'Are you from Hyderabad?'

'Yes.'

The man switched to Hindi and introduced himself. A Gujarati on a student visa, he had been fired from six IT jobs. He showed his SQL book and said, 'You Hyderabadis come on H-1B and take F-1s' jobs.'

'Please give me a calling card.'

Sreenivas paid in cash, wished him good luck and left.

He called home and spoke to his parents. Familiar voices in a foreign land comforted him. He entered the loo. A new world. Left tap: hot water, right tap: cold water; a dirty curtain; a white bathtub. Sreenivas came out, drank water and asked FBG, 'What is your name?'

'Selvam. Why did you come to America?'

'My manager told me to join the job.'

'There are no jobs for me. What the heck you guys do?'

A Tall Man came out of a bedroom, saying he had arrived here in January 2008 and, even six months later, remained jobless.

No job means?

Later, Sreenivas met a tearful man in a bedroom and asked him in Telugu, 'What happened?'

He had left his wife without consummating his marriage.

'Why can you not bring her to USA?'

'Where is the job?'

In the evening, strolling on the pavement, the Tall Man, Dhaval, told him that their flat, accommodating several H-1Bs, was called a 'guesthouse'. Strange: during his government stint, a guesthouse meant a residence for dignitaries. Not a cramped dump like this. They entered a liquor store. The endless brands—of whiskey, beer, wine—amazed him. On the way back, Dhaval said Faizan stuffed the fridge with frozen food, buying them not from an Indian but a Pakistani grocery store. They discarded the unused packets in a week; he brought new ones. Dhaval demanded food expenses from the 4M management, wanting to buy what he liked. (He never got any.)

People keep food in the fridge for a week? Sreenivas had so far used it only for storing vegetables, buying other groceries, such as milk, in limited quantities every day. But here, everything flowed in abundance. Even alcohol. A huge bottle of Red Label sat on the living room table. 'Why did you buy alcohol when there is a bottle in the house?'

'That's for the friends of H-1Bs here. It's cheap and tastes no good. I prefer quality wine.'

They poured wine into their glasses and lounged on the balcony. The landline rang.

'The phone is ringing,' he told Dhaval.

'I don't care.'

Only he and Naman didn't have a mobile, so Sreenivas rushed to take the call.

Vishnu: 'Hello P.K., how are you?'

'I am fine.'

'Tomorrow, 11 a.m., I'll take you and Naman for lunch.'

'Thank you.'

Sreenivas finished dinner and retired to a bedroom. His roommate, the Telugu man, still cried in a low hum. He wanted to savour his wine-induced bliss, so he shifted to the living room, carrying a blanket and a pillow, lying on the couch. Selvam hadn't switched off the TV. No one owned the place, so no one cared—like a college hostel. His flatmates popped up to use the attached toilet, disturbing his sleep. Dhaval, as tall as Sreenivas (6'2"), had advised him to sit and pee, as it'd cut the noise. But no one bothered. He fell asleep at around two-thirty.

In the morning, Selvam was watching a speech by Tamil Nadu chief minister Jayalalitha on the desktop. He had not used the headphones or reduced the volume. Sreenivas said 'good morning'; Selvam said nothing. He freshened up, made coffee and returned to the living room.

'You look excited today,' Selvam said.

'Yes, I am going to meet Vishnu for lunch.'

Selvam wore a curious expression. Years later, Sreenivas would blog about it: 'It something like you watch from the other ship while Titanic is sinking where your rejected girlfriend is dying.' He loathed Selvam's pity but kept quiet. He finished his coffee and put the cup in the sink.

'Don't leave it there,' Selvam said. 'Clean it.'

'The sink is already full with unclean stuff.'

'Clean it.'

Sreenivas washed the utensils and went to the bathroom. Another new world: warm water from the shower. He had hardly bathed in warm water in India because heating it on the stove took a lot of time. But in the promised land, he just had to turn the knob. He got dressed and wore shoes. A strange confusion pulled him: body in the US, mind in India. Something felt off … fishy. Still, he was excited about meeting Vishnu; he had brought a shirt for him.

Vishnu drove them to a South Indian restaurant, Mirchi, in Iselin. The sumptuous buffet delighted Sreenivas. They served themselves lunch and took their seats. Vishnu asked him, 'Do you have any questions?'

'Yes.'

'That's fine. Please ask at the end. Let me start with why are we here today? You have a job but not a project. So you don't get paid till you get a project.'

Project?

'I have a job, right, then why no salaries?'

'That's what I'm trying to explain. You have a job, that's why you got an H-1B visa. But you don't have a customer, so we don't pay salaries till you get a customer.'

His mind froze. His heart broke. It finally made sense—the whole 'where's the job' chatter. He had left India, his wife, his kid for this? What was this world?

A 'cult' almost exclusive to Indian H-1B workers. A cult whose first gateway led to a 'guesthouse'. A cult that would now rule his mind, body and soul.

A cult so old it even had a name: 'desi consultancy'.

6

Manu rushed through the John F. Kennedy International Airport, hoping to reach the college as soon as possible. He had refused the pick-up offer from the Indian Student Association, thinking he'd take a bus. But, outside the airport, New York overwhelmed him, so he asked a middle-aged American about the Bridgeport shuttle. 'You know what,' he said. 'I'll take you.' Manu didn't get him. The man asked whether Manu wanted to use the restroom. He did; it was a long flight. Did he want to drink water, eat something? No, thank you. He picked up Manu's suitcases and loaded them in the trunk. Crap, a cab driver! Manu couldn't say no. His first conversation in the US cost him $350.

The cab settled on the I-95. In less than two hours, it'd reach Bridgeport, a booming industrial town a long time ago, but now struggling with crime and poverty. Its university, too, had experienced a simultaneous decline. It had 9,100 students in 1970;[2] by 1992, it dipped to 1,300.[3] College buildings languished empty. Bars, restaurants and stores had shut shop. Illegal drugs ruled the local economy.[4] In 1990, the university announced an end to its liberal arts programmes, severed links with the law school, fired around fifty tenured faculty and ordered the rest to take a pay cut of 30 per cent.[5] This caused a two-year strike—the longest in the history of American higher education—driving away thousands of students. The ones on campus, fearing gunshots and mugging, considered it 'depressing' and 'dead.'[6]

A $22 million debt threatened to shut the university.[7] But then it met a saviour. The Professor Religious Academy, an affiliate of the Unification Church, a 'cult' founded by the Reverend Sun Myung Moon, accused of brainwashing followers, splitting families, evading taxes.[8] By paying the school over $100 million,[9] it could nominate 60 per cent[10] of Bridgeport's trustees for the next ten years. In 2002, with the church stopping its major donations, Bridgeport needed a fresh financial fillip.[11]

In August 2008, however, Manu headed to a changed university. It had 'more than 4,750 students' in 2007, its annual report puffed with pride, an 'increase of more than 18 percent over the last year'.[12] From 2005 to 2007, enrolment had increased by '115 percent in mechanical engineering', '178 percent in electrical engineering' and '196 percent in computer science'.[13] By 2008, Bridgeport became the 'fastest-growing university in New England'. The School of Engineering 'continued its impressive growth, enrolling more students in its master's degree program than any other university in New England, including MIT, Harvard, and Northeastern'.[14]

In the same year, a satirical outlet, *Radar*, published the list of 'America's Worst Colleges'. The University of Bridgeport 'swept the competition in every category' for not only its 'meager academics, post-apocalyptic campus and downright shady administration' but also its 'ghetto-type atmosphere', where students feared 'for their lives'.[15] The city's crime rate, increasing by 11 per cent over the last two years, was 162 per cent higher than the national average.[16] Yet the enrolment had continued to rise, benefitting from the 'aggressive recruitment of international students',[17] who constituted one-fourth of the student body.[18]

Indian hustlers had saved an American university.

Manu reached the electrical engineering building to register for classes. His batchmates surrounded a senior who, in 'thick Gujarati' and snatches of English ('this course is good', 'this professor will give you A'), gave them advice. Manu chose his own courses. Accustomed to following instructions—from parents to teachers to educational consultants—many young Indians found the freedom in America unsettling. So their seniors acted as surrogate parents—suggesting courses, jobs, internships—freeing juniors from independent thinking. A loner by choice, raised amongst conformers, Manu vacillated between the two extremes.

The accents troubled him most, making lectures hard to follow. While talking, he masked his incomprehensibility with an obedient nod accompanied by an 'okay'. The education loan made him cut costs. Manu bought frozen masala rotis, cooked Maggi and hardly went out.

He also joined a non-profit Christian organisation, Bridges International, hoping the conversations with American students would solve his accent problem. As a member, he attended a church, Black Rock, every Sunday. He was a silent presence, but his friends—James, Kane and Riley—drew him into chats. After praying, they wound up at another member's house. Those meetings had banter and board games. Manu sat alone.

Over the last six months, he hadn't fallen sick. Diseases hounded him in India: asthma, TB, fever, stomach disorder, throat infection. But in Bridgeport, he never visited a doctor; his stack of medicines remained untouched. In the new world, technology manifested magic: buses' dollar-ingesting machines released tickets; portable alarms summoned the cops in less than two minutes; labs stayed open the entire night. Fewer bullies, too. He didn't miss his Hitler Family. America provided freedom, not restrictions. The freedom to choose his own courses, for instance, from not only electrical engineering but any programme, unlike P. Indra Reddy, where the principal selected the electives. No one sat on his shoulders, judging and mocking. Manu could finally breathe.

The next semester, he met an acquaintance who was about to quit his gig at an Indian restaurant. Would Manu like to replace him? He hadn't found a part-time job. Submitting resumes to the library, dorm and dining hall had yielded nothing. The extra money would pay for his food expenses.

Manu worked during the weekends. He joined as a server but discharged diverse responsibilities: wiping glass tops, cleaning the restroom, washing dishes. His shift lasted for twelve hours, from nine in the morning to nine in the night, and three such days earned him around $300. But after some weeks, the owner hardly called. Manu lost interest and quit.

He needed a full-time job to clear his loan. But for someone unable to bag an on-campus gig, a corporate career looked like a mirage. Manu shared a recurring worry with his friends on online chats: 'If I don't get a job, I'll have to return to India.' His life could transform, though, at the start of the fall semester when Bridgeport hosted a career fair. It would give him a rare chance to meet recruiters, make contacts. His last chance.

Wearing a suit and holding resumes, he entered the career fair. He approached the booth of an IT company. An electrical engineering student, he had no background in IT. But a job was a job. The recruiter, an Indian man, asked no technical questions and said, 'We are looking for candidates in SQL and UNIX.' Manu spoke to several such desis and dropped his resume.

Later, in his room, he picked up a company's brochure. Much of it made sense—technical requirements, contact details, comforting help ('free training in Java, Bootstrap')—but one assurance did not: '100 per cent job guarantee'. Manu had sought a job for months, and failed, but this firm promised one?

But a job was a job. He had submitted his resume, fulfilled his dharma. If those promises were true, then he'd get a call or an email. Manu had no reason to be suspicious: America wouldn't allow fraud. He uploaded his resume on Dice, Indeed and Career Builder. Waited for weeks. Applied for jobs.

Nothing.

Time raced past. An international student had to find a job within ninety days of graduating. Failing to do so risked deportation. Manu had no close friends on campus. Nobody to guide him through the job hunt. So he turned to a familiar recourse: Mamaji. He introduced Manu to his friend Gyan Prakash, an IT professional in New Jersey.

They spoke over the phone. Gyan told him to join a 'desi consultancy'. The latest buzzword in his life, it often popped up among conversations with peers. A consultancy meant an IT firm that provided training, a job and 'rent money or something like that for a year'. What else? No clue.

Gyan came to Bridgeport in December 2009, after the last semester's finals, to pick up Manu. An assertive figure, he would help Manu find a job and teach him American life. He pointed towards a speeding vehicle on the highway. 'What's that?'

'A car.'

'It's an SUV. Sport Utility Vehicle.'

Gyan's car—yeah, not an SUV—stopped outside an apartment complex in Piscataway, New Jersey, Manu's new home. An Indian man, in his late twenties, opened the door. An empty living room, except for a few chairs and a table. A staircase, adjoining the dining room, led to the first floor. After Gyan left, he checked the bedroom upstairs. A crumpled comforter on the floor, some pillows on it. Nothing else in the rest of the room. Manu entered the bathroom: it didn't even have a bar of soap.

The DMNT Solutions office, comprising a few employees, looked just as bleak. In a vacant room, he watched SQL tutorials every weekday for eight hours. He didn't know anyone in the company; no one knew him. DMNT Solutions covered his accommodation, and an employee dropped off groceries every few days. It wouldn't pay him till he got a client, and Manu, with no IT experience, couldn't find one without training. Weeks passed. No sign of training.

'I'm fed up,' he pinged his Bridgeport friend, Ramesh. He shared his worries with his mother. She blamed him: 'Why did you go to the US if you did not do anything?' The loan stress fogged his brain. Only three things mattered: a job, a job, a job. Any job. Grocery store, shoe shop, desi consultancy. Any salary. $25, $20, $15 per hour. Manu would do anything to save his ancestral house.

Gyan often met him at the DMNT guesthouse. Every conversation cleared and created confusion. 'You can't apply directly for a position. These websites, Career Builder and all, won't work.'

But if he got a job, it'd be in IT. Manu had studied electrical engineering. It wouldn't be easy, said Gyan, to find an electrical engineering job. Even there, he'd run into MATLAB and VLSI codes. All worries met the same answer: desi consultancy. 'You're a fresher. Nobody will look at your resume. They need experience.'

One day, he asked, 'You'll have to put five to six years of experience on your resume. How do you feel about that?'

'But it's a lie, right?'

'Then you are on your own. You will not find a job in the United States.'

This shocked Manu. Working off-campus (illegally)[19] for some cash was one thing; adulterating his resume with six years of experience, something else. A coin toss: play the game, pay the loan, lose himself; or, return to India, earn a pittance, lose the property. Heads they won, tails he lost.

7

Virgil never cared for politics; he never voted—even though he identified as a Republican and called himself a 'Fox News junkie', someone who adored capitalism and distrusted unions. Politics appealed to folks with fancy degrees and ten-dollar words, not 'illiterate hicks' from the boondocks.

All that would change now.

Because he was unemployed even after 10,000 applications. The same old challenge: fixing the big picture—this time, not a code but his life. So Keep America At Work turned into a mission. On his website, using 'first grade math', this high school dropout would investigate the source of his scars: the 'villains' of his life.

Virgil followed the election campaigns, remaining sceptical of Barack Obama. 'Am I the only one that noticed he could not lead us in the pledge of allegiance?'[20] he wrote on Keep America At Work. 'If he can't do something as simple as that, how in the hell can he lead us in any of our other traditions??'[21] A few months later, Obama's comment on the working-class people in industrial towns coping with job losses annoyed him further ('they get bitter, they cling to guns or religion or antipathy to people who aren't like them or anti-immigrant sentiment or anti-trade sentiment as a way to explain their frustrations').[22] But in the subsequent months, the Illinois senator began to convince and convert him: that if someone could get him a job, it'd be Obama. In November 2008, Virgil stepped out to vote. He voted blue.

He wrote daily on Keep America At Work—at least one post a day, on some days more—trying to detect a pattern. After a year of railing, however, he wanted concrete evidence, hard numbers, to prove his point. Because many refused to believe him, echoing his state six years ago: 'ten-feet tall' and 'bulletproof'.

Sometimes, he relied on his own experience. 'My theory of why so many of us can't find work is that 1) our corporations have taken the selection process away from the manager that actually needs the help and turned it over to the HR dept. 2) HR … has turned to a buzz word matching system which makes them more efficient and able to process many more resumes.'[23]

The website featured a new section: The Wall of Shame, comprising firms offshoring jobs in the recent past (Dell, Nokia, Flextronics[24]—the list kept growing). Pegging the lowest middle-class income at $1,000 a week, he pulled out the annual salaries for all occupations and concluded: 'There are 26 million people in America that make above what I consider poverty. There are 107 million people in America that make less then what I consider poverty. Now do you see why your retailers, manufacturers and raw material producers are coming to us with their hat in their hand?'[25]

He repeated the figures in a different piece, explaining how offshoring had dented the American middle-class. 'Yes, I am well aware that the Wall Street Journal, CNBC, Bloomberg and Fox Business refuse to even consider these facts because I have repeatedly tried everything to get this information in front of them.'[26]

So he contacted someone who did, the White supremacist website, VDare. 'A Displaced Texas Programmer', stated the headline of an April 2009 post, 'Analyzes the Pattern of Low Salaries and Immigration That Leads to American Job Loss'. 'I document how American businesses eliminated over 1,200,000 jobs that paid an average of $96,000,' read a part of his letter, 'and replaced them with jobs that paid only in the $34,000 range. The transfer of wealth, perpetrated by our corporations, that prefer immigrant labor, is the actual cause of our economic crisis.'[27]

His curiosity spawned a new chapter: 'caste'. He searched online and shared a piece on Keep America At Work. 'The so-called upper caste men would enter any house of the Dalits and do anything with the women they wanted,' he quoted the Dalit rights activist Martin Macwan. 'So, for example, a higher caste man has come and entered the house where a woman is alone. He sets his shoes outside the house. If the husband comes from the market and sees the shoes, he understands somebody's there, so he won't go inside. He will go back to the market.'

'Is this the future you want for your children?' Virgil wrote below the excerpt. 'It sure as hell is not the future that I want for any of my children, which is why I do what I can to stop America from becoming ChinAmerica with IndiAmerica overseers.'[28]

An Indian recruiter from a consulting firm, ObjectWin Technology, contacted him about a project for the Office of the Attorney General in San Antonio, Texas. It needed a programmer with FoxPro experience. Virgil nailed the interview. He got hired for $50 an hour.

But how did he get a project? That too amid recession? What changed? Nothing. He got the job because the gatekeepers let him in. This red-blooded, freedom-loving Texan was going to enrich a villain. A desi consultancy so vicious that the Department of Labor (DOL) had penalised it. The 1998 American Competitiveness and Workforce Improvement Act had granted enforcement powers to the federal agency.[29] It possessed limited authority, though, as it could investigate a firm in four exceptional conditions.[30] One of them hinged on an H-1B worker's complaint. But since an employer owned the visa, and not the employee, such complaints were rare because of the fear of retaliation. The DOL investigation, concluding in 2008, declared ObjectWin Technology guilty of 205 H-1B violations, ordering it to pay back wages worth $206,541[31] to forty-three foreign workers—the eighty-third highest amount among 2,321[32] such penalties.

The long-term project rejuvenated him. He met an ObjectWin employee at work, an Indian man, Sathvik. They had to reverse engineer the Attorney General's case management system. Virgil liked the work; he liked Sathvik. They ate lunch together, chatted and took cigarette breaks. He told Sathvik about his employment troubles. His colleague had faced no such problem. During a smoke break, they cracked the puzzle: buzzwords. So Virgil copied the format of Sathvik's resume.

They created a system in two months. But the Great Recession choked the project. Back to the hellhole.

Months passed.

Even the new resume failed. That must mean something—but what? The HR departments' buzzwords obsession didn't explain it all, because if that were the case, he'd have barged in, as he had copied the format. What was he missing?

Virgil chanced on an article. An Infosys employee, Promila Awasthi, an American citizen of Indian ancestry, had sued the outsourcing giant.[33] As he continued to read, the pieces aligned. 'Infosys management routinely disparaged Americans', including Awasthi, 'as not having "family values" and stated that layoffs in America are good because the jobs will be outsourced. [It] ridiculed her for celebrating Thanksgiving, telling her she should not celebrate it because she is Indian and therefore must work on that day.'

The Wall of Shame welcomed a new entry.

'Infosys management ridiculed her children for celebrating Thanksgiving, and called them "ABCD", "American-Born Confused Desi", and "IBCD", "Indian-Born Confused Desi", insulting terms used to criticize people of Indian ancestry who are Americanized.'[34]

It kept getting better.

'Infosys management ridiculed Mrs. Awasthi for celebrating Christmas, saying "we" do not celebrate it. They repeatedly discussed the quality of her work by explicitly commenting on their expectations for "a woman your age".'[35]

So this was both rejection and exclusion. A way to maintain hierarchy. A way to assert supremacy. At least a part of the puzzle revealed itself.

What was that word again? Ah, yes: 'caste'.

8

After meeting Vishnu, Sreenivas returned to the guesthouse and wept in the living room. His flatmates entered and left, but no one consoled him, no one asked a thing. Maybe they had cried a thousand times, too. He went to the bathroom and washed his face; the tears kept dripping. How could they not? All dreams shattered. Everything, zero. All in less than twenty-four hours. Why did 4M force him to leave his job in India? Why did 4M give him a job when it didn't have a job? What should he tell his family?

Was this Dream America?

His father had given him $1,000—enough for the return flight. But when he calmed down, he accepted his fate. Sreenivas had done nothing wrong; why should he quit? The next morning, he visited the 4M office: all desi employees and except for Faizan and the receptionist (a Punjabi woman), all South Indians. Vishnu called Sreenivas to a cabin to prepare his resume. He opened MS Word on his laptop and typed his employee's name: 'Kumar'.

Kumar? P.K. Sreenivas. Kumar was his middle name.

'This is America. You have to go by Kumar. Not P.K. or Sreenivas.'

His new name: Kumar Pandruvada. The next change: resume. Consulting the list of IT skills on his laptop, Vishnu grilled Kumar. Each question followed the same pattern. If Kumar said he knew Java, then Vishnu wrote 'Java' on the resume. If not, he popped another question—'do you know .Net?'—and so on. By the time he finished, just the 'Technical Skills' section filled half the page, ranging from 'Software' to 'Hardware' to 'Tape Libraries' to 'SAN'.

The next order stunned Kumar: fake your resume,[36] put ten years of US experience. 'If we tell vendors you've just arrived from India, they'll pay less hourly billing.'

Vendor? Billing?

'Your resume must be at least eight pages. We can't go less than this.'

Vishnu chose different Fortune 500 companies, different US states and different years. Every line, every lie, manufactured a new Kumar. His mind kept buzzing with a question: Why should he fake his resume when he had worked for ten years? Kumar countered and pestered Vishnu. He finally barked, 'Get out.'

Vendor[37] calls exploded; Kumar panicked. His own resume confused him—the clients, the locations, the years. Vishnu directed him to track vendor and client names on a spreadsheet. He stuck the eight-page resume on the guesthouse wall, trying to memorise his identity. But the question continued to irk him: why was he lying to get a job?

The puzzle unravelled slowly. Vishnu submitted the resume to a vendor, who called Kumar to verify. That vendor forwarded it to another vendor. When the second vendor rang, Kumar had to say he worked for the previous vendor. He couldn't remember the chain for every call. Vendors called from different American states—and Andhra Pradesh. Almost all of them Indians, carrying strange curiosities: 'Are you from Hyderabad?' 'Do you speak Telugu?' 'Do you know Tamil?'

Vishnu continued to train him. 'You'll get a fixed annual salary for the first year'—$55,000 (less than the starting pay of an undergraduate techie)—'so the billing rate is irrelevant to you. The company is paying $100 per month to you, and other H-1Bs, because we are providing free accommodation and food.' That 'salary' also included working on 4M's in-house projects.

Kumar found some solace in a Sai Baba temple in Iselin. He visited it on Thursday afternoons. During that time, he didn't check his phone. The clients, the vendors and the employer could wait. As a young adult, his fervour for Hinduism had matched his patriotic zeal, making him absorb a foundational belief: that Indians were 'soft people'. But America began to challenge his every key assumption: about his countrymen, his country, his own self.

He got a call from a Boston-based vendor who had submitted his resume to an American 'prime vendor'. Another new term—maybe it meant the 'first broker'. He spoke to an American man who told him that the firm didn't take phone interviews, and since his resume mentioned Boston, an in-person conversation would be ideal.

Boston?

So Vishnu had changed his resume again? How would he go to a faraway city without a driving licence, car or money? He called Vishnu.

'Take a bus.'

He took a bus. But he had no money for a motel. The middle vendor, a man named Raghav, allowed him to spend the night at his company's guesthouse. It was a sparse high-ceilinged apartment crammed with Indians—all desperate to get placed. A stranger, from a different company and a different city, unsettled them. Unlike them, this 'immigrant', hogging limited space, stood a sniffing distance away from their dream. Except for one 'North Indian', the rest of them, 'South Indians', looked hostile. Kumar devoured the leftover bread and curry in the kitchen. Most occupants slept on the cold floor. So did Kumar, without a blanket or a choice.

A few days later, he got a call: 'Congrats, you got selected.' The vendor told him to wait though as 4M hadn't signed the contract. Kumar called Vishnu. He refused to sign, saying the vendor had withheld 4M employees' salaries.

'If the vendor is not good,' he emailed Vishnu, 'then why did you submit my resume?'

Vishnu screamed on the phone. 'Don't send such things in business emails. Come to the office and talk about PO, MSA.'

PO, MSA?

He found out later that PO meant Purchase Order and MSA Master Service Agreement. Each vendor sent a PO to the other vendor in the hiring chain, agreeing on pay rates. The MSA, attached to right to represent contracts, forbade other middle vendors from poaching an H-1B worker.

He met more 4M employees in the guesthouse. One of them surprised and impressed him: Khan. Entering the US on an H-1B visa in January 2008, he had secured a project in Texas. Not long after, his father died. Khan flew to India, leaving his car and leasing his apartment. He also lost his job. When he found a project after returning to the US, Vishnu refused to sign the PO and MSA. Khan stormed through the 4M office, flinging tables and chairs, smashing glasses and furniture. Vishnu and his boss panicked; they signed.

Kumar got a phone interview. A four-member panel: one Indian and three Americans. The Indian man began: 'Where did you stay in Boston?' Visiting it once, he hardly knew anything about the city. Kumar improvised an answer, but the interviewer tightened the screws: which street? What locality? He stammered and stopped—his silence said everything. The man hung up.

The prime vendor emailed Vishnu, rejecting Kumar.

'Take it easy,' Vishnu wrote to him.

Take it easy?

Kumar wanted to howl. Why should an Indian insult him in the US when he had decade-long experience? A raw rage seized his body. He took a cab, reached the 4M office and met Vishnu's boss.

'I want to change my manager.'

'H-1Bs have no right to choose their managers.'

'Then give me tickets to India. I want to go back.'

'What is the problem?'

'Vishnu. Fake resume. Why should I fake my resume when I worked for ten years? I will go with India resume only.'

'We will get less billing.'

'I do not care about your billing. I care about my ethics and values.'

4M had rejected two offers, said Vishnu's boss, because of the billing rate, $65 per hour.

'Do not test my patience. I have seen what Khan did so, please, let me not repeat it. Let me go with India resume, India experience and get a customer to you.'

'Background check will go to India. It will kill time.'

'That's fine. Because for everything, you say, we send it to India legal team, it doesn't matter, let the background check also go to India.'

Kumar walked towards the office of the man heading the finance team. Vishnu's boss scampered behind him, saying, 'Please, this is a small issue. Let's not make it big.'

He uploaded his original resume on the career portals. His rate dipped; his demand soared. Kumar's work experience distinguished him from his peers (many on fake resumes).[38] The vendor calls now requested 'proxy' support—'proxy phone interviews', 'proxy skype interviews', 'proxy project work'—for their H-1B employees. The duplicity of Indian IT workers, profiting from this scam, shocked him. 'I am sorry,' he'd tell the vendors. 'I am not the kind of person you think.'

He got an in-person client interview in Silver Springs, Maryland. His original resume filled him with confidence. Kumar explained his previous jobs and told the hiring manager, 'If I get selected, it will be my first onsite project.'

He did. An opening after six endless months. He also found out that he had lost the case against the corrupt bureaucrat. It disappointed him, but he had left the past, beginning a new chapter in a country, where 'law' was 'ultimate'.

9

DMNT Solutions had not begun to train Manu—even after a month. Gyan drove him to another consultancy, Unitech Infosol. They met a turbaned man, Manpreet Singh, who said the company wanted to 'place candidates in LoadRunner and testing'. Manu moved into a new home the next day: the Unitech guesthouse. The two-bedroom apartment, in Lawrenceville, New Jersey, had just one occupant. In no time, three more desis joined. Unlike the DMNT accommodation, the Unitech guesthouse bustled with short-term visitors. A TV stood near the living room door. A two-seater couch touched the opposite wall. Two nails on its right wall hung clothes. Jackets covered the backs of chairs; their laps held IT books. Suitcases, shoes and floaters lay on the carpet.

Since Manu's roommate kept the light on till late at night, he crashed on the living room floor, laying one comforter on it and the other on himself. During the day, he sat on the carpet, leaning against the couch, placing his laptop on a carton. The company paid for the groceries. The consultants took turns cutting vegetables, cooking and washing utensils.

Unitech Infosol gave him an offer letter. After ninety days of unemployment, he needed a job—at least on paper—to maintain his immigration status. His designation: programmer analyst. Annual salary: $50,000.

Every morning, Manpreet picked up the consultants from the guesthouse. The office was a standalone two-storey house, less than two miles away, in a residential locality, Hamilton. The ground floor opened to two rooms: one for the accountant and the other for Manpreet. Two more on the first floor: a server room and a classroom. Several sheets detailing SQL concepts marked the basement walls, helping employees during interviews.

They assembled in the classroom every morning, poring over instruction manuals on the Unitech Google Groups. Facing a whiteboard, Manpreet taught them QTP, LoadRunner and software testing in hour-long lectures. After the lunch break, they practised the testing sessions on desktops.

Manpreet emailed Manu a five-page resume. He recognised three things on it: 'Technical Skills'—such as 'Internet Explorer, MS Word, MS Excel'—and his first and last name. The rest? A 'fictional travelogue'. In February 2003, at age seventeen, he had worked as a QA tester in Hyderabad. By June 2004, he had moved to Philadelphia, as a QA tester, for a healthcare organisation. He then joined an auto insurance firm in Maryland, working for two years, followed by a four-month project in Indianapolis. Since March 2010, he had worked at a medical tech company in New Jersey as a senior QA engineer.

Manpreet sent it to different vendors. A fabricated resume could land Manu interviews, but how would an electrical engineer, with one-month training, clear them—pass off as a consultant with seven years of experience?

Well, he wouldn't.

Gyan had informed him about a 'proxy interview',[39] where an experienced professional, often from the same consultancy, attended a phone interview for another employee. The applicant either put the phone on call forward before the interview or handed it to a colleague in the same room. The consultancy magic worked. A Unitech consultant had bagged a job and left the guesthouse.

'How is your marketing going?' A friend pinged him in April 2010.

'Not yet but will start soon. Probably by next month, I will get a job.'

'Good going.'

'But it'll be tough it seems. Because we'll show six years and a friend said he is having a hard time.'

'Yeah, that's common in software.'

'Oh …'

'We keep many things on our resume which we don't know. Don't worry.'

April, May, June: still jobless. Manu's mother blamed him and stopped sending him money. He contacted other desi consultancies but didn't tell Manpreet. Some firms emailed him job requirements, seeking his signature on the 'right to represent' agreements. Some emailed him embellished resumes. Others probably submitted (fabricated) resumes without informing him. He didn't know how many versions of his resume, carrying what levels of exaggerations, reached clients. Soon, around a dozen companies marketed him.

'I have changed the resume years,' Manu messaged a Euphoria Protech employee, 'and if there is another modification, please guide me.'

'Sure. U wanna go with 5 yrs resume?'

'Yes. Is it okay?'

'No probs, can't you manage 7 yrs?'

'Yeah, I can though …'

'Send me 7 yrs.'

'Recent project I am keeping as QA analyst, not QA lead.'

'Ya, don put lead.'

'Anything else I need to change?'

'Nothing. U will get a call from Neha. She is from Dambert Techno Solutions. Client is Silicon Synergy.'

Every week, something new.

'Can you provide two references?' Another vendor messaged him.

'Yeah sure.'

'Send me, urgent.'

'On the recent project, right?'

'Ya, do you have official ids?'

'No. Doesn't work?'

'No.'

Unlike Manu, a seasoned player would have requested a consultant at the same client for a reference from the company's official email ID. Desi consultancies had built a dense network; their employees swam in it.

July: still jobless.

'I don't think my consultancy is going to place me,' he wrote to Ramesh. 'Probably the house would be sold man. We will be on footpath.'

An email from a desi vendor, ZNK Solutions, perked him up. It needed a QTP Analyst for a biotech company in New Jersey. On the client call day, he sat near Manpreet who faced a table covered with sheets distilling key concepts. The phone rang on time; Manu handed it to Manpreet. For the next twenty minutes, he tackled the questions with confidence, poise and humour.

Manu got the job. He had to report to the client's corporate office, collect his badge and ask for the manager Guan Zi. But when he met Guan, she told him he wasn't in her team. Or in any team. He had nothing to do. A week passed: no work.

The office was five miles away. Carrying a GPS, walking non-stop—not stopping even when it drizzled—he reached work in two hours, with beads of sweat clinging to his back. Nothing to do for weeks. To kill time, he searched for second-hand cars online.

He earned around $4,000 every month. The payment flowed through a multi-hooped channel: the client paid the vendor, ZNK Solutions, which paid the consultancy, Unitech Infosol, which paid Manu. He didn't know the billing rate or Unitech's hourly earnings. The Purchase Order—signed between Unitech Infosol and ZNK Solutions, specifying his per-hour pay—never reached him. His salary, deposited in his bank account, came at least a month late. No idea why—he never asked.

One day, a middle-aged woman stood outside his room, which he shared with a few colleagues. Manu stepped out to meet her.

'Your contract has ended,' she said. 'You have one more week to wrap your things up.'

'But I thought it was a three-month project.'

'The project is over, next week is your last week.'

Soon, Manpreet found a full-time job and quit. Now Manu had no one to market his resume. Back to nothing. He spoke to Gyan.

'Why don't you join Infocon Logix?'

It sounded like another generic consultancy.

'I know about this company. It has placed a lot of candidates.'

Manu was still uncertain. Because even after a year, and two consultancies, he had secured just one short project. He was desperate for shelter. The jungle had begun to roar.

10

'One thing I need to make clear,' Virgil wrote on Keep America At Work. 'I am not against people from India wanting to move here and become American's and embrace our lifestyle. I am not against people from any country wanting to do the same. I have had the pleasure of working with some great people from India, and I have enjoyed getting to know them. I'm against sending our work offshore because it puts American's out of work. Nope, this is not a protectionist talking. This is necessary for our survival.'[40]

But not all days were nights. He had met a woman. Molly Clarke. They connected immediately, and Virgil knew it was special. Joyous, comforting, healing. He hung out with her at a different time—after the Attorney General project—when cash flow, and financial confidence, was not a problem. But when he realised that his life would give him nothing but long penury, he bailed on her. The new life imposed new rules. As a friend had told him some years ago: 'When poverty enters through the front door, love leaves through the back door.'

Keep America At Work helped him build a committed squad. Matt, an IT recruiter, had contacted him in the early days of the website. Followed by Navy veteran Andrew Gardner, Virgil's colleague on a Vegas project. Kyra, a Denver resident, used to be a software analyst. Brad Miller had worked in a bar in Vegas. Gavin Lynch, a technical writer.

Matt, like Virgil, had a terrible itch. Jobless for months, he examined the American economy and politics, posting his conclusions on Keep America At Work, explaining the free trade agreements, the 'submissive and ignorant' Americans and the Department of Labor's spurious unemployment rates.[41] Kyra ran an online journal for unemployed Americans. Brad, a lifelong Republican, investigated the Grand Old Party.

So did Virgil. He concluded that its leaders snubbed regular Americans and revered the status quo: cutting taxes on corporations, snipping workers' safety nets, lowering minimum wage—all unwilling to restore the 'balance' between the interests of businesses and citizens. His research produced a report card. First, John Boehner ('you wouldn't know how to create jobs if it was a rattle snake that bit you on the shin').[42] Eric Cantor ('you are a cheap despicable self serving individual that would throw the people of America under the bus just so that you and yours will not have to pay their fair share of taxes').[43] Rick Perry ('another right-wing extremist?').[44]

The world beyond his desktop made no sense. He explained his findings to the people in Harper—cautioned them about the rising tide of decreasing wages—but they looked indifferent. Fellow coders, too. 'Virgil, you're saying it's going to rain,' said a programmer on the FoxPro mailing list, 'but the sun is shining.' As if the media's ignorance and indifference—the 'Fox propaganda'—didn't frustrate him enough.

'Are you alive?' A message from Max, Virgil's childhood friend, a Gillespie County employee.

'Yep, woke up at 2:30 with an idea for an article and couldn't go back to sleep.'

'Hope you didn't have a liberal brainstorm <grin>.'

'Yep, wrote my best article yet.' He shared the link.[45] 'You going to be down there? I need to go to Kerrville and get cat food, shampoo, etc. It's hell being the poorest person in Harper nobody in Harper will do business with.'

Virgil's Harper Fix-It Shop—an extension of his lawn mower repair shed—had remained dormant for months. His town folks wouldn't trade with him because he didn't have the parts; he didn't have the parts because he didn't have the money. Before the chicken or the egg came the bullshit of unemployment and the indifference of the unaffected. 'Here in my hometown I am shunned because I will not get a job,' he wrote on Keep America At Work.[46] He could neither reason with them nor make them believe. They bitched about him, called his website pointless and wanted him to compromise. To any question, they had a standard reply: there were 'jobs everywhere'.

Virgil had trusted the healing hands of capitalism his entire life. An ardour reflecting his faith in the American dream, as capitalism was patriotism. But in his unemployed years, he had seen its seamy side: a system victimising the victims, isolating and lampooning them. His posts often recalled the land he loved, reminding others what they had forgotten—'there is a saying in America: United we stand, divided we fall'—as if they lived in a different country. But Harper folks needed no education because, unlike Virgil, they knew American capitalism very well: every man for himself playing a game he couldn't afford to lose.

One morning, Max emailed a link to McDonald's job openings.

'You actually consider that to be a job that will provide a better than average future?'

'No, these are keep the lights on jobs till you find a good one.'

'You don't get it. I'm not settling for stuff like that. I will create a future for myself or die trying.'

11

Kumar took a $2,000 loan from his employer and reached Baltimore. But of course, 4M owed him—around $30,000, an amount he'd never get. No point bemoaning the past though. Now he'd sew his heart and start his life: a new chance, a new Dream America.

He stayed in a motel, then rented a room for $750 in an Indian man's house. But it wasn't a room—it was a basement. It had a washer, a dryer, a makeshift toilet and nothing else. Not even central heating. Kumar carried a folding bed, but the January cold left him helpless. Even mundane activity, such as going to the toilet, hurt. If he forgot his slippers, the icy floor pricked his feet. The rats tripled the torment. They scurried at night and mocked his sleep, as if they paid the rent.

Kumar woke up early, finished his morning prayer and walked for forty minutes in the soul-shaking cold to reach the office. A puzzling sight at work: Indian techies obeying a hierarchy, like the Hindu caste system. F-1 college graduates languished at the bottom of the pyramid, hoping to secure stable work permits; above them, H-1B workers who could work in the country for six years tied to their employers; and at the top, green card[47] holders who, unbothered by visa sponsors' shackles, had attained foreign workers' dream: freedom.

An ocean of new experiences and insights, he flowed. 'One has to remember,' he emailed a friend a few weeks into the project, '70% of software jobs are held by Hyderabadis and the rest by Tamilians, Bengalis, Gujaratis, etc, but others don't respect Hyderabadis and within them there are lots of regional and caste feelings. We criticize Americans (not all) and interpret them wrongly, but when it comes to help, we exploit our own people. I was fortunate that a foreigner rescued me, otherwise I would be paying huge rent to an Indian.' He had moved to a room in an American colleague's house for $550 per month. 'I have great respect for Indians, but after interacting with some of them, I'm fed up (remember not all, I am not generalizing like the Telugu media), but 90% of them have a crab mentality and ego problem. Every day, I spend four to five hours to upgrade my skills to get a second (standby) job in case the economy goes for a toss.'

The Great Recession proved him right. The client fired him, along with countless employees and contractors. An unemployed H-1B faced a crushing possibility: leaving the US. Kumar had to find a project in less than a month—that too during the Recession. The background check for this job lasted as long as the job itself.

Kumar wept.

He cleared his desk, packed his belongings and reached the bus stop. Heavy hands, hard snow: howling heart, blurry future. Even his location was uncertain. For the time being, Baltimore. Best case scenario: a job from here. Worst case: move to the 4M guesthouse, look for a job from there, and what if he found nothing?

A fortnight passed. Kumar had stopped cooking and praying. The uncertainties continued to multiply. He emailed a friend. 'Nothing is permanent on this earth as I have thrown some of the beloved books and other stuff in dustbin yesterday to reduce it to four big boxes. Irony is, we Andhraites are crazy about America, ra! But Life is not that good here is my personal experience.'

When he reached the guesthouse, a searing pain surged in his left hand. Kumar dashed to a doctor in Iselin. She told him to visit Edison downtown for heart-related tests. Vishnu called him. 'Who asked you to come to the guesthouse? Vacate immediately.' It only accommodated fresh arrivals from India, he said, not someone like him. If he stayed, he'd have to pay rent. Another clarification: for the duration between the projects—the 'bench' period—he'd have to pay his employer's taxes. Kumar was too shocked to process anything. 'What about my Maryland salaries,' he wanted to ask. Vishnu hung up.

4M intended to commit both immigration and tax frauds. The law mandated H-1B employers to pay foreign workers soon after arriving in the US and considered non-payment on the bench illegal. Such crimes produced penalties or arrests—or both. A desi consultancy seldom gave bench salaries, but still ran the payrolls, paying the taxes, to follow the law. It later recovered the same amount from the consultant. A benched H-1B worker decayed in a corporate cellar, where he paid the company to keep his job.

Most body shops, devoid of projects, 'benched' their employees when they came from India. A guesthouse, then, assuaged their immediate anxieties: providing shelter and food in a country, where they had no home, no salary, no contacts. Assailed by worries, they could leave the US or inform the cops. But a 'safe house' kept them hidden (and quiet).[48]

Kumar discarded most of his belongings and packed his luggage with one hand. Scanning his contact list, he found an HRDI colleague in Maryland who let him crash at his place. Kumar didn't have a car; Khan dropped him off. He applied for jobs, but the bleak reality cornered him soon: he wouldn't find a project in thirty days.

Enough.

He'd return to India and end this torture. Kumar informed his friends and relatives. His brother-in-law, in Detroit, had planned a West Coast trip. Would Kumar like to join? He had no money; his relative bought the flight ticket.

Kumar visited the Grand Canyon. The sunrise and sunset mesmerised him; he bought photos from a professional photographer. In Los Angeles, he posed against the backdrop of the 'HOLLYWOOD' sign. He prayed at a Balaji temple.

The devotee got a call mid-vacation. An employee at a reputed consulting firm, Amit Mhatre, wanted to hire an IT worker for a project in Harrisburg, Pennsylvania. Not a corporation this time but a state agency. Mhatre checked his IT expertise and informed him about the overtime hours.

'Will you pay for them?'

'Yes.'

Kumar left the trip and moved to Harrisburg. The first week in a motel, then an apartment through Sulekha.com. The two-bedroom house had three desis. They soon increased to over half a dozen, filling the living room. Working for the same client, they took turns using the loo in the morning. Kumar called it the 'Dubai model'. He had reached an agreement with his flatmates: on the nights he cooked, they'd clean up after him. But they did not. They also stuffed their tiffin with the overnight food, leaving nothing for him. Their entitlement annoyed him no end. So did their stinginess. He had bought a GPS along with his second-hand dodge van (thanks to another $2,000 'loan' from 4M). On weekends, a flatmate vanished with it. It cost less than $100, but the guy would still not buy his own.

A young Telugu man, Sadananda, perplexed him for a different reason. He often left the house with a packet of frozen chicken. But why? Why not cook at home?

'Where are you going?' Kumar asked him one evening.

'My boss likes chicken.'

Chicken?

'What are you doing there?'

'I cook chicken.'

'Why are you going to boss' house to cook?'

'Because he does my job.'

In July 2009, Kumar went to the JFK airport to pick up his wife and son. A few weeks later, he took them to a neighbouring town, Hershey, to visit its chocolate factory. They returned often. Another haunt—a Balaji temple in Pittsburgh.

The left-hand pain persisted. Sometimes it swelled so much that he struggled to wear a shirt. One day, he couldn't lift his neck. He drove to the nearest hospital. The doctor found nothing abnormal and gave him a neck collar. The temporary fix provided some respite. Kumar consulted a doctor near his apartment, Naina Rathore, who diagnosed the problem: carpal tunnel syndrome. She handed him a wrist brace—its metallic plate gripped his left palm—and recommended physiotherapy.

He met with a physiotherapist for a few weeks, but the wrist brace had worsened the pain. Back to Rathore. 'This is not India that I can prescribe injections. What can I do? This is America. Bear the pain.' Kumar showed her the MRI test result. The same answer: carpal tunnel.

The (unpaid) overtime work had made him literally sick and, soon, the Recession killed the project. Kumar vacated the apartment and requested a friend to drive him and his family to his sister's home in Detroit.

He met a spinal cord specialist, Theodore Shivley, who recommended a surgeon and faxed him the test results. 'My patient will see you for the following problem: cervical C5 disc herniation.' It made sense now. Not carpal tunnel but a slip disc.

The doctor didn't have dates for surgery. Shivley told him to rush to India. Dream America: twelve years. The promise to his father: two years. Real America: one-and-a-half years. A life drenched in humiliation and pain. But now at least his family was with him. Kumar knew the next step, his final step: he bought three flight tickets and buried his Dream America forever.

12

Infocon Logix was a much bigger company. It had four guesthouses: one for women, two for men and one for the office. Manu's guesthouse in Edison split into two levels. One bedroom on the ground floor, two on the first floor. A billiards table and a few chairs filled the basement. He moved into an empty room but soon shared it with roommates, a Nepali and a Hyderabadi man. Like the Unitech flatmates, they chatted late into the night, so he took the living room floor.

Every weekday, around a dozen consultants assembled in the office basement, learning SQL, UNIX, Informatica and Ab Initio. An in-house instructor taught SQL, while a trainer from the Hyderabad office the rest of the courses. After the month-long training, vice president Prakash Sarraju told Manu to add an Infocon Logix recruiter, 'Graham King', on Google Chat, who would market his resume. But Graham never came to office. It struck him later that, like many consultancy recruiters, he worked from the company's offshore office in Hyderabad.[49]

This feature dominated the desi consultancy ecosystem. Companies milking cheap labour, after all, needed more cheap labour to sustain them. So they hired recent college graduates on meagre salaries and taught them the art of fake resumes, 'proxy' interviews and relentless marketing. Desi recruiters had become so infamous for their duplicity—ensnaring H-1Bs to toil for their own firms, the middle vendors, by obscuring the actual clients—that they adopted American names to evade suspicion. Some failed that requirement, too. A recruiter once changed his name to 'Kevin Pietersen', the famous English cricketer. Another slapped the following disclaimer above a job description: 'Please do not submit Muslim candidates.' If post-liberalised India had moulded the Indian identity, making it self-serving and cut-throat, then desi consultancies provided its most literal exemplification: Indian recruiters with fake names colluding with Indian techies on fake resumes to snatch jobs from deserving applicants.

Infocon Logix handed a resume to Manu: seven years' experience, five end clients. Two options for 'proxy': Prakash and Nitish, the manager of operations. But even with their expertise, and several interviews, he failed to find a project in the first six weeks. Graham emailed him another opportunity: a tester position at an insurance firm in California. On the day of the client interview, sitting in the guesthouse miles away from Prakash, Manu put his phone on call forward. And, just like that, he got the job.

About to earn money for the consultancy, he reached its office in Edison to sign the contract. A small establishment—one room, a few workstations—comprising two employees: Mahalakshmi Deshpande, the HR professional, and the accounts manager, Santhosh. Sometimes Prakash dropped in to check for updates. The Edison place operated as a modest front-end, processing payrolls and maintaining documents. The business' heart, training and placing candidates, throbbed in the guesthouses; Prakash had a room in one of them.

Mahalakshmi asked Manu to carry two blank cheques and explained the next steps in person: he'd earn an annual salary of $60,000 in the first year and then on a 70:30 'percentage basis.'[50] If Infocon Logix got $100 per hour, it would pay him $70 and pocket $30. It would also charge $10,000 if he quit before twelve months. Mahalakshmi handed him the contract. He wanted to peruse it, but she rushed him, saying, 'sign here', 'sign there'. He signed wherever she pointed. She kept the contract; he didn't receive a copy, nor asked for it.

Besides Infocon Logix's salary, the project's implementation partner,[51] an American multinational, would give him a per diem allowance of $150. Almost $45 an hour: a lot of money. But Santhosh told him that the consultancy had reduced his salary from $25 to $15, almost equalling an intern's pay, as it didn't 'give so much to a consultant on OPT' (Optional Practical Training, a year-long work permit, with an extension of seventeen months, for foreign graduates of American schools).[52] Manu did not protest. He could *not* protest. Because he didn't own the visa, his employer did.

Desi consultancies' coercive contracts, imposing a hefty fine for quitting, solidified such silence. They also sued their employees for just changing companies. American courts, honouring different state laws, judged these cases with varying yardsticks. They interpreted some clauses as penalties (illegal) and some as liquidated damages (legal). Desperate pleas pervaded countless court dockets, where cash-strapped H-1Bs, unaware of their rights, represented themselves. Many times, they lost. If guesthouses dangled the chains, then courts affixed them.[53]

Infocon Logix paid for Manu's San Francisco flight ticket and gave him $500. Gyan lived in the same city. Sweet luck twice: desi consultancies rarely paid for travel, and he could split the living costs with Gyan. He stayed in a two-bedroom apartment with Gyan and three Andhra IT workers.

The job demanded automated testing, but Unitech Infosol and Infocon Logix had prepared him for manual testing. Unlike a normal job, he had no time to settle. Because this was an exam, whose questions changed by the hour, overseen by several invigilators: his manager, Andrei, and the software developers—Mukesh, Nikesh and Harshal—whose scripts he had to validate. Everyone in the team, much older and more experienced, carried an air of confidence. He'd have to fulfil responsibilities, meet deadlines, exceed expectations. Accomplish all this without raising suspicions. Manu couldn't reveal his identity, his past, his present. A recent college graduate had become a spy.

One day, Andrei came to his cubicle and inquired about the location of a file used to activate an insurance claims database.

Crap, an out-of-syllabus question. His fingers raced on the trackpad, opening and closing windows, settling on what he considered the right answer.

'Is that the location?'

'Yeah, I got confused. I will take a look and let you know.'

'You don't know?'

Andrei took the mouse and effected some clicks. Job done.

'Why couldn't you find it?'

'I got confused with different folders.'

'Okay.' Andrei left.

Damn, he knew. But not just Andrei.

'Hard times,' he had pinged Ramesh after joining the project. 'They got doubt man.'

Manu had approached a few employees for access to ETL tools.

'Why what happened?'

'They asked you don't know this, you don't know that, what have you done in your previous project. They asked so many questions.'

'Why are they asking now? Did you run into problems while testing?'

'No, did not get access.'

'What about documentation, I'm sure every project has documentation.'

'Yes.'

'Look at the summary or the list of contents. I'm sure it will have accessibility to tools. Don't be scared man. God be with you.'

'Thanks man. Hope they don't remove me. Because they won't even say. They will just have a meeting and the next day my ID won't work. And when I'll ask, they will say you no longer work here. :('

'My friend, you are going to a job with 9 years of exp right? Of which you have 6 months exp? Even a genius will have problems.'

'No man, 3 months only.'

'So, it's only logical you will have problems. It's not like Matrix where Keanu Reeves downloads information at the speed of light. How many years did u show? 5, 7, 9?'

'7 years.'

'Gulpppppppppp.'

':('

'7 years, wow. No wonder I am not getting a job. I am showing only 2 years in India. So you showed you worked for 7 years in USA? Wow. So you started working from 17 years?'

'Lol.'

Clients fired incompetent 'freshers' like Manu. Some fumbled the charade, and a tiny mistake exposed them. They hardly got a reason, and most managers didn't escalate the issue. Corporate America didn't consider fake resumes transgressive because it had redefined transgression itself: a dullard sucking resources, sinking profits. So, as long as the job got done on time, no matter how, it was business as usual.

Manu browsed online forums, consulted his friends and asked the Infocon Logix instructor: nothing. He tweeted: 'Need Help in Business Objects Data Service Designer :('

He pinged Prakash the next day. 'Do you know someone in Business Objects Data Services Designer?'

'Ya, y. You need help?'

'I need some overview, so I can work smoothly.'

'Call Narayan. He will help you. I'm emailing both of you.'

Narayan answered Manu's questions and explained the basic concepts. He advised Manu to read the relevant manuals and check a YouTube link. Manu often pinged Nitish ('Is PDM different from BRD and Mapping document?') and Prakash ('How can we import a file in Unix?') who resolved his queries.

A young Indian stopped by his cubicle. He introduced himself, smiling, 'I'm Vikram.' At one point, he asked, 'Hindi aata hai na?' You do understand Hindi? Finally. Someone who spoke his language. Manu relaxed in his presence and, in the subsequent weeks, walked to his cubicle, popped a question and Vikram obliged.

'You know I'm just a fresher,' he said once. 'This is my second project.'

'I know. We have all come like that.'

Manu had taken a risk. Vikram could inform other Indians in the team who, like 'hungry tigers', would pounce on him and get him fired. Weeks passed. He and Vikram never discussed his secret. Eventually, the job eased up. 'Man, frankly, we don't need seven years of experience,' he messaged Ramesh. 'Even a noob can do.'

A decent salary hadn't changed his lifestyle. He still slept on the floor; he had still not bought a car. Loneliness followed him in the city, exacerbating during the weekends and vacations. Not that he lacked options. His flatmates soaked in the heady American nights on weekends. Sometimes they spent the nights in hotel rooms. They asked Manu as well, but he cherished his own world, where routine and solitude—and video games!—reigned supreme. He played *League of Legends* and *MMORPG* with strangers online. One of them, Reid, a Rhode Island resident, had gifted him a PlayStation. The gesture moved him. They had not even met.

Around seven months had passed since he joined the client. His contract would expire in a few more weeks. He contacted a director at the implementation partner to check for an extension.

'I spoke with Mark and he said he will not need you past December 22,' came the reply. 'He wanted to make sure I told you that you have done a great job.'

13

When you were a nobody from a nobody town, and no firms glanced at you, and no locals gave you business and no one understood that a part-time job solved nothing, then all you had was a monitor and a keyboard. So Virgil wrote emails, many emails. To news channels (Fox News, CNN, CBS), rebuking them for not telling the right stories. To newspapers (the *New York Times*, the *Washington Post*, the *Wall Street Journal*), sharing his ideas on fixing the world economy. To universities (Harvard, Berkeley, Yale), championing a global trade protecting workers across continents. To government agencies (the Department of Labor, DOL; the Department of Veterans Affairs, VA; the Texas Workforce Commission), flagging workplace discrimination in the IT industry. To Donald Trump: 'You want my vote?'

No reply, sometimes his emails bounced. As if he didn't exist. As if he was a ghost—a side character in his own story. 'I'm outside, looking in, and the door is locked,' he emailed a fellow activist, Bob Hall. 'Who holds the key? If I knew, I would open it.'

From 2008 to 2010, Virgil had secured at least one contract a year. Even though short-lived, it helped his annual pay reach around $30,000. But in 2011, he got just one remote project, much shorter than the previous ones, hurtling his yearly income below the minimum wage. He survived on unemployment cheques and food stamps; readers' donations and Google Ads contributed a few hundred dollars. He failed to sell a property. Real estate thrived on perception; Virgil couldn't afford haircuts. Holes studded his shoes, making his toes peek out. The repair shop, too, was bare as ever.

In May 2012, when the unemployment benefits expired, he was broker than broke—the 'brokest' ever. He applied for a food service worker position, 'the lowest of lowest jobs', at the VA. Even there he had a plan: once inside the civil service haven, he'd scope out the IT positions reserved for internal applicants. The next day, the VA rejected him.

An email to Bob the next month.

> I don't want years' worth of work wasted if something happens to me like getting arrested because I can't pay child support, etc.
>
> http://www.godaddy.com
> vbierschwale
> scotty1miller
>
> That's where it can be renewed if something happens. My real estate site, virgilbierschwale.com, went down today, and there's no money coming from anywhere. Let's just say I'm putting my affairs in order <grin>.

Keep America At Work sank, too. Virgil didn't have the hosting fee, $7. His internet hadn't worked in a while; he used a buddy's computer to check emails. 'I don't have a clue, how I will get a break,' he emailed Molly, 'but I still keep trying.' He'd later tell Bob, 'Hell, I'm the closest I've ever been to blowing my brains out.'

A lifeline appeared. An initiative of the DOL and VA, the Veteran Retraining Assistance Program (VRAP) would provide $1,473 per month to veterans attending approved institutions for a year and 'employment assistance'. Virgil contacted the Cleveland Institute of Electronics (CIE), as he had liked its correspondence course in his Navy days. But certified for half-time, it'd only give half the benefits, $737. He emailed the school, asking if he could enrol in two degrees, making his study full-time.

When that didn't work out, he contacted Austin Community College (ACC). Certified for full-time, it listed his preferred course, the

Associate of Applied Science in real estate brokerage licensing. But it required him to attend an orientation programme at its Austin campus. 'I guess I will have to drop out,' he replied. 'I qualify for VRAP, which means I have no job, no money, no gas. Austin is out of the picture.'

Virgil struggled to find a college that even knew about VRAP. He asked on the VA website about applying to both the electronic engineering technology and software engineering degrees at the CIE. Got a convoluted answer that ignored his question. So he applied to just one programme.

In September 2012, he received a letter from the VA denying his claim to benefits: 'You are not enrolled as a full-time student.' He appealed the decision, emailing the chronology of events to the DOL, VA and CIE. 'I have already had all my utilities shut off except electricity, which will shut today if I cannot pay $96. I was counting on this lifeline, but I now realize it was but a boat anchor.'

Over two weeks passed. Virgil wrote to Arizona Senator John McCain (a Navy veteran) and the veteran's office at the Senate. Nothing. 'Right now, CIE is the only port in the storm,' he emailed its guidance counsellor, checking if she had heard anything from the DOL or VA, 'so I want to leave it open until they tell me it's no longer an option. At that point, I will no longer have anywhere to turn, and I might as well just give up, lay down, and kick the bucket, which would give our so-called Veterans Administration one less vet to deal with.'

The VA replied two weeks later. 'You meet the basic eligibility requirements for VRAP, you are just not attending school full-time therefore payments cannot be made.' Which meant joining ACC. Which meant going to Austin. Which meant spending money. Which meant, well, back to the hellhole. 'Do you realize I am broke? How do you expect me to attend anything other than correspondence courses? Do you even give a damn if I live or die?'

An ACC employee apologised, assuring him he could take online classes. Virgil visited its Fredericksburg campus and finished the admission process. The school also wanted his Phoenix and Capella transcripts for financial aid. 'I can't get them,' he replied. 'I have zero dollars, not even a penny.' The college called it an 'institutional' policy.

'Then you will lose a student because I have told you I don't have the money to pay for anything, and I will tell the G.I. Bill I meet all the requirements for their VRAP program and you refused to participate even though you are a certified G.I. Bill Institution.'

He kept emailing Capella University, explaining his predicament. No reply. Another email: 'I don't want to jeopardize your school's accreditation, but I have tried every route and got zero meaningful response, which forces me to contact the agencies that accredit your school. I don't want to do that, so perhaps you can help me?' The threat worked; customer care told him how to collect his transcripts. But ACC wanted the official—and not online—transcripts. Which needed money. 'I hate to escalate this to the Board of Trustees,' he emailed an employee, 'but I've no option.'

He applied for the mechanic maintenance position at the VA in Kerrville. The reply read: 'You were not among the most highly qualified candidates, and your name will not be referred to the employing agency.' He forwarded it to Max. 'Guess they just want me to blow my damned brains out and give up like you do. Bastards.'

14

Kumar met with an uncle in Hyderabad, a radiologist, who checked his test results and recommended ten-day bed rest. He lay on a low plywood cot the entire day—a rolled towel balancing his neck—only standing up for bathroom breaks and morning ablutions. He ate on the cot and avoided taking a shower for the first few days. The inactive period made him restless, but the treatment worked its magic. Kumar inquired about his professional prospects: it would take him at least six months to find a job. Only one place delivered in weeks.

While flying to Detroit in December 2009, he sat in a wheelchair, as the slightest mobility aggravated the pain. He slept on the carpet in his sister's house and applied for jobs lying down, keeping the laptop on a wooden table over his tummy. An Indian outsourcing giant, Wizsys, hired him for a contract in Clayton, North Carolina, and ordered him to join the project as soon as possible. Kumar still needed rest, but for Indian H-1Bs, choices were as rare as unicorns. He flew to Clayton, worked for a week and returned to Detroit to drive his dodge van. A twelve-hour journey, relentless snow, a fragile wrist—so fragile that he drove with one hand at times. A man missing his family, facing an uncertain future: he cried, multiple times.

The client had fired many full-time employees, outsourcing the IT work to Wizsys. Even though not on Wizsys's payroll, he had to finish the dirty job: meet the American worker, get his sign-offs on the 'knowledge transfer' documents and replace him. An African-

American man, Ronald, who had worked at the firm for two decades. Ronald and Jack, a White man, sat in such a low-ceilinged server room that visitors had to hunch to enter it. They didn't appreciate his presence, especially Ronald who, considering him a Wizsys employee, shooed him away. Kumar moved to the canteen. Obeying the company protocol, he couldn't tell them that he didn't work for Wizsys or decide their fate. He understood their anger, and the guilt pricked him.

One morning, he met an old woman smoking under a tree outside the building entrance. 'Today is my last working day,' she said. 'I have two college-going daughters. I have a house on mortgage. I don't know why Indians are taking all the jobs, even in accounting and finance.' Kumar struggled to sleep that week. Or process anything: why did the American companies not care about their workers? Why was the US government so indifferent? Had his dream become someone else's nightmare?

The Wizsys team lead in Chicago, Ramanan, phoned and grilled and dismissed him, like an IAS babu deriding a clerk. The Indian hierarchy again: Ramanan worked for a famous firm; Kumar, an obscure consultancy. During a conference call attended by Wizsys's employees and Kumar and Jack, Ramanan spoke to him in Tamil.

'What is he saying?' Jack asked Kumar.

'I don't know. He is talking in Tamil.'

Jack complained to the client's chief financial officer (CFO), who escalated it to the Wizsys delivery manager, Saraswathi. Kumar complained to Saraswathi, too. Once the CFO asked Kumar, 'Do you've any caste problem with Wizsys? Why are they harassing you?' The question embarrassed him; he didn't expect an American to know about the caste system. 'It's not caste. But even I don't know the reason.'

To extend his H-1B visa, he needed letters from all the firms in the hiring chain to establish his employment. He requested the client manager: received it on the same day. 4M also gave the letter. Wizsys refused. 'Two thousand contractors need the letter,' Saraswathi said. 'It's not possible to give it to everyone.' Kumar pleaded and begged.

Wizsys never provided the letter, ending his stint in less than four months. His master, Vishnu, barked: 'Find another project.'

A new client, a new town: Helena, Montana. This project too, like the Harrisburg one, for a state agency. The office resembled a 'big house'. No Indian colleagues, a pleasant change. Complemented by a relaxed work culture—he wore shorts once a week—and weekly potlucks. Once, a project manager, Harold, wanted a picture with him. Paying tribute to *Harold & Kumar*, Harold and Kumar stood beside each other and beamed at the camera. Another colleague said he awaited Kumar's citizenship oath—'we call it the American dream'. It moved him.

Montana's beauty bewitched him: expansive mountains, transparent lakes, curious animals—a deer stared at him through the office window. He hiked to soak it all in. 'After visiting Kashmir, I felt that kind of beautiful place on earth is Helena,' he'd write on his blog years later. 'If you are in the USA and did not visit Montana, then there is no excuse.'

Only one thing pierced his bliss: 4M. Vishnu demanded a $3,000 money order—without 4M's name or address—for the green card application. Kumar reached a post office, made the unusual request and got scolded. He called his master. Vishnu screamed: 'Send money today.'

Why is he asking for money? Why does he talk like this?

Kumar sold his freedom for $3,000. An H-1B visa remained valid for a maximum six years. After that, a foreign worker could stay in the country, via yearly extensions, if his company had applied for a green card.[54] But since country-wise quotas decided its allotment and Indians dominated the H-1B programme, they had to wait for over ten years—around fifteen for someone like Kumar, without a master's degree—to become permanent residents.[55] Most consultants hung on to their employers during that period, because changing a green card sponsor caused more delays and doubts. This leash delighted American corporations and Indian body shops. If, by allowing firms to own the visas, the H-1B programme began the foreign workers' 'enslavement', then the long green card queue made it permanent.

A dance academy intrigued Kumar. A woman named Amy told him that the belly dance class met every Thursday. He enrolled. Among the students, he was the only man, the only Indian. The first man in Helena, said the instructor, to learn belly dance. The class had diverse participants: a doctor, students, part-time workers. Kumar enjoyed it so much that, one weekend, he drove 100 miles to attend a workshop; he even bought a book.

Downtown Helena had several dance classes. Kumar used the discount coupons and explored them. Once, in a pub for a Zumba class, a young American woman sat beside him.

'Where are you from?' she asked.

'Hyderabad, India.'

She took a piece of paper, scribbled on it and showed it to him.

ఇదో రకం చెట్టు

The Telugu for okra. How did she … he looked at her.

She smiled and said: 'Bagunnara?' How are you doing?

It amazed him. A former exchange student at Hyderabad Central University, Madeline had visited West Bengal to attend a friend's wedding. She showed him photos from her trip and recounted her experiences: the train journey, the pretty sights, the income inequality. Kumar added her on Facebook and bumped into her often.

One day, Amy introduced him to an American couple who taught at a local university. Kumar saw a huge bookshelf near their house's entrance. It had tomes by Swami Vivekananda, Mahatma Gandhi and other spiritual figures. Even his favourite, the Bhagavad Gita. The couple welcomed him. First, basic questions: his name, his hometown, why did he come to America? Followed by: did he, like other Indians, also have a 'caste name'? Whenever he had discussed Hinduism with Americans, that question—of caste—always came up. Kumar hadn't resolved the religion's contradictions, including questioning how its hierarchy served a Brahmin like him, so it needled him. But this one had a simple answer: Sreenivas, his father's first name; Pandruvada, his village's name. Withholding his controversial views, he highlighted the unfortunate differences between India's rich and poor.

'You talk like a philosopher,' said the hostess.

Philosopher. A new word.

The living room seated around a dozen people. Many musical instruments. Some looked familiar: a harmonium, a damaru, a dappu. He sat on the floor. Like the others, he held a bunch of chits clipped together. Each slip held one line—from a different holy scripture: the Bible, Quran, Bhagavad Gita and more.

They started chanting.

Musical instruments complemented the voices in unison. A Shiva chant boomed; dappu beats lashed. When a line in Sanskrit popped up, the professor nailed the diction. The experience cleansed him; he kept returning for more.

In October 2011, his six-month project got over. Kumar emailed his friends and colleagues. 'I am truly leaving with mixed feelings. Excited for the new opportunity but sad to leave a great work environment and comfort zone where I had many wonderful moments.'

Kumar and Madeline planned to meet downtown. He reached mid-afternoon and waited. She came on a bike, leaving her shift.

Why did she bother, he said, he could have driven to her place.

Madeline smiled. 'I just wanted to say bye.'

15

Infocon Logix gave Manu a new recruiter, Jackson Edge (real name: Jaikrishnan Hegde), who received an email from a vendor wanting to hire an ETL tester for a global bank. Jackson provided Manu's contact information, location and availability. He also attached Manu's resume; this version presented a different consultant, told a different story. A resume filled with specific skills, satiating corporate America's buzzwords obsession. A new position, a new Manu, a new chameleon in the jungle of IT.

After clearing the vendor interview, Manu turned to Prakash for proxy. On the client call day, he and some Infocon consultants assembled in Prakash's room. He wanted to give them a live demo: a guru inducting his followers. Manu switched on the call forward; Prakash's phone rang. Over the next twenty minutes, he answered questions, assuaged doubts, cracked jokes. The vendor called a few days later: the client had said yes.

He flew back to his old life, San Francisco. Infocon Logix had also applied for his H-1B visa. This time, too, he earned a meagre salary, less than $25 per hour. But he no longer worried about the loan. Manu had paid more than half of it by December, and his father gave the remaining amount. Work also didn't bother him. 'Looks like it's relaxed,' he wrote to a friend.

Not so much after a week.

'Man, this thing is killing me,' he pinged his Unitech roommate, Bala.

'What thing.'

'Test objectives, dunno whom to ask :(This Monday I have to report my status.'

Another message a week later. 'Man, still having hard time with damned test objectives and cases.'

'It's due today right?'

'Yeah. It is simple yet highly complex if you know nothing about the process, and no one to help like last time.'

Manu spent hours trying to find a solution.

'Oh man, new problem arrived :('

'Ah haa?'

'I'm telling you, never ever never ever never ever switch jobs.'

'What happened?'

'I have to do dry run in Autosys.'

'What's the problem?'

'I don't know dry run.'

Another ping to Bala the next day.

'Now I have to count when they'll kick me out.'

'Why?'

'Those test objectives were not correct.'

Bala messaged him later in the day. 'So what happened?'

'Nothing. I think I can write a book called "How to lose your job even though you are experienced!"'

'Lol.'

'Lol.'

'Man, still having a hard time. Today the lead blasted me. I can't baby sit you.'

Manu pinged Mandeep and Vishal: did they know anyone who knew Autosys? No luck. Prakash gave him a consultant's email, but that didn't work either. Stuck in similar quandaries, many techies 'outsourced' their work to IT professionals in India for a few hundred dollars. In the desi consultancy world, where an H-1B's pay enriched several companies—the prime vendor, the middle vendor(s) and the employer—a harried worker on a fake resume changed his identity once more. Aping an outsourcing corporation, he became a corporation himself, making his dehumanisation voluntary and destined.

Manu's manager, Pulkit Ahuja, emailed him. A meeting invitation, but just for the two of them. Strange: this hadn't happened before. He met Pulkit in a conference room. Without a smile or greeting, he said Manu spent a lot of time online. Manu said he only checked his email for work. Pulkit looked unconvinced; the meeting ended.

'Now I am in jail,' he pinged Bala.

'What happened?'

'Got warning.'

'For what?'

'They said I am too much online and not proactive.'

'As in, on the websites?'

'They did not say that.'

'So you are talking to me on iPhone haha.'

'Yeah man :(And this is not the first time. Last time also my manager was shouting at me ... you don't know this.'

'Lol.'

'Lol.'

'Man, maybe I will go back to India. I will stop taking this stress. What is the most they can do? Fire me.'

'Idk.'

'Me neither, lol.'

Manu stopped checking even personal emails on the office desktop. But he made little progress. Pulkit called him to meet again. On Friday evening, the office buzzed with weekend anticipation. So did Manu. He had bought a video game, *Diablo III*, and hoped to unlock newer levels in the next two days. But what explained this meeting? In the conference room, Pulkit spoke about the budget constraints and said, 'Today is your last day.' When they came out, he asked for Manu's badge. He followed Manu to his cubicle and told him to email his timesheets. Manu couldn't even log out properly; Pulkit continued to stand behind him. Once he finished the formalities, Pulkit escorted him to the entrance. Pulkit said nothing—not even bye—as he shut the door.

16

By discriminating against American techies and exploiting Indian H-1B workers, desi consultancies had ravaged Virgil, Kumar and Manu. (Virgil lucked out with the ObjectWin project. Desi consultancies rarely hired Americans.) But if a sharp law eliminated the rogue players, would the new H-1B programme benefit both foreign and American professionals? A typical IT hiring chain looked like the following: H-1B Worker → Employer → Middle Vendor(s) → Prime Vendor → Client. Devoid of desi consultancies, it'd become H-1B Worker → Prime Vendor → Client. The Indian outsourcing giants, or huge IT body shops, often played the role of prime vendors. Their recent actions, too, had raised major suspicions.

In October 2013, American federal prosecutors accused Infosys of committing 'systemic visa fraud'.[56] They alleged that the firm had brought foreign workers to the US on tourist visas to work full-time, revised their contracts to represent them as off-shore resources and trained them to deceive immigration officials. Since foreign nationals couldn't work full-time on tourist visas, the company submitted 'invitation letters' to the US consular officials containing alleged false statements about their purposes of visit, such as for 'meetings' or 'discussions'. Infosys also created a 'Do's and Don'ts' memorandum for its employees: 'Do not mention activities like implementation, consulting, design & testing, etc., which sound like work'; 'do not use words like work, activity, etc., in the invitation letter'; 'do not mention anything about contract rates'.

After an investigation of more than two years, the firm paid the US government $34 million[57] in a civil settlement—the largest amount ever in an immigration case.[58]

Like many IT behemoths, Infosys prized H-1B visas. In 2015, *InformationWeek* published a list of the biggest users of the guest worker programme and their employee demographics in the US.[59]

Company	*Petitions Approved*	*Visa Rank*	*Per cent Indian*
Cognizant Technology Solutions (CTS)	15,680	1	99.6%
Infosys	8,991	2	98.1%
Tata Consultancy Services (TCS)	6,339	3	99.7%
Accenture	5,793	4	95.4%
Wipro	4,803	5	99.6%
HCL America	2,776	6	99.4%
Tech Mahindra Americas	2,657	7	99.4%
IBM India Private	2,500	8	87.3%

Outsourcing visa. That's what Indian Commerce Minister Kamal Nath had called the H-1B in 2007.[60] In 2013, all the top ten H-1B sponsors were outsourcing companies.[61] Six among them, Indian multinationals (TCS, Infosys, Wipro, HCL, Tech Mahindra and Larsen & Toubro), while the rest employed a vast majority of Indians. Next year, same.[62] In 2013, the five biggest recipients of the H-1B visas—Accenture, Cognizant, Infosys, Tech Mahindra and Wipro—paid an annual median salary of about $64,000. Amazon's H-1Bs $95,000, Apple $115,000.[63] Cost-cutting 101, desi consultancy style.

Because the rare Department of Labor (DOL) investigations had also found the big bosses guilty of visa abuse.[64] Some multiple times, paying astounding back wages.

Company	*Back Wages*	*Employees Affected*	*Year*
Wipro	$82,726	1	2014
Infosys	$45,101	11	2012
Tata Autocomp Systems	$153,279	9	2014
Cognizant	$509,607	67	2008
	$1,692	1	2015
	$63,720	24	2017
	$4,096	1	2015
HCL America	$560	1	2019
	$8,999	1	2017
Tech Mahindra Americas	$326,337	11	2015
	$6,777	1	2015

The DOL found H-1B violations in 2,708 cases from 2005 to 2023.[65] Cognizant's back wages ranked twenty-third, Tech Mahindra thirty-seventh, TATA Autocomp 136th.[66] Even though Tata Technologies paid no back wages, it shelled out a rarer fine—civil monetary penalty (CMP)—worth $16,575, ranking ninety-eighth among all CMPs.[67]

Wipro, Infosys, TCS, Cognizant and HCL evoked intense revulsion among H-1B techies on Indian immigration forums. They called the collective 'WITCH' companies, bemoaning the long work hours, low salaries and favouritism.[68] 'I have been to six different locations across the USA in the last 6 years,' read one such post, 'and observed that if the account director is from a certain region from India, then only people from that region get promoted. Let me know your thoughts.' It got one reply: 'The Sun is hot, the moon is cold, the grass is green. What else, Captain Obvious?'

But their most common complaints unravelled the 'EB-1C green card[69] fraud', which needed just over one year of experience as a manager at the multinational's home branch. Unlike the other categories, 'EB-1C' didn't need an employer to prove it had hired an exceptional foreign professional. Or that it would pay her a prevailing wage. Or that it couldn't find a suitable American. Many companies sent such employees on an intra-company L-1A visa, which had no annual cap. The quick processing time, taking around a year—as opposed to other decade-long green card categories—sweetened the deal. Indian workers railed about it, anonymously, online: 'How can I sue [Cognizant Technology Solutions] CTS for EB1C fraud?'[70] 'How Can We Stop Rampant Abuse of EB1C India by TCS, CTS?'[71] 'Why Does the USCIS [United States Citizenship and Immigration Services] Not Punish the EB1C-India Green-Card scam?'[72] Over 34 million people had endorsed a 2012 petition to Congress, called 'Stop EB-1C abuse and fraudulent filing'.[73] They tweeted to USCIS, informing the federal agency about the '#EB1CFraud'.

The WITCH corporations had also faced a long list of other corruption charges. Epic Systems,[74] Computer Sciences Corporation[75] and Simonelli Innovation[76] sued TCS for stealing trade and intellectual properties. Five US law firms—Zhang Investor Law, Bernstein Liebhard, Bragar Eagel & Squire, the Rosen Law Firm and Howard G. Smith—filed class action lawsuits against Infosys on behalf of shareholders and investors for issuing misleading statements to inflate short-term profits.[77] Accused of bribing an Indian government official and violating the Foreign Corrupt Practices Act, Cognizant agreed to pay $25 million to settle the charges.[78]

WITCH workers had also sued their employers for wage theft. An Infosys employee filed a lawsuit against the company for withholding his overtime pay, exceeding 1,000 hours.[79] It had paid $26 million in 2007 for similar accusations.[80] TCS settled for $29.75 million in a class-action lawsuit for allegedly robbing its employees' tax refunds.[81] Cognizant, too, reached a $5.7 million settlement with its employees, compensating them for underpaid overtime work.[82]

Infosys was stuck in another loop. In 2017, it agreed to pay $1 million to the state of New York to settle visa fraud allegations that mimicked its 2013 settlement: that the firm had brought foreign professionals on tourist (instead of H-1B) visas and paid them 'significantly less' wages as compared to equivalent American or H-1B workers.[83] The state prosecutors alleged that Infosys created a '"Do's and Don'ts" memorandum' for its employees to 'deceive US Consular officials' and submitted fake 'invitation letters' that misrepresented the 'true purpose' of their visits.[84] Two years later, Infosys settled another case of visa and tax frauds, paying $800,000 to the state of California for allegedly importing foreign professionals on—what else but!—tourist visas.[85]

Like true globe-trotters, the WITCH companies had angered workers in multiple continents. Over two dozen lawsuits in the 2010s in North America alone—and for one reason.

Erin Green was promoted to lead Infosys's global immigration team in June 2013. But his supervisor, Vasudeva Nayak, assigned his 'immigration "operations" responsibilities' to 'less experienced' or peer-level employees in India, alleged Green's lawsuit complaint,[86] 'with no prior US Immigration experience'. Nayak criticised Green and gave him vague performance goals. When he informed Nayak about managers awaiting long-overdue promotions, Nayak replied, 'Not everyone can be CEO'. Only those employees would get promoted, he said, who entertained 'more role and responsibility'. Green termed it the 'Catch-22' situation. Because 'only South Asians' got 'more responsibility' and subsequent promotions.

Nayak 'consistently lowered' his American team members' scores, alleged Green, reducing a Black employee's rating from '1 to 3', with '1+' being the highest, without justification. He also excluded Green from managerial meetings and 'spoke [in] Hindi' in his presence. On his US visit, Nayak disrespected Green in front of his team and once screamed at him on the phone at night, saying Green was 'conspiring' to get Nayak fired.

Green filed an internal discrimination complaint. Nothing happened. Five months later, Nayak awarded him his lowest performance rating, telling him to concentrate on 'operational issues'. Catch-22 again: Nayak had ordered him to recede from operational focus. On a conference call, he 'verbally assaulted' Green's subordinate, a White manager, reducing her to tears. He 'berated' another woman in the team 'to the point of tears' at least twice and threatened 'her return to India'. Demoting

Green's 'long-tenured Indian subordinates', he even illustrated the 'concept of a perceived Uncle Tom' in an 'Indian-dominated' company.

Green approached the US legal team. Infosys hired a law firm, Jones Day, to investigate the charges. But its employees grilled him instead, asking irrelevant and leading questions. It also considered him a 'suspected whistleblower' for a government investigation into the company's immigration-related compliance. (Green denied the charge.) Nine months after the probe, Infosys fired him for having used his work computer for personal use several years ago.[87]

The complaint referenced another lawsuit quoting an Infosys manager. 'There does exist an element of discrimination. We are advised to hire Indians because they will work off the clock without murmur and can always be transferred across the nation without hesitation unlike [a] local workforce.'[88]

Many White American workers, like Green, had sued the WITCH firms for racial and employment discrimination. They weren't alone.

In early 2011, eighteen IT professionals—belonging to different races and national origins—sued Cognizant and its client, Molina Healthcare.[89] They alleged that Cognizant paid 'kickbacks' to their supervisor, Amir Desai, Molina's CIO, to replace American employees with Indian H-1Bs. The outsourcing giant applied for forty visas, allegedly submitting 'false statements' to the DOL, stating that the foreign employees wouldn't affect the company's American workforce. After the approved applications, Molina fired about forty Americans. By January 2010, the once diverse IT department comprised around '80%-90%' Indians.

Desai told Molina's senior HR professional, Supriya Sood, that the 'upper management' had given him 'orders' to fire Americans and hire Indians. In October 2010, Sood and Josephine Wittenberg, the former HR Director, investigated and concluded that 'the upper management indeed discriminated' against 'American workers' in 2009 and 2010, 'including the plaintiffs'. Molina, for example, 'allowed its Indian staff' a 'long lunch' break to 'celebrate Divali', alleged the lawsuit complaint, after which they didn't return to the office. Non-Indian employees received no such benefit. The managers 'discouraged' the Christmas,

Thanksgiving and Fourth of July celebrations, 'assigning mandatory work' during such holidays. Staff meetings, often conducted in Indian languages, excluded American employees.

Desai promoted 'only Indian nationals' to senior management positions and once 'verbally abus[ed]' a non-Indian manager. An Indian professional's incompetence deactivated Michigan's health plan database for a week. He faced no consequences. But when a non-Indian database administrator made 'mistakes not nearly as serious', he lost his job. Despite 'many complaints', the CFO and CEO—John and Mario Molina—'refused to allow any investigation'.[90]

Professionals from more races and national origins sued the WITCH firms, including African-Americans.[91] Davina Linguist[92] led Infosys's Diversity Recruiting Program in 2012. Responsible for increasing its non-South Asian workforce, she testified against the company's discriminatory practices in the *Koehler v. Infosys Technologies Ltd*[93] case. She stated the firm's composition had remained around '93% Indian' during her tenure and her team 'found little to no support' for the 'Diversity Program'. Explaining her 'personal experience of discrimination', she revealed that the IT multinational had rejected close to '12,000 U.S. applicants'. During her deposition, the firm counsel tried to 'intimidate' her by asking 'irrelevant and harassing' questions about her 'home life, family members, [and] children'. Infosys demoted Linguist. Her replacement had 'no relevant experience'. She resigned.[94]

More Black employees sued the WITCH firms. So did Indian-origin green card holders.

When Subash Thayyullathil[95] noticed Infosys importing Indian B-1 workers, alleged his lawsuit petition, he requested it to 'get proper work visas' for them. For at least one employee, it could still apply for an H-1B. He procured a client letter, too. But Infosys 'failed to process' the visa on time. He informed the firm that the 'misuse of visas' had risked the project. Infosys 'reacted negatively', desiring 'greater profit'. After two months, he 'again raised concerns' about the 'fraud and misuse of visas'. Infosys ordered him to move to India in two weeks—without a reason. Forced out of the project, he witnessed another instance of 'visa fraud'. He filed a whistle-blower complaint. The company fired him.[96]

But the employment discrimination charges weren't confined to the US alone.[97]

The Brisbane City Council (BCC) outsourced its IT work to HCL in 2013, eliminating fifty-five jobs, claiming that it would save $7.9 million over five years.[98] In 2018, a Queensland workers' collective, the Australian Services Union (ASU), accused the BCC of exploiting Indian techies in a 'systematic and brazen' manner and 'discriminating against' Australian professionals.[99] HCL employees worked '60 hours per week', ate 'meals on the job' and got no 'overtime'. If they didn't obey, they'd lose their jobs to other pliant Indians. 'In local government, we have never witnessed such blatant wage theft, exploitation, and discrimination,' stated the ASU,[100] 'including breaches of the National Employment Standards and Award. It is disgraceful that it is Australia's largest council that seems to be complicit in this.'

Now what? Would fixing both the villains—the mom-and-pop body shops and the outsourcing giants—fix the problem?

Not so fast—not so simple. Because this implicated more players hiding in plain sight. American corporations leaned on countless allies. Virgil, a one-man shop struggling to survive, had just begun his research. Every turn threw up more questions than answers. But wandering in the graveyard of broken dreams, he encountered an ally, someone who knew the problem, someone who had the solution. A professor who knew where the 'dead bodies are buried'.

III

THOUGHT CONTROL

17

Norman Matloff, a computer science professor at the University of California, Davis, investigated the H-1B programme for a simple reason: he cared for his students. The sluggish economy in 1993 made them sweat for jobs. Some worked in Macy's as sales clerks. The 1990 guest worker programme, swelling the labour pool, had exacerbated their desperation. It perplexed Norm.[1]

Born to 'one-and-a-half immigrants',[2] he grew up in East LA and San Gabriel Valley. After a short stint as a Silicon Valley programmer, he secured a PhD in pure mathematics from UCLA in 1975, then joined the UC Davis faculty.[3]

As he intensified his H-1B research in the mid-1990s, something else, too, stirred: the tech industry. Its first wish: increasing the annual H-1B quota. Its eternal move: the 'thought control' tactic implanting the 'STEM[4] crisis' notion in public consciousness. The Information Technology Association of America (ITAA), an industry trade group, released a study in 1997.[5] So did the Department of Commerce (DOC).[6] They came to the same conclusion: that the country wilted from a STEM workers shortage.

Prodded by the ITAA, the DOC co-sponsored a two-day National IT Workforce Convocation in Berkeley. *The New York Times* published a piece on the front page, quoting the ITAA chief, Silicon Valley executives and noted academics, confirming an acute labour shortage.[7] Other media outlets sang the same tune.

But a report by the Government Accountability Office (GAO), the congressional watchdog, flagged 'serious analytical and methodological' errors in the DOC and ITAA studies.[8] The American media ran countless pieces and news segments, featuring critics of the STEM crisis. The Institute of Electrical and Electronics (IEEE)-USA published profiles of 500 unemployed engineers amid the tech boom, calling them 'Misfortune 500'.

Senator Spencer Abraham (R-Michigan) introduced the American Competitiveness Act in March 1998. It aimed to reform H-1B rules, increase the annual cap from 65,000 to 85,000 and create 20,000 scholarships for low-income students to study STEM. As if Silicon Valley had handed its megaphone to Capitol Hill. The tech giants devised a two-fold solution to combat the 'labour shortage' problem: expand the H-1B programme in the short term and increase scholarship and training funds for native workers to reduce the reliance on foreign workforce in the future.

Norm testified before Congress on 21 April 1998. For him, the H-1B issue pivoted on a three-letter word: age. Junior employees earned less, needed fewer benefits and, without marital pressure, toiled overtime. He cited the examples of vocal proponents of labour shortage (Intel,[9] Sun Microsystems[10] and Cypress Semiconductors[11]) whose hiring patterns—evident from their employment web pages, recruitment literature and lawsuits—demonstrated a tilt towards younger techies.

Age discrimination hurt American programmers as young as thirty-five.[12] An *InformationWeek* survey of hiring managers found that only 2 per cent of them preferred to hire an applicant with over ten years of experience.[13] A *Network World* survey stated that 'the younger the manager, the less likely he/she' would have hired an older programmer.[14] Another study concluded that, on average, it took 'three more weeks for a laid-off programmer or engineer' to land a job for each year of age.[15]

Sun Microsystems's employment webpage categorised workers by their experience levels: entry level (0–2 years), intermediate (3–5 years), senior (6+ years). A position for senior software engineer on

Intel's website set the cut-off at five years of experience. Oracle, four years. Best Buy, two years. And they weren't outliers.[16]

Industry folks themselves admitted—or deflected—the age discrimination problem. 'The half-life of an engineer, whether hardware or software, is only a few years,' said Intel's chief operation officer, Craig Barrett, at a stakeholders' meeting.[17] In March 1998, Bay Area TV hosted a debate between Norm and Intel's HR vice president, Coetta Chambers. Norm said he could forward her the CVs of several well-qualified engineers and programmers, helping her remedy the firm's 'desperate labour shortage'. She greeted the offer with 'awkward silence'.[18]

The 1993 National Survey of College Graduates—sponsored by the National Science Foundation—estimated that 57 per cent of computer science graduates continued to work as programmers six-and-a-half years after college. It plummeted to 37 per cent after fourteen-and-a-half years and 19 per cent after twenty-and-a-half years.[19] Many quit the industry after an endless unemployable period, making the attrition rate largely involuntary. The sceptics, though, mentioned career changes or entrepreneurial ventures. But it should have been true for other majors, too, such as civil engineering where, after twenty years, 52 per cent of graduates still worked in their fields.[20]

The firms claimed to covet coders with 'hot skills'. Norm called it a 'red herring'.[21] General programming talent mattered much more. 'We're not looking for any specific knowledge because things change so fast, and it's easy to learn stuff,' Bill Gates told the *Wall Street Journal* in 1994. 'You've got to have an excitement about software, a certain intelligence.' A manager at Microsoft, Jim McCarthy, echoed that point in his 1995 book, *Dynamics of Software Development*. But Microsoft's own employment web page demanded: 'State your skill sets'. So did numerous other firms. Their resume-scanning machines, sniffing 'hot skills', snubbed many applicants.

The companies' hiring rates confirmed the American programmers' woes: that they received (more than) enough resumes but selected a small portion.[22]

Firms	*Hiring Rates*
American Management Systems	2%
Broderbund Software	1%
Ecbridges	2%
Microsoft	2%
Qualcomm	4.5%

Industry lobbyists said that the low figures indicated multiple offers or professionals 'testing the waters'. So Norm provided the list of offer rates—accounting for 'hot skills' techies called for in-person interviews—underscoring the employers' selectivity.[23]

Firms	*Offer Rates*
American Management Systems	Under 25%
Broderbund	30%
ECbridges	20%
Flashpoint Technology	25 to 30%
High-tech job fairs	6%
Microsoft	25%

Besides, if demand dwarfed supply, salaries would have soared. But the Bureau of Labor Statistics (BLS) data showed that programmers' pay, including those with 'hot skills', had increased by just 7 per cent from 1996 to 1997.[24] The other surveys and recent college graduates' hikes produced similar results.[25] The demand for software H-1Bs, however, danced to a mythic tune. From 1990 to 1995, software engineering jobs grew by 35 per cent, but the demand for H-1B coders surged to 352 per cent.[26]

Industry lobbyists called the annual cap expansion temporary because they posited a long-term solution: 'education'. Norm offered several programmers' testimonies—published in the mainstream media and academic journals—that highlighted their inability to get hired despite high-tech degrees.[27] Retraining, tech lobbyists' favourite mantra, solved nothing either. Because a 'competent C programmer', said Norm, could write Java code 'within a week'. 'Fully up to speed' in two weeks, like an 'old pro' in a month.[28]

Finally, the H-1Bs: overworked, underpaid, indentured. And overwhelmingly young, at a median age of twenty-eight.[29] Analysing the Labor Condition Applications (LCA)—filed by employers while requesting H-1B workers[30]—a former DOL official and an immigration lawyer reported in their book that computer programmer positions in New Jersey and Texas (marked by a high concentration of H-1Bs) paid 21 per cent and 11 per cent less compared to the national average.[31] A 1996 DOL audit had concluded that 19 per cent of H-1Bs earned less than the LCA wages.[32] Over time, it got worse: Manu and Kumar's underpayment began at 40 per cent.

But the tech firms changed the conditions year after year. They first proclaimed an overall programmers' shortage in 1997, then whipped out a shortage of coders experienced in a particular sector (say, banking).[33] Even the 'retraining' issue illustrated their obstinacy. The companies wouldn't hire an older programmer who had taken a course in Java because they insisted on actual work experience. The tech industry's shifting goalposts suggested to Norm that the 'labour shortage'—'in the manner' they had 'defined it'—would remain 'permanent'.[34]

The 'STEM crisis' paranoia was an old story. It started in the early 1950s when the US obsessed over lagging behind the USSR in scientific talent and innovation. Four more alarms rang in the next six decades, creating a cycle of 'boom and bust'.[35] Its third episode starred a fabled federal agency, the National Science Foundation (NSF).

In April 1987, NSF's Policy and Research Analysis (PRA) division—headed by Dr Peter House—released a paper predicting a looming shortfall of 675,000 American scientists and engineers by 2006, starting from 1982.[36] The figure rattled policymakers, academics, politicians, journalists. It boomed in Congress, political debates, scientific conferences, lecture circuits, media outlets—you name it.

Indicting the country's priorities and values, it created widespread panic, the 'equivalent of shouting fire in a crowded theatre'.[37]

NSF director, Eric Bloch, gave at least fifty-five speeches from 1987 to '90—some in congressional committees—agonising over the imminent shortage.[38] He cited the PRA projections in his 1986 written Senate testimony, too, requesting an $89 million increase in the agency's 1987 budget for science and engineering education.[39] NSF's funding for the Education and Human Resources Directorate had risen and fallen along with the predicted shortfalls of scientists and engineers. It ballooned to $700 million in 1968 following the 1957 Sputnik launch, then nosedived to $47 million in '83—a drop of 95 per cent—a year before Bloch headed the NSF.[40]

The '675,000' figure remained conventional wisdom for years. But in October 1990, the president of the National Academy of Engineering, Robert White, asked why 'young people' were 'increasingly reluctant' to seek STEM careers.[41] Because, far from a 'shortfall', the US suffered from a glut of engineers. It led to such societies as the American Association of Concerned Engineers and Young Scientists Network, seeking support for their plight.

More experts joined: Allan Bromley, the president's science advisor; Alan Fechter, executive director, the National Research Council; Janet Norwood, the BLS commissioner. Rep. Howard Wolpe (D-Michigan), heading the House Committee on Science, Space and Technology, ordered a Congressional probe.

The PRA paper had concluded that the decade-old stable participation rate of twenty-two-year-olds in natural science and engineering, and their declining numbers, would cause a huge shortfall. But it had ignored demand—in a flexible responsive market. Even the supply side was weak, excluding STEM immigrant workers and transfers from related fields. Wait, it did factor demand. A 'proxy demand', as House called it.[42] His team had used the average degree production from 1984 to '86, an inflated level[43] due to the defence spending boom.

The PRA produced and distributed at least ten drafts of the 'underground literature' featuring different figures and years of the shortfall.[44] How could the NSF, though, release such a sloppy report? Had it not undergone a peer review?

The NSF identified nine reviewers, associate director of the General Accounting Office, Jim Wells, told Wolpe. But his team found that 'no formal review had occurred'.[45] Reviewing the study in early 1989, NSF's Science Resources Studies Division questioned its data, claims and assumptions. It stated that 'shortfalls' and 'scarcities' could be misinterpreted as 'shortages'.[46] House fired a 'vitriolic response', accusing the reviewers of 'not honestly seeking to help improve the outcome'.[47] Bloch also berated the Office of Technical Assessment (OTA) director in a fourteen-page letter when it didn't endorse the report. OTA's assistant director, John Andelin, called it an 'off-the-record attempt to silence dissent and intimidate dissenters—even those in another Federal agency'.[48]

By late 1990, when Bloch left the agency, the NSF itself disagreed with the PRA study—publicly. The new director, Frederick Bernthal, stated that the 'supply of scientists and engineers at both the BS and PhD levels' mostly kept up with the demand.[49] He assembled a mini task force, headed by Jim Hayes, to determine the 'NSF position' on PRA's projection. On 2 January 1991, Hayes emailed a few NSF officials, including House. It read: 'Shortfall or Not?'[50]

The Office of Legislative and Public Affairs scoured old files to check if Bloch had mentioned '675,000' or 'shortage' or 'shortfall' in his speeches.[51] The editor of *Science* magazine refused to publish the 'NSF position', calling it 'garbage'.[52] House revisited his study in 1991, expunging 'scarcity' from its title, eliminating the '675,000' figure and agreeing that the paper couldn't address the numerical strength of American scientists.[53]

On 8 April 1992, Wolpe interrogated House in exacting detail. 'Clearly, what has happened here is that the entire affair has been used to manipulate the political agenda of … the … NSF. One has a sense that the goal was to create the impression of a crisis to lend urgency to the effort to double the NSF budget. Everyone, including I think most of the media, accepts as a given that NSF's pronouncements are the result of good science. This was not good science, this study that you produced. If you had performed this analysis for a member of Congress privately as a private kind of action, initiative, you wouldn't be here today; we would not be here today. But you work for the National Science Foundation and a different standard, I think, must apply as we deal with this question.'[54]

Six years later, during his Congressional testimony, Norm took this story further. 'I urge people on the committee to look at the work of Dr Eric Weinstein. He's a math professor, well, a mathematician at MIT. He's found a smoking gun on the salary issue.'[55]

Weinstein had accessed a confidential PRA paper, where the analysts did consider a proper demand before the 'infamous scarcity study' was circulated.[56] They wanted to publish their findings, but 'according to government sources', wrote Weinstein, House 'suppressed' the study.[57] They observed that the PhD-level pay rose from $52,000 in 1982 to $75,000 in 1996, nearing '$100,000 shortly beyond 2000'.[58] They proposed a solution to fix the 'pessimistic scenario': 'A growing influx of foreign PhDs' suppressing domestic salaries but only 'to the extent' that the international students still pursued doctoral programmes in the US 'as a way of immigrating'.[59]

The analysts knew its impact on American scientists and engineers. 'The relatively modest salary premium' might be 'too low' to attract 'able potential' graduates, driving them to 'alternative career paths' in 'business or law or management'. For them, 'the effective premium for acquiring a PhD may actually be negative'.[60] The same paper proposed automatic green cards for foreign graduates.[61]

Wolpe clarified that the NSF's wish to double its budget didn't trouble him. Something else did: the flawed study influencing major legislations in the country. One of them was the Immigration Act of 1990.

Why did the Act matter? It created the H-1B programme.

18

Austin Community College snubbed Virgil. Seven months had passed since he applied to VRAP. Hungry wallet, unsold washer, empty future. He contacted the American College of Technology, which—finally—accepted his application.

Over the last two years, a new sidebar had popped up on Keep America At Work: 'Significant Milestones'.[62] Updated every few months, it encapsulated his research via several articles: why firms preferred H-1Bs over Americans, how monoliths like Walmart decimated small businesses and how 'as few as six corporations' dominated the mainstream media. It ended with: 'In November 2012, we found the best description of all the events.' The puzzle's last piece, the reason for his destruction, explained in the book *Who Stole the American Dream?* by Pulitzer Prize–winning journalist Hedrick Smith.[63]

Virgil read a sample chapter available online. Matt had sent him the same document some years ago: a thirty-four-page letter,[64] written in 1971, for the members of the U.S. Chamber of Commerce by Lewis F. Powell, Jr, a leading corporate attorney about to become a Supreme Court justice. Proposed in an era when American corporations had suffered political setbacks due to government regulations, consumer activism and trade unions, the Powell Memorandum aimed to restore the scale of power. It challenged corporations' 'apathy and impotency', thundering out searing maxims to seize control: 'strength lies in organization' and 'political power is necessary'.[65]

Corporate America nodded. It formed lobbyist organisations, swelled their memberships and flooded them with money. It opened think tanks and revived dormant ones to push policies benefiting businesses. The U.S. Chamber of Commerce doubled its membership and tripled its budget, employing dozens of lobbyists. By the late 1970s, corporations overwhelmed Congress: they deployed 130 advocates for every elected member.[66]

Since the mid-1970s, America bore little resemblance to the country post-Second World War, where fair wages, progressive taxation and increased productivity had launched millions into the middle class. As Virgil pieced together the history of the American economy, he found out that free trade only freed its beneficiaries. The offshoring fire razed domestic manufacturing and raised ghost towns. At the same time, corporations kept scouting newer countries for cheaper labour. He called it a 'game of musical countries', dismantling the middle classes at home and abroad, which donned a new avatar in 1990: the H-1B programme. This was not a 'system defect'—this was how the system worked. The numbers captured that climax better than words: in the 1970s, the ratio of CEOs' salaries to workers' wages was 40:1; by the early 2000s, it jumped to 367:1. History had done a somersault, returning the robber barons.[67]

'My investigation is done,' Virgil emailed a friend. 'Now I need to get my income to the 50K level as a start.'

The VRAP classes gave him hope. 'After a year with no income, I might get a small check by next week ($450),' he emailed Molly. 'If so, I will treat myself to a shrimp dinner, or maybe even a steak. After all, it has been a very long time.' He bought 9.38 acres of land, reactivated his real estate licence and ordered business cards. On the front: 'Virgil Bierschwale. Are you having a hard time selling your property in Texas?' On the back: 'KeepAmericaAtWork.Com. We are not out of work because the economy is bad, the economy is bad because we are out of work.'

Virgil believed that the DOL, honouring its VRAP promise, would end his unemployment woes. But the actual promise swallowed his hope: 'Staff should encourage the veteran to go to the American Job Center or sign up for the Wagner-Payser services virtually.' He had done that—for years. Squatted on USAJobs.gov since forever. Emailed many DOL officials. 'I don't need somebody to help me find a job as I can do that perfectly well,' he wrote to a friend. 'I need somebody to bust open the doors.'

After weeks of silence, a reply. The DOL's assistant state director in San Antonio wrote to him. 'We have received your email regarding your employment with the VA in Kerrville and need for assistance. Please call my office.'

Virgil called from his mother's phone, then sent a follow-up email. 'Thank you for your help. I would love to get back to work in Information Technology, but there are no jobs like that here, and the ones that are, I have applied for and heard nothing. If I can pay my child support, and keep this place, I would be happy even if it is a clerk position (can't do manual work anymore). At the VA I could buy back my military time, and once I had the degree, I should work my way up.'

The DOL official directed him to a Texas Veterans Commission employee in Kerrville. Virgil had interacted with him. Sweet guy but clueless about IT. Like others, he thought there were millions of software jobs, so Virgil's resume must be the problem. He never got the real problem: more workers than jobs.

'What exactly do they not understand,' he emailed Mike Thornton, who ran layofflist.org. 'I spelled it out and they don't seem to get it. It's like I'm talking Chinese or something.'

Enough employers everywhere, including one in his own backyard, the insurance giant United States Automobile Association (USAA). The biggest firm in San Antonio—employing over 30,000 people across the country—called the 'community pillar'. A former CEO, Robert F. McDermott, had an expressway named after him. Founded in 1922 by twenty-five Army officers to insure each other's vehicles, it broadcast countless ads celebrating veterans. Less than 100 miles away, a Navy veteran had applied for countless jobs. Not a peep.

Virgil found a buyer for the ranch that had slipped out last year. At last: rain in the desert after three-and-a-half years, $30,000. He split the amount into six $5,000 cashier cheques. Beside the original 12-by-32 feet cabin, he attached two more cabins: an 8-by-12 for laundry and restroom and a 12-by-28 with a six-foot porch. He also bought a car, settled the utility bills and networked for real estate. $2,000 left. Two months—the span of good times.

Besides the DOL, Virgil had also contacted the Department of Veterans Affairs multiple times for employment help. His pleas went unheard, and the agency routinely rejected him for the 'lowest of lowest jobs'. Writing to other agencies, such as the Texas Workforce Commission and Equal Employment Opportunity Commission, yielded nothing either. The government had spoken by staying silent. No point waiting: the 'cavalry' was 'not coming'.

So, months later, still unemployed, he resurrected to fight his next fight. He set Google Alerts for his latest obsession: 'H-1B'. Around the same time, in April 2014, a pro-immigration lobbying group, FWD.us, co-founded by Mark Zuckerberg, celebrated its first anniversary.[68] Its board members ruled Silicon Valley, heading Microsoft, Netflix, YouTube, Yahoo!, Qualcomm, Groupon. Accompanied by Zuckerberg's op-ed in the *Washington Post*, its launch had got extensive media coverage.[69]

Virgil began his investigation from the DOL's website, which maintained an annual database of all Labor Condition Applications (LCAs). The spreadsheet contained close to 500,000 records. Each corresponded to over a dozen fields: salary, designation, location, company's address, number of workers requested, occupation codes and so on.[70] To tabulate the data, he taught himself MySQL and PHP. He compared the number of existing jobs to the visas awarded[71] in each profession and uploaded his findings on the website.[72] The highest paying jobs—in computer and mathematical occupations—had suffered the most. 'Which is why,' he wrote to a *Forbes* journalist, 'there is no outcry from the rest of the white-collar and blue-collar groups.'

Virgil kept analysing the data: categorising LCAs by salaries, signifying underpayment; switching occupation codes to depict pervasive similarities; changing the years to underscore the problem's longevity, and on and on. Corporate America called H-1Bs 'the best and the brightest', so he investigated that claim, too. Virgil revealed that specialised occupations produced a small percentage of applications, while around 65 per cent went to system analysts and computer programmers. 'Folks, I spent nearly three decades working in these positions,' he emailed reporters, economists and Bill Gates, 'and I can guarantee, you do not need to be the best and brightest to be exceptional in these fields. Mark, trust me. I will continue digging. That is a promise.'

19

Kumar finished a thirty-six-hour project in Boston, then a three-month contract in New Jersey and searched for jobs. Most recruiters operated from India; simple conversations turned painful. If he mentioned the 'Mountain Time Zone' while job-hunting in Helena, they said, 'What?' Some hung up. Many called after 5 p.m., cornering him in Telugu slang: how much he knew, what he did not know, how he did not know what he did not know.

Is this an interview?

The rate negotiations echoed flea market bargains: $60, too high; can you do 30, how about 35? A desi consultancy offered him a position in California for $25 an hour. The vendors dismissed his skills, identity and preferences. They just wanted a 'body' at the 'client site'.

Is this recruiting or human trafficking?

The IT industry profited every party in the body shop chain—except the H-1B worker. If the end client paid, for instance, $120 per hour for a consultant with six years of experience, then the prime vendor scooped up around $40, the middle vendor(s) $30, the desi consultancy $25 and the H-1B worker $25.[73] Someone scrambling to defend a fake resume—risking his identity, sanity, dignity—earned almost the same as his employer risking nothing. As the consultant gained experience, his earnings should have increased, but the company kept finding creative ways to steal his wages, as Kumar found out every few months, making him helpless and mad.

He got an interview with a middle vendor, Magentoy, and a prime vendor, Xscind, hiring for a government client in New York. He asked Magentoy's recruiting director, Tim, for a salary of $85 per hour. Tim agreed to $65. Weeks passed. No confirmation. After some more silence, Xscind said yes.

Another chance.

This job, unlike the previous ones, demanded extensive travel. He had to cover around thirty data centres from Staten Island to the John F. Kennedy International airport, travelling to at least two of them daily, shelling out over $100 in tolls and gas. But the billing rate—$65 per hour, making his share $48.75—comforted him. The overtime income would also help him buy flight tickets for his family. Kumar waited for the payday. Like every project, he'd get the first pay cheque after forty-five days.

The day came.

$25?

Didn't Tim say $65? Didn't 4M specify 75 per cent? He called Vishnu.

'Magentoy is paying $46. 4M is recovering money for the previous projects.'

First, they paid late, and when they did, they brought 'all old shit'—some 'bench loan' or the other—and withheld his salary. 4M didn't show the purchase order this time too, so he didn't know if it earned $46 or more? Or did Tim cheat him—was that why he never committed the $65 rate on email? Kumar called him.

'Your salary got reduced because you aren't qualified for a senior role.'

'How does an illegal vendor decide my skills?'

Tim said he had worked as an IT manager with the client. His previous experience, in fact, taught him the middle vendor game. Kumar emailed Nick—the prime vendor's accounts manager—saying he wished to transfer his H-1B to Xscind, earning what he deserved: $85. His phone rang. Pete, his team lead, told Kumar he couldn't join Xscind, as it had signed a year-long contract with Magentoy. The call from Pete, a Xscind employee and his boss, served as a veiled threat:

obey or disappear. Tim controlled his money, Pete controlled his work and Nick controlled who controlled whom. Business partners for years, they had captured a goat, poaching his pay cheques.

So not just Indians, Americans, too, milked the H-1B programme?

Tim forbade Kumar to enter his hours in Xscind's portal. Tim did it himself. Their overtime hours differed—sometimes by as much as 50 per cent. Kumar protested; Tim spurned him. A colleague, Dean Lane, told him that the client paid Xscind around $125 an hour. American techies earned $85 and received transportation costs (75 cents per mile). Magentoy also fired Americans and hired Indians on F-1 and H-1B visas. That's how a recent Telugu graduate, working on a fake resume, had replaced an African-American employee. The billing rate dipped from $85 to $45, enriching Tim, Nick and Pete. Once, during lunch, Kumar ribbed Tim, indirectly, about his underpayment. Tim smiled and said, 'We learned corruption from you Indians.'

Kumar fought for his overtime pay. Vishnu always gave an excuse, and it never made sense. Like a revolving satellite, he orbited around Nick, Tim and Vishnu for his 91.25 hours of pay ($3,500). His supervisor, Duan, a Xscind employee, asked Tim and Nick: 'Why is Kumar not getting his overtime? Why are you making him work like a slave?' He wouldn't assign more work till Kumar received his pending payments. Xscind fired Duan.

Tim, who was himself conning Kumar, warned Vishnu over an email. 'I have already paid your company 76.25 hrs. He should be PAID IMMEDIATELY. Failure to provide this payment no later than his next pay period, I'll be forced to submit a complaint to the NY Labor Board and the US Department of Justice.'

Suspecting Kumar had stoked Tim, Vishnu threatened to fire him. Kumar requested them to come on a conference call, wanting to prove Tim had sent that email. Over a long chat, they resolved their differences. Kumar got his overtime pay (after unending delays).

By early 2013, around two years into the project, the work eased up. Kumar finished an assignment and approached the team lead, Stephen. Got more work, finished it, asked for more. 'Not like this,'

Stephen said. 'I can't create work. It has to come from the client. I give you permission to use Facebook.'

An idea flashed and everything aligned. He added his Facebook friends to a group and began writing—or flowing, like a waterfall. Soon, he found an audience: a distant cousin from Chicago, an IT professional from West Bengal, a body shop owner from Sri Lanka. The Bengal man's suggestion captivated him: why don't you make it public (as opposed to a closed group)? It'd start a new journey. Kumar named the Facebook page: 'H1B Indians Immigration Boat, A Confrontational Book'.

An early post on it read: 'IDEA OF THIS BOOK. I am a small bolt in BIG ship of H1B Indians Immigration Boat, writing it honestly is the matter to me. Idea is to tell H1Bs "do not break your wonderful life in offshore to come and suffer like me". Our many guys Indians rip Indians for dollars here. To write a book like this, I do not think more experiences matter because according to me experience means, repeating of first year. If FT jobs fine, otherwise no life for H1Bs.

'I am not against India or Indians but openly sharing my experiences to take your inputs to improvise. My friends and cousins have been contacting me about studies or jobs in America ever since I land here. I have been sparing lots of time to explain individually by phone or email. At a later stage I realize, it would be better if I write all my experience in a nut shell. Hence I got this idea. I apologize if I hurt anyone.'

Kumar spilled onto a long document—flowing into thousands of words—explaining an H-1B's journey from India to America. He divided it into multiple Facebook statuses. When he exceeded the word count, he lunged into the comment section. He had a simple motivation. During his Dream America phase, he had no guiding light, not even a fast internet connection, so he wanted to help others, honouring what he had emailed his friend once.

Life is like a candle, ra. It should burn to give light to others.

Kumar was writing the book—and the book was writing Kumar.

'In Montana, one American Lady changed her name as INDIA and few of American friends visit India each year. Friends there can read Bhagavad Gita in Sanskrit and they are from America. Then I understand religion is a bricks between humanity.'

'One time, an American Land lord asked me questions which I do not have answers: 1) If your country is great then what are you doing here? 2) If your country is great then why people do not change? 3) If your country is great then why corruption in all walks of life?'

'Never mind if my Indian buddies don't like to hear about this—tell the story anyway. You are free to speak your mind and no one can stop you. Being critical of our own countrymen is the only way we can get them to improve their behavior.'

Kumar's Facebook group had a man named Raghav Kishore, a recruiter for a desi consultancy, VersIT, in Boston. They had first interacted in 2008 for a project in the city. Raghav helped him crash in his consultancy's guesthouse. They never met but became Facebook friends and, years later, Raghav called him a few times. An erstwhile Hindu, now a Christian, he fired a series of questions: why does Lord Krishna have so many gopikas? Why does Shivalingam look like a penis?

Kumar berated and shunned him.

But when his Facebook page gained popularity, Raghav contacted Kumar again. This time with an offer: correcting Kumar's grammar. His newer posts ended with acknowledgements: 'thanks for reading, team, Kumar and Raghav'; 'edited by Raghav'; 'TRUTH POST Editor Mr. Raghav'. His collaborator's designation didn't bother Kumar because Raghav agreed with him, opposing the sordid practices of the industry. He admired two qualities the most in Raghav: his communication skills and his anti-caste stance. 4M's discrimination and 'bossy' green card Indians had reshaped his views on caste. This 'Hindu fundamentalist' Brahmin had experienced the humiliation of segregation.

But a maddening contradiction still rankled. What made him different from body shop owners? After all, both belonged to the same country, worked in IT and served American overlords. They also raced towards the same end: pleasing the Almighty. But he was different—in his heart, he felt; in his conscience, he believed. Kumar absorbed a simple principle to stand out: that gods lived inside, not outside, him. He'd rewrite his life, challenging every tenet of the desi consultancy ecosystem. He'd change himself, empower others and practice equality, irrespective of caste, religion, nationality. Soon even Facebook fell short, for he had too much to inform, rant and rail. He chose a more accessible website. A platform that wouldn't let him hide behind a laptop—or hide at all. He had a lot to atone for, a lot to answer. This 'casteist violent mind' would get a rebirth.

Kumar would open a YouTube channel.

20

Manu applied for jobs using his own resume, even informing Jackson to 'keep original projects'. One evening, he got a call from Julia, a recruiter at Graymond Services, who was looking to hire a tester for a telecom firm, Cell America. He explained his previous projects; she submitted his resume to the client. He got an interview. Prakash had stopped giving proxies, so Nitish directed him to Hari, an Infocon employee in California. Manu sent Hari his resume and told him the interview's date and time. Hari aced the interview; Manu got the project.

He rented an apartment six miles from work. A daily cab ride cost $40. The recent bench period, worth $4,000, had escalated his stress. 'Life is free,' he told a friend, 'but living is expensive.' To save money, he trekked to the office every day in the paralysing winter.

He bought a car: a silver 2013 Ford Fusion. Two days later, on an overcast Christmas afternoon, he walked to his apartment's parking lot. He opened the car's front door and snapped the area near the steering wheel. Sat on the passenger seat and clicked the same spot again. Two photos of the side-view mirrors. A photo of the backseat and the speedometer. A mid-shot picture of the licence plate: 'Illinois, R51 6753, Land of Lincoln'. Manu uploaded them on Facebook: 'I bought a new car :) How is it?'

He messaged his father. 'Hello Daddy. How are you doing?'

'I am ok :-)'

'I bought a car.'

'Good. Drive carefully. Don't be rash or careless.'

'Yeah.'

'What about a wife :-)'

'I don't think I am going to marry. Too much responsibility.'

'You are afraid :-)'

'You can say that.'

'You must take responsibility and face it. You will feel lonely after sometime.'

'Yeah that's true.'

'And this loneliness will be your greatest enemy and handicap. It is better to try and fail rather than not try at all.'

'Yeah.'

'You must not lose faith in the system even if chances of reward are remote :-) Some body may be liking you—you also need to respect others feeling :-)'

Cell America didn't give him a cubicle. Manu shared a table with other contractors. One day, a senior executive addressed the employees and consultants in the hall, discussing the general operations, upgrades and updates. He wanted a cordial work environment, he said, where nobody troubled their colleagues. If someone reported a hostile employee, he'd act on it right away. Manu's last project, in Herndon, Virginia, had a haughty desi boss. Annoyed by her accusations and screams, he had resigned. So this assurance comforted him. He finally found someone in corporate America who understood compassion and valued respect, someone who treated people as people. Manu never complained. No one mistreated him. Even people from other teams acknowledged him and remembered his name.

'What are your new year plans,' a P. Indra Reddy acquaintance pinged him.

'Not much, will stay in Illinois. Illinois likes me :)'

'You like Illinois?'

'Of course. If someone likes me, I also do.'

'Racha, awesome. You should write film dialogues, dude.'

'Lol, na.'

Manu began making plans. He knew that, in the long term, he'd have to work in New Jersey. Overcrowded with Indians, the state never appealed to him. But at the moment, Cell America and Illinois suited him just fine. Maybe he could work here for a year—maybe a year more?

He wrote to Mahalakshmi. 'I'm with Infocon Logix from February 2011. Will you guys do a green card for me?'

She replied, 'Please send me your updated resume. I could open a case for you.'

Once his boss asked him, 'Can you work on Sundays?'

'Yeah, sure.'

'You'll be paid overtime.'

'No issues.'

She didn't know that he'd have worked for free.

One afternoon, Julia called him. His contract had ended.

'Any specific reason?'

She hung up.

Manu remained seated. Surrounded by colleagues, staring at the monitor. Cold and blank. After an hour, he wanted to wail. He went to the pantry, sat on a chair, lowered his head on the slab and the floodgates burst open. He wept—silently.

'Are you okay?' a woman asked him.

'Yeah.' He looked up at her. 'I am fine.'

Later that evening, he sat on his living room mattress. Two-and-a-half years, five projects, four cities. Failed to stay anywhere for long. Failed to find a home. Failed to get respect. Hire, grill, fire—no stability, no dignity.

Manu wept.

How long would this last? This uncertain, fearful life. Manu never wanted the world for himself. 'What I wanted was an ordinary life,' he'd have said if someone asked. 'Just like … living normal you know? Having normal salary.' He sought to save money, send some home. His mother had quit her job. He wanted to support her, move ahead, rebuild his life. But now he only had crushed hope. He worked at Cell America for two more weeks and returned to his temporary home—the only home he had ever known—the Infocon Logix guesthouse.

21

Back in 1998, suspecting the tech industry was trying to undercut American workers, Bill Clinton had threatened to veto Senator Abraham's legislation but eventually approved it. After that, he flew to Silicon Valley—for a fundraiser tour. The American Competitiveness and Workforce Improvement Act created an 'H-1B Dependent' employer.[74] The category needed one of the following three conditions: a company with twenty-five or fewer full-time equivalent employees and at least eight H-1Bs; or twenty-six to fifty full-time equivalent employees and at least thirteen H-1Bs; or fifty-one or more full-time equivalent employees and 15 per cent or more H-1Bs.[75]

Such a company had to submit three specific attestations on the LCA. It pledged to not fire an American worker ninety days before and after filing the visa petition, place its employee(s) at a firm that hadn't fired (or intended to fire) an American worker ninety days before and after the placement and ensure good-faith steps to hire an American worker before applying for the visa.[76] But these requirements vanished if an employer paid an annual wage of over $60,000, or if the foreign professional had a master's degree or equivalent.

Norm's investigation—compiled in his updated Congressional testimony[77] and a long H-1B research paper[78]—exposed the loopholes. Corporate America claimed the 'best and the brightest' H-1Bs solved the 'shortage' of native STEM workers. Talented techies, however, earned much more than $60,000. 'Genius-level' wages hovered around the $100,000 mark; $60,000 was, in fact, the median national salary in IT at all education levels.[79] Tech salaries increased by about 10 per cent every year, but the threshold figure never changed.

Now, what about 'H-1B dependent' firms? LCA conditions tucked a key provision: 'total'. Most companies sought H-1B visas for computer programmers. A company's workforce also included non-tech professionals, such as HR, accounts and marketing. An employer, as a result, could hire much more than 15 per cent of its technical personnel as H-1Bs and still evade the restrictive label.[80] By isolating the heavy users of the H-1B visas, the Act conveyed a misleading message: that a few (Indian) outsourcing giants had tainted the guest worker programme.

Or, as Norm put it, 'Intels Good, Infosyses Bad': 'racial scapegoating'. 'Large American firms', he explained, relished 'cheap labor' as much 'as anyone else'. Sun Microsystems had 'bragged' about employing programmers in Russia at 'bargain prices'.[81] General Dynamics imported H-1Bs from England who, the employment agency told the firm, would 'work for as much as a 40% pay reduction' compared to domestic salaries.[82]

The 'natives versus immigrants' narrative didn't explain this debate either because firms craved indentured workers. So green card holders (or permanent residents), changing companies at will, encountered the 'same discrimination'. The IEEE's chairperson of the workforce committee, Shankar Lakhavani, a man of Pakistani origin, said, 'Many immigrants like me, who are American citizens, would like a crack at these jobs.'[83]

'Be wary of H-1B visas in the USA,' stated an Australian publication, *Fairfax IT*, quoting computer graphics guru Carsten Haitzler. 'You basically get shackled to a company. Being a non-American in the USA is almost like being a second-class citizen.'[84] A 1998 *Washington Post* piece stated that firms 'dangled' the 'green card' promise to retain their employees.[85] H-1B workers had also formed their own interest group, Immigrant Support Network, to lobby the Congress to ease their shackles. Its director, Murali Devarkonda, said in a TV panel discussion, 'This is legal human rights violation in America. You [as an H-1B] are an indentured servant. A modern-day slave.'[86]

The 1998 Act almost doubled the annual H-1B cap from 65,000 to 115,000. The next year, the tech industry lobbied to triple it. A 1999 paper by BLS researcher Carolyn Veneri found that existing data didn't support the STEM crisis claim.[87] Her study posited that the computer science field, evicting programmers, made the unemployment rate meaningless. So a 'former engineer, now a sales clerk at Radio Shack', summarised Norm, counted as an '*employed* [sales person]', not an unemployed engineer.[88] Even the DOC recanted its report, stating it couldn't 'conclusively' establish an 'overall IT worker shortage' due to data 'limitations'.[89] The IT Workforce Data Project—a four-part series on the IT labour force, sponsored by United Engineering and Alfred P. Sloan Foundation—found no shortage either.[90]

But the 96-1 Senate result proved that nothing mattered. 'Once it's clear [the bill] is going to get through, everybody signs up so nobody can be ... accused of being against high tech,' said Robert Bennett (R-Utah). 'There were, in fact, a whole lot of folks against it, but because they are tapping the high-tech community for campaign contributions, they don't want to admit it in public.'[91] Tom Davis (R-Virginia) said, 'This is not a popular bill with the public. It's popular with the CEOs.'[92] A 1998 Harris poll concurred: 82 per cent of Americans opposed the cap increase.[93]

Sometimes, actions screamed louder than words. On the afternoon of 3 October 2000, it was announced that no voting would take place during the day, and the House members could go home. But the voice vote still happened that evening—in front of forty members.[94] The bill sailed through.[95]

Clinton approved it on 17 October 2000, increasing the annual cap to 195,000, amid the tech industry downturn. Even a wilted market, however, didn't deter corporate America. Its use of H-1B visas rose by 14 per cent the next year.[96] It dipped in 2002, but only due to an unprecedented high-tech bust.[97] The firms fired American workers and ordered them to *train* their replacements, young Indian H-1Bs. If the displaced professionals refused, or contacted the media, they didn't get their severance. Several companies were accused of this practice, some in courts: Dun & Bradstreet,[98] Netscape,[99] Siemens,[100] Sun Microsystems.[101]

One engineer rebelled in his own way. Born into a middle-class family, Kevin Flanagan grew up in Long Beach, California. He secured a bachelor's degree in computer science and philosophy from California State University. After working for McDonnell Douglas as a programmer, he moved to San Francisco and joined Bank of America in 1996. A colleague called him a 'programming god'. Another said, 'Every time I got stuck on a program, he'd unstuck it in, like, ten seconds.'[102] Kevin had little to complain; he had bought a house in Pleasanton Hill.

In 2002, his firm signed outsourcing agreements with TCS, Infosys and Accenture. The Indian H-1Bs poured in; his peers evaporated. The lay-offs whittled his small team down to one member: Kevin. In early 2003, Bank of America ordered him to train his replacement. The forty-one-year-old was 'disgusted'.[103] On his last day, Kevin collected his belongings, packed them in boxes and placed them in his Ford Ranger's trunk. He sat in the front seat, put a 12-gauge Remington shotgun to his head and pulled the trigger.[104]

After the 2000 Act died, George Bush signed the H-1B Visa Reform Act of 2004 that reverted the annual quota to 65,000 but added 20,000 visas for master's students. It expanded the DOL's investigative authority, increased visa fees and revised the wage structure. The federal agency defined the 'prevailing wage' as the 'average' salary paid to 'similarly employed workers' in a specific occupation and area.[105] It intended to reduce wage depression and save H-1Bs from exploitation. An actual wage corresponded to the wage rate of similarly qualified and experienced workers in the same position at the same firm.[106] Before the 2004 Act, a firm had to pay a higher amount between the actual wage and at least 95 per cent of the prevailing wage. The new law changed it to 100 per cent.[107] It also restructured the salary slab from two levels to four, accounting for experience. Many interpreted it as a victory for American workers. IEEE-USA called it a 'meaningful prevailing wage requirement designed to ensure that H-1B workers receive the same pay as American workers'.[108]

Once more, not so fast.

Because Level I, the lowest salary, equalled the seventeenth percentile of the total wages surveyed for an occupation in an area. Level II, thirty-fourth. Both way below the median, resulting from the choices made by the DOL. Level III, fiftieth. The previous pay bands corresponded to the seventeenth and the sixty-seventh percentiles. The extra categories, II and III, had increased the underpayment options in the law itself.

Even the prevailing wage definition, explained Norm, had 'gaping loopholes'. First, as opposed to setting a strict and substantial wage-floor, the DOL permitted firms to set salaries. The LCA allowed them to choose from a vast range of wage surveys—from government agencies to private companies—whose differing methodologies, producing diverse figures, enabled employers to pick the cheapest option. Second, surveys masked actual differences between jobs; they didn't factor 'hot skills', for example. A specific software skill could command as much as a 20 per cent salary increase in an open market. Third, the prevailing wage was based on the job, not the worker. A company, as a result, could under-classify a position, fill it with a highly skilled worker and save a hefty amount. Fourth, job titles varied across surveys. Some, for instance, contained both definitions of a software engineer—the ones performing complex and simple work—automatically depressing the former's salary.[109]

Wage theft so smooth it could only be legal.[110]

The actual wage had a muddy definition, too. Why compare 'the best and the brightest' H-1Bs, asked Norm, to ordinary professionals? Was this the pro-worker reform? 'The industry lobbyists have hereby reached,' he wrote in his newsletter, 'new levels of clever deceit.'[111]

Around three years later, in fall 2007, a comprehensive immigration bill, almost doubling the annual visa cap, failed to pass in the Senate. On 15 November, Microsoft's chief lobbyist, Jack Krumholtz, wrote a letter[112] to the secretary of the Department of Homeland Security (DHS), urging him to extend the duration of the Optional Practical

Training programme from twelve to twenty-nine months.[113] The federal agency received letters from the U.S. Chamber of Commerce; Yale, Columbia, Johns Hopkins University; the top executives of Microsoft, Intel and Qualcomm.

OPT allowed a foreign graduate from an American university to work in the country for a year. It had no annual cap or minimum wage requirement.[114] Corporations drooled over it for another reason: a discount of 7.65 per cent[115] per hire, as they didn't have to pay the Social Security and Medicare taxes. An amount that would surge to almost $2 billion by the next decade.[116]

'The F-1 visa program was established to "educate the world"', explained Norm, 'especially the impoverished countries. OPT was intended to supplement a foreign student's book learning with some practical experience to take back home.'[117] The F-1 visa, too, required students to state that they'd return to their countries after their studies. Yet the OPT had 'devolved' into a 'holding pattern', allowing an employer to buy more time till its employee got an H-1B visa. The twenty-nine-month OPT period would further increase their chances to clear the annual lottery.

Desi consultancies loved the OPT programme. They could hire a techie on an even cheaper salary, transform him into a resource with 'six years of experience' and steal a bigger cut from his pay cheque. Squeezing its benefits, they visited third-tier colleges to lure vulnerable applicants. Manu, like many graduates, had worked on OPT in his first year of employment. That's how Infocon Logix paid him $15 per hour in San Francisco.

April 2008: DHS increased the OPT duration to twenty-nine months, creating a parallel guest worker programme. Unlike H-1B, it ran through regulation, so the extension didn't require legislation. 'The DHS took this action under an obscure law that says in "emergency" situations', wrote Norm, 'an administrative agency can, in effect, make its own laws.'[118] If the OPT would make foreign students effective professionals after leaving the US, then the emergency had to be in their own countries. 'Well, which countries does DHS have in mind, and what emergencies do they have? The only "emergency" is the urgent need for both major political parties to get campaign donations from the industry lobbyists in this election year.'[119]

The tech industry, however, wasn't just satisfied with ruling Congress. Commanding an army of allies, it had mounted a 'thought control' ecosystem manufacturing truths about—and toying with the rules of—the H-1B programme. On 15 May 2007, Cohen & Grigsby, a renowned Pittsburgh law firm, held an annual immigration conference. It featured a discussion on the Program Electronic Review Management (PERM) application. A key step in green card approval, it required an employer to 'test the labor market' in the job's 'geographic area' to ensure that it had 'no able, qualified, and available U.S. workers' willing to accept the job offer.[120] A condition excluded from the H-1B process, thanks to the American Immigration Lawyers Association's lobbying.[121]

'What do we typically use as our three other recruitment sources?' Lawrence Lebowitz, vice president, Marketing, asked his colleague on the panel, Jen Pack.

'Most of the times, it would be the newspapers' websites in conjunction with the physical print ad and the employer's website.'

'Our goal here of course is to meet the requirement,' Lebowitz said, facing the audience. 'But also do so as inexpensively as possible, keeping in mind our goal. Our goal is clearly not to find a qualified and interested US worker. And you know that in a sense sounds funny, but that's what we are trying to do. We are complying with the law fully, but our objective is to get this person a green card and get through the labor certification process. So certainly, we are not going to try to find a place [to advertise] where the applicants are going to be the most numerous. We are going to try to find a place where we can comply with the law and hoping, and likely, not to find qualified and interested worker applicants.'

The firm released the conference videos on its website. The Programmers' Guild, an activist group opposing the H-1B programme, uploaded a five-minute clip onto YouTube, adding dramatic music and subtitles.[122] In less than a week, it got over 54,000 views and 500 comments.[123] Several media outlets covered it. Senator Chuck Grassley

(R-Iowa) and Representative Lamar Smith (R-Texas) rebuked Cohen & Grigsby, demanding an explanation.[124] None of this was a newsflash though. Seven years ago, attorney Joel Stewart wrote that, 'Employers who favor aliens have an arsenal of legal means to reject all US workers who apply.'[125]

Norm exposed the less obvious facets. Lebowitz worked as an adjunct professor of immigration at the University of Pittsburgh School of Law. Its business school had devised a programme called 'Katzport' that paid the 'H-1B fees' for its foreign graduates to ... 'Cohen & Grigsby!'[126] Besides, people had only watched a minuscule portion of the released videos. Just 'part 9 of 20'—that too, a 'small excerpt'. The 'other outrageous segments', no longer available online, detailed other loopholes.[127] In video 12, for example, attorney Pack explained ways to obtain a prevailing wage '$10,000 to $15,000' below the market rate.[128]

Some weeks after the 'TubeGate' incident, a network engineer, David Huber, saw a Cisco job ad in the *Chicago Tribune*. He called the number, and the company's telephone operator directed him to an immigration law firm, Fragomen.[129] Spread in over 170 countries, it served many Silicon Valley giants. The same playbook as Cohen & Grigsby: a newspaper ad 'complying with the law', 'hoping' 'not to find' a 'qualified' American. This scandal also got major news coverage, even sparking a DOL investigation.[130] 'This provides yet another example,' wrote Norm, 'that contrary to the industry lobbyists' claim that most abuse of the H-1B and green card laws is by Indian body shops, the abuse pervades the entire industry, including big household-name firms such as Cisco.'[131]

A few years later, something else happened, though, that astounded him.[132] The president (almost) met a victim of the H-1B programme. During a Google Hangout session, in January 2012, a Fort Worth resident, Jennifer Wedel, asked Obama a question.[133] 'My husband has an engineering degree with over ten years of experience. He was laid off three years ago and is yet to find a permanent job in his field. Why does the government continue to issue and extend H-1B visas when there are tons of Americans like my husband with no job?'

'Well, Jennifer, I don't know your husband's specialty, but I can tell you there's a huge demand around the country for engineers. Now, obviously, there are different kinds of engineers. So a civil engineer, for example, right now may not be getting as much work because we're not building our infrastructure as much as we should. Where you're seeing a lot of specialised demand is in engineering related to the high-tech industries. Now the industry tells me they don't have enough highly skilled engineers. If your husband is in that field, then we should get his resume and I'll forward it to some of these companies.'

'Why do you think the H-1B program is so popular with big corporations?'

'Can I ask you what kind of engineer your husband is?'

'A semiconductor engineer.'

'See, it is interesting. Because the word we're getting is that somebody in that kind of high-tech field should be able to find something right away. And the H-1Bs should be reserved only for those companies who say they cannot find somebody in that particular field. I'll follow up on this because I'm interested in finding out and maybe we can get some information as to why your husband has been having trouble getting placed. We want to encourage more American engineers to be placed.'

After Obama's town hall, the Wedels's phone rang often. The Texas Workforce Commission, recruiters, headhunters, journalists. Even the White House. But over two months later, reported the *Fort Worth Star-Telegram*, 'the phone is quiet, the emails are no longer flooding in, and the long-sought-after job interviews—which had begun to be scheduled—have petered out.' Jennifer's husband, Darin, had to remain in North Texas due to a custody agreement for his daughter. Even with such a restriction, however, the Wedels thought he'd soon find a job. 'I mean, he's the POTUS,' she said. 'But it seems not even the leader of our country can get [my husband] a job.'[134]

22

USAA continued to tick Virgil off. Driving in San Antonio, he had noticed many Indians around its headquarters, making him suspicious. In July 2014, USAA Careers tweeted, '@USAA isn't just talking the talk. They are out there meeting and making hiring commitments to our service.'

'Yeah, right!' he replied. 'Says an unemployed Navy veteran with 30 years of technology experience.'

He emailed the CEO, inserting the exchange's screenshot. 'I see stuff like this by leaders such as yourself, AND I WANT TO BELIEVE IN YOU, but the stories I hear from others like myself that learned their technology in the service tell me ya'll are doing a great job talking the talk, but that's it. Case in point, as of now, you've 29 IT jobs open.'

Virgil copied them from the USAA website: developers-programmers (20), information security (3), IT (3) and systems-network engineering (3). 'I can apply for all of them, and I'll not get an interview even if I tell you I am an unemployed veteran with nearly three decades of experience at ALL levels. And you'll never know it, but I'm one of the best at reverse engineering any non-working system due to procedural, hardware, or software reasons, AND I can develop the solution to ensure it won't happen again AND track the process using Juran and Deming. Now the one thing I can't do is write a resume that will impress you. Probably because I don't care if you've a certificate or a diploma, but I DO CARE that you can hold your weight. After all, that is what the military is about, isn't it? Taking raw recruits and building their skills.'

Virgil shared a Keep America At Work article[135] explaining why American software types could 'no longer find work' due to 'the gatekeepers in the HR or the caste system'. He also spoke about, and marked, his ex-colleagues on the email. 'I've done what I can. I hope you'll do what you say you will when you say, "We hire Veterans" simply because many of us have been thrown under the bus.'

23

Kumar shot an early video for his YouTube channel—Kumar Exclusive, a name suggested by Raghav—in his apartment's living room. Wearing a polo shirt and a cap, he stood close to his cellphone camera. On the left wall hung his son's drawings, his work schedule and a picture of Kumar and his wife. A lamp, standing near the door, filled the room with warm light.

He recounted his journey from the late 1990s, speaking in a measured tone. Sometimes he looked at the camera, sometimes up, collecting and crystallising his thoughts. He looked like a mentor—an elder brother—trying to educate young Dream America aspirants. He spoke about 'many guys' in Hyderabad 'approaching middle-men' for visa petitions. 'Don't pay money to anybody. Because if someone is offering a job, he has to bear all the expenses. If he is not, then what is that you ... you ... can expect once you come here? I am repeating. If you are paying money to come to America then it is unethical.'[136]

His initial videos described the American work culture. 'Remember, a king in India is like a soldier in the US,' he said, referring to an IT manager becoming a contractor. 'So let go of that ego.' He emphasised a foreign worker's priorities. 'Immigration. Project. Health. If two are down, you may have to leave the country.'[137]

He released more videos: 'F1 visa preparation complete check list', 'Experience about life in India & USA', 'Political analysis of Indian democracy'.[138] Each of them stacked hundreds of views. The channel remained sunny for the first six months. But in November 2013, he dimmed the lights for the first time. Kumar recorded a video, sitting in his car: 'The Dark Side of H1B Life in America.'[139] It soon cut to: 'H1B—Episode 6—Helpless and Hopeless Life in America.'[140]

'I am not against India, Indians, Indian Incs and vendors. I am speaking from my heart. Problem is multiple layers, layers for no reason. Unethical layers. Unethical practice. Layers just forward your resume to multiple Indian vendors, who take $20 to $40 per hour. Because of that an H-1B, or an OPT student, lead a pathetic life. You approach the top 10 American vendors. Don't contact Indian vendors.'

An ideal project involving a desi consultancy employer should have looked like the following—H-1B Worker → Employer → Prime vendor → Client—containing entities essential to the hiring process. But plonking between the prime vendor and the employer, the 'layers' drained an H-1B's pay, fattening their coffers. Such middle vendors materialised in various ways: sometimes, the employer inserted a layer (via his friend's company who knew about a job at the client); sometimes, a middle vendor lured an H-1B, using the prime vendor's job posting, and inserted itself into the chain; and sometimes, a desi hiring manager at the client inserted a layer by colluding with a middle vendor and so on.

'Who is a vendor?' Kumar had once asked on his YouTube channel. 'An Indian on a green card who has opened a body shop. It is a whole shitshow. In fact, why is this necessary? Why can't an H-1B directly apply through a consultancy?' He couldn't because the middle vendor(s), partnering with his employer or the hiring manager or some other party, could sink a project. H-1Bs might not have unionised with any force, but in project after project, they saw its exasperating counterpart: the union of companies.

In mid-2014, Kumar moved to a different floor at work, where he met two Indians, Mani and Ruchi. A few days later, Mani made a strange request: he wanted Kumar's bank details. Kumar provided it and got $1,000 in his account. Mani asked him to come to an ATM. He did this with others, too. $1,000 was not a small amount. What was he up to?

Mani spent a lot of time on his desk phone, sometimes stepping out to receive calls. He soon told Kumar: 'proxy' interviews. Proud of 'helping students', he earned around $500 for each proxy, attending at least one call every day—some days more. He also had a literal partner-in-crime, Ruchi, as a female proxy. Vivacious and jovial, Mani kept it light and ribbed Kumar for this reason or that. Kumar warned him to stop his unethical business; Mani challenged him to record his calls on camera. Kumar loathed his fraud; Mani called him Mahatma Gandhi. Kumar said a human being's true purpose lay in 'doing something for the society'; Mani: 'my life, my family, my future'.

His friendship with Raghav, over a year old, continued to deepen. They had still not met but often exchanged emails centred on H-1B scams and Kumar's videos. If many Indians, like Mani, mocked Kumar for his idealism and dismissed any discussion about the H-1B abuse, then Raghav listened to him, agreed with him, empathised with him, as a friend, ally and safe space. 'When I was in India, I was happy, lots of respect for Indians, religions, etc,' Kumar emailed him in late 2014. 'But today I am on the edge of lose complete faith on Indians who do business in IT and other Indians because every day someone sent a filthy email to me due to too many of my communication channels. Reasons are simple. I was born in India. We have hate each other.

'I told a good American peer I do not know whether come to America is a bliss (expose to best of best) or sin (squeeze blood by fellow Indians). I lost faith in all systems in India while working in Government and due to injustice of justice systems, losing faith in Indians here which are doing business. We get crush between castes and corruption in motherland and then between fellow Indians and immigration systems in a foreign land. How pathetic.'

Most corporate crimes hinged on a few villains: an individual, a group, a company. But the H-1B scam, implicating countless Indians, turned an entire society complicit. Many perpetrators, like Mani, looked like regular people: pious, polite, patriotic; profiting companies, raising kids, paying mortgages. Yet their corruption and callousness—and a lack of remorse—elicited distinct discomfort. They did it because they wanted to do it, because everyone else did it, because they could get away with it. They had also kept this industry hidden because it benefited them.

But even their honest compatriots in America had buried this secret, as H-1Bs represented modern India's (rare) success story. Their country celebrated them, as affluent and brilliant, and America showcased them, as part of the 'model minority'. Any criticism of the H-1B programme, then, felt like criticism of India. Such evasions and delusions incensed Kumar no end. 'We Indians are in an extremely unfortunate state,' he had said in a video once. 'I don't even know what "India Shine" means.'

24

Manu's next project in Delaware, his longest, lasted just eight months. He knew that such short periods had continued to diminish his worth as an employee. He was not, what could be considered, a valuable 'resource'. A valuable resource worked long projects. A valuable resource never questioned, never retaliated, never got fired. A valuable resource became rich, making his consultancy richer. But an H-1B worker without a client, earning no money for his visa sponsor, was a dead weight, like Manu had become for Infocon Logix.

After the Delaware project, he returned to the guesthouse and began going to the Infocon office. One afternoon, he encountered Prakash. 'What are you doing, man? Are you alright? Go outside and take deep breaths.' Prakash had told him more than once to 'Go to India, market yourself and get yourself a job'. For someone struggling in the US, finding a job from India, that too on his own, was impossible.

Infocon Logix assigned him a new recruiter, Tara. Paying (his company's) taxes during the bench period had destroyed his savings. Manu had also shelled out $790 for his green card application. He couldn't afford to pay Infocon anymore. In late May 2014, his second month of unemployment, he requested his employer for 'an unpaid leave of absence'—from 26 May to 6 June—because he had fallen sick and would 'not receive salary for the foregoing leave'. The next month, a vendor, Kyra Jameson, contacted him for a data warehouse tester position. She asked for his professional references. Manu emailed the contacts of a project manager and a team lead at a healthcare multinational and a university hospital, covering up his new fake resume. She sent him a SQL test. He scored twenty-one out of thirty, making his proficiency level 'advanced'.

He followed up: 'Are we moving forward with the client interview?'

'Although your SQL experience was strong we can't move further due to your lack of healthcare experience and the dishonesty displayed from you and your employer around your resume. We found a resume of yours listing your last position in Delaware—and notes in the system from other recruiters who spoke to you about it.'

The unemployment stress made his temples itch. Manu approached two desi consultancies to market his resume. He once relied on an unusual proxy. For a Skype interview, an Infocon colleague sat beside him outside the camera's view. Whenever the recruiter asked a tough question, she pinged him the answer on Google Chat.

Still no offer.

In late July, a recruiter, Carl Smallwood, contacted Tara for a data quality analyst position. She sent Manu's resume. It listed a new email ID ('highangelofflight@gmail.com') and a new phone number. Fabricated resume, inverted name ('Mitra Manu'). Manu spoke to Carl, who had submitted the resume to the client. Carl emailed him soon: 'I received another resume from Infocon Logix with your name on it that was completely different.'

'Sorry Carl. Please don't consider that. I cannot even complain because they hold my H-1B and my green card is in process. I hope you understand. Sorry once again.'

Manu wrote to Tara. 'Please use this resume (attached)'—listing the original clients—'because even if it is double submission it's ok because it has the same projects. You can change the technologies but don't change projects. Please. I have to ask my mom for money. She is a divorcee and not working. I am 30 years old and asking my mom to pay in her old age instead of supporting her. Is it fair? I have a loan of $22,000. Prakash anna told me to leave the country and go to India and I have to live on my mom's money till I find a job? And what do I do with the loan? Somebody trusted me and gave money and I have to tell them I will not pay? Is it ethical?'

One day, Tara got an email for a contract position in Wichita, Kansas. She emailed his resume, saying, 'He is local to Kansas.' Even though Manu had gained some experience, the vast IT field still stumped him. Sometimes, he cleared the interviews on his own, like his last project, but sometimes he needed help or, in this desperate situation, absolute assurance. So he forwarded that email to an Infocon colleague who gave the proxy. He reached Wichita in less than a week.

On the first day of work, he met his manager, Jack Wilson, and a Nepali man, Aditya, who handled knowledge transfer (KT). Manu familiarised himself with the office: got access to software tools, figured out the place for stationery, explored the canteen downstairs. The next step: house hunting. He settled on a first-floor one-bedroom apartment, signing a year-long lease. He liked the place. It was spacious and affordable: $300 for rent, $50 for utilities.

During a KT session, Manu picked up a sheet of paper, drew ETL's diagrammatic representation and showed it to Aditya.

'Oh, this is what they explained at the consultancy?'

What?

'I am not talking about consultancy.'

'I know. In consultancy, they explain everything.'

The Nepali guy had an 'Indian mentality'. Aditya flattered the American colleagues and taunted Manu. He mentioned 'consultancy' again, implying Manu's dubious work experience. Just a few more days. After the KT, he wouldn't face Aditya again. Manu would also start repaying his loan. It had only been a week; he had plenty of time.

Jack stopped by his cubicle the next day. 'Do you have a minute?'

Manu followed him to a room.

'So you took an apartment?'

Yeah.

'Are you married?'

No.

'Today is your last day.'

He waited for the explanation.

'That's why we hire contractors.' Jack laughed.

A quiet Manu left the building.

Back at the apartment, he didn't cry, as if even tears had given up. His mind obsessed over other worries: the loan, the one-year lease and, ugh, New Jersey. What was worse than being broken? Being broken and lonely. No one to call or text—to complain, share, rant. He found solace in an online portal: the Suicide Project.[141] 'A website for sharing stories of desperation and depression … and ultimately of hope. We hope that by allowing people to share their stories of despair, they can find a reason to live, a reason to survive another minute. Another hour. Another day.'

Manu created an account—for the moment that was enough. Another hour. Another day.

A week later: *Screw this.*

He emailed HR.

If I do suicide, these three are responsible.

Jack Wilson

Eva Miller

Aditya Adhikari

I hold these two criminals since they hire even when the background test is not complete.

Jack Wilson

Eva Miller

I hold them responsible for fraud charges up to $30,000 for breaking the contract of six months.

Jack Wilson

Eva Miller

I hold them responsible for blame game, politics, and screwing innocent people's lives.

Jack Wilson

Eva Miller

If I leave this country without paying my debt of $30,000 these two are responsible.

Jack Wilson

Eva Miller

If they did not want me, why did they select me? They could take a Skype or a face to face interview. But they just want to waste the company's resources and others' time. I will tell this to the whole world by mailing the police of Wichita, FBI, and the President of the United States, and I don't care if Jack Wilson and Eva Miller hire a gunman to kill me because they are criminals already. Please forward this to the upper management? This should be prevented in future.

The vendor called, telling him not to contact the client. Manu scolded her.

'Sorry, it didn't work for you.'

'This is not the way to do business. You at least need to give some notice.'

'Don't worry, you'll get paid for one week.'

'I am not talking about pay. Did I say anything about pay? I am talking about respect.'

25

The H-1B programme had left Manu, Kumar and Virgil dejected, disillusioned and devastated. But American corporations, media outlets and politicians spread a contrasting message, parroting its endless virtues. The tech industry's potent weapon, think tanks, had helped spread that optimism, publishing pro-H-1B reports, year after year. As opposed to incendiary rhetoric, hard data seemed unbiased. But you had to know the game—the intricate ways in which even numbers could lie—to understand how it was gamed. Norm, who had co-founded the statistical department at UC Davis, knew this world in all its expanse: its merits, limitations, deceits.

So a May 2013 Brookings report baffled him. It concluded that H-1Bs earned 20 per cent more than comparable Americans.[142] Because in his recent study, published in the journal *Migration Letters*, he had found the exact opposite: that they earned 20 per cent less.[143]

The Brookings researchers, Jonathan Rothwell and Neil Ruiz, had accessed H-1Bs' wages through economists Magnus Lofstrom and Joseph Hayes's Freedom of Information Act request to USCIS. The 2010 visa petition forms, or I-129, for new and renewed applications listed foreign workers' ages, salaries, degrees, occupations and industries. Rothwell and Ruiz used the 2010 American Community Survey to get the corresponding data for American workers.

Norm read the Brookings report and wrote an e-newsletter post. 'Let's begin by discussing Brookings' H-1B data itself. They claim that this data is representative, but it is certainly NOT representative. Why not?' Because I-129 forms mentioned salaries 'at the time of hire'. 'Workers in general tend to get periodic raises in the years AFTER they are hired, right? Well, not if you are an H-1B.'[144] The National Research Council (NRC) study stated that H-1Bs got smaller pay hikes as compared to American workers. The 'H-1B advocacy groups', too, claimed foreign workers often received 'no raises' at all.[145] Even industry lobbyists had complained that the law forbade increments to green card–sponsored H-1Bs because it'd 'force the employer' to 'open up recruitment again' for Americans, who might take it for a 'higher price'.[146]

'The analysis says that,' added Norm, 'salaries in general grow at the rate of 10% per year, and since the visa is good for 3 years, and can be renewed for 3 years, the average H-1B has held his visa for 1.5 years.' Which meant his salary would have increased by 15 per cent since his filed petition. 'Suppose, as indicated above, he has gotten no raises. He is then underpaid by 15%—but the Brookings data wouldn't show it, because it only shows salary at the time of hire.'[147]

The study also assumed that the 'wage difference' between a 'bachelor's and a master's' remained the 'same' as the one for a master's and a PhD.[148] Norm had calculated those differences for his 2013 Economic Policy Institute (EPI) paper for computer science graduates.[149] Master's and bachelor's, \$6,703. PhD's and master's, \$21,543. 'Since, as the industry lobbyists love to point out, an H-1B is much more likely to have a PhD than Americans, this produces a major bias in Brookings' findings. They are not comparing H-1Bs to comparable Americans, in this case, NOT comparing PhDs to PhDs.'[150]

Then, the region.

The analysis had no variable for it. The BLS estimated the average salary for software developers in Chicago as \$89,990. San Jose, \$116,610.[151] Since H-1Bs clustered in the high-cost-of-living regions, it had produced 'another major error'. The findings had 'numerous other flaws', but something else troubled Norm more.

'Brookings, like any not-for-profit organization, survives through contributions. And it is a fact of life that these organizations cannot afford to do many, if any, studies that are counter to the goals of the donors. But unlike many other organizations that have clear agendas, Brookings presents itself as ideologically neutral, with a motto of "Quality, Independence, Impact." Its Web address even sports a .edu domain.

'Independence, nice concept. But how independent can Brookings be on tech issues when its annual report lists a contribution from the Bill and Melinda Gates Foundation in the $2,500,000-4,999,999 category? (This is the highest category.) There are also contributions from Microsoft, Google, and so on. Is it any wonder that Microsoft people are usually invited as featured panellists in conferences Brookings holds on the H-1B issue? I'll say, with considerable understatement, that it's impossible for researchers to be impartial with Microsoft/Gates' millions hanging over their heads. Bias doesn't have to be as flagrant as fudging data; it can be more subtle, such as telling only part of the story.'

Rothwell and Ruiz had shared their study with another H-1B critic, Ron Hira, an associate professor of public policy at the Rochester Institute of Technology. He blogged about it for EPI's website.[152] The researchers had used 'proprietary' data, he wrote, which—'exclusively held' by them—excluded others from 'critiquing or reviewing' it. Skimming through the report, he found a 'few peculiar items'. It included just 105,000 workers, while the USCIS database had 193,000.[153] Hira 'repeatedly pointed' out the 'serious discrepancy'; the researchers 'dismissed' his concerns. They only agreed when he kept explaining 'why their data didn't make any sense'.

They also made 'questionable analytic choices', failing to compare 'apples to apples'. The law required H-1Bs to hold bachelor's degrees or the functional equivalent, but the study considered an 'expansive' definition of comparable American workers, including 'all computer occupations'—many of which didn't require bachelor's degrees—such as computer support specialists. Jobs that H-1Bs didn't do. This category had a 'significant share' of all computer occupations and 'relatively low wages'. By doing so, Brookings had 'systematically' lowered the 'reported American wages', making 'H-1B wages appear higher'.

Next year, the *Washington Post* published a long report on the think tank. 'Over the past decade, a new business model'—emphasising 'expansion and fundraising'—had 'taken hold' at Brookings.[154] Its 'public seminars, research papers, congressional testimony and op-eds' often matched the donors' interests.[155] The researchers had adopted 'market-oriented stances on key issues'.[156] Several 'recent Brookings studies', noted the piece, 'have been singled out for criticism by academics and others' who attributed the lopsided results to its 'association with corporate donors and other wealthy interests'.[157] The *Post* investigation provided two major examples: student debt and high-tech immigration. The 'critics suggested' that, in Brookings's July 2012 study, a 'methodological error' had 'understated' the outsourcing firms' use of the H-1B programme.[158] It referenced the May 2013 analysis as well, where the critics had objected to its 'flawed assumptions'.[159]

Analysing the think tank's annual reports, the piece revealed that Brookings's revenues had shot up from $32 million in 2003 to around $100 million in 2013. Corporate donations increased from 7 per cent to 25 per cent and overseas contributions, including 'foreign governments and trade associations', rose from 6 per cent to 22 per cent.[160] The researchers said the 'fundraising imperative' had 'changed the environment'. They had to now 'review the costs and financial benefits of their work' and attend 'seminars and receptions with donors', some held abroad, comprising top Washington lobbyists.

The tech industry moulded the public perception of the H-1B programme through another ally: universities. Corporations doused them in donations—new buildings, lab equipment, endowed professorial chairs. Stanford University, for instance, had Gates Hall (Microsoft), Huang Center (NVIDIA) and Hewlett Hall and Packard Hall (Hewlett-Packard). In June 2001, Tata Consultancy Services had launched the Software Industry Center[161] at Carnegie Mellon University (CMU) and, fourteen years later, donated $35 million to it.[162] (Its parent company, Tata Group, had given $50 million to Harvard Business School in 2010.[163]) In 2004, the Bill and Melinda Gates Foundation had gifted $20 million to CMU.[164] Infosys founder Narayana Murthy sat on Cornell's trustee board.

Universities profited from the guest worker programme. International students, hoping to work on H-1B visas, paid much more tuition than their American counterparts. The schools also coveted government funds to cope with the 'STEM labour shortage'. Unlike corporate America, they could hire *unlimited* foreign workers and, unbound by the prevailing wage requirement, set their own pay scales. These provisions had resulted from the American Competitiveness in the 21st Century Act of 2000. Support our legislation for an increased H-1B cap, said industry lobbyists, and we'll make sure you get unlimited H-1Bs at academia-level salaries.

They both won.

Years later, that relationship spawned a new chapter: research parks. The universities hired H-1Bs (on much-reduced pay) and, for fat overhead fees, 'loaned' them to firms. A sleight of hand that saved companies enormous costs. All of it was technically legal, but a scandal at Wright State University[165] in 2015 caused the resignation, demotion and termination of at least three college officials.[166]

The 'selfish' and 'empire-building' universities baffled Norm.[167] 'Isn't academia supposed to be a purer world, one whose central goal is the noble pursuit of truth?' he asked in his newsletter. 'Isn't the very notion of a university symbolized by Harvard's motto, Veritas? Academia's refusal to fix the real problem is disgraceful.'[168]

In 2011, an Agnes College professor, Madeline Zavodny, published a paper on H-1B. It compared the native employment rate to the population of foreign-born STEM workers with advanced degrees from American universities in fifty states and the District of Columbia from 2000 to 2007. She concluded that a 10 per cent increase in the share of such workers increased the US-born employment rate by 0.04 per cent. Or an extra '100 foreign-born' STEM workers were associated with an additional '262 jobs' among natives. Or '2.62 jobs' for every foreign-born STEM worker.[169]

Those figures spread, like a scent out of a bottle.[170]

Newspapers: *The New York Times*,[171] *The Wall Street Journal*,[172] *The Indian Express*,[173] *The Boston Globe*,[174] *The Economic Times*,[175] *San*

Francisco Examiner,[176] *New York Daily News*,[177] *Financial Times*,[178] *NBC News*,[179] *Business Standard*,[180] *The Hill*,[181] *Bloomberg*,[182] *Forbes*,[183] *Fortune*,[184] *DNA*.[185]

Politicians: Senator Ted Cruz (R-Texas),[186] Senator Orrin Hatch (R-Texas),[187] Senator Richard Blumenthal (D-Connecticut);[188] Representative Mike Quigley (D-Illinois)[189] and Representative Erik Paulsen (R-Minnesota).[190]

Think tanks: Chicago Council on Global Affairs,[191] The American Action Forum,[192] American Freedom Institute.[193]

Lobbying groups: U.S. Chamber of Commerce, Partnership for a New American Economy,[194] American Immigration Lawyers Association,[195] Information Technology Industry Council, National Immigration Forum,[196] American Immigration Council,[197] Compete America,[198] Business Roundtable[199] and, of course, FWD.us.[200]

Even the White House.

Obama's Executive Office released a July 2013 report, 'The Economic Benefits of Fixing our Broken Immigration System', whose seventh page featured the '2.6 jobs' figure.[201] It appeared again in a 2014 White House blog.[202] Zavodny's study had become the new sun in the H-1B world: it shone everywhere.

Norm read the paper and first objected to its term 'foreign-born'.[203] Because many foreign-born 'STEM students', he explained on his blog, were 'either naturalised US citizens or permanent residents' who had never been 'H-1Bs or foreign university students'. So a lot of STEM workers in her 'foreign-born' category were 'actually Americans'. She did 'not make this clear' and was 'likely unaware of it'. Zavodny had included a 'separate number for H-1Bs (183 instead of 262)', but countless people 'on [Capitol] Hill and in the press' would have interpreted 'foreign-born' as 'H-1B'.

Zavodny's study intrigued a Silicon Valley programmer, R. Davis. He contacted Norm in late 2014 about his opinion on its statistical method. Norm had criticised her 2003 paper—which concluded that data provided little support that the H-1B programme depressed wages—but told Davis to contact her. He did, and she shared her data and code.[204]

While attempting to duplicate her results, Davis noticed something odd: the native employment rate. It averaged around 65 per cent, making the unemployment rate 35 per cent, 'much higher than', he wrote on his website, the reported figure. Zavodny had also counted 'those not in the labor force'—the retired and the self-employed—as unemployed.[205] The paper didn't mention it anywhere. The 'native employment rate' appeared thirty-two times; 'labor force' and 'self-employed' not even once. Davis found the self-employed workers' classification especially 'problematic', as the 'sideways movement between' the private sector and self-employment registered a change in employment. The dubious definition had altered the Y-axis dataset, skewing the result.

He also subjected the study to different start and end years. Like Zavodny, he did find the '2.62' figure for 2000 to 2007. But as the periods changed—from 2002 to 2010, from 2003 to 2011 and so on—the results became more negative, pointing to a 'loss of native jobs'.[206] The extended timeline revealed the study's sensitive nature to the first and last years.

A 'fundamental' challenge 'using cross-state comparisons' to show a 'relationship between immigrants and jobs', Zavodny explained in the paper, was that they gravitated towards the job-yielding regions. So 'evidence of high immigrant shares in states with strong economic growth and high employment' could be the '*result* of greater job opportunities', not 'the *cause*'. Cross-state comparisons would then 'show an artificially high impact of immigrants on the native employment rate'. To avoid 'overcounting', she had relied on a 'two-stage least squares (2SLS) regression estimation'.[207]

Her assertion alarmed Davis. Because Zavodny had not used 2SLS regression to calculate the '2.62' figure. She had used an OLS regression. Besides, a relationship between A and B didn't mean by default that A caused B. Crowing roosters were associated with sunrise, went a famous saying, but they didn't cause the sun to rise. 'The study does avoid causal language in the following case,' Davis wrote, quoting a part on page 4. 'An additional 100 foreign-born workers ... is *associated* with an additional 262 jobs among US natives'.[208]

But then the claims got bold.

Page 10. 'This implies that every additional 100 foreign-born workers … *led* to an additional 262 jobs.'[209]

Page 13. 'An additional 100,000 such workers could *lead* to an additional 262,000 American jobs.'[210]

Bolder.

Page 8. '100 FOREIGN BORN WORKERS = 262 ADDITIONAL JOBS.'[211]

Page 8. 'Every additional 100 foreign-born workers … *created* an additional 262 … '[212]

Page 13. 'Bringing in more highly skilled workers will *create* American jobs.'[213]

The study's gaping holes made Davis conclude that 'Zavodny's own numbers' did 'not support' her '2.62' claim. Besides 'no evidence of causation', she presented 'very weak and arguably flawed evidence of correlation.'[214] While discussing Davis's findings with a *Science* reporter, Norm said the 'dominant variable' in her graph was 'not the number of foreign workers' but 'state'. Jobs and foreign workers shared 'essentially no relationship' but 'state to state' showed a 'big difference.'[215] In the states with 'big H-1B usage, such as California, New York and New Jersey,' he added on his blog, 'the data are basically flat! Within states, an increase in the number of foreign-born STEM workers with advanced degrees is NOT associated with a trend of increasing STEM employment for natives.'[216]

But the mainstream media made Zavodny's result look like a self-evident truth. The journalists need not be stats whiz, however, to mention two facts. It was a working paper yet to be peer-reviewed, and it was published by a conservative think tank, American Enterprise Institute, and an immigration research and advocacy organisation, Partnership for a New American Economy, founded by Michael Bloomberg.

Zavodny first ran the regression for 2000 to 2010, concluding that 'none of the estimates are significantly different from zero.'[217] She hadn't found a significant effect of foreign-born workers on native jobs. In an email exchange with the authors of a 2015 book, *Sold Out: How High-Tech Billionaires and Bipartisan Beltway Crapweasels Are*

Screwing America's Best and Brightest Workers, she revealed that the study's sponsor had told her to discard the last three years' data—from 2008 to 2010, due to the Great Recession—and try again.[218]

She did—and Silicon Valley winked.

26

The 'thought control' ecosystem revered another economics professor: Giovanni Peri at UC Davis, Norm's colleague. He released a (working) paper in May 2014.[219] Examining wages and immigration in 219 Metropolitan Statistical Areas (MSAs) from 1990 to 2010, he and his co-authors, Kevin Shih and Chad Sparber, concluded, 'One percentage point increase in the foreign STEM share of a city's total employment increased wages of native college educated labor by about 7-8 percentage points and the wages of non-college educated natives by 3-4 percentage points.'[220] *The Wall Street Journal* carried an excerpt (and a graph): 'Want a pay raise? Ask your employer to hire more immigrant scientists.'[221]

The newspaper's enthusiasm for the study matched R. Davis's: he attempted to reproduce the findings.[222] Peri's team had relied on the Integrated Public Use Microdata Series (IPUMS), an individual-level population database for information on, among others, wages, employment and nativity. Davis used the same source to recreate the *WSJ* chart. But his and Peri's plot had a glaring difference: the exclusion of San Jose—a city in the 'heart of Silicon Valley'—with the 'largest share of foreign STEM workers.'[223]

The IPUMS contained data for 303 MSAs. Eighty-four cities, however, lacked data for one or more years featured in the study (1980, 1990, 2000, 2005 and 2010). Subtract 84 from 303, 219, the MSAs in the paper. But Huntsville, Newburgh and Middletown, despite missing the data fields for 1990, were included in the *WSJ* chart. Yet San Jose, with over a million points each year, was not.

Davis wrote to Peri asking for the spreadsheet containing the values of the 219 MSAs in the *WSJ* plot. He obliged. The MSAs in the IPUMS table that didn't contain values for 2010 weren't included in the graph. But the ones with missing values for 1990 but not for 2010 did appear in Peri's chart. Stamford, though, like San Jose—despite containing all the values from 1980 to 2010—did not appear in the *WSJ* graph, a city that had the 'largest percentage change in real native college-graduate wages from 1990 to 2010'.[224] San Luis Obispo—which had values for 2000, 2005 and 2010—wasn't included either. The excerpt did not mention these exclusions. The *WSJ* piece stated, '33 cities saw a decline in foreign STEM workers and 25 of those cities saw an outright decline in wages for their college-educated populations'.[225] Out of them, however, 31 had no data for 1990, whose values, presumed Davis, came 'from an undefined source'.[226]

'I asked Mr. Peri for the source of his spreadsheet but received no response,' he wrote on his website. 'When I asked for the data'—to replicate the outcome—'[Peri] said he checked with his coauthors and they convinced him the right avenue of action is, as they spent several months organizing and cleaning the data, it should be available through the journal that publishes the paper.'[227]

The next year, in July 2015, the *Journal of Labor Economics* published the peer-reviewed version.[228] It featured an 'instrumental variable', an entity (Z) that had a direct correlation with the variable X but influenced the variable Y only in association with X. So, according to a famous example, in the relationship between smoking (Y) and depression (X), Z could be a lack of job opportunities. Z affected X—unemployment leading to depression—which influenced Y (an increase in smoking). But Z and Y didn't have a direct correlation.

Peri's study had used the 'H-1B driven increase' as an instrumental variable, which affected foreign STEM workers' share of a city's total employment (X), to find the changes in native wages (Y). The researchers had chosen the 1990 to 2010 period and divided it into three parts—from 1990 to 2000, 2000 to 2005 and 2005 to 2010—

to 'exploit the large variation in national H-1B policy that occurred between 2000 and 2005 relative to the other periods'.

Norm commented on the methodology in his newsletter. 'I have long stated my reservations about the very broad scope of many of the papers of this type.'[229] It included a wide variety of H-1Bs. But the most contentious part of the guest worker programme—related to the displacement of American techies and the (law-codified) underpayment of foreign workers—occurred in computer fields. 'Mixing together lots of different occupations can mask some effects, dilute others and produce contradictory results. ... [Take] the famous Simpson's Paradox (regression version), under which the algebraic sign of a relationship can change when data is amalgamated.'[230] The public debate on H-1B primarily concerned tech workers, added Norm, not marketing executives or financial analysts. 'Congress and the press will take [Peri's] research to have implications specific to the hiring of engineers on temporary work visas—even though [it] does NOT do this.'

Norm's next disagreement tackled a term marking many pro-H-1B papers (including Zavodny's): 'foreign-born'. Numerous foreign-born techies had entered the country at a very young age—such as Google's co-founder, Sergey Brin, who migrated as a six-year-old—making the dataset questionable. 'The public debate concerns foreign nationals on work visas, NOT workers who came to the US as children and are now either permanent residents or naturalized citizens.'

He also discussed the model's fragility. 'I am a former statistics professor ... I continue to teach and do methodological research in the field. My specialty is regression analysis. I use [it] in my own research on H-1B, but I know that it is a very fragile tool, as Simpson's Paradox often vividly shows. Part of [Peri's] paper uses a particularly fragile form of regression analysis called "instrumental variables". IVs are quite popular among economists, but are rarely used elsewhere. Even among economists, IVs are controversial.' Norm linked to a 2007 *WSJ* piece—'Is an economist qualified to solve the puzzle of autism?'[231]—which, quoting Nobel Prize-winning economists, raised persuasive concerns about the efficacy of instrumental variables.

Peri's paper, according to Norm, suffered from another disconnect. 'I teach my students and consulting clients that regression analysis is most useful if its results jibe with other information one has.' What were the 'hot button' questions here? 'Are H-1Bs paid fairly, relative to their market worth? Are [they] typically "the best and the brightest", as claimed by the lobbyists? … Is there a tech labor shortage, the putative raison d'être for H-1B?' All of them had produced strong 'negative research.'[232]

A simple 'thought experiment', added Norm, resolved the underpayment issue. The H-1Bs sponsored for green cards were de facto immobile, so they couldn't get the best deal in the labour market. That made them, on average, 'underpaid relative' to their true value. 'Basic economic theory, not to mention plain common sense, establishes the underpayment issue. Similarly, if H-1B is such a boon to native skilled workers, why have their wages been flat for the last 10+ years, as shown by other research?'

In 2015, the *New York Times* published a piece detailing how the financial ties between agricultural behemoths and university professors influenced their research.[233] It stated Monsanto had recruited Kevin Folta—a University of Florida professor and a long-term defender of genetically modified foods—for 'biotechnology outreach', quoting email exchanges between him and the executives. *The New York Times Magazine* published an essay the same year, titled 'Debunking the Myth of the Job-Stealing Immigrant',[234] citing a 'leading scholar', Peri. But the *Times* failed to mention that he, too, had taken money from the industry. In fact, almost no media outlet, supporting his findings, disclosed the fund's source.

'Many immigration scholars regularly cited in the press have worked for, or received funding from, pro-immigration businesses and associations,' revealed a 2017 *Atlantic* piece.[235] 'Consider, for instance, Giovanni Peri … whose name pops up a lot in liberal commentary on the virtues of immigration. Peri is indeed a respected scholar. But Microsoft has funded some of his research into high-skilled immigration. And New American Economy paid to help him turn his research into a 2014 policy paper decrying limitations on the H-1B visa program.'[236]

Norm pointed out something else, too. 'The bibliographies in his papers almost never cite any work that has findings that are unfavorable to the H-1B program, when in fact one is supposed to cite all relevant prior work. These are major academic transgressions.'[237]

The Peri study even enamoured the White House's Council of Economic Advisors (CEA). Discussing increased worker productivity, the 2014 CEA report[238] referenced Peri's 2014 working paper on the fifth page. Another Peri paper popped up on the next page. Three more on the ninth page. Two more on the tenth page, and on and on and on and on. 'Peri and his coauthors,' wrote Norm, 'were basically the *only* ones cited.'[239]

'The CEA report does cherry pick from the existing literature on immigration economics,' said *Financial Times*.[240] 'For instance, there are thirty-three mentions of Giovanni Peri, all of them favourable. He's the pro-immigration economist's pro-immigration economist.' The CEA only mentioned 'George Borjas [an economist at the Harvard Kennedy School], well known for his scepticism about the employment and wage effects of immigration, three times'—and did so to 'contradict his findings'.

While discussing high-skilled immigration, the CEA relied on a 'single Peri paper', wrote Norm, 'ignoring a mountain of negative research.' It didn't consider two Congress-commissioned studies—by the NRC and GAO—which had shown the pervasive underpayment of H-1B workers and stated that the size of the H-1B IT workforce alone depressed wages. 'Such obvious bias in selling the policy to the American people is unconscionable.'[241]

IV

FIGHT

27

In mid-January 2015, Virgil discovered a YouTube channel. He watched one video, then another, then another. Even though the accent confused him, the videos confirmed his long-standing hunch: that corporate America had reduced H-1Bs, like Americans, to mere pawns. He left a comment: 'Can I get a copy of your book?'

'Thanks for watching,' Kumar replied. 'I am still writing and yet to make a hard copy. A friend of mine Raghav is helping.' He shared his Facebook pages and a video, 'LiA Episode 57, Confrontational Book.'[1] 'Please like our pages and subscribe to my channel.'

'I will check it all out, and I want to ask you a favor, and I understand if the answer is no.' Virgil proposed unemployed Americans and immigrants file a class-action lawsuit against corporations. 'If we sue and win, the immigrants will lose. If we lose, the immigrants will win but ultimately they too will lose, because too many Americans are getting forced out of work.'

'Sure, I do not want any American to be displaced because of an H-1B.' Kumar said 'unethical layers' hired Indian master's students and H-1Bs for less pay. 'So ultimately the middle-men greedy for money' benefited by 'dragging people like' him to America.

They exchanged close to half a dozen emails daily. Some days more. Virgil shared his past life: the Vegas house, the Attorney General project, the endless unemployment. Kumar explained the duplicity of body shops, the dishonesty of H-1B workers, his desire to change his narrow mindset.

Virgil continued investigating the H-1B programme. Kumar complemented Virgil's findings with his own analysis, unfurling endless discussions on visas, offshoring, limited jobs. 'I don't know the solution,' he told Kumar. 'But I have many questions and the skills to get the answers, and if I live long enough, I will get back to work no matter what it takes.'

'I empathize and do not know whom to blame for me here. My dreams, dollar dreams, America dream, or my Indian employer or Indians or US client who promotes outsourcing.'

'Trust me, it's not your fault. It's the law of demand and supply.'

Virgil had sold his car and iPad; he used the internet and phone at his mother's house. His website shut down because he couldn't afford the $10 hosting fees. Po again, po as hell, po all the time. Po: when you were 'too poor to add an "or" to it'. He emailed Kumar. 'I might as well give up and commit suicide for all they care because I'm but a disposable commodity. Don't mind me, but if I don't come up with 2,500 asap, I will lose my home and land, and I can't buy a job, and when I ask for help, the response is "Get a job".'

Kumar made a YouTube video.[2] 'Donate $50, one hour of your salary, to a badly displaced American. He worked as an IT manager who is now without a job. He will save his small land and four dogs.' Kumar also wrote a long Facebook post ('Dear friends in America, I would like to introduce my friend Mr. Virgil Bierschwale …').

The next day, Virgil received $200.

'Dang, didn't expect,' he wrote to Kumar. 'Especially since you need your money based on what you told me. Thank you.'

'No problem. I used to send $200 to my father but I stopped to pay credits here and when I called him he said, repay loans and come back asap. Instead of sending it to him, I sent to you. I did not do anything great.'

Over the last few weeks, as Virgil struggled to save his land and cabins, Keep America At Work became, if it was even possible, more and more grim. Several posts described his desperation and plight. 'Folks, I'm at the end of my rope,' read one such article on 4 February.

'NOBODY will hire me in a job that will allow me to afford my land and the sheds I live in. All those Veterans Organizations that say we help our vets will only do so after you commit suicide.'[3]

He had bared his heart many times before. Nobody cared; nobody replied. It wasn't news; it didn't happen. But in early February, American techies changed from ghosts to humans. Southern California Edison (SCE), an electric utility company, had fired its IT employees and ordered them to train their replacements, Infosys and TCS workers.[4]

This news reached the politicians. Jeff Sessions (R-Alabama) cited the SCE layoffs in his Senate speech.[5] Two months later, ten senators—including Sessions, Bernie Sanders (D-Vermont) and Richard Durbin (D-Illinois)—wrote a joint letter to the attorney general, the Department of Homeland Security (DHS) and the DOL, urging them to investigate the utility company.[6]

A few days after the SCE layoffs, Virgil emailed a *Breitbart* reporter. 'I might have a good story for you. By now you've probably read about the SCE deal. I can't get into USAA no matter what. So I created a spreadsheet for you that shows all work locations of San Antonio.' Three firms, requesting H-1B workers, dominated the list: HCL Technology; Infosys; and an obscure entity, Yash & Lujan Consulting, Inc. 'The Yash one has an address on I-10, and USAA is two miles away. Just imagine.'

Two weeks passed. Still no money. First, he'd lose the cabin, then the land. He called the cabin-leasing company. Without a payment plan, it would have just taken the cabin when Virgil wasn't home. But he wanted to make this decision at least. He wouldn't let anyone treat him like a (dishonest) deadbeat. It all happened in front of him. A huge trailer arrived at his doorstep. And just like that, he had nothing left.

He wrote a post on Keep America At Work.[7] Its headline: 'Thank you Dept of Labor and Veterans Administration for making me realize you have no honor', referring to their VRAP 'employment promise'. Under it, pictures of the barren land. Many concrete blocks, earlier holding the cabin, strewn all around. More than a dozen plastic jugs—he had stored them for long, planning to grow plants in them using the wicking garden technique. A white refrigerator. Two mattresses. Disposable plates. His dog Lexie, a crossbreed of a Japanese chin and an eskimo spitz. Near the pickup, the Japanese chin Titus. A barbeque pit in front of the oak trees. A table, a recliner, an office chair. His plans. His dreams. His defeat.

Two days later, Virgil sat on his recliner, Lexie and Titus on his lap, looking at the area that used to be his living room. A thought struck him: 'A beautiful day to die.'[8] He posted it on the website, describing his desperation, like a man talking to himself. 'I can't believe I was thinking that. But after writing to everybody from the President of the United States of America to the Veterans Department and Department of Labor and many lesser authorities like the Attorney General of Texas, I have come to the conclusion that they don't give a damn about Americans in America as long as they can become millionaires by selling us out. … So tell me. If the government will not come to my rescue. And private industry will not hire me. And civil service (veterans administration among others) will not hire me. And I don't have the funds to start a business. Nor the credit to borrow … What exactly am I supposed to do?'

A *Wall Street Journal* reporter, Joshua Edwards, contacted Kumar, wanting to write about recent foreign graduates working for shady body shops. The story intrigued him, as imminent legislation would increase the OPT extension's duration from seventeen to twenty-four months. 'Joshua asked me how to prove this scam?' Kumar told Virgil. His subscriber had shared an email where a desi consultancy employee, Manasi Hariharan—'manasi@fundamentalit.us'—asked for a $3,800 H-1B fee.

'Your first clue is the email id.' Virgil retrieved its 2015 LCA applications: five, all in Houston. 'This tells me they are in this business.' He landed on 'fundamentalit.us', which directed him to 'fundamental-infotech.com'. Virgil scanned its domain information and found the registrant's name and email ('Joel Reddy', 'reddy@ fundamentalit.us'). A Google search of Joel Reddy led him to Reddy Drivesol, which shared Fundamental Infotech's address. A Joel Cheruku owned Reddy Drivesol who, Virgil presumed, was Joel Reddy, the owner of another company, HXN Integrators.

Kumar received another email from a subscriber, Ashok, who inquired about Soluwork. Virgil sleuthed again. Several companies listed the same location as Soluwork: 5 Independence Way, Suite 300, Princeton, New Jersey. 'Now you would need to go there to see which ones are in Suite 300, as that info was not in the data files and who knows, that might be a great story for a reporter.'

'Earlier also friends sent addresses like this. I called and the call went to India. I told him I wanted to visit, he said hurriedly, "No no, only desktop lady is sitting there" (see his English). What if I go? Can I have a right to go with a cell phone camera and shoot and post it on YouTube? Is it an offence? Only a media personnel must do?'

'I don't know, but I'm creating something that will allow an address search hoping that it will uncover some snakes. Your WSJ friend might be interested in that spreadsheet as it looks like they're running a lot of companies from that address.'[9]

Joshua sent them a list of the OPT workers—and their employers—at 5 Independence Way. 'This all started because of an email you received from Ashok that someone at Soluwork was trying to get money for H-1B processing. We need proof of that in an email. Did he get that proof? Can we check? Any email that Ashok has from Soluwork could show a pretty large operation.'

Kumar emailed Ashok. 'Show me proof. 1) Did you pay money? Do you have bank receipts? 2) Did they send emails, documents, physical copies to sign? 3) Scan and send everything.'

Kumar followed up. No reply. The story died.

'Today I interviewed a young woman from India,' Joshua wrote to Kumar and Virgil. 'She worked for a "desi consultancy" that changed her resume, charged her for H-1B processing, and asked her to take part in significant fraud involving other workers' names and social security numbers. There is proof. She wouldn't let me write about it, even if her name is not used. That has happened now, probably 20 times or more. It is truly awful that young people who know they could stop the exploitation of their peers choose not to help out of fear and, to a certain extent, selfishness.'

But Joshua had another chance at the story. He procured a list of companies hiring from 'problem schools': 'VSquare/VForce Infotech, SCM Data/MMC Systems, Beta Soft Systems, Canvas Infotech, Xceltech'. Virgil extracted their LCAs, converted them into tables and arranged them in Excel files. Each contained the job title, location, LCA status, visa class and salary. The pay ranged from $45,000 to $53,000, 'substantially less than what an American' would have made.

'I love data like this. You are an excellent digital forensics expert, Virgil. I appreciate the help. Kumar, you have many contacts. I need one who will talk about their first-hand experience. My editor decides tomorrow if we throw everything we have at this story, or call it a day.'

This story, too, died.

Or did it?

Because a few months later, in May 2015, Virgil emailed Kumar an article in an Indian newspaper, *DNA*: 'Two Indian-Americans arrested for H-1B visa fraud in US'.[10] Hiral Patel and Shikha Mohta, Jersey City residents, had been 'charged with one count of conspiracy' to import and harbour aliens and 'obstruct justice'. The violation carried a 'maximum potential penalty of five years in prison' and a '$250,000 fine'. They had committed the same crimes as countless body shops over the decades, including 4M and Infocon Logix: lying to the DHS that their foreign employees had full-time jobs in the US, paying them only when they got a 'third party' project, 'generat[ing] false payroll records' to cover up non-payment of wages and so on.

And which companies did Patel and Mohta own? The ones frustrating Joshua for weeks: SCM Data and MMC Systems.

28

Between June 2013 and January 2015, Kumar had exposed a small portion of the H-1B scam on his YouTube channel: the unethical 'layers', the unpaid travel expenses, the wage theft during the bench period. But Virgil's[11] first email, a 'live example' of a victim, moved and miffed him. He made a video the next day. This time, he didn't hesitate or halt. Or prepare a script. Or refer to his notes. This world deserved to be burnt—and Kumar flicked a hungry match.

'A student appears for visa interview in India, show he has enough funds for studies and living. But the reality is he looks and inquires for illegal part-time jobs. After coming here, he or she does a lot of illegal part-time jobs. So where is the money, when he or she went for the interview when he or she show a lot of money? Is it fake—is it hype? After coming here, he or she cannot get a job just like that. But there is a back-home loan, of 20 to 30 lakh rupees, then Indian employers encourage'—the match blazed, the secrets scampered—'… a proxy call, a fake call.'[12] He revealed the scam's extensions. 'Proxy Skype call,[13] proxy project support, fake POs, fake MSAs. Fake transportation bills to avoid taxes. What is this? Are we learning anything from America or are we breaking every single rule here?

'When an H-1B attend a visa interview in India, he will tell the US consulate he has an in-house job. He or she get a visa. But the reality? He doesn't have a job. That is truth. The so-called Indian middle vendors or employers will suck his blood, if he goes with his original resume. Because everything is fake here. "Seven years of experience", junior; "10 years of experience", senior.'

This industry allowed just one gateway to freedom, but even when it materialised, free immigrants didn't unshackle but tightened the chains. 'After all this struggle he get a green card. Then, he become another employer. Like college ragging, in the first year they do, and when he enter the second year, he do the same ragging for the juniors.'

He ended the video with a tribute—hinged on his love, admiration, inspiration; restlessness, exasperation, despair: America.[14] 'Truth is, America kicked out poverty and racism—to a maximum extent. American government pays unemployment wages for locals. When will we kick out poverty and racism? What I learnt from America is humanity, equality and unity. But where is our humanity? Did we come here just to promote discrimination—either caste, religion or region? What are we? Truth is, we die for dollars.'

Kumar uploaded twenty-four videos in the next five weeks. Almost all brimming with fire: 'how to avoid illegal layers'; 'lie, fraud, king H-1B life in America'; 'H1B Episode 39, H1B scam.'[15]

As his channel changed tenor, so did his subscribers' messages. Most came from India, flagging a common concern: body shops demanding thousands of dollars to file H-1B visas. 'Hi Mr. Kumar,' read one such email, 'please find below an employer who is asking for money.'

He forwarded it to Virgil.

'They're coming out of the woodworks,' he replied. 'I believe you will attract a lot of attention with this movement you've started.'

Kumar had received hundreds of emails and comments. The inquirers comprised a diverse bunch—a business school graduate, a video editor, a call centre worker, a medical representative, a twelfth grader, an Indian worker from Canada, someone with a 'hospitality background', a post-doctoral candidate from Durban, a final year engineering student, a medical student, a college principal, a lawyer from Bangalore, an Infosys employee, an IBM employee and countless others—wanting to further their professional prospects: how to select the right university, how to choose a 'genuine consultancy', how to tackle the vendors' payment problems, which country: US or Australia, H-1B or Dubai, how about Canada, or Germany, what was the most coveted IT skill set, how to prepare a resume and on and on.

Some suggested topics for future videos.

'What about L1 visa abuse? It is worse because you only require manager label.'

'Please do a video on the rights of H-1Bs, billing rates, how to survive, etc.'

'Please make an English version of some videos.'

Some praised him.

'Your recent video touched my heart.'

'I feel proud of you as an Indian.'

'American tech professionals have been trying to spread this message for decades, but no one pays attention coz we are labeled racist, bigot, xenophobic. We need H1B folks to expose this nasty game for the better of both the immigrant and American workers. Thank you.'

Some inquired about marriage: 'What should I check before committing to an H-1B visa holder?'

Some offered general advice: 'Don't use bad words like pimp, because digital is forever.'

Many objected to his abusive language and broad generalisations; many ridiculed his English. One complaint, however, recurred so much that it became a subgenre.

'You are always insulting our country.'

'Don't talk like a communist.'

'Don't you think you are "anti-India"?'

Raghav had also gotten more and more annoyed with the H-1B programme's abuse and its beneficiaries' entitlement. He continued to encourage Kumar, fuelling his grievances, correcting his grammar, suggesting titles for videos.

'The problem with Mani or anyone who draws more money is they underestimate others saying not showing interest or talent,' Kumar emailed Raghav. 'He always says: if you are complaining, means you do not have talent.'

'Without fraud, ask him to move. Let's see how long he'll last? Resume fabrication, Proxy Interviews, Back Door Hiring, On Job Support and bogus skills are part of majority desis Life.'

'Yes. When I say this, a MS student from IL wrote, Do not jeopardies Students life in USA.'

'Jeopardize? As soon as finishing master's in USA, instead of 0 Years they start from 8 Years.'

'TRUE.'

'Those who do all frauds think they're so great for fooling America and they try to lecture about life and moral values. Moreover they ridicule honest people who make less living than them.'

A minute later, Raghav emailed again. 'But what they lose in life is character.' Kumar never forgot the next line. 'When character is lost, everything is lost.'

29

Kumar recorded a video in early 2015, 'Edu Episode 53, Students FAQs—BTech, MS in USA.'[16] 'You have to ask yourself: If I finished my BTech, why did I not get a job? Ask your principals, lecturers. Email your MLA, MP, district collector, honourable chief minister, even the honourable prime minister. You email—what is there? Youth is future, right? This is after you do RCA, Root Cause Analysis, on why you couldn't get a job. If nothing wrong, then ask them, where are the industries, where are the companies? If they are not, then why are you giving permission to BTech colleges? Close them.'

Towards the end of the video, he revealed another secret of foreign guest workers, implicating tens of thousands of Indian masters' students. 'Every student knows where he is applying. See, for example, you get a seat in IIT Chennai, IIT Assam—[or in] an [obscure] engineering college in Srikakulam, on the Orissa-AP border—so don't you know which college to apply? You know better than anybody else. Same thing here, whether it is unrecognised or fake university like Tri-Valley, they know well in advance. I don't believe how media projected. I don't believe they are ignorant. They know. They all want to come to America, study for less money.'

The Student and Exchange Visitor Program[17] (SEVP) had approved Tri-Valley University (TVU)—a for-profit institution in Pleasanton, California—to admit international students in February 2009. DHS, during a site visit that month, confirmed capacity for 'approximately

30 students'.[18] But the school prospered at a blinding speed: May 2009, eleven students; September 2009, seventy-five; January 2010, 447; May 2010, 939. September 2010, 1,555[19]—over 95 per cent from India and a vast majority from Andhra Pradesh.[20] As the enrolment surged, so did the earnings. Starting with an initial investment of $5,000 in 2008, its revenue jumped to $4.19 million in September 2010. Its president and founder, Susan Xiao-Ping Su, bought a 6,384-square-feet house. She commuted to college in a Mercedes-Benz.[21]

On 19 January 2011, ICE raided the school, accusing her of running an immigration racket. The federal laws imposed three employment conditions on international students during semesters: a) they could only work twenty hours per week; b) they could only work on-campus; and c) they could get a Curricular Practical Training (CPT), making them eligible for internships in relevant fields, only after the first year.[22] TVU violated all of them. It handed out CPTs in the first semester, allowing students to work off-campus full-time and take all courses online. They spread to different states—from New Jersey to Virginia to Texas—working at a dollar store, a 7-Eleven, a tobacco shop. Five hundred fifty-three of them listed a Sunnyvale apartment as their address. Many hadn't seen the college.[23]

ICE called it a 'sham university'.[24]

Andhra Pradesh's NRI cell disclosed that TVU had appointed two consultants for the South Asian region, both in Hyderabad, and six out of its eighteen board members hailed from Andhra Pradesh.[25] The raid got wide media attention in India. 'We are even afraid to get a traffic citation. Why would we go and commit fraud,' said a student's husband. 'Most of the students that joined the university are [from] well-to-do families in India.'[26] Another said, 'We paid a lot of fees, we wasted a lot of time and money, a lot of us are feeling nervous and it's totally depressing students.'[27] They had three options: report to ICE and pick a day to leave the country, depart on their own or transfer to a different university. A week after the raid, thirty-five of them met with Indian consul general, Sushmita Gongulee Thomas, in San Francisco.[28] They also drafted a petition, requesting the DHS and ICE to consider their plight.[29] The Telugu Association of North America (TANA) posted the petition on its website. 'Ultimately, we want to protect the kids within the boundaries of the law. They are not here to break the law,' said its president, Jayaram Komati. 'This is no fault of the students. It is the university not living up to the norms of society.'[30] The organisation contacted lawyers and requested Californian congressman Pete Stark to allow the students to move to other accredited universities. The American Telugu Association (ATA), too, hosted a conference call with a law firm, attended by over 300 students. Like TANA, ATA spoke to 'various US Senators and Congressmen' to help the 'victims'.[31]

ICE slapped ankle monitors on them to track their movements, creating a furore. 'We have conveyed to the US authorities,' said the Indian Ministry of External Affairs, 'that the students, most of whom are victims themselves, should get fair and reasonable treatment and the unwarranted monitors must be removed.'[32] The Indian external affairs minister, S.M. Krishna, told the US secretary of state, Hillary Clinton, that, while the US investigated Tri-Valley, its students deserved 'humanitarian considerations' and the chance to transfer to a different university. She promised to 'personally intervene', ensuring them justice.[33]

In May 2011, a federal grand jury indicted Su on thirty-three criminal counts.[34] Five months later, the United States Attorney Office charged four Indian students—Vishal Dasa, Tushar Tambe, Ramakrishna Reddy and Anji Reddy—with conspiracy to commit visa fraud.[35] In November 2011, the district court of Northern California called the TVU students 'victims of fraud', helping the Indian diaspora emerge from this ordeal with conscience, reputation and self-righteousness intact.[36]

So did this story end here? Did the students really not know anything? Was it just a rogue university? Only (former or potential) Tri-Valley students could answer these questions. But where do you find them? Whom did the Indian students, wanting to study in America, contact in moments of confusion and indecision—especially those interested in an unknown school? Fellow applicants. Where did they interact? Online. Now, since thousands of them moved to the US every year, they must have frequented famous websites that archived such discussions?

Damn.

All hiding in plain sight.

Indian immigration forums.

When Indian students had applied to TVU, it was so new—and so obscure—that they didn't know its accreditation status. So they checked its website. But littered with grammatical and spelling errors and limited information about the courses—many taught by Su herself—it was an amusing mess. Its mission statement read: 'To make Christian scientists, engineers, business leaders, and lawyers for the glory of God, with solid academic professionalism and Christian faith, therefore to live out Christ-like characters, value and compassion in the world, to make an impact and shine as its light.'[37]

Prospective students discussed the college on immigration forums. 'TVU provides hassle free admission,' wrote one of them. 'Gre, gmat not mandatory, tofel is pretty much the only requirement. Low semester fee, OPT, CPT from the day the course starts. No tests, no mandatory online classes, a perfect way to bypass the visa process!'[38] Charging only $16,000 for two years, TVU's exponential growth resulted from a 'referral' and 'profit-sharing' system. Referrals earned a student up to 20 per cent of the tuition fees. If that person referred someone else, the original referee netted around 5 per cent: a classic 'pyramid scheme.'[39]

Among the countless TVU threads on immigration forums, the one on Trackitt, titled 'Tri-Valley University—CPT, OPT',[40] generated the most interest. It began on 5 April 2010, nine months before the raid, and stacked over 600 comments. An initial post read: 'I, in fact all the members reading this thread, agree that TVU is a non-accredited university. In such case how is it possible for SEVIS [Student and Exchange Visitor Information System] to give it a recognition and also how USCIS is issuing I-20 with or without CPT.'[41]

An American school didn't always need accreditation for SEVIS approval.[42] In such a case, ICE required it to submit letters from three accredited institutions that accepted its credits. But these students knew nothing about those schools—or whether Tri-Valley had those letters. So they continued to air their desperation. 'I want to enroll in any programme of any university which gives full time CPT from day 1 and is the cheapest,' wrote a Trackitt user. 'I'm on H-4 status, how long will it take to convert to F-1?'[43] H-4 visas were reserved for the immediate family members of H-1Bs, such as spouses or children. In 2010, H-4s couldn't work full-time in the US. But a student visa removed that restriction. Tri-Valley provided an F-1 status and instant CPT—a sudden chance to mint money.

'Tri-Valley University's F1/CPT/OPT option is to make my spouse legally eligible to work/gain some MS course related work experience for a couple of years,' added Sathishkvvsm, who had started the thread, 'before the economy gets better and companies starts sponsoring H-1s again.'[44]

'My wife is in same boat as yours. How can I contact you?'[45]

This pattern recurred throughout the thread: Indian husbands, and their wives, discussing ways to enter Tri-Valley and the repercussions of such a decision. Two weeks after the raid, Andhra Pradesh's NRI Cell submitted a report to the chief minister. '[It] shows how many from [Andhra Pradesh] who went to Tri-Valley had a spouse living in the US,' read a *Times of India* article.[46] A source quoted in the piece said, 'Many of the spouses now facing deportation and federal charges had taken admission in Tri-Valley within just three to four days of landing in the US with the help of agents.'

But did they, as reported before, work part-time jobs, or did this secret hide more secrets?

'I am also looking for some training especially in QA or BA field,' wrote Khushboo143, an H-4 TVU applicant. 'Can you give me some pointers ?? or any contacts ??'[47] Saimallipeddi, another H-4, asked, 'Contracters are not ready to apply H-1 without client letter so i am trying to do M.S online. So is it possible to do M.S through Tri-valley university?'[48] An H-4 from Memphis commented, 'Not even 1 consultancy is ready to offer H-1 ..u beleive or not all the consultancies are advising to go for TVU n get CPT.'[49]

So desi body shops eyed TVU, knowing its 'Day-1 CPT' would provide a cheap, sizeable workforce. The demand for such workers was so high that it sometimes looked like the only criterion for landing a job. 'I have a pending offer waiting for me to get F-1 then get CPT,' clarified a Trackitt user.[50] After several months, Khushboo even got a reply: 'If you want a training in BA/QA, you can contact me ... We are IT consulting company based in fremont, CA.'[51]

Staying true to internet discourse, the Trackitt thread spawned different topics. The discussions intensified when the moniker RisingSun joined. Unlike others, RisingSun didn't inquire about but defended the university, sharing information only privy to a TVU administrator. Even innocuous questions about the school annoyed RisingSun who flung a series of insults ('I really sugest tht you go to see a Doctor (mental department) to talk about all of your thinking!').[52] Their responses also implied close association with—or direct ownership of—Tri-Valley ('my University will never give you peopel any Job!').[53]

Soon, the thread turned into the university's help desk: students lobbing queries at RisingSun who answered with ease. RisingSun's answers even matched some posts: 'TVU has received hundred of statsu change approval, many wifes are pursuing their higher education, and many VISAs are approved every single day!'[54] At one point, RisingSun itself completed a part of the puzzle: 'Many company can not affrod H1 any more (for H1 there a certain salary uplit in each state).'[55]

It all made sense.

RisingSun referred to the H-1B programme's prevailing wage, which varied according to the geographical location. 'We actually have several partner companies, [that] ask us to conver their employee into F1 so that they can work for them with the entire company's budget cut.'[56] So Tri-Valley not just triggered illegal immigration but also helped desi consultancies slash costs during the Great Recession. The fog lifted: the visa mill occupied the centre of this network; on one end lay the Indian educational consultancies; and on the other, body shops.

Indian students may have been desperate but not dumb. Many knew about the school's questionable reputation, so they didn't enrol directly. They instead got an I-20 from a third-tier college, cleared the visa interview and, once in the US, switched to Tri-Valley. 'Only a little more than 100 students who had obtained visas from the US consulates in India were TVU bound,' said the NRI Cell report.[57] The Trackitt thread, as usual, corroborated this: 'I applied for change of status from H4 to F1 visa using I20 from university "A" and my F1 visa got approved 2 days ago. ... But now, i want to change from university "A" to university "B" due to some reasons, can I change my univeristy at this point? Or do i have to study for some time in university "A" before moving to Unoveristy "B"?'[58]

'Guys ... Don't agree or seek admission into all online degree classes,' cautioned Hanna, 'as it is against the rules of F1. Try to find other schools that are offering on campus classes and are still suitable for your personal situation. Hanna, Admissions counselor, University of Northern Virginia.'[59]

A few months ago, an employee from the firm Lorvin Overseas, Vinod Babu, had written on Orkut, 'Most of the universities in USA give legal permission of 10-20 working hours per week, so Students looking for part time jobs in gas stations and motels they hardly earn $6 to $7 per hr. But there are few Universities UNIVERSITY OF NORTHERN VIRGINIA which gives legal permission to work 40 hrs a week. So that u can work full time in IT firm we can help u in getting Free Admission in the University and job assistance.'[60]

Like TVU, UNVA popped up often on the Trackitt thread. 'I have 4.5 yrs exp gained in MNC's in Chennai,' wrote an H-4 holder. 'My husband also suggested to go to unva atleast ... the university offers CPT soon.'[61] The day after the Tri-Valley raid, another user said, 'UNVA requires physical presence for 2 classes per semester while 1 class can be taken online. They are ... following the rules to the T.'[62]

Well, no. Like TVU, UNVA lacked accreditation, allowed foreign students to work off-campus from the first semester and partnered with Indian educational consultants.[63] Authorised to issue around fifty I-20 forms, it had 2,400 students—90 per cent from India and an inordinate proportion from Andhra Pradesh.[64] In July 2011, ICE raided UNVA, forbidding it to enrol international students.[65]

Several other 'Day-1 CPT' colleges had also become popular. 'Herguan, SVU [Silicon Valley University], ITU [International Technological University],' wrote a Trackitt user, '... are also same category.'[66] California, due to lax regulation, had attracted a swarm of such schools. 'I name few more universities here in bayarea,' said another, 'Herguan, Silicon Valley University, ITU, NPU [Northwestern Polytechnic University], CTU they follow similar model.'[67]

The Trackitt thread didn't remain peaceful. One feud—between the accounts Nishant1981 and Usher—devolved into a 'North Indian–South Indian' fight, where the former called Telugus unethical, who had disgraced all Indians. Usher accused him of stoking 'regional disparities'.[68]

'I called Herguan today,' said Nishant1981, 'and asked them to give me the names of 3 accredited schools that will accept their credits, and the admission officer first said he did not know. Then he said that information was confidential and will not be released to non-students. Boy, this time the good guys have a chance to expose all these liars—officials, consulting firms, students—who cheated and we had better not stop applying pressure.'[69] 'You wait and watch, when Herguan and ITU are raided [by ICE], we will see more Andhraites with collars.'[70]

The federal agency proved him prophetic on 2 August 2012, issuing Herguan a notice of intent to withdraw its SEVP[71] certification.[72] It had 450 students—400 from India.[73] Like Tri-Valley, it had lied about its 'in lieu' of letters,[74] distributed 'Day-1 CPTs' and paid a referral fee ($1,200).[75] They shared another connection: TVU's founder, Su, had worked as an adjunct faculty at Herguan.[76]

When ICE officials visited the college in November 2010, its CEO, Jerry Wang, directed the students to move to 'California within a week and take in-person classes'. If they didn't, the school would cancel their visas. 'We can't go at such a short notice,' a student emailed her computer science class. Wang apologised and offered '$500 if they returned for six days of class'.[77] But in a world of more than one Tri-Valley, he had committed a blunder. Around a quarter of students dropped out, joining an unaccredited college down the road: ITU.[78]

Like TVU, ITU paid a $500 referral fee. Like UNVA and Herguan, it often appeared on the Trackitt thread. Indians, once more, flooded the campus, 94 per cent. ITU students, stated a *Chronicle of Higher*

Education piece, followed an 'unusual schedule': they attended 'each class only three weekends per semester, all day Saturday and Sunday'. That was so because they worked full-time in 'New York, Ohio and other states' and returned to campus when required. The university considered them 'full-time students'. In February 2011, many Indian students 'jostled for space at ITU's registration desk', holding 'checks and paperwork', looking 'friendly but nervous', seeking a 'transfer from Tri-Valley'.[79]

A few years later, ITU's faculty affairs director, Concepcion Saenz-Cambra, exposed the college in a lawsuit: how it circumvented the 'federal statutory requirements', undermined qualified individuals from 'overseeing SEVIS compliance' and 'intentionally fail[ed] to track' students' addresses.[80] The school awarded passing marks to countless students who never attended classes—some received A grades. A faculty member once wanted to 'fail a student for cheating', but Provost Karl Wang dissuaded him to help the student 'keep his visa'. The professor disagreed, then resigned. ITU also 'regularly accept[ed] students with low-level English proficiency' and in 'recent years' with TOEFL scores 'as low as in the fifties'. Its ESL (English as a Second Language) director, Patty Wiggin, was told to draft false letters to SEVIS certifying students' proficiency in English. She also resigned.

On 16 April 2015, Saenz-Cambra received an email about an 'exceptional' techie at 'Tesla Motors' who might not get his H-1B visa extended.[81] Could he apply for a 'master program at ITU' and get an 'F1 visa?' The firm would cover 'his tuition and other fees'. When the Tesla employee couldn't complete his application on time, the HR vice president, Mark Lipscomb, appealed to the college, on Tesla Motors's behalf, to grant his case 'special consideration'. Wang emailed Saenz-Cambra, calling Tesla a 'good and well respected company' and encouraged the university staff to 'establish a relationship' with it to facilitate 'internship' opportunities for 'other students'.

Such full-time job arrangements, explained the lawsuit complaint, thrived in ITU. 'Many large Silicon Valley employers' hired the college's foreign students for 'full-time "internships"' to avoid the hassle of procuring H-1B visas. It benefited the companies in at least three ways:

unlike the H-1B, the F-1 visas didn't have an annual cap, or a prevailing wage requirement or high fees. This deception ensured a cheap visa in any year, on any salary, for anyone.

Like TVU, ITU approved full-time jobs for students that had 'nothing to do with their studies'. One such student joined Beta Soft Systems as a 'recruiter' (the same firm investigated by the *WSJ* reporter Joshua). Another 'intern[ed]' at a 'gas station'. At least one more tried earning internship credit by working for his 'own company'.

In June 2015, Saenz-Cambra and several staff members informed the Board of Trustees about the school's violations. In a meeting next month, Wang told her and other department heads that, 'If [they] want to work for him, [they] have to do what he tells [them] to do or [they] can leave.' The college officials 'continued to threaten' Saenz-Cambra. In March 2016, ITU fired her. She sued after five months.

She found justice after four years.

The college coughed up $1.17 million in 2021 to settle the visa fraud allegations.[82] Around four years later, Tesla's CEO and Trump's then senior advisor, Elon Musk, said he'd 'go to war' to defend the H-1B programme. Bizarre threat coming from someone whose own firm had subverted—or gone to war against—the H-1B and F-1 programmes by colluding with a visa mill. Much before helming the Department of Government Efficiency, Musk had shown how his own company could cut costs by defrauding the US government. This was poetic corruption: charity, after all, began at home.

30

Trackitt comprised diverse Indians. But one immigration forum had a collective voice, a distinct personality. Its members shared crucial commonalities: young men from Andhra Pradesh working for desi consultancies or studying (or interested) in visa mills. They bantered in Telugu, deploying testosterone-charged humour, using GIFs and memes—especially those of comedian Brahmanandam—to convey their approvals and frustrations. They toyed with the English language: famous turned 'pamous', please 'flease', uncle (anybody above the age of thirty-five) 'vuncle'. Founded in 2009, it had collected over tens of thousands of registered users in a few years. By the end of the next decade, that number exceeded 75,000. Unlike most Indian immigration forums, it allowed its members to share images, videos and other multimedia content. Countless posts featured erotic photos of actresses and models. A common topic? 'NSFW'. It resembled an Indian engineering hostel—a 'safe space' for repressed masculine energy—spilling sexual fantasies and professional annoyance. Its name, too, was simple, direct and (almost) innocent: AndhraFriends.com.

On 24 April 2015, around a month after Kumar made a video on Indian MS students in the US, a thread appeared on the website: 'List Of Cpt Giving Universities Pros/cons'.[83]

'Hi all … I have decided to apply to [these] universities,' wrote a user named heartlavender.

University 1:

Sullivan University is tri- semister … meaning one has to pay 5000$ every 3 months. masters program will be over in one year …

Advantages: CPT will come. you can work anywhere in US. no radius limit.

Dis advantages: The course will be over in one year and then there will be only one chance for H1b. So for that one chance [we] have to spend 24000$.

Note: Sullivan univ is strict in SOP. if you copy, it will reject your admission.

University 2:

Wilmington University, Delaware …

These people will not deal with international admissions through phone. have to meet in person or email …

University 3:

Harrisburg University, Delaware …

I don't know the rules … I will post them as soon as I get info.

The basic rules that have to be followed for universities selection.

Rule 1: look for 2 years program (so there will be 2 chances again to apply for H1b – 2016 and 2017).

Rule 2: Ask university whether we get CPT and work only certain radius to the campus. (Some universities have this rule … that one shouldn't work outside 150 miles radius)

Rule 3: Whether there is any current bad talk or case on the university … [like] tri valley …

As the above comment—and countless others on the forum[84]—exemplified, young Indians not just used 'Day-1 CPT' schools to enter the US but also continued staying in the country under imminent threat to their immigration status (say, if their OPTs expired and H-1B petitions failed to clear the annual lottery or if USCIS rejected their applications or if they got fired). Such schools gave them F-1 visas—a legal status—and enabled them to work full-time and apply for visas again. More comments poured in, showing how AndhraFriends users played immigration laws like violins.

'A university in chicago called Knowledge systems institute apparently gives CPT. But [you] have to go to the university once a week.'[85]

'Those who studied at Stratford university will not be given admission at Gold[ey] Beaco[m] University [GBC] is what I heard … I spoke to them once.'[86]

'Harrisburg University … Monthly once college … They give a lot of course work apparently … like Sulivan university, it is not possible to copy paste, strict [against] plagersim.'[87]

'Even wilmington univ will not give admission to those who did their MS from stratford, I found out. 2 years MS course. easy assignmetns (it's okay if you copy). CPT from day 1. working anywhere in USA acceptable. no radius limit. Once a month [you have to] visit the univ for classes. A safe university where there will be no case or enquiry for the next 2 years.'[88]

'Have to go everyy otther weeek in Gee bee ceee, brother.. radiuus strict.. They will give admission only if it is NY/NJ/PA/DE.'[89]

'Sulli**van gives cpt from day 1. There is no radius limit, can work anywhere. GRE, toefl not required if you have masters degree from USA.'[90]

'… 1) I**T**U

'2) harris***BUrg

'3) Sulli** van

'4) G**b***C

'5) there is one in florida and one in indiana.…

'6) glo****be Minnapolis …'[91]

'The problem here is not the second masters .. my opinion is that it is not correct to look for short cut .. playing with rules means playing with fire …'[92]

31

After Manu got fired, he didn't tell anyone at Infocon Logix to market him. He was tired. Nobody asked him either. Maybe they were tired, too. The clock kept ticking; the debts kept mounting and the vendors had stopped calling. Maybe returning to India made sense?

He finally found a project in New Jersey. Hired as an ETL tester, he made sure to detect at least one bug every day. If he excelled at his job, then his boss, Tanuja Banerjee, wouldn't fire him. By the end of the first month, he flagged around 100 defects. But some technical portions—such as the dimension tables, slicing and dicing technique and SQL Developer—confounded him. So he consulted Infocon Logix's Nitish and the QA lead Lajos. He also relied on a tester, Dhruv. Manu stood near his cubicle once, waiting for him to return.

Tanuja saw him.

'Come here. What do you want from him?'

'I had some Rally related query.'

'He is not working here anymore.'

A colleague, Chaddha, told Manu that Dhruv quit after arguing with Tanuja. 'A Nepali woman used to sit in your place. She also left because of her.'

One day, Manu found a defect and approached a developer. He was busy. Manu contacted him again: still busy. Third time: the same response. Manu escalated the issue to the scrum master. She informed his manager.

In her cabin, Tanuja banged her hand on the table and screamed. 'Why did you send it to the scrum master? Who told you to give it to the scrum master?'

'Based on my experience, scrum master is the bridge between the developer and tester. So if there is a problem, I should coordinate with her.'

Tanuja calmed down. She began checking her emails, but then—she flared up again. 'Why did you come to that meeting?'

What? How is it related to this conversation?

She once asked him about an assignment.

'I'm working on it.'

'Why is it taking so long?'

'Lajos is also, you know, giving me work, so—'

'The offshore team can complete it in two hours. Why does it take you the whole day?'

'If you want I can do it one hour but don't expect quality.'

'I'm not saying compromise on quality.' She mellowed down. 'Okay, continue.'

One day, Manu contacted a business analyst, Sarah, for an ETL-related query. She informed his manager.

Tanuja called Manu to her room and, yes, yelled again: 'Why are you going to Sarah?'

'No, I had a request.'

'If you have a request, you have to come to me.' She continued screaming. 'I'm your manager. Sarah is not your manager.'

Another teammate, Navika—an H-1B worker on her first project in the US—also changed her behaviour. Manu had taught her testing in her initial weeks, but after Tanuja's frequent yelling, Navika also started the 'monkey-see-monkey-do' business. She became rude, disregarded his presence, tossed terse replies. She gossiped in Hindi at work, treating the office like a college canteen. Once, collaborating with her to resolve a problem, Manu walked to her cubicle; she was chatting with a colleague. As he explained the ETL's workflow to Navika, she snapped at him.

'Looks like another Tanuja Banerjee,' the colleague told Manu.

'Ditto.' He walked away.

Manu stopped talking to her.

Months passed. Tanuja's anger turned into a routine. She called Manu to her room every week and shouted at him. Trivial reasons. Sometimes, no reason. When it went from bad to worse to unbearable, Manu rubbed his face. He'd do it at the office, he'd do it at home—he'd do it whenever the humiliation seized him—turning his face red. Sometimes, he rubbed it so hard that his temples oozed blood. The scars remained for days.

He struggled to sleep. On days Tanuja screamed at him, he lay awake till two in the night; insomnia hounded him for a week. Manu shared the ever-escalating stress with his mother and Mamaji. She told him to not worry—in her usual loud tone—and that if the job bothered him so much then he should return to India. Ditto Mamaji, a spineless man, echoing his sister. Manu called Gyan who told him to complain to HR. No point: nobody would listen to a lowly contractor like him.

Hoping to diversify his prospects, in his eighth month of the project, he prepared for the Principles and Practice of Engineering exam. But a few days before the test, he couldn't focus or sleep. Tanuja's insults kept stinging him, making his head heavy. The pain continued to press and persist. Manu had to find a way out—he couldn't bear it anymore. Every week, same story. Technical problem, any problem. Every week, twice a week. Not just in her room but also in front of others—and no one cared. They had hired a person, not a dog. If they tightened the leash, he'd bite. He created an account and wrote an email recounting his harassment. He sent it to three parties: Tanuja's boss' boss, the local police and the New Jersey FBI.

He emailed his father. 'Hello Daddy. Because of too much stress at work I am becoming mentally ill :('

'It is not because of stress but loneliness. You have no one to talk to and nobody wants to hear because others have no time. There are too many Indians where you live and they are bigger crooks than real

Americans. Please talk to my sister and brother in law in Columbus. I know how difficult it is to suffer from loneliness.'

'No, at office they torture a lot. I kill time by playing games or doing creative work, so I don't feel that lonely. But they yell. I do not feel good.'

'Please ask [your uncle or aunt] for advice. What you wrote is not good and takes a toll on mental health. Do I tell them?'

'Na ... I don't think we can do anything. They will continue the same and I am a contractor and they will kick me out if I complain and I am not lucky in getting another job. I guess I have to suffer :('

The pounding existential threat receded the next day. Should he have not sent that email? Maybe they had read it and fired him? Either way, he'd do what he had to do. He just had to wait one more day, as he had taken a holiday on Monday to write the exam. Manu wrote it with a heavy head—didn't do well.

Tuesday morning brought rain. He usually reached the office at 8 a.m., an hour before the others. But that day, he arrived fifteen minutes earlier. He swiped his badge; the door opened. It surprised him. He handed his ID card and laptop to the security personnel. She refused to accept, as his badge still worked. He kept them on Lajos's desk and left. The next step was absolutely clear. His H-1B would expire in September 2015, and he had to pay his employer's taxes till he found a job, an option he could no longer afford. No problem, one chance—the last chance. Two months. If he found a project, great, but if not, he'd stop running. He'd sit, collect himself and fly back to India.

32

Virgil interviewed with the VA for a food service worker position. A few days later, an email: he had got the job. Finally. Stability, income, future after twelve blind years. Now, even if he didn't find programming work, he'd keep this job, pay his loans and mend his life. And once inside the VA, he could open more doors: maybe a job in IT?

After accepting the position, he got an email from HR. 'A subject must show good faith by making written arrangements to repay the debt, or it may be a disqualifying factor under the suitability of "Criminal or Dishonest Conduct".' His troika of torment had knocked again: the loans for the IRS, college and child support.

Virgil contacted an IRS employee, Ruby, who sent him a letter on 21 May 2015. 'A review of your financial condition indicated that demanding the due balance would impose an undue hardship. Your accounts are currently suspended from collection.' Good, one problem solved. He emailed the letter to HR.

'Thank you. However it is from the Taxpayer Advocate Service that reports to Congress. You will need to make payment arrangements with the IRS for your federal debt and provide a plan for this office to continue the hiring process.'

A string of emails and follow-ups produced comforting news in the subsequent weeks. His student loans got deferred to the next year, and the child support stated that it would deduct $212 from every pay cheque. Virgil also hoped to close the IRS loop once Ruby returned from her break on 29 June. Each day of delay pinched. His initial date of joining, 31 May, had raced to 12 July, which meant he wouldn't get paid before the end of the month. 'Now I have to figure out how to raise $1,200,' he emailed a friend, 'so I can get my land before someone else and I need to do that yesterday.'

Virgil contacted Ruby on 30 June. 'Sorry to bother you as you're probably still getting caught back up. Was wondering if they decided anything?'

'They first said since you can't pay, it can stay uncollectable. Then said he needs to give a small amount. I have not heard from them yet.'

Two weeks passed.

'I apologize it is taking time. I am working with a collection unit to review all your paperwork and assist us in your payment plan. I thought this would be simple. I will get back to you by July 28.'

She emailed him the next day. 'When you get a chance, please call me. I've good news.' The IRS had agreed on a $25 monthly fee; it expected the first instalment on 28 August. Virgil sent the IRS letter to the VA. Now, 12 July had become 9 August.

Then, dead silence from the VA, except a phone conversation about his 'very high' blood sugar level, 12.1.

Weeks passed. Countless emails. Nothing moved.

He wrote to Senator Jeff Sessions: 'A large number of unemployed Americans are itching to abandon the Republican party. Today is August 6, 2015'—he had got the job on 27 April—'and they have still not brought me onboard and my depression over this nonsense is winning at the moment. I have written the President [Obama], the Vice President [Joe Biden], Senators Cruz and [John] Cornyn asking why won't you help me. The only one who responded is Congressman Lamar Smith's office. If you expect me to vote for Cruz and Cornyn who laugh at us displaced Americans while bringing more temporary workers on non-immigrant visas, that will NOT happen.'

Cornyn's office replied a few days later and, like Smith, sent him a privacy release form, which asked for his name, grievance, personal details and signature. 'With all due respect Senator, I did my time in the Navy, and the VA claims to support and hire veterans. I didn't destroy my credit, and I believe I deserve better than this.' Virgil filled, scanned and emailed the form.

And waited and waited and waited.

Nothing.

An email from Kumar. 'Can I send money through credit card?'

'Money is always welcome, but you really need to take care of yourself.'

Virgil received $250. 'You should not have done that. But thank you very much. I hope it didn't put you in a bind.'

The VA offered him a *new* position: housekeeping aid ($11.36). With weekends, he could make $591 per week. Again, inside the VA, he'd try for computer jobs reserved for internal applicants. He had also got a coding gig, which meant he could, once again, hope to buy back his land. 'Am I worried it will fall apart again?' he asked a friend. 'Of course, but it is what it is, and I need to get on with my life.'

Virgil finished all the formalities in the coming weeks—the fingerprint scan, the physical test, the TB shot—and then, the VA fell silent. Again. More than six weeks had passed since the second job offer. He emailed Lamar Smith's office, explaining his predicament, and forwarded it to his cousin, Dorothy, a quality assurance professional. 'Perhaps you can explain it to momma because she does not get it, and I'm too stressed she doesn't get it. There are 4 options in life. 1) Get a job with the private sector. 2) Get a job with the government service. 3) Start your own business. 4) Suicide. I do not want option 4, but I have exhausted all three. Some people might live with others and smile and be happy with nothing, I can't. All I want is buy my land back and put me a shed on it.'

'Your skills are not marketable. You had plenty of time to teach yourself .Net which is the most desirable skill in IT, besides big data. You have data mining and analytical skills but are not working in the latest technologies. If data mining or .Net don't interest you, then you should leave IT and pursue something else. Another high growth area is software testing. Look at entry level positions and build a new resume. An active market of small companies and entrepreneurs post one-off jobs on bulletin boards for low hourly rates. However, they are all better than zero and you are building fresh skills. If you are interested. You would work best in a self-employed role where interaction with others is minimal.'

'I do .Net and data for a living. There are millions of us in the same boat.'

'Data mining is the number 1 hot career. There are not a million working with big data. It's actually difficult for the basic Indian skillset. You should research that more.'

'Matt Schmidt [his school friend] committed suicide. He was big data for PayPal. Email Norm Matloff and do your homework.'

'You asked me for input, it wasn't what you wanted to hear, so now I'm the fool? No problem, don't bug me again if you don't want a discussion.'

'You are not discussing. You are talking about something you have no knowledge about. But you are right. There is no family no more. I will be glad when I no longer have to be around any of you. So I will never contact you again.'

On the same day, he wrote an article on Keep America At Work and emailed it to Kumar. Its headline: 'Is suicide the only option?' A week later, Virgil received a notice to renew his website. He had no money. His last fight, his only hope, would also desert him, and he could do nothing but watch. He got another notification the next day: Kumar had donated $250.

Virgil followed up about his job in December. The VA directed him to the Office of Personnel Management (OPM). He emailed. 'It has now been 211 days since I got a Food Service Worker position and 65 days since I got a Housekeeping Aid position. Could you help me?'

The OPM employee said individual agencies determined 'qualifications and eligibility criteria' for selected applicants so, for the specific hiring questions, he should 'contact the VA HR'.

'Folks, while they may make their decisions, they told me to contact you. Their hiring is through you as is their background checks. Surely, somebody somewhere in the OPM can do what is necessary to resolve this? Is this the way you take care of veterans who served our country?'

33

In May 2015, Kumar's project got over—without a reason. Five days later, he recorded a video. 'There is a saying in Telugu: neither mother feed the kid nor allow her to beg. Neither the Indian employers get a project nor sign contracts for projects you get on your own. I don't know why. Lots of issues. Beyond control.' He removed his glasses. His voice remained calm, like a benign soothsayer reading his death sentence. 'See, if a prostitute has children and if they are held by the centre's manager, she can't run away. That is how H-1Bs live. You cannot leave this guy for another body shop. You can but you need money. I don't find words more than ... indentured servitude. What man.' He looked up. 'Because of craze America we come and get stuck, fall in this melting point. One, we can't go back, second, we can't continue life here.'

Over two months passed. Still no project. Reaching the edge of his exasperation, Kumar did what he had always done: he made a video.[93] Wearing a chequered shirt, he sat in the living room. A lamp, facing his back, glowed in the corner—the only light in the room. 'When I did my hardware diploma, I went shop to shop and asked for a job. Whether pay or without pay.' His face softened as he continued:

> After I get exposure, I put it on my resume and walk into the next company. So when I came here, I fight my employer, I can't go with fake resume. Billing low and all, I don't care. I want to try with my own skills. Same thing, why don't the students do when they come

for MS? After you finish your master's, you approach Indian Incs who take you for ride. And you don't know anything, you want quick money, because back home you took loan—you have a pressure, tension, whatever—so you do all kinds of fake. Because Indian Incs force you to do, and you want to do.

Why do you build your career on crime?

You get $5,000 a month, no matter what, in spite of 25 million Americans displaced. Indian Incs want easy money, they push you to US clients by fake or whatever. Or proxy. Proxy support. You don't know Control Panel. You pay 1,000 bucks and you are dependent on somebody.

Where is your career?

You do BA, QA, testing, Java, .Net. You keep on roaming, right? You have no foundation, right? Indian Incs charge you 2,000 for training. If they really spend that amount, then you are up to the mark, but they throw 500 bucks in Ameerpet, and somebody online train. Or you pay.

So what you learn?

I don't like to complain about master's students. I get their situation, I empathise, and I am recording this video for you to understand. You have to tell him, I don't want to fake my resume. As Indians, if we get trapped in scams or frauds, then nobody can save you. Your parents take huge bank loan. Build your career wonderfully, right? How much time do you need? Prepare 100 interviews. Why are you giving 500 bucks to a fucker, and he has to attend your call? Don't you feel ashamed?

We get stuck here because we don't have basis, self-confidence. Only thing we have is money, man. What is so great when we earn illegally? Where is our character? When character is lost, everything is lost.

If Kumar hoped to shake his core audience—recent Indian graduates working for desi consultancies—then he had accomplished his mission. Because, unbeknown to him, he added a new chapter to his life: AndhraFriends.com.

'Kumar Srinivas Pandruvada About Ms and Life in Usa,' read a thread's title on the forum. 'How many of you agree with his discussions in youtube?'[94]

'Dude google him he is very famous now a days. He is fucking annoying with all his youtube videos exposing loop holes and businesses in USA.'[95]

'He seems to be a psycho … the batch that cry cry cry.'[96]

'I have to meet this idiot once. Someone bring him [here].'[97]

'Why is he scolding america this much and then waiting here to get GC? If he has any Gaand mein dum, ask him to go to India and create jobs … Those who ruin us in Usa are our own people, starting from consultancy, stupid raskals.'[98]

'If I find this shameless son of a whore, I will hack him to death till his intestines are out, motherfucker idiot … [Even though] he studied English literature, he has no clue how to speak english properly. What the fuck does he mean when he says students show they have money to do ms and then pay for it while doing a job … what the fuck you son of a whore … how the fuck does it matter to you how they get the money? He is making a scene as if he is some american losing jobs … america has driven racism off it seems … this chooth must be abandoned in the country side of Texas … then he will know if racism exists or not … '[99]

34

Manu hadn't visited India in the last seven years. What kind of a life awaited him? What kind of a job would he get? Would he even get a job? At least it would be better than the H-1B phase. At least, in his country, no one would throw him out. He wouldn't have to worry about documents, immigration status or time. He'd survive, somehow, even if he had to beg.

Infocon Logix assigned him a recruiter: Joy. Joy James. Manu contacted a few consultancies as well. Even contemplated joining one, emailing it to check if it provided a guesthouse till he found a project. Whenever he had tried for a job in the past, he got countless calls, but nothing this time. His process remained the same: giving the recruiter's contact to vendors. So what happened: did Joy, wanting higher cuts for his employer, reject offers? Or did Prakash punish him for his short projects: cutting his prospects, forcing him to leave the US? A vendor recently told him that Infocon Logix's rate was 'too high for this role'. Did that happen more than once?

Manu needed two solid interviews to save himself from the jungle. But he had run too much for too long. Over a thousand applications in the last month. Just two client calls. But even a job wouldn't guarantee a stable life. It had happened many times before, from California to Illinois to Kansas. Hope dangled like a carrot; whenever he lunged for a bite, it moved up. This time, he wanted to walk away. If the carrot cared, it would come get him.

He emailed his father. 'Can I stop by your home and put my luggage? Mostly I will leave for Delhi because most jobs require in person interviews.'

'When, because I am moving around.'

'I am planning to book my tickets for June 5. No need to come to the airport because my life has become very uncertain. Might get an offer and end up cancelling.'

'Manu, before you start, please make sure you have settled all loans because with your Indian salary you cannot.'

'Can you explain if I could clear them why would I come to India? I paid $10,000 to my employer and all money is lost. Forget it, I will find another place to stay.'

'I cannot explain anything because you have not been transparent with me. Americans will hound you like dogs if you leave debts. With whom did you discuss before you paid your employer?'

'There is nothing to be transparent. There are laws to maintain legal status for H-1B. They have become strict. That is why I call it "Slavery Visa". My consultancy signed up saying my salary will be 60K per year. If it is less, then either my visa is not renewed or my employer is in trouble. Look at my attached W2, it has $62,007.70 in the gross amount. How come it is showing that when I was unemployed for six months and I get less than $30 an hour? The law says I shouldn't give money and they have to pay me even if I don't have a job. But if you need more transparency you have to check with an immigration attorney and understand the laws better. Then you will know why I gave so much money for nothing. I know it does not end well. But I will get what I deserve.'

With the India return almost certain, Manu needed a data point. He emailed Ramesh. 'Hey man, planning to come back. Do you have any vacancies in your place? Don't want to stay in Hyderabad anymore ... too much drama. Hope to get a government job. Life has become a joke ^.^'

'Wow dude. There are plenty of Quality Assurance jobs in Bangalore. They pay well. In my company, the salary is less.' Ramesh worked in Kerala. 'You are talented. You can get a job in Delhi,

Mumbai, Chennai, Calcutta. What about GC? Didn't they start your process?'

'Freak green card man. I don't need it. Can't get a project in six months, what will I do with green card?'

'Well, welcome back. It is the missing USA part you have to get through. It is terrible. And getting adjusted to the Indian climate, attitude of people, smells, traffic, cleanliness is not easy. People ask questions such as beta at your age, why are you not married? Being stuck in the US without a job is horrible. Consultancies are blood sucking vermins who make money off consultants and throw them into garbage. Take care buddy, sorry things did not work out.'

'Na ... it's ok. Life is great in our country only if we are wealthy.'

'Yes, but at least we are not third class aliens in a foreign country with little rights.'

The day came close; he got his affairs in order. He owed around $40,000. With no money—or hope—to clear the loan, he turned to his only option: emailing a law firm dealing with consumer bankruptcy. Manu met with the attorney and explained his situation. The attorney said he'd prepare and send the bankruptcy documents. The next step: car. He had bought it for $32,000; he'd sell it for $10,000. He reached a Ford showroom and met an employee who called several prospective buyers. No interest from anywhere. Manu told the showroom person he had filed for bankruptcy and left the car at the facility.

Days passed. Joy marketed his resume, so did another consultancy recruiter. Manu, too, kept applying.

Nothing.

He bought two one-way flight tickets: New York to Mumbai, Mumbai to Hyderabad. Manu just needed to discard the extra stuff, which would make his luggage exceed the baggage limit for international travellers. He got rid of three laptops, a printer and other household items. He had to leave something else behind, but his heart refused to allow: his PlayStation, Reid's gift. Manu had carried it everywhere—guesthouses, motels, apartments. He had played on it for hundreds of hours, slept beside it, found quiet solace in its ownership. That PS had given him joy, memories, friendship. Couldn't leave it here, couldn't carry it with him. He'd entered the country empty-handed, had to leave it feeling empty.

Manu took a cab the next afternoon and reached the airport. He checked in his bags. Overweight. He trashed the extra stuff. Still overweight. He transferred a few items to his handbag, threw more stuff out and paid for the extra luggage. Now the literal last steps: clear the security check, enter the flight and fly out. For one last time. To never return. Manu was blank. If only he had saved some money. Nothing grand, around $3,000. It could have carried him through the first two years in India. Manu had $500 at the moment, Rs 30,000. Five-and-a-half years and $500—less than $100 per year—less than $10 per month.

He had failed in a country where countless Indians earned, succeeded, settled. Many, working for desi consultancies, must have endured similar exploitation—many much more. Yet they swallowed it all, prompting a natural question: why didn't they leave? They could, after all, return to their own country, to a life of lifelong freedom. Their refusal then hid a national embarrassment: that 'slavery' in America surpassed freedom in India.

Manu couldn't stay though—no matter how hard he tried. Life had snatched too much from him too early, and he had nothing left to give. He still craved a family. Seven years had passed—so much had changed—but his mother hadn't. Still irritable, still controlling, still confrontational. Mamaji was no better: expert at fumbling, masking, blaming. His dad, the same. He wouldn't call him ever. Manu had fled the wild only to become an animal. And now the same jungle called him again, as if restless to complete their story.

35

On the night of 20 December 2015, nineteen Indian students left for the Rajiv Gandhi International Airport in Hyderabad. In less than twenty-four hours, they'd land in America; in less than three weeks, their classes would begin; in less than two years, if everything went well—and everything usually went well—they'd find high-paying jobs. The vintage American dream, flashing (at least) $60,000 per year.

But Air India officials barred them from flying. They were headed to 'blacklisted' colleges, popular on AndhraFriends for years, Silicon Valley University (SVU) and Northwestern Polytechnic University (NPU).[100] The 'blacklisted' label spread in the Indian mainstream media. Both colleges issued statements, rubbishing the allegation.[101] (NPU threatened to sue Air India.[102])

But this story didn't end there.

On 22 December 2015, Etihad Airways forbade twenty students from flying out of Hyderabad. The same reason, the same schools.[103] They camped out at the airport hoping to get permission; they got nothing. The Ministry of External Affairs of India advised the SVU-NPU cohort to 'defer their travel' and the others to 'do due diligence to ensure' that their institutions had 'proper authorisation and capacities'.[104] Sushma Swaraj, then the external affairs minister, tweeted, 'The information so far is that SPU [sic] San Jose and NPU Freemont are not blacklisted. But they are not reputed either.'[105]

2 January 2016: the U.S. Customs and Border Protection cancelled the visas of eighteen Andhra Pradesh and Telangana students at the New York airport. They said the officers detained them for hours 'without drinking water and food', threatened to bar them from entering the country for five years if they didn't return home and refused to provide reasons for denying entry.[106]

Many Indian students, as per the media reports and AndhraFriends posts, had identified the guilty parties. 'They all agree that the recent fear of attacks by the Islamic State,' reported *Deccan Herald*, 'has heightened the security blanket in the US affecting Indian students.'[107] Others accused the Ministry of External Affairs of negligence, journalists of distorting the news and the US government of fraud, wanting to 'inform Modi sir'.[108]

But this story didn't end there.

Because unlike other visa mills, SVU and NPU were non-profit institutions. Which meant their tax filings—detailing their costs, revenues and surpluses—were publicly available. Following TVU's tradition, NPU's tax form read: 'To Provide An Advance Education And A High Technology Learning Envilroment That Motivats Students ...'[109]

'Envilroment' and 'motivats'. Bonus points for at least spelling 'education' right. Also, if 'advance education'—as opposed to 'advanced education'?—was an Easter egg, then its ingenuity had to be admired. 'Advance education': education supplied beforehand. More: 'NPU Seeks To Prepare Its Students To Begin And Enhance Their Professional Careers In Computers, Engineering, And Business Through Study In Both Undergaduate And Garaduate Curricula.' 'Undergaduate' and 'garaduate' in the same sentence. It even got its own name wrong, constantly misspelling 'Polytechnic'. 'Polythechnic', 'Polythcnic' and 'Polytechic' appeared throughout. So did 'domitory', 'tution' and, of course, 'knowledlgle'.[110]

Their tax returns showed how these institutions had flourished over the years.

Northwestern Polytechnic University[111]

FY	*Revenue*	*Expenses*	*Income*	*Surplus*
2011	$11,760,985	$7,361,073	$4,399,912	37%
2012	$9,533,188	$7,185,874	$2,347,314	25%
2013	$12,808,198	$7,462,499	$5,345,699	42%
2014	$38,776,089	$10,617,510	$28,158,579	73%
2015	$72,891,536	$19,362,455	$53,529,081	73%

Silicon Valley University[112]

FY	*Revenue*	*Expenses*	*Income*	*Surplus*
2011	$1,843,371	$2,382,963	-$539,592	-29%
2012	$1,934,025	$688,871	$1,245,154	64%
2013	$1,379,070	$2,501,212	-$1,122,142	-81%
2014	$3,668,833	$3,253,988	$414,845	11%
2015	$20,324,268	$7,019,903	$13,304,365	65%

Pause for a moment to digest those numbers: NPU earned 73 cents surplus for every dollar in 2014 and 2015, rivalling the drug trade boom. SVU, similar, 65 per cent in 2015.

Founded in 1984, NPU had survived as an obscure institution under its president, George Hsieh, a Chinese immigrant, for around two decades.[113] But when his son, Peter, a trained corporate lawyer, joined the enterprise, it unveiled a much more ambitious plan. In the winter of 2013, the college tripled the funds for recruiters—$74,000 for one trimester—and directed them to India. The tuition earnings leapt to $12.7 million.[114] It paid $1.7 million to educational consultants in 2014, spread across Hyderabad, Mumbai and other Indian cities, a 1,400 per cent increase. The revenue shot up—by over 213 per cent—to around $39 million.[115]

The Hsiehs had perfected the formula.

By 2015, the school spent $800,000 on foreign recruiters every trimester. The number of students on visas rocketed from 1,634 in 2013 to 3,728 in 2014 to 9,024 in 2015. New York University, with the largest population of international students, had 13,178 foreign students in 2014-15.[116] NPU, more popular in Andhra Pradesh and Telangana than in the US, ranked ninth.[117] By early 2016, Indians had a 95 per cent share of its student population. They got an incredible deal. Dirt-cheap tuition—around $12,500 per year—and a $500 discount every trimester for each referral.[118]

But the lax admission criteria also attracted slackers who failed their courses, risking their visas and the college's revenues.[119] 'We need to solve the grade distribution problem,' George emailed the administrators in 2014, 'once for all.'[120] And he did—by hand. A student, repeating a computer science credit, had got an F: George made it C+. He altered another student's score, by hand, from D- to C+. One by one, he improved academic fortunes, slashed immigration troubles and enriched the university's coffers. Over 600 grades got facelifts: F became C+, C moved up to B, B to A-. By the spring of 2014, the issue of low grades vanished: now instead of an F, a student got a W, which meant he had withdrawn from the class.[121] How could you flunk a course you never took?

In May 2014, a teaching assistant failed several students. George's wife, Wen Hsieh, an administrator, emailed the course's professor. 'For those students who hardly learned a thing and should repeat the course, a grade "W" would serve the purpose ... This grade does not affect the student's GPA, and hence for those students who rely on bank loan (from India) can have a chance to continue their studies here (when GPA is below standard and the student is placed on academic probation status, the loan is terminated).'[122] He obeyed.

By mid-2014, a new rule lowered the failing bar by 20 per cent. A grade of 40 per cent qualified as a passing score—anything less than that a 'W'—and 59 per cent a C. The college didn't inform the accreditor, even though its faculty handbook stated that only 'an error in computation' could change the grades and 'no other reason.'[123]

But this story didn't end there.

Because NPU and SVU had accreditations from a century-old agency, the Accrediting Council for Independent Colleges and

Schools (ACICS). NPU highlighted the recognition in its publicity materials to Indian recruiters.[124] An accredited school's graduates could apply for federal loans; their H-1B petitions fell under the master's degree quota. These incentives lured more students, benefitting the schools. ACICS had also approved Herguan two years after the ICE raid. By May 2016—a year after the university's CEO admitted to visa fraud—it had still not revoked the accreditation.[125] UNVA and ITU? ACICS.

An NPU employee sent a long letter to the accrediting body in late 2014, listing blatant violations by the college.[126] Before ACICS's site visits, the letter alleged, the college told key faculty to return to the campus from their full-time jobs elsewhere. When the agency arrived in 2012, the 'professors spent the day in offices where they normally didn't sit' and 'taught classes with slides' provided by the administration.[127] Another time, in the mid-aughts, the school didn't have a librarian, an accreditation criterion. So, to clear the inspection, NPU did an NPU-like thing: it rented a librarian from another institution. To verify the allegations, the whistleblower listed the names of the suitable interviewees and enclosed the photocopies of their LinkedIn pages.[128]

What did ACICS do?

It requested the university to provide its enrolment chart and describe how it maintained the programmes' 'stability'. It also asked for signed job descriptions for full-time faculty members and, well, the librarian. A year-and-a-half later, it invited an NPU instructor as a speaker in its annual conference. His presentation's title: 'The Acculturation of Foreign Students Into Your University'.[129]

In June 2016, the office of Massachusetts Senator Elizabeth Warren published a report on the watchdog.[130] First finding: ACICS had a 'history of accrediting schools accused of numerous violations of federal and state law'. It continued to approve seventeen institutions that had been 'sued, investigated by, or reached settlements with state and federal governments for defrauding students or engaging in other deceptive practices'. Twelve of those were on its 'honor roll'. It once certified a college in Florida, FastTrain, that had used 'exotic dancers' for recruitment. In May 2016, it held a training 'session for school officials' on 'how to evade attorney general lawsuits'.[131]

Second finding: ACICS had 'ignored obvious signs of wrongdoing'. A former financial aid director at ITT Technical Institute, an ACICS-accredited school, called its reviews a 'dog and pony show' and its 'entire business model' a 'rubber stamp', allowing suspicious players to 'profit' from 'federal student aid'.[132]

Third finding: ACICS-approved institutions showed 'poor student outcomes'. The report cited a *ProPublica* investigation that found that only about '35% of students' graduated 'within six years'—'the only major national accreditor' whose schools graduated 'fewer than half' of their intakes.[133] The other metrics were as embarrassing.[134]

Now what about the watchdog's watchdog? The National Advisory Committee on Institutional Quality and Integrity (NACIQI), revealed the Warren report, had 'historically overlooked' the main criterion—students receiving meaningful 'education and training'—and instead focused on whether the accreditors followed the 'technical bookkeeping criteria'. It could recommend renewal or denial of recognition or grant additional time for accreditors to 'come into compliance'. But it often gave them another year to fix the problems. It rarely prevented an agency with current compliance issues from 'accrediting new institutions'.[135]

The Department of Education's staff report to NACIQI in 2011 had 'identified fourteen issues' with ACICS. Overlooking 'dismal student outcomes' or state and federal investigations, NACIQI 'did not recommend' its termination, suggesting it take twelve more months to 'come into compliance'. In July 2013, the Secretary of Education granted the accreditor a three-year term. Since then, the state or federal authorities had 'investigated, sued, or settl[ed]' with fourteen out of the seventeen ACICS-certified schools.[136]

In early 2016, NPU tried to salvage its pride. True to its history, it adopted a unique approach. It invited a few 'community leaders'—all Telugus—to visit its campus and address the media. NTV Telugu covered the event, where a Telugu reporter asked a Telugu dignitary about an American university in America in ... Telugu. 'We have Mr Appi Reddy from TATA [Telangana American Telugu Association].[137] You have toured the college, please tell us about the rumours and what will you tell the new students?'[138]

'All the classrooms are perfect,' Appi replied in Telugu, standing beside Peter Hsieh. 'We will provide proper advice and feedback. They are trying to improve the branding and quality, so we appreciate them.'

That clip, shared via a YouTube link, did multiple rounds on AndhraFriends. Appi fascinated its members, inspiring countless discussions. Many followed a pattern.

First, a question.

'Who the hell is Appi Reddy?'[139]

Then, an answer.

'TIGER MAN ... WHEN HE WALKS ON THE ROAD CLOUDS SEPERATE.'[140]

'Who is this appi reddy?'[141]

'Not a name, it's a brand.'[142]

'Who is this hero man, give clarity?'[143]

'Future IT minister for Telangana, appi anna. Youth tiger appi anna.'[144]

So, well, who was Appi Reddy?

'Hindus new god Appi Reddy Anna.'[145]

Okay, let's be serious. If AndhraFriends folks asked the question, then they knew the answer, too. Appi, for instance, featured in a famous post: 'Most rich consultancy owners in US.'[146]

'Which consultancy?'

'Microinfo but build up is like Microsoft.'

'Lol our guy is crazy about Publicity.'

Their Anna celebrated his birthdays with committed pomp. Several YouTube videos captured such parties, where young recent graduates fed Him cake, clicked His photos, danced with Him on strobe-lit floors, singing, clapping, swaying, hugging, sipping beer, smoking hookah, drenched in urgent masculine energy.[147] MicroInfo's anniversary celebrations, too, had a similar flair.[148] The 2015 one featured V6 News Telugu, a channel in Telangana, Appi's home state.[149]

'Lmao is this who appireddy is ... i know this guy way back in 2011. In a consultancy in Dallas, he used to help arrange students in their rooms and [did] other maintenance work, like an office boy. He used to have a nice large tummy and wear hollister t shirts … now he has set up a consultnacy and giving buildup on this level, huh?'

A YouTube channel, 'Appi Reddy', detailed his backstory: his place of birth, his educational qualifications, his career.[150] '2002 South Africa. Betrayed by a consultancy which promised to get them a job. After facing many issues moved back to India after 1 year.' 2004, London: 'Started life doing Odd jobs. Went all till attaining a Respectable position and Rised like a Phoenix.' 2007, a picture of the Statue of Liberty and the word 'America'. Followed by a photo of a pensive Appi. 'Started as a recuteir. Learnt every thing abt consulting firm and Determined to setting up his own company.' Cut to a picture of his office: a swivel chair, a desktop, a printer—and a portrait of Mohandas Gandhi on the wall. A text on screen: 'Everyone suffers some injustice in life, and what better motivation than to help others not suffer in the same way.'

Like countless desi consultancy owners, Appi had amassed enormous wealth and wielded immense clout. But the AndhraFriends crowd discussed him for another specific reason.

'When will the Labour NPU SVU students stop the broker business under him.'

'Innovation crime by appi to harbor npu batch from onboarding from India to client place. End result is American families are gone for toss they are into drugs, child sex videos divorce, food stamps, etc.'

'As long as you are rich, thats all matters … if we stick to ethics, we will be just boot lickers.'[151]

36

Virgil was still stuck between the VA and OPM. A week before his fifty-eighth birthday, in December 2015, he contacted the Equal Employment Opportunity Commission, wanting to file an age discrimination complaint. Rewinding his life, he explained how his blood sugar level had raced to 15.1, far above the normal, 6. Two weeks later, he emailed over two dozen OPM and VA officials—'Why will nobody stand up for veterans in America'—marking a few lawyers and journalists, repeating himself (once more). Two hundred fifty-one days since the job offer, 251 days of unemployment.

The American presidential race intrigued Virgil. 'It's not just you,' he emailed an acquaintance. 'I also contact senators, but they don't listen. It will take a catalyst, like Trump winning, for them to listen.' Trump had released his immigration reform plans in August 2015. They featured several draconic provisions: building a wall across the US-Mexico border, ending birthright citizenship, deporting criminal aliens. He also addressed the H-1B issue; Norm blogged about it. 'Trump's proposals for handling illegal immigration are vintage Trump, some sensible, some off-the-wall, but on H-1B, the man gets an A+.'[152] Trump had identified two key problems with the guest worker programme: corporations snubbing Americans techies and most foreign workers earning low wages. He didn't scapegoat the Indian outsourcing giants either. But the vintage Trump surfaced two days later: reversing his stance, parroting the industry party line: 'Intels good, Infosyses bad.'[153]

Virgil's friend told him about a mom-and-pop financial firm wanting to hire a veteran American programmer. FirmLoan had recently shifted from Los Angeles to Kerrville. He printed two versions of his resume, drove to Kerrville and dropped them at the office. The founder, Ralph, called the next day. They had a pleasant chat, some of it centred on Virgil's Navy days. They also discussed his low credit score. He tried to explain the horror of the past thirteen years but, like most folks, Ralph didn't seem to get it. Virgil would find out soon: if he got the job, his phone would ring.

He waited. The night before, he had fought with his mother, saying he'd be better blowing his brains out. 'She should not hear that, and I should not think that,' he told Joseph, another unemployed programmer. 'I thought I would get a job offer today which is why I'm depressed.' Around fifteen minutes later, the phone rang. Ralph wanted to meet. Virgil asked for an annual salary of $72,000. Ralph offered $36,000, with a $1,000 bump every two months. Not ideal, but no choice.

A few weeks later, the VA called. It wanted to start the employment process again. Bizarre: no explanation. Virgil finished the e-QIP and fingerprint tests and got another call. He got the position. After *eleven* months. Now: the VA or FirmLoan?

He drank a can of Miller Lite.

It would be foolish to reject a government job. Ralph's business might fold; the VA would remain. FirmLoan only paid $800 more; the VA made him eligible for internal IT jobs. Or: how about the VA and FirmLoan? Evenings and weekends at the VA, weekday afternoons at FirmLoan. Ralph agreed. By the end of May, Virgil had two jobs and sixteen-hour workdays. 'As of today, I'm making about 67,000 per year,' he emailed Molly. 'Will know for sure in less than a month. If so, I'll celebrate.'

At the VA, Virgil collected garbage from different hospital wards and swept and mopped the rooms. After a week, he had to work in a faraway building, so he grabbed the mop bucket and headed out, thinking he'd return to trolley the cart. As he left the premises, the supervisor stopped him. 'I want you to push the cart and drag the mop bucket behind, so you can do it all at once.' The guy wasn't rude. But the order meant something else to Virgil: of how low he had sunk. Once an ace coder for corporations, he now had to toil like a 'slave without a brain'. Last year, while waiting for the VA to respond, he had emailed an economist: 'If all I want to do is mop floors, that might be one thing. But what if I want to reach for the stars?'

He told the supervisor, 'That won't happen.' He collected his belongings and left the building.

At least he had the FirmLoan gig. Which meant he could afford some land. A fellow realtor informed him about a 7.23-acre stretch. $80,000: a down payment of $1,600 and a monthly instalment of $625. Virgil agreed.

'Can't afford a mower or a cabin yet,' he emailed its picture to Kumar, 'but I finally have seven acres with a water well and electricity.'

'Are you living there now? You moved to your mother's home right?'

'Still at my mother's. No place here. I hope to buy a ten-by-twenty building next month.'

'Ok. I wish you good luck whole heartedly.'

'Thank you. I wish you the same.'

Virgil created a website, H-1B Hunting Licenses, which categorised the 2015 LCAs by the employer, job title and prevailing wage level. He soon added two new features—city and zip code—followed by the green card data and the years 2013, 2014 and 2016. Frequenting online coding tutorial W3 Schools, he taught himself JavaScript and developed another model. Now clicking on a firm's name—or an occupational code or location—transformed the website into a United States map dotted with numerous pins signifying each LCA. A drop-down menu allowed the user to plug and play.

'This is the first of the many maps,' he emailed the Programmers' Guild founder, John Miano, 'and if you have a request, let me know.'

'We should get you to work on the Programmers Guild website!'

'I wrote them all the time and got no responses. Because I believe this issue is bigger than programmers, and they seem to be only about programmers. As for working, I'm all ears <grin>. Depressed because

I've been back to work since Feb for a measly salary of 39K at a job I worry will not last, and I can't afford to buy a small shed to put on the land I bought.'

Ralph, a seventy-year-old man, made for a tough boss. Sitting in a wheelchair with an oxygen cylinder hooked up, he looked too frail to work, once even nodding off mid-conversation. Two months ago, Virgil had emailed his concerns: Ralph's fading health, his inability to trust Virgil, the 32-bit operating system managing 64-bit machines and more. 'I'm not trying to take over, but if you and Ron and the guy in California would focus on sales and let me handle the software part, in a year, you would be pleasantly surprised.'

No reply.

In September, Ralph's VB6 programs failed. Virgil asked if he could test them on Ralph's computer. That system didn't work. Virgil took a look: the mouse had a dead battery. Ralph said he still couldn't print anything. Virgil asked if he could check the printer, then showed Ralph he had sent instructions to a printer not in the office.

'I haven't selected it yet.' Ralph opened MS Word, chose a printer and printed a blank sheet of paper. 'It's ready now.'

'That doesn't select the printer for your VB6 program.'

Ralph yelled. 'Yes, it does.'

Virgil screamed back, grabbed his printer and stormed out.

Three months: from barely middle-class to nearly homeless.

37

Kumar had a new boss at 4M, Vijay, who arranged an interview at an energy company via an outsourcing giant, Data Consulting Services (DCS), and a 'layer', Futuristic Techno Solutions. He cleared the interview and joined the project. This company, too, had replaced American professionals with (Indian) DCS workers. Kumar had to take 'knowledge transfer' from the displaced employees and document the process. Working from home in the first week, much to his relief, saved him the embarrassment of meeting them. He rented a motel room in Long Island with an Indian contractor, Fahad, working on a fabricated resume (and a fake green card).

One evening, driving home from work, Kumar got a call from the DCS manager Madhav. Someone had restarted the server. Madhav shouted at Kumar: why had he left Long Island? Why was he not at the client site? What happened to the server? Kumar said he'd check tomorrow and report. Madhav kept screaming.

He walked into a hands-on meeting the next day. Facing a projector, Madhav grilled around two dozen DCS employees. The thirty-minute meeting produced no meaningful result. Except for one: Madhav fired Kumar and Fahad in the conference hall. Fahad requested Madhav to step outside the building. Kumar stood in the hallway, watching them from afar. Fahad touched Madhav's feet. Kumar was convinced that Fahad had tried to bribe Madhav. When Madhav entered the building, he fired Kumar again. (Fahad had saved his job.)

Vijay directed Kumar to get his timesheets approved by Madhav. 'Otherwise, we won't pay'—around $5,000.

Locked out of the DCS portal, he contacted Madhav.

No reply.

Emailed, called, texted. Cajoled, pleaded, begged.

No reply.

Another email to Madhav and a DCS manager who had taken his interview. 'I have been requesting to approve time sheets and there is no response from DCS. Employer and vendor won't pay without it. Why are you harassing H1Bs?'

4M's finance department emailed him after a month. 'Your November hours are not yet approved in the DCS portal.'

Kumar wrote to them again. 'I did not get salary because DCS and Futuristic not released the amount. As per labor laws, H1B worker must be paid for the duration worked. Otherwise I will complain to DOL.'

He kept his word and filed a DOL complaint against DCS and 4M.[154] An officer, Joe, called Kumar, giving him two choices: allow the agency to visit 4M's office with a complaint in his name or show up with an anonymous complaint and summon the records of random employees. Neither option suited him. In the former, 4M would most likely retaliate and fire him; in the latter, his employer—knowing its fraud—might not share Kumar's file. The officer suggested a third route: change your employer and file a complaint with your name. But almost all desi body shops charged around $6,000 for an H-1B and over $20,000 for a green card. This, too, didn't work.

Joe replied, 'Our hands are tied.'

The DOL's indifference had defined its very ethos. Constrained by law, it could only check the LCAs for 'missing information or obvious inaccuracies'.[155] It lacked the authority to verify any labour condition, such as workers' wages, and so would approve (deliberately) inaccurate LCAs even when it knew they were inaccurate.[156] The Government Accountability Office found the H-1B gatekeeper so toothless that it once recommended transferring the LCA review process to the Immigration and Naturalisation Services (USCIS's predecessor), which actually verified visa sponsors' information.[157] None of this was by accident: Congress wished to expedite the Labor approval, making the hiring process smooth for businesses.[158]

Unlike the H-1B programme, the Fair Labor Standards Act unshackled the DOL, authorising it to launch varied inspections to detect non-compliance.[159] H-1B workers' enslavement and exploitation didn't just result from callous companies. The law itself ensured that they remained enslaved (by making their employers own the visa) and exploited (by tying DOL investigations to four exceptional conditions).[160]

Kumar got an interview at a prestigious financial services firm, YBMyles Crown, through a prime vendor, Arkonsys, in early 2016. It had received his resume via two body shop owners: Balanath Ponduri from GridInfo Services and his friend Aadesh Koneni from Sharp Business Tech. The twelve-month project in Columbus, Ohio, offered the possibility of an extension. The interview panel comprised hiring manager Rudra Kolla and his colleague Mario. Kumar got an email: YBMyles had selected him.

But Arkonsys objected to middle vendors; it'd only sign the contract with 4M. Balanath and Aadesh threatened Kumar, saying they'd tell Rudra to fire him. Ignoring the threat and leaving his family in Webster, New York, he rented a two-bedroom apartment close to the office. Very early in the project, Rudra came to Kumar's cubicle and said, 'Come out.' With his back resting on a wall and hands on his waist, he said, 'Where is my money? How did you enter the project after bypassing my friend Aadesh? You think you can survive here?'

Kumar explained that the prime vendor had removed Aadesh, but Rudra didn't budge. 'I set the billing rate as $75 to promote Aadesh's business. You ditched my friend, I will fire you.' Their bond had another layer of solidarity: the same caste, Kamma.

'I am a worker, you are a manager. You are not supposed to talk to me for money. Please call my employer if you have lust for dollars.'

'Get out. Get my money.'

He called Vijay from the parking lot. Vijay screamed: Tamil, Hindi, English; insults, taunts, abuses. 'Don't talk to the manager about layer issues.'

'You please listen carefully. I did not talk about billings, he only started.'

Kumar entered the building after an hour, when Vijay and another 4M manager, Arun, spoke to Aadesh and Balanath. Vijay also called Rudra to discuss the kickback. Later, Rudra told Kumar he knew nothing about Windows Admin, that he got a 'second chance' on humanitarian grounds because he had a family. Otherwise, if he were on OPT, Rudra would have already fired him.

Kumar worked twelve hours a day, including weekends, coordinating with the Indian offshore team. In the first few months, he accumulated around 500 hours of overtime. Arkonsys agreed to pay but not Rudra. He kept obsessing over his own bribe—$25 an hour, to be shared among him, Balanath and Aadesh—assuming Kumar earned $75 per hour. He often called Kumar to his room: 'Where is my money?'

Eddie, an Arkonsys employee, told Kumar the real rate: $65.

'Listen, you idiot,' he told Rudra, in Telugu. 'The prime vendor confirmed the amount. $65.'

'Where is my money?'

Kumar called Eddie.

'Our conversations must be getting recorded. Don't call and say the hiring manager is harassing you. We know Indian hiring managers are corrupt here, but we can't help it.'

Kumar confronted Vijay, too. After several phone calls, he agreed: yes, $65. But Kumar would get $55, as 4M had to accommodate the kickback. Which made his share, $41.75, a fortnightly salary of $3,300. His first pay cheque showed $1,900. He emailed Vijay. 'I was not paid for the last bench period. So I am not clear on the gaps. I just need whatever I get from the American prime vendors for both the projects. I commute 800 miles on weekends and pay rents and advances in NY and Ohio. I have relocated at my own cost to Webster and these issues put me in great financial problems.'

Vijay said 4M needed to 'recover' the last project's amount. But recover what? He had earned $25 an hour. Second pay cheque, another email. 'Dear Sir, what is my LCA rate?' Vijay had agreed to shell out the DOL wage. 'I have to give $1,300+ rent in New York and $400+ here. I am begging my roommate to hold on until I get my next pay. Kindly do justice. I left with no tears.'

Kumar continued to find solace in Raghav who, even years later, remembered his initial fire. 'You must stop making videos and start concentrating on your book.' He contacted a 'trusted Christian publisher', WestBow Press. 'My dear friend Kumar is writing a secular book about life in America and will disclose a lot of information on visa fraud and loopholes of corporations and immigration systems. Kumar also went through comparative religious study and acknowledged Jesus as living God and still at learning stage as he began to read Bible. We look forward to publishing his book through you soon.'

Helping 'Christian authors self-publish their message', WestBow Press asked for $5,000. Kumar couldn't afford it, so he dropped the idea, but this pattern—of Christianity's involvement—had persisted with Raghav. His nudges had sharpened during the YBMyles project when, on long phone calls, he lectured Kumar on Christianity. He had done the same in New Jersey. If Kumar protested, itching to spend time with his family, then Raghav would say, 'What family? We're talking about eternal world and life after death.' Raghav sent him a Telugu Bible, instructing Kumar to read it in fifteen days, wanting him to finish the last step: releasing a 'testimony video' saying 'I saw Jesus'.

Kumar didn't.

But otherwise, Raghav remained a solid ally. 'If anyone having questions, please ask them to email h1b@usa.com,' he had emailed last year. 'I can give you access or if anything comes addressing your name, I'll forward it to you. However will copy you on every conversation. Created this as I found it available and to make our work look professional.'

4M kept paying Rudra, but it never satiated him. He wanted more and more—and as soon as possible. He refused to provide the client letter for Kumar's H-1B extension, calling it a 'company policy'. USCIS issued a request for evidence (RFE), demanding additional proof of work (such as, well, the client letter).[161] He continued telling Kumar that his project was about to get over. It became a routine: he appeared before Kumar, took him to a conference room and harassed him for kickbacks. In the project's eighth month, Kumar accompanied Rudra, sat opposite him and switched on the cell phone camera, holding it under a table.

'See sir, I cannot say you are taking but I am getting $25.'

'So talk to them and—'

'Last time you told fuck Aadesh. But I cannot, right?'

'Is there anything I can do to help you?'

'Employer is pushing me to stay here for RFE. Once I clear it, I will only go, sir. I am not a beggar. Otherwise, Vijay said he paid $35,000 to Aadesh and you. If I get it, I will leave.' Kumar rewound the harassment of the last eight months. 'That is why I prepared ... I thought of die writing everybody's name. Then my wife called, "Do not commit suicide because of these issues, let us go back to India."'

The camera moved to a new position, filming Rudra's left leg. 'Arkonsys sent proof they are paying $65. I am getting $25. Then who is taking, sir?'

'You talk to your employer and figure out.'

'They said they paid to Aadesh. Because he warn, hiring manager will fire. He threatened 4M. Vijay said he talk filthy. If you tell me to leave without RFE clear, I have to die, sir. I have no choice. Employer saying stay, you say leave. What would you do if you were in my situation?'

'I feel for you. I mean, there isn't anything—'

'Because in my lifetime, nine years, no American boss brought me to room like this several times and torture, sir.'

'What do you think—'

'Employer telling touch the feet of your hiring manager and beg ...'

'Chee, chee, chee. Ba, ba, ba.' Rudra chuckled.

'See sir, nine years I worked. I can fuck off this project and get out now.'

Rudra laughed.

'But I don't want to leave just like that. Where is my money?'

'Money-a? Ask your employer.'

'I will call HR. I will call ethics cell. Everybody I will call, sir.'

'Okay, what are you expecting?'

'Sir, I will not complain anyone. Let me stay peacefully till my RFE is done.' He repeated his commitment. 'On call I never miss. I drive eight to ten hours in snow.'

'I feel bad for you.'

'I get tears. It is not worth coming here, sir. Professionally I am good. Technically I am good. Because you are not getting money and you scold me, it really hurts me a lot. If you want $25 per hour, I will beg somebody and give it, sir.'

His phone shook. 'Why are you harassing me this much?'

He screamed. 'I am mentally down, sir.'

His voice broke. 'I will jump from this building.'

He broke down. 'Where should I go? I have a family. I have kids.'

38

Manu reached Hyderabad after a twenty-hour flight. His mother and Mamaji had moved to a two-bedroom house, his loan collateral property, in Secunderabad. Outside the main door, he smiled at her and said, 'We are meeting after seven years!' She didn't react—he found it odd. But she came to his room later that night and asked him the whole story. He explained his recent past and shared his plans.

Mamaji helped him apply for his Aadhaar and PAN cards. Manu scouted for jobs; he kept getting rejected.[162] He even attended a walk-in interview in a faraway city, Roorkee, for a research fellow position at the Indian Institute of Technology. But he didn't have a PhD—failed again. After returning to Hyderabad, he completed the bankruptcy application, spoke to a judge over the phone and buried his past life.

Two months passed: still jobless.[163] Manu met Nitish, who had moved to India, at the Infocon Logix office.

'You can work as a trainer. How much salary do you want?'

'At least Rs 10,000 should be there.'

'What Rs 10,000? You will get Rs 25,000.'

For someone struggling to find a job for years, Manu began his online training sessions with a lecture on how to prepare a resume. Most of his students had recently graduated, so he taught basic and advanced software testing concepts over a fortnight in ten hour-long classes. Every alternate class concluded with an assignment. Some students called to ask questions. Some appreciated him. ('You took a good class. God bless you.') He taught new students every month.

Even though Manu went to the Infocon Logix office and used its email ID, he worked for a different firm, Softpro IT Logic, or its US wing, Prompt Techsol. Like Prakash, many consultancy owners operated multiple body shops in the US. If their business just needed cheap and unfree labour—of which there was no shortage—then why stop at one firm? This strategy also obscured dirty trails. If the DOL debarred a company from exploiting the H-1B programme, then its owner could always open another consultancy—under his relative's or wife's name—and continue minting money. Some body shops had become so notorious that their owners established different companies to mislead H-1Bs. Such deceits produced more deceits. A consultancy owner, for example, could use his second firm to issue a 'client letter' to an H-1B worker employed by the first company, helping him clear the visa interview. The cloning tactic had found so many takers that, like the guesthouses, fake resumes and 'proxy' interviews, it, too, deserved to grace the body shop playbook.

Softpro IT Logic, around twelve kilometres from Manu's house, in Uppal, functioned as an offshore office, marketing and training consultants. It followed American work hours, stretching his day from six in the evening to three at night. He stayed at the company's guesthouse on weekdays and returned home on Saturday afternoons.

Manu loathed night shifts. Days were nights, nights were days and sleep had vanished. He hit the bed at four in the morning. Hours passed before he slept—or, at times, not sleep at all. The daylight savings, pushing his schedule by an hour, exacerbated his insomnia. The skin below his eyes itched and flaked. He developed dark circles, and the Tanuja flashbacks still overwhelmed him. He rubbed his face, rubbed it hard, rubbed it often. His temples oozed blood; he sweated in the cold shower. Manu visited a psychiatrist who prescribed him antidepressants, Stalopalm and Clonotril. But neither the 0.25 nor the 0.5 mg dose worked. He needed at least a 1 mg tab to calm down and sleep. The side effects crashed in soon: the pills supressed his hunger and blunted his feelings.

His month split in two halves. First: training, second: bench sales and recruiting.[164] Now he was the Graham, Jackson or Tara to many

Manus across the sea. Bench sales—finding projects for benched employees—meant forwarding job positions to them and setting up vendor interviews.[165] Recruiting involved luring an H-1B or an OPT, on a different consultancy's payroll, to work on a project where Infocon Logix was a middle vendor or a potential employer.

Manu posted a 'fake job', copy-pasting the requirements uploaded by a different company, on Monster, Dice and Indeed. Most desi recruiters followed a similar template, and deceit ruled such hiring. But he chose 'brutal honesty'—or at least as much as this world allowed. He ensured all job ads carried the Infocon Logix logo. Many recruiters didn't mention their consultancies on the call, fooling desperate applicants. Manu cold-called them, saying Infocon Logix would place them. He asked for their years of experience and told them that finding a project might take time. Almost all resumes had six to seven years of experience, making it impossible to differentiate a fresher from an experienced professional. But Manu had played this game for so long that one proper conversation separated the actors from amateurs. The recent graduates sounded eager—too eager—to please. He'd say, 'So you have worked for six years. Can you tell me about yourself?' Most times, they blurted out, 'Actually, I just graduated.'

He once received the resume of an African-American applicant. Manu spoke to him and forwarded it to Infocon Logix's HR manager in New Jersey.

She called him. 'Hey, why are you sending this American guy's resume?'

'He wanted a job.'

'Do only for Indians. Not Americans.'

This is racism.[166]

Manu kept quiet, but he didn't want to recruit anymore.

His mother hadn't changed—her caustic temper kept him in a shell. But sometimes he tried. 'I earned Rs four lakh per month in the US,' he told her once. 'Now I make that much in a year.' She replied, 'Tumhara time bhi aayega'—your time will also come. A few weeks later, chatting with Mamaji's friends, she said: 'I told him not to leave the US. He used to earn a lot.' Manu left the living room. When Manu shared with her that he wanted to see a psychiatrist, she informed Gyan; he said Manu suffered from 'psychosis'. Insults dropped like pigeon shit. While talking to an old friend, she had said, 'Yeh toh baap ke mooh se nikla hai'—he was born from his father's mouth.

One evening, he accompanied his mother and a family friend, Sharma Uncle, to the army canteen to buy a backpack. When they returned home, she said, 'You did not do namaste to Sharma Uncle.'

'I did. He must not have noticed.'

'You did not.'

'I did.'

When Mamaji came home, she made him call Sharma Uncle. 'Did Manu say namaste to you?'

'He did not.'

'You did not do namaste,' she screamed. 'You can't even do namaste!'

'I am not getting a job, and you are stuck on namaste? What namaste? To whom?'

Nothing new though. If he brought bottles of mineral water home—because the house didn't have a water purifier, and he didn't want to drink (once boiled) water from the dirty earthen pot—she didn't speak to him for weeks. If he played computer games, she scolded him. If he drank wine to fall asleep, she shouted, 'Today he is drinking alone. Tomorrow he will get all his friends and drink with them.'

One afternoon, she told him to keep the prasad in the pooja room.

'Let me get the key.'

She yelled, telling him where to find it.

'I know, don't worry.'

'You don't know anything.'

'Why are you shouting? I said I know where it is.'

The next day she sprained her leg while cooking. She screamed in pain and screamed at Manu. Avoiding an argument, he went to his room. Most fights followed a pattern: a trivial reason, her screams, the history channel.

Because of you this happened.

Because of you that happened.

'Because of you I got married.'

'Because of you your dad left me.'

He left for the office in the afternoon. His phone rang in the evening: Mamaji. Manu stepped out, climbed a few flights of stairs and reached the terrace.

'Why are you harassing your mom?' he shouted.

'I'm not. Do you even know the meaning of harassing?'

Then Mamaji opened his mouth and shit flowed.

'You don't do anything at home … you always play games … you always keep the light on … you always waste electricity … we have to cook for you … you waste time … you ask for money … you drink alcohol.'

'Who are you to tell me all this? You didn't even pass tenth class.'

'Just leave the house.'

'Give me a few weeks. I have a lot of luggage.'

In less than a month, Manu left the Hitler Family.

V

HOPE

39

By 2016, Virgil had become a known name among H-1B critics. If someone wrote even one piece interrogating the guest worker programme, he emailed them: told his story, shared his findings, advocated a fightback plan. He'd top it up with the message, 'United we stand, divided we fall.' But the anti-H-1B and pro-worker stance didn't always align. Because some 'fought' for their own gains. So he admired very few activists: attorney Sara Blackwell (who, representing displaced American workers, had sued Disney);[1] the authors of *Sold Out*, Michelle Malkin and John Miano; and his favourite, Norm.

That list used to feature one more name: Keith Parker ('K'). A former IT professional, he had sued a WITCH firm and won, exposing the systemic rot in the body shop business, attracting immense traction. K inspired H-1B victims, for he had scripted a rare success story. He had shown that a regular worker, appealing to American courts, could find justice. K's victory also vindicated America: that the land of the free and the country of immigrants shielded innocents and shamed offenders.

He and Virgil exchanged emails for years. But by May 2015, a distinct pattern emerged. 'I've been sending stuff to Keith Parker who supposedly is working with Senator Sessions and ICE and other police organizations,' he emailed the technical writer Gavin Lynch. 'But when I wrote to him yesterday about my trouble with the VA job, I never heard nothing and with me, trust is everything so I'm not sure whose side he is on, except for maybe his own.'

An email from Kumar. 'Whistle Bowler sent LinkedIn request.'

'Keith? He doesn't talk to me anymore. Guess I ticked him off when I said quit doing photo ops and lead, follow, or get the hell out of the way.'

'He only sent today. Think he found my videos.'

'Yeah, he watches my site occasionally. Probably how he found you. I don't think he's a bad guy. I guess I'm too aggressive and demanding for him.'

A few months ago, Virgil had told K about introducing Kumar to Sessions.

'You'll have to go through me.'

Ain't happening.

Not because he didn't trust K but because such bottlenecks created weird control, and he wouldn't play that game.

In March 2016, Kumar emailed Virgil, summarising his conversation with the DOL agent, Joe, about the complaint he withdrew.

'You need an attorney if you go this route. An American attorney.' He recommended Miano or Blackwell. 'One thing you have that nobody else has come forward with (that I am aware of) is PROOF that you have been BENCHED and NOT PAID.'

'Yes. Do you want me to contact one in Webster or Rochester or New York?'

'If they are not up to speed on immigration, h-1b's, etc, they will do you no good. Keith won his case. I'm not sure who represented him, but I'll write to him and see if they will talk to you. He is a good guy who will bat for you.'

On the same day, Virgil forwarded K's email to Kumar. 'I've a great attorney for him.'

'Keith just called.' Kumar wrote to Virgil after two days. 'He will call again after talked to few guys. Thank you.'

'Good luck.'

Kumar sent regular updates to K and his attorney about the YBMyles project. K wanted to enter its building wearing a body-rigged camera, executing a 'sting operation'. Kumar refused; the CCTV would spot K and get him fired. But he contributed in every other way. He forwarded the accounts of other H-1B victims—his YouTube subscribers—along with long emails on his own harassment and the overall scams of Indian body shops. Kumar also implemented K's suggestion: recording the kickback conversation with Rudra. After months of interactions, K suggested something else: suing 4M and YBMyles. Uncovering such a huge scam could get Kumar a 'whistle-blower visa (the U visa)' and impressive prize money.

Raghav dissuaded Kumar, saying only an employer-sponsored green card guaranteed permanent residency. But K insisted. His attorney once told Kumar that not reporting crime meant supporting crime. He pinched Kumar's most raw nerve. Not long after, K emailed a PDF document. A part of it read:

K. Coleman Parker LLC
Whistleblower Protection & Immigration Compliance
8761, Michael Rd # 215
387-183-4702
Keith.parker@kcparkerllc.com

> The parties agree as follows: This agreement is made by and between Kumad Pandruvada ... Consultant [Keith Parker] agrees to represent Client in the matters in the following case(s) to with: "ANY AND ALL CLAIMS ARISING FROM OR RELATED TO IMMIGRATION VISA ISSUES WITH YBMyles Crown, 4M Techgroup AND OTHERS, OR ANY CONTRACTOR THERETO OR SUBSIDIARY OR AFFILIATE of the above mentioned. TO INCLUDE BUT NOT LIMITED TO ANY QUI TAM OR FALSE CLAIMS ACT ACTION AS RELATOR, whether state or federal law claims".
>
> Client shall agree to a contingency fee agreement in the amount of 10% (ten percent) of any and all awards less expenses to Client from said representation as Consultant or as Realtor for any and all claims whether by civil lawsuit, FALSE CLAIMS ACT or by qui

tam action. Further, Client shall provide payment for or reimburse from proceeds to Consultant for necessary and reasonable expenditure, including, but not limited to: Court transcripts, filing fees, depositions, travel, lodging, meals, expert(s) to include consultants necessary for the litigation and all other costs of Court and expenses incurred. This will be deducted from award.

In any event Client receives no monetary award the Consultant is owed nothing.

Therefore, I, Kumad Pandruvada, having read the foregoing Contract to Employ Consultant in full and understanding the terms herein, I agree that said Contract is fair and reasonable and I hereby employ Consultant.

There has been no promise or guarantee by Consultant relating to the outcome of these cases.

CLIENT:______________________________________
Date:______________
Address: ____________________________
Telephone Number(s): ______________________
CONSULTANT: _______________________ Date:________________

Kumar signed and sent it.

In early 2017, K's attorney filed the lawsuit. 'Relator Kumar Sreenivas Pandruvada brings this Qui Tam False Claims Act on behalf of the United States against "4M" and "YBMyles" to recover penalties and damages arising from false records and statements, misuse of visas, forcing employees to work by threats, threatening to revoke visas and mental abuse.' Working with 4M since July 2008, Kumar knew the 'intimate details of 4M and YBMyles's schemes to use the H1B, H4 and F-1 visa program' to 'manipulate the visa system' and, privy to 'emails and other documentations', could prove such violations. The factual allegations section detailed 4M's scams, covering almost all the projects, including bench wage theft and Rudra's kickbacks. It also exposed desi consultancies' modus operandi: 'fabricating resume(s)', 'professional references', client letters; bribing managers; providing on-call 'job support' and much more.

The accusations read:

'Count I—Violations of the False Claims Act.'

'Count II—Violation of the Immigration and Nationality Act.'

'Count III—Violations of the Trafficking Victims Protection Act'.

Defendants 'knowingly' held 'non-immigrant employees and Relator's immigration documentation such as I-797, I-129, and green cards (I-140)', preventing them from getting 'any other employment' and threatened them with 'revoking visas and deportation'. A 'threat of deportation' alone, the complaint concluded, supported the 'claim for forced labor'. Now Kumar waited for his prayers to come true, reserving his hope and heart in the country where 'law' was 'ultimate'.

40

Virgil worried about losing his land again. He emailed Miano. 'I'm willing to develop the website or merge my two sites and yours into one if it fits your needs. All it takes is money <grin>. Seriously, I soon need to come up with $625 to keep my land. You find a way to make that happen and I will resolve the things you want.' A day before the due date, he wrote a Facebook post. 'In 2002, I was making $540 per day. Overnight, that changed, and it took me a decade to understand, but I can describe it in one word: caste. Google Dalit if you don't get what I'm talking about.' Virgil requested the property owner for some more time. He wrote to Miano again, saying, for $2,500, he'd run the website and support it for free.

'We have the money for that,' Miano replied. 'We should discuss.'

An unemployed programmer joined a (rare) organisation that fought for unemployed programmers. Virgil ordered a 12-by-28 feet cabin with a four feet porch and, in late December 2016, got the best birthday gift: a wooden home in his patch of wild. But once he finished revamping the Programmers' Guild's website for a one-time fee, he struggled again. As always, he needed cash yesterday. At least $933 per month to save his land and cabin. He interviewed with the VA: housekeeping aid ($11.50 an hour).

A few years ago, he had met a techie, Lee Davis, who shared his passion: discussing technology and drinking beer. Lee had created a tip acquisition software to stop crime. A telecom giant bought his firm; he worked for it. Lee hated the corporate world. He quit and rebuilt a more robust version. Over 50,000 schools and businesses used his product, including law enforcement agencies. Davisoft Tech's annual revenue exceeded millions of dollars. Lee lived in Kerrville and often visited Harper. They met at the same bar and followed the same routine: ordering pints and 'talking shop'.

'Just thinking about you.' An email from Lee. 'How's it going? What does your timeline look like on the cabin? Call me.'

'Phone is off. Got to go to San Antonio tomorrow to do employment physical. Been trying to raise twenty for gas all day with no luck. Cabin is good until Monday.'

'I've 20 for you if you want to run by here.'

'Appreciate that but I have to catch a seven thirty shuttle at VA. Will go to my mother's and borrow it from her. All this has made me more determined than ever to get some type of web-based app that can get me income.'

'I hear ya on the motivation. Glad to help if needed.'

Virgil got the VA job in the first week of July—and, once more, hoped for a new beginning.

41

Manu had no mother, no home, not even an illusion of it. No father, either. Or extended family. So he had to search for a home, and he lived in a city where the wells called to the parched. The answers swirled all around. Manu found one in his inbox, among countless emails from visa consultancies: a permanent residency in Canada. An easy and convenient way to immigrate, the Canadian PR had many success stories. But it demanded a hefty investment, and he had minimal savings. He applied for a bank loan of Rs 2 lakh.

Manu contacted an immigration consultancy, Americaz Global. He spoke to an employee, Sonali, and asked about his chances if he got a low IELTS score. She assured him that he would get a good score. Manu paid Rs 67,850, submitted the transcripts for a World Education Services evaluation and registered for IELTS. Americaz sent him a book to prepare for the exam. He got an Overall Band score of 6.5. Listening: 8.5, Reading: 5.5, Speaking: 6, Writing 5.5. The counsellor, Sandeep, told him to rewrite the test, as he needed '6 in Reading and 6.5 in Writing' and failed to fulfil 'the criteria of 67 points'.

'Can you try with this score? I know you are also working hard on my application. If I don't get the visa, I will not ask for the money. I was actually in the US and the only reason I came back because I didn't have a permanent status and H-1B is modern slavery.'

'We understand, but as per the immigration requirement you need at least 67 points. Your score doesn't meet that criteria.'

No point writing IELTS again. It was expensive, and his score wouldn't improve. Manu called Sonali. The same spiel: write the exam. He emailed her. 'I am not working with Americaz because Sandeep said he won't apply with my score. Can you continue with the same score for the express entry or return my amount?' When Manu didn't get an answer, he contacted two other employees. 'It is a request to refund my fee. I requested Sandeep to proceed with whatever I have, but you know Indians are arrogant, and India is an undeveloped country—no wonder our economy is going down—so he didn't. I requested Sonali for the refund, but she is not responding. I have been in the United States and Indians do a lot of fraud, that's why I had to return. Please check with her and refund the amount or I'll have to file legal proceeding.'

Manu got an answer the next day. 'We regret the inconvenience and understand your concern. However, our agreement, signed by you, clearly informs that refund would not be processed if the applicant can't meet the required IELTS score (clause 7(m) and 7(p)). Your score does not fulfil the criteria, which is a major requirement for the Canada PR. We suggest you take time, re-appear for the exam and continue with the process. Until then, we'll keep your case on hold.'

'I had asked Sonali what if my score is low? She did not reply. Just because your employees are incompetent, you cannot start blame game with customers. I would not have requested the money if I had not been kicked out of the house. I do not want anything—I will find a way. Do not respond.'

42

The many empty cubicles surprised Kumar. The reason shocked him: an FBI investigation. Rudra 'coached' him for the interrogation. 'YBMyles Crown advertised this position. Arkonsys contacted your employer—don't mention Balanath and Aadesh—just remember this chain: YBMyles → Arkonsys → 4M. Now tell me, who took your interview? How did you get the job?' (The FBI never interviewed Kumar.) So what happened? Several threads popped up on AndhraFriends in not just December 2016 but also years later.

'They are saying there is a main [guy], director level …'

'Hired over 100 full timers in last few yrs in 90k to 110k paygrades.'

'Plus from his [friend's] consulting companies with monthly 1,000 dollars kick backs from each candidate.'

'It seems there is something like NGO day in [Crown].'

'If an employee transfers 100 dollars to an NGO … then [Crown] matches that amount.'

'[From the director's] batch it seems around 50 members transferred 10K each …'

'I just heard from a friend that … some big fish along with others used 130 consultants [and] charged kickbacks to bring the candidates onboard. Used [the NGO day scheme] in association with a Telegu organization, so in an audit they caught and removed all 130 consultants. As of now, the news is Unofficial and yet to be confirmed.'

'On Ohio Manager floor, 20 HR ppl came … They took each [consultant] in the room … what is your experience, what the fuck did you do after coming to the US, where were you slaving before … whom did you bribe (and how much) for this job, who took the interview … after verify[ing] everything for 2-3 hours, they told the consultants to pack their bags it seems. Except for one or 2 resources, they said namaskar to everyone else …'

Spread across the different US states, AndhraFriends members spilled more secrets.

'Similar story—Dallas Verizon …'

'One big Vendor in Ohio area gives a brand new car every year for [Crown's] nationwide managers … and sponsors world tours for their families …'

'My friend, a director in tcs, pitched hyundai a proj in south korea. After presentation he supplied hookers it seems. My friend said it is quite common. Our people have done all rotten things.'

'There is a company in midwest where a developer's billing is 130 … vendor gives labourer 60, the rest vendor and manager eat.'

'Another story: I [once] shared a ride with a TCS engagement manager for several hours, just two of us. [Big MNCs] spend according to clients habits. If the client turns out to be horny, then it is just fire. He booked an entire strip club for the whole night … just for 2 guys …'

'If they investigate correctly, then desi managers and FTEs will go to jail. Cts, infosys, wipro all acct managers pay for yr end gifts, sponsor holidays, give cash for cars …'

An AndhraFriends user posted, what seemed like, a Telugu newspaper clip.

'In a major bank fraud in Columbus, 130 people were fired … because of illegal money transfer … It is rumoured … some are directors and managers working on visas sponsored by a big Indian software company …'

'Because of [YBMyles Crown] … Code of conduct 22 Cognizant employees fired … are any of them your friends?'

'2 years back same thing happened with tcs I guess.'

'My sixth sense says kumar uncle is the whisteblower.'

Kumar at last got his last date: 1 February 2017. He recorded a video. It opened to his room: a mattress, a couch, bags, jackets, books and toilet paper rolls scattered all over. A smiling Kumar on a small separate screen superimposed on the bottom left. 'Yesterday only came to know my project is ending. I am partially vacating. Because a lot of corruption issues, mental torture by hiring manager.' Cut to: Kumar outside his apartment, his car trunk crammed with clothes and a huge plastic container. Followed by: Kumar on the highway, late in the night, driving back home.[2]

Rudra called him in Webster. His project had got extended. Kumar returned and, tired of this nonsense, emailed Eddie. 'Why Rudra Kolla scared to write in business email to you by saying project ending? Why does he comes to me daily and speak in filthy Telugu Indian language to get out as project over? Something is seriously wrong with him. When project is there till April 2017, how come he is pushing me out? I do not know how to put a check point to this? I told Mathew his boss about his torture but so tragic, he forward that email to Rudra and rest you can imagine—double torture.'

He wrote to Virgil in early March. 'I am counting hours in USA. March 15 Employer has to file h1b. Job ends on April 6, corrupted hiring manager said. No new project, no road ahead.'

This time, it really got over. Weeks passed. No project. The endless exasperating cycle—of finding a project, wage theft, harassment, negotiation, humiliation, losing a project—had left him hollow. Dream America had died countless times. But he had to live, and there was just one way. The only way.

Kumar decided.

A ping from Raghav. 'If you go to India—you'll subjugate your children. Your kids will get sick. Physically, mentally, emotionally.'

Another ping at 10:28.

'OH MY—I can't imagine that Hell of Education. No Sports, No games—STUDY STUDY—BY the time they come to high school—they'll be in pitiful situation.'

Kumar didn't reply; Raghav didn't stop.

10:29: ‘I beg you—don’t spoil your kids future Sir. Don’t let them live in shit Sir.’

10:30: ‘Just because we’ve seen all the shit in India, does it mean our children also have to go through the same shit??????’

12:07: ‘Please don’t think like that Sir. By Patience and Long-suffering let us endure everything Sir.’

12:08: ‘I’ve no words to ease your pain. I pray God will comfort your heart and give you peace. If your father wants you to be there, why you came to US?’

13:09: ‘I respect your family values and sentiments. That is your personal and I don’t comment on them. But I as a brother guide you to be wise in life.’

Kumar stayed.

43

After establishing a successful IT business, Appi Reddy scaled another peak of American affluence: philanthropy. He created AHR Foundation, which supported poor children's educational needs.[3] He adopted a village in Telangana, Dondapudu, making it 'Digital Dondapudu'. Its 218 villagers, reported the *Hindu*, got 'basic computer training' to 'conduct digital transactions'.[4]

The next step? Hollywood. Appi served as an executive producer on a faith-based sports drama, *Slamma Jamma*. It told the story of a young Black man who, after a prison sentence, finds solace in God to win the national slam dunk competition. When the film released, a Telugu news channel, TV9, interviewed Appi inside a multiplex. It also spoke to a few audience members, all Indians, who called the movie 'very good', 'very inspiring'.[5] But the *Hollywood Reporter* found it 'hoary' and 'melodramatic'.[6] *The A.V. Club* called it the 'nadir of faux-inspirational filmmaking' whose 'ineptitude' was 'charming'.[7] Appi continued his juggernaut though. (Who cared for film critics anyway?)

As regional vice president of the Telangana American Telugu Association (TATA), he diversified his rise. In June 2015, celebrating Telangana's first anniversary, TATA invited an entrepreneur and a philanthropist, Srinivasa Manapragada, as the chief guest. A Telugu film website covered the event, highlighting the sponsor: Appi, 'an inspiration for hundreds of Telangana students'.[8] TATA also hosted an event for Telangana chief minister's officer on special duty, Deshapati Srinivas.

The Telugu media again mentioned AHR Foundation and MicroInfo.[9] A few months later, TATA celebrated the second anniversary of Telangana's formation at MicroInfo's office (where the 'Bay Area Youth Icon Appi Reddy' gave a 'spellbound speech').[10]

Such events helped Appi cosy up to political power. But they were overshadowed by Telugu associations' biennial conventions. Because these glitzy fares featured film stars, singers, dancers. Prominent politicians appeared as chief guests. News channels showcased the spectacle.

Telugu associations were spread all across the US. There were so many of them, and many with only state-level presence, that it was near-impossible to estimate their true number. A few big ones—such as the Telugu Association of North America (TANA), American Telugu Association (ATA), North American Telugu Association (NATA) and North America Telugu Society (NATS)—had been around for decades, headquartered in different states. This vast spread elicited a simple question: if all of them wanted to promote and protect Telugu culture and solidarity, then what was the need for so many of them?

Yeah, that word again: caste.[11]

In the early 1900s, the US restricted immigrants from the Eastern Hemisphere. The Immigration and Nationality Act of 1965—passed during the Cold War and civil rights movement—largely abolished that discrimination. Using their class and caste capital, Telugu doctors migrated to America in huge numbers. From the 1970s, they sponsored their family members' visas. A few Telugu organisations had popped up in the country by then, but TANA, formed in 1977, united them all. The Kamma caste dominated its initial membership, monopolising the top-brass positions.[12]

But it split in 1991. One version blamed the Congress leader Marri Chenna Reddy who, after becoming the chief minister of Andhra Pradesh in 1990, encouraged the Reddis to form their own organisation. Another pointed to an election where a Reddy was about to become the first president, but the Kammas ensured that one of their own continued to head the organisation. So the Reddis created ATA.[13] But political and regional discord splintered ATA and TANA, too. The former produced

NATA, the latter NATS.[14] The intercontinental distance hadn't mitigated but heightened caste rivalry. A battle for supremacy raging for around … 700 years.[15]

Kammas and Reddis made for fascinating arch-rivals, rooting their resentment in differences and similarities. Both Shudras, they fought the dominance of Brahmins, owned large rural lands and yearned for Kshatriya status so much that they commissioned caste histories.[16]

But they also had two major differences.

First, geographical. Kammas clustered in the fertile Krishna and Godavari deltas; Reddis controlled the arid Deccan plateaus, including Telangana and Rayalaseema (so much so that the region came to be colloquially called 'Reddiseema'). This territorial segregation seemed to follow a cartel-like logic: one area, one boss.[17]

Second, political. By the 1930s—responding to economic depression and higher taxation harming their farmers—Kammas, moving from being pro-British to nationalists, helmed the Andhra Communist party. Reddis gravitated towards the Congress.[18]

After India became independent, Andhra Pradesh's warring castes raced towards the political throne. By the early 1980s, the scorecard, comparing their chief ministers, read: Reddis 6, Kammas 0. But then a Kamma film star, N.T. Rama Rao, took centre stage, serving a long term as the chief minister in the late 1980s, followed by his son-in-law, Chandrababu Naidu, in the late '90s and the early aughts.

Even though the fissures between Kammas and Reddis widened, they continued to share a significant commonality: education (and its close connection to caste). They established private engineering colleges from the 1970s, making Andhra Pradesh one of the first Indian states—besides Karnataka and Maharashtra—to privatise higher education. Via caste-based trusts, they created educational societies that dominated the state's technical educational landscape. A link so prominent that institutions were associated with castes. VR Siddhartha Engineering College in Vijayawada, the first private technical institute in the state, and Vignan University and KL College of Engineering, in Guntur, were called 'Kamma colleges'.[19] Listed as 'Kammavari' on caste-based websites, these institutions also included several medical colleges.[20]

Some educational empires, such as Vignan Tutorials, began as coaching institutes and grew into schools and engineering colleges.[21] Its owner, Lavu Rathaiah, became a Congress leader. The founder of Gandhi Institute of Technology and Management, M.V.V.S. Murthi joined the Telugu Desam Party (TDP). Manu's alma mater also had a similar backstory. In his decades-long career, P. Indra Reddy contested elections from both the TDP and Congress before succumbing to a road accident in 2000. This triangulation of education, business and politics—topped off by caste—consolidated in Andhra Pradesh decade after decade,[22] racing to its next natural destination in America, where they met again: the H-1B programme.

Kumar had attended the Telugu associations' conventions and made videos on them, explaining their caste connections. 2010, NATS, New Jersey; 2015, TANA, Detroit.[23] He emailed Virgil describing TANA's convention. 'Interesting topics: 1) Politics. 2) Immigration, Student Visas, Education in USA for my writings to guide students. 3) IT companies business meetings.'

He had visited the convention's twentieth edition. A Kamma politician inaugurated the landmark anniversary, receiving a lifetime achievement award: then Union Urban Development minister, M. Venkaiah Naidu. It also starred more politicians, film stars, public intellectuals.[24] Over 10,000 people thronged to the three-day event from India, Canada and the US.[25] Like TANA, many Telugu associations had non-profit status, tax-exemption privileges and impressive revenues, especially in the years they hosted the conventions. (TANA and ATA held them in alternate years to avoid conflict.)

Organisations	*FY*	*Annual Revenue*
TANA	2023	$7.88 million[26]
ATA	2022	$4.62 million[27]
NATA	2022	$3.21 million[28]
NATS	2023	$3.44 million[29]

But Kumar received an email in June 2016 that added a new layer to their story:

> I am from Hyd, been here for 14yrs, US citizen now. You are doing a great job of making a case for genuine well deserved people. But I think we should provide a bigger picture to the audience. The "body shop" owners—what do they do? They groom, support, and nurture politics back home. They formed a cartel[30]—a vicious circle where things go as per understanding with each organization. When they grow, they become tax-free. After the formation of Telangana, the situation has become worse. Now they promote region/caste/party/group politics.
>
> They bring political leaders, actresses doing "recording dances", promoting double meaning songs in the name of culture. Do you know what such actresses do? I have seen them with arrangements of prostitution with $3,000 to $5,000 a night. They have 2 or 3 managers for negotiation and secrecy. We are already a laughing stock in the non-Telugu community. These poisonous organizations are ruining Indian culture in general and Telugu pride in particular.

In 2018, the United States charged a couple—Kishan Modugumudi ('Raju') and Chandra Kala Purnima Modugumudi ('Vebha')—with importing 'aliens for sex trafficking'.[31] The government alleged that the pair had taken five Tollywood actresses to 'Telugu and other Indian conferences' to identify 'potential customers' for 'commercial sex acts'.

'Victim A', said the criminal complaint, submitted a document to the US embassy officials, stating that she intended to visit the country as an honouree of the Telugu Association of Southern California (TASC). It later changed to 'NATS'. During an interview with law enforcement officers, 'A' provided two more invitation letters: one from TANA and the other from the Telangana People's Association of Dallas (TPAD). B's visa application's notes stated, 'Model to ATA event in Illinois for 1 week.' C: 'Going to function in Detroit, 40th anniversary of Detroit Telugu Association'. D: 'VJ, invited by TLCA [Telugu Literary & Cultural Association] to appear at cultural events'. E: 'Telugu and Kannada major actress; invited by ATA as guest'.

Law enforcement officials contacted the TASC president and a NATS official. Neither knew 'A'. TANA and TPAD's presidents also confirmed the invitation letters were fake. Even though the investigation didn't identify Telugu associations as perpetrators, they had at least functioned as gateways of sexual exploitation.

Even in the YBMyles scandal, the AndhraFriends users had mentioned an 'NGO day' scheme where consultants transferred their kickbacks to a non-profit organisation, and the client matched that amount—doubling it in essence—presuming it to be a charitable donation. They identified a 'director-level' employee, the president of a ... Telugu association in Ohio, a scam that spread to many states and companies over the years.[32]

Casteism and capitalism: both 'upstairs-downstairs' structures sustained by an eternal promise. Upstairs, there's always someone to venerate. Downstairs, there's always someone to subjugate. And the H-1B scam had made them meet—like long-lost brothers in a Bollywood film.

44

Manu searched for an alternative: how to apply for a Canadian PR with a low IELTS score. He found his answer in the Saskatchewan Immigrant Nominee Program (SINP), which allowed foreign nationals to migrate to a province in western Canada. An 'International Skilled Worker' needed sixty points out of 100 to be eligible. Based on education, work experience, IELTS score and age, Manu scored sixty-one. SINP listed a handful of occupations. 'Information systems analysts and consultants' was one of them.

He approached a different consultancy, Glonect Solutions. It would cost him Rs 75,000; he had to pay Rs 40,000 upfront. His case manager, Sagar Arora, sent him a PDF file listing the supporting documents. The 'Settlement Funds' section stated that the applicant must maintain a 'minimum amount' of CAN$ 12,164 for 'at least 3 months' before applying and keep it through the 'entire process'. Manu emailed his documents. Sagar requested a few more, including the last six months' bank statements showing Rs 6.5 lakh.

Manu had no money. But he had to find a way—he had to leave India. A colleague told him about a bank employee, Bhargava, who, for cash, could give him the letter. Manu met with him, paid Rs 10,000 and got the letter. He emailed Sagar the remaining documents, including his last six months' bank statements (balance: Rs 1,08,780) and Bhargava's bank letter stating the amount in his fixed deposit (FD) account: Rs 6 lakh.

The Saskatchewan government sent him a letter three weeks later. 'You must have proof of $12,164 CAD in your account(s) for at least 3 months prior to your application and maintained throughout the entire immigration process. Please provide bank statements or letters from your financial institution indicating balances and transaction history of the account(s) from July 24, 2016 to today's date. Also your term deposit was only put in place in October 2016 and matured November 2016. Please provide proof of renewal and funds since July 24, 2016.'

Bhargava said he couldn't arrange the FD renewal letter. But he'd make the money appear in his statement for a longer period for another Rs 10,000. Manu paid. He sent Sagar his bank letter specifying the account balance, Rs 75,491. 'In this amount is less than previous, but it's ok right because it still meets the minimum requirement of 6 and half Lakhs?'

Sagar said Manu needed to show the 'renewal FD' for Bhargava's bank. He wrote to his father, asking for a loan ('I will return once I get nominated—3 to 4 months or before').

No reply.

He opened MS Paint and imported the bank letter. Changed its date, altered the font, revised the account balance—from Rs 75,491 to Rs 6,75,933—and emailed it to Sagar.

'I have sent the pending documents to SINP,' he replied. 'Now we need to wait for their response.'

45

At the VA, in his forty-second professional year, Virgil, once a 'Fox News junkie', joined a union. Wanting to apply for IT jobs reserved for internal applicants, he emailed his resume to different union leaders, introducing himself, describing his skills, telling his story. He demonstrated his recent software experience by providing a link to the Programmers' Guild website.

No reply.

Lee emailed him the next month. 'I may do the Harper tour this afternoon. You game?'

'Always game. Down to my last 20, so probably won't be much bar time.'

'What is the least you would leave your current job for?'

'I make 28,730 right now. Probably take double or around 1,000 a week.'

Virgil soon wrote him a long email. Despite the budget constraints, Lee wanted to hire two full-time developers. So Virgil proposed a plan and pitched his services as a product manager, who understood the system's features, enhancements and requests while supporting it. Lee donated $650 the next day.

'Thank you, wasn't expecting. That is like two weeks salary for me these days.'

In a subsequent drinking session, Lee asked Virgil if he'd like to join his firm. Virgil first hesitated—thinking good friends wouldn't make good colleagues—then agreed. Lee had one condition: Virgil would have to delete everything related to his H-1B activism. It didn't bother him, but he had to think about his customers.

A job, a full-time job: Virgil's desperation, frustration, decade-long fight. And he had it now—granted, at a modest salary ($42,000 per year), but it provided an opening at least. He wrote an article on Keep America At Work.[33] 'I hope you will understand should I pursue this path. I'm trying to figure out how to say this so bear with me. For fifteen years, I have fought a battle most will never understand until it happens to them … I have a chance to get a steady job which will allow me to buy some land and put a tiny house on. But it means I must shut down all of my keep America at work type websites. I hope you do not consider me to be a quitter. But without a massive financial support to truly make a difference, I simply have no more to give, and it is time that I build a life for myself.' He forwarded that article to Norm.

Virgil joined Davisoft Tech in September 2018, working from home. Every morning and evening, he had a Skype call with the developers. He also researched automated software solutions, which would free Lee from relying on expensive programmers. That explained his hiring because he had little else to do.

With the new cash flow confidence, he dreamt big: buying a house. But most properties in Harper, priced at around $200,000, exceeded his $100,000 budget. So he found a real estate agent, Bierschwale Land Company, operating in a town forty miles away, Junction. A property caught his attention: 1,100-square feet, two-bedroom, one-bath. Plus a two-car garage, a back porch, a patio. Oak trees lent comforting shade. The house came for $119,000. He contacted the realtor, checked the property and gave an offer: $115,000. The realtor agreed. Virgil applied for a VA-guaranteed loan, but his low credit score, 648, could crush his hope again. He sent a letter explaining his job and house discrepancies. Much to his relief though, the loan got approved. He hoped to settle the deal on 21 December, but it happened after six days.

'Today is my 61st birthday,' he emailed the loan company employee. 'Just wanted to say thank you for helping to make this possible.'

'Happy Birthday!! I hope it was the best birthday present :) Thank you for your service to our country!'

An email to Lee two days later. 'For some reason I can't send this to you via text.' A close-up shot of the kitchen sink. On the right drainer, a bag full of ice; on the left, a dozen cans of Miller Lite.

He wrote to Norm the same day. 'After 16 years of hell, I bought a house. Just an fyi so that when others reach out to you, you can tell them to keep trying.'

VI

SECRETS

46

After two short projects, Kumar looked for a job. Months passed. His savings bled. Just three months of work in the last six months. In October 2017, 4M fired countless benched employees, including Kumar. He panicked. If he couldn't find an employer in two months, he'd have to return to India. But even a new company would want the last two pay cheques for the visa transfer; Kumar had none. He contacted Raghav: could VersIT file his H-1B?

'Our management is saying they'll charge. I'll connect you to our HR Mr Rajendra. You talk to him and ask half or whatever you think is fine. (Please don't think bad, we had bad experiences from candidates, so they put some policies for everyone.)'

'Thank you sir. Could you let me know how much? Do I need to arrange ASAP?'

'Process will start after placement. On Monday you'll get all clarifications.'

Rajendra told him the amount: $10,000. Kumar said he didn't have the money—could he pay once he got the project? Rajendra agreed. Kumar emailed Raghav. 'Thanks for you and your great team helping me in most difficult times. I hope you will guide me if delayed any interviews and crossing 60 days time, right?'

'No worries. We'll try for client letter if we get nothing by Thanksgiving.'

'I do not know how to thank.'

'God is Faithful. We can count on our living God, who answers our prayers through his works in our lives.'

Raghav wrote to him a week later. 'www.biblestudytools.com/topical-verses/prayer-bible-verses. Search for these references in your Telugu Bible and note them down.' Raghav and a VersIT recruiter, Gautham, marketed Kumar's resume. But nothing clicked for weeks. Raghav continued to encourage Kumar in his own unique way.

> *Dear Believer,*
> *Are you in troubles and problems?*
> *Is your boat of life tossed about and not able to go forward?*
> *Is the wind against and the circumstances not favorable?*
>
> Don't worry. The disciples of Jesus were also under the same conditions. Keep your faith and don't lose heart. Do you believe your God? If yes, then, believe His promises and be happy. Know that HE is with you always! Amen.

In the early days of their professional relationship, Raghav had an unusual advice for Kumar:

> I'm closing all google accounts (gmail). Henceforth, you communicate with me only to this address. You shut all your gmail as well. If you've YouTube, change your email access. Create a new email.
> Regards,
> Raghav Kishore
> ROfficial@ProtonMail.Com

ProtonMail, an encrypted email service based in Switzerland, was exempted from US surveillance laws. Raghav told Kumar to deactivate his YouTube channel, too, so his H-1B activism wouldn't pop up in the background check. 'Please don't think I'm trying to tame you out of FB and YT. I want you to properly use your time. We must give importance to soul than flesh. You contain with Bible—you can win anyone, anytime. First you work on New Testament. Complete it soon.'

Raghav wrote to him five days later. 'Read about Epic Tool. Minimum Billing $100/hr. Best Technology.' The next day, the old

Raghav. 'Over 100 million copies of the Bible are sold each year. The Bible has been translated into 2,883 languages. The Bible is God's word. The Bible is historically accurate. The Bible never contradicts itself'—and on and on.

In early February, Kumar finally landed a project: the IT department of a government client in Maryland. Three firms sat between VersIT and the client: the prime vendor Cyber Techsol and two layers, Ohzion and iTech Infologic, all Indians. The first problem came in the first week. When Raghav entered Kumar's designation (senior security engineer) and work location in the DOL portal, it produced a Level IV wage, $120,000. Raghav said his firm couldn't afford it; iTech paid VersIT the same amount. He'd enter a different job title and try again.

Using his 2016 tax returns, Kumar, on Raghav's instruction, transferred the first instalment of his H-1B fees, $2,000, to a VersIT employee, Gopi Ranga. Raghav contacted Kumar again about the LCA. Even the new designation, systems engineer, had a high salary, $95,000. But if VersIT got $120,000, Kumar asked Raghav, why couldn't it pay him $95,000?

'Still unaffordable.'

So what now?

'Don't tell anyone and vacate your stuff from the office. Email them the next day that you've fallen sick and quit the project.'

'What about my ID card?'

'Leave it on the desk.'

Kumar emptied his cubicle and filled his car. But later that evening, he pieced together his past. 4M fired him because he didn't have a project. But he had almost clinched one a few months ago, via an outsourcing giant, paying over $70 per hour. Due to a software glitch in his MS Word, he had told Raghav to submit his resume. Raghav had sent it through his VersIT account. The firm objected to a middle vendor; Raghav made him exit the hiring chain. It perplexed him: why did Raghav send the resume through VersIT's email? And then? He didn't have a project; 4M fired him. Raghav ordered; Kumar followed.

Dear Believer, are you in troubles and problems?

Then VersIT, like most desi companies, charged for the visa and didn't provide an offer letter. Raghav didn't share the LCAs either and now instructed him to quit this project, too? How would Kumar survive without a project? He had to apply for an H-1B in April; he had less than a month. What if he didn't find a project? What if he had to leave the US? What would happen to him, his family, his future?

Is your boat of life tossed about and not able to go forward?

Kumar couldn't quit this project; he wouldn't quit this project. He searched for 'H-1B transfer' in his inbox and found a desi company, Avatar Infosol. He emailed its recruiter, 'Rocky Jones', who introduced him to the owner, Deva Ram. A remarkable coincidence, for Kumar had known him and his brother, Harsha, for a long time.[1] Deva said he'd file the visa from a different body shop, ByteCore Consulting. Kumar asked what his salary would be. 'Do not ask anything now,' Deva said. 'That we will see later.'

Kumar didn't argue. Now he just had to inform Raghav: their friendship would continue, but the professional collaboration would end. Raghav lost it.

Is the wind against and the circumstances not favorable?

If VersIT had to leave the project, he said, then Kumar would have to compensate the company for the financial damage: $5,000. If Kumar refused, then VersIT wouldn't provide him with the no-objection certificate. Several years ago, while discussing the prospect of making the Facebook page public, Raghav had said, 'Truth shouldn't hide, and everything must come to light.' Everything had indeed come to light. All those years of collaborations; counselling H-1B applicants; discussions about the body shops, the caste system, the greedy desis; friendship, solidarity, brotherhood; all of them collapsed into a price point: $5,000.

They fought over the phone.

Kumar emailed him. Subject: 'You screwed up everything'.

'CALL ME URGENTLY.'

Like a true desi body shop employee, Raghav wanted nothing in writing. Was that why he switched from Gmail to ProtonMail?

He hadn't shared the password of h1b@usa.com either. What did he do with it? Did he forward all the subscribers' emails as he had promised? Who was this guy?

Kumar wrote to Raghav. '4M didn't collect money for h1b, VersIT collecting. 4M sent offer letter and LCA, VersIT won't. You told, Cyber won't pay if leaving in the middle of the project. Then I will bring K to get my hours worked. Please don't mess up with me. $2,000 return asap.'

No reply.

Two days later, he emailed again to settle his confusion, sorrow, debt. It still made no sense. 'You are a good person trying to help me. But your company is doing a crime like taking h1b fees and not sending offer letters, etc. What hurts me, despite our long friendship, how come you are not supporting while collecting the money? If VersIT professional, they will send offer letter. If VersIT professional, they would not take $2,000. Because of our brotherhood, you may get it. Otherwise, they do not, right? Why you do not understand this simple logic? If you do but still support them, then I have to consider I was exploitation right? I do not because you were the only person helping me through worst times. I am grateful for the work you and Gautham did. 4M did not do it in 10 years. But you are not on the side of justice. Think and email, Sir.'

No reply.

He sent an email with the subject 'VersIT collecting h1b fees from applicants' to Reporth1babuse@uscis.dhs.gov. VersIT had dropped off the project by then as Ohzion, honouring their agreement, had paid the required amount, and ByteCore applied for Kumar's visa.

'He took money for H1B and abscond,' Kumar wrote to Virgil. 'When I ask him to return, he shouted at me. See he joined hands with me to write H1B book. I did not know I will get cheated by him like this.'

'I was worried about him. Never had a good feeling.'

Kumar emailed a Mumbai-based journalist a week later. 'Are you in USA now? I am no longer associated with h1b@usa.com or my friend Raghav. So email me directly if any questions.' While researching his book proposal in late 2016—centred on the abuse of the H-1B programme—the reporter had discovered Kumar Exclusive and sent a few questions to h1b@usa.com. When he didn't get a reply, he wrote to Kumar, introducing himself and copy-pasting the same queries. H1b@usa.com answered five days later.

That journalist was me.

'Dear Kumar, I'm not in the US yet. I've a book contract, but I'm trying to sort out the visa issues. If everything goes well, I'll be in the US by June.'

This exchange triggered a four-year-long ritual. Kumar sharing his story, me asking questions; Kumar unveiling different scams, me picking my jaw off the floor. A few days later, he introduced me to Virgil. By mid-April, going to the US looked near-impossible, as I didn't meet the criterion for a foreign journalist's I visa. I didn't have a job in the country; working on a book didn't qualify as one. When I moved to Delhi on 1 May 2018, I still needed another protagonist. I had emailed and called many but got no meaningful response. One afternoon, though, I chanced on an email draft, where I stored my reporting notes. 'This guy returned to India, contact him.' Under it, a link: Manu's Facebook profile.

47

Virgil found another ally, Hilarie Gamm—the author of a self-published book, *Billions Lost: The American Tech Crisis and the Road Map to Change*[2]—with whom he exchanged regular emails. 'I now realize this job is only a buddy helping me out with no opportunity to use my skills and no hope of advancement. So I'm begging for a janitor position at the local VA until I can draw early social security at the end of the year.'

By early 2019, he joined the VA. 'I'll try to manage 30 hours per week for my day job for as long as they will keep me,' he emailed a friend. 'But not sure as in nearly eight months I've done eight hours' worth of work.' With his new cumulative earnings—totalling around $72,000—he hoped to enter the middle class again. But it also meant intense hustle: working for Lee from 8 a.m. to 2 p.m., then driving to Kerrville, then toiling at the VA. The sixty-one-year-old had never been so tired. One night, he fell asleep at the steering wheel and almost hit a truck. On the third night, he crashed into a deer. The fifth night: a deer died. The next day, he quit.

Virgil had spent years investigating the H-1B programme, relying on DOL data. But since LCAs didn't solicit information on clients, the links between them and body shops remained hidden. That changed in November 2018, when the federal agency revised the applications to 'better protect American workers, confront fraud, and increase transparency.'[3] Now third-party firms had to list the 'secondary business entity'—or the client's—name and address on the LCAs.[4] This crucial feature, implemented after twenty-eight years, gave new clues to sleuths like Virgil.

I, too, wanted to find out. Did USAA, for example, hide a secret? The DOL portal would give me the answers, but the LCA spreadsheet for just one financial year—running into hundreds of megabytes—took a few minutes to open. Wouldn't it be nice if a website allowed me to plug and play, saving me time and hassle?

Hang on.

Someone had made such a website. 'Can we find out which staffing company supplies H-1B workers to USAA (or the associated body shops for any client)?' I emailed its creator. 'Because if we can get "X" for every scenario (H-1B Worker → Employer (X) → "Layers" → Client), then it would open a new can of worms.'

Virgil replied fifteen minutes later. 'h1bhuntinglicenses.com/2019 apps.php. Select secondary business entity name in the list. Enter USAA and hit submit.'

I first wanted to check the H-1Bs directly hired by the insurance giant. For this, too, I used Virgil's website. I selected 'employer name' from the huge drop-down menu and first typed 'USAA', then 'United Services Automobile Association'. Found four results: all for 'USAA Real Estate Company'. Maybe its hiring practices were fair? I then clicked 'secondary business entity name' and keyed 'USAA'. The new page blew up—and so did my mind. But even this didn't represent the true extent because many consultancies mentioned the full form on the LCAs: 'United Services Automobile Association'. Now I had two huge spreadsheets revealing USAA's professional links, and to examine them, I reported my findings in the following format:

Third-Party Consultancies	H-1B Dependent Consultancies	Consultancies Paying Back Wages for H-1B Violations	Consultancies Hiring Visa Mills' Graduates	Consultancies' H-1B Workers at Client	H-1Bs Earning Much Less Than Median Salaries
A	B	C	D	E	F

Where,

A = the number of unique third-party consultancies obtaining certified LCAs for H-1B workers for a client (such as, in this case, USAA) in FY 2019.[5]

B = the percentage of third-party consultancies being 'H-1B Dependent' (which, created by the American Competitiveness and Workforce Improvement Act in 1998, measured if a company had a heavy composition of, or bias towards, H-1B workers.[6] It's a binary estimation: a company is either H-1B Dependent or not).[7]

C = the percentage of third-party consultancies, investigated by the Department of Labor (DOL) for H-1B violations, which paid back wages to their employees in the period 2005 to 2023.[8]

D = the percentage of third-party consultancies intending to sponsor green cards for visa mills' graduates in FY 2019.[9]

E = the number of H-1B workers, with visas sponsored by third-party consultancies, corresponding to the total certified LCAs for a client.[10]

F = the percentage of H-1B workers at the client, hired via third-party consultancies, offered much less than the median salaries (Level I and II). H-1B employers could choose from four prevailing wages—Level I, Level II, Level III and Level IV—equalling the 17th, 34th, 50th and 67th percentile of the total wages surveyed for an occupation in an area. Level I and Level II then, considered for this analysis, were way less than the median salaries (50th percentile).[11]

A higher percentage of consultancies gravitating to visa mills and committing H-1B violations showed that they preferred—and exploited—mediocre foreign workers. A higher percentage of H-1Bs earning much less than the median salaries contradicted their 'best and the brightest' tags. And a higher percentage of H-1B Dependent consultancies proved that they excluded (or discriminated against) American professionals. So this table represented the ultimate debasement of the H-1B programme: consultancies exploiting foreign workers, profiting visa mills and snubbing American techies.

But before calling a parameter 'higher', we had to first evaluate the 'average'. The above criteria were conservative. I considered, for example, just fifteen dubious entities,[12] famous on immigration forums as 'Day-1

CPT' colleges, for the visa mills investigation (even though the actual number is much more). Then, analysing the data in the USCIS, Student and Exchange Visitor Program and Work and Hour Division datasets over the last two decades—which contained information on H-1B Dependent consultancies,[13] SEVP-certified schools and consultancies paying back wages for H-1B violations—I found the following probabilities for an average H-1B firm:

H-1B Dependent	Paid Back Wages for H-1B Violations	Hiring a Visa Mill's Graduate
5%[14]	<1%[15]	<1%[16]

If a client, for example, had 200 third-party consultancies (a huge hypothetical figure!) then, in a normal scenario, around 10 of them would have been H-1B dependent (5 per cent), two would have paid back wages (1 per cent) and two would have hired visa mills' graduates (1 per cent). This gave us a yardstick to determine if an American client, via third-party consultancies, exploited the H-1B programme.

To find out more about USAA's contractors, I combined the two spreadsheets—with the client names 'USAA' and 'United Services Automobile Association'—and filtered out the duplicate contractors.[17]

Third-Party Consultancies	H-1B Dependent Consultancies	Consultancies Paying Back Wages for H-1B Violations	Consultancies Hiring Visa Mills' Graduates	Consultancies' H-1B Workers at Client	H-1Bs Earning Much Less Than Median Salaries
295	73%[18]	18%	21%	1,450	82%

Well.

Two hundred ninety-five third-party consultancies obtaining certified LCAs for 1,450 H-1B workers in one year. Virgil had applied for over a decade—and yet, nothing. They were all here: the 'villains' of his life. Every metric—consultancies preferring H-1B workers, committing H-1B violations and hiring visa mills' graduates—was damning when compared to the stats of a regular firm. H-1B dependent? Fifteen times. H-1B violations? Eighteen times. Visa mills? Twenty-one times. These figures erased all ambiguities. What happened to Virgil, and others like him, was not an accident but, as Kumar said once, a 'planned murder'.

HCL America and TCS alone comprised 41 per cent of the total certified LCAs for USAA in FY 2019. The other big players—such as Accenture (4), IBM (74),[19] Ernst & Young (1), KForce (12), PricewaterhouseCoopers Advisory Services (2) and Wipro (14)—contributed 9 per cent. Desi consultancies dominated the other half, including Manu's employer, Infocon Logix; Appi Reddy's MicroInfo; and a firm popping up in Virgil's investigation, Yash & Lujan (Y&L) Consulting.

The numbers, though, revealed only one-half of this story. The other half needed the voice of H-1B workers. But scared of getting fired and deported, they swallowed insults, endured exploitation and kept quiet. I saw this fear myself. In 2018, during my first year of reporting, I contacted many H-1B workers. No one agreed to an interview—not even anonymously. Some college acquaintances, working for desi consultancies, began ignoring my calls and emails. That silence taught me a foundational lesson: that, burnt for long, H-1Bs could only trust their own distrust.

The internet, however, gave them an armour that life did not: anonymity. Helping foreign professionals find employment, the website MyVisaJobs.com published profiles of varied firms and allowed employees to post 'reviews'. It cracked open the last piece in the puzzle: the voice of H-1Bs, threatened and muzzled over the last three decades.

But anonymous reviews also raised concerns. What if they lied? What if they hid ulterior motives? What if they wanted to avenge some other grievances? All valid questions, but on MyVisaJobs, hundreds and hundreds, if not thousands, of desi consultancies had awful reviews. Countless complaints mirrored the experiences of Manu, Kumar and his YouTube subscribers. Many contained verifiable leads on employee lawsuits, DOL investigations and 'sister concern' companies.

Much before MyVisaJobs, H-1Bs had themselves created two websites, DesiCrunch.com and Goolti.com. Like their successor, they functioned as whisper networks, where H-1Bs warned each other about shady firms. Many reviews on DesiCrunch and Goolti, both long defunct,[20] matched the ones on MyVisaJobs. Anonymous tips, whisper networks, suppressed grievances in those thousands of comments: the reviews on MyVisaJobs transcended the rants and rails of foreign workers; they wailed the oral history of the H-1B programme.

Anonymous complaints could be risky, too, as many body shops were mom-and-pop operations, but even then, negative reviews rained on the website. Among USAA's contractors, at least eighty-one (or 27 per cent) had scathing reviews. A 'BOGUS company', wrote someone named Venturpalli on Yash & Lujan Consulting's MyVisaJobs page in 2018. 'They say they have [a] sister company name "Sistema Technologies" that is BOGUS as well.'[21] Another commenter said an employee, Meena Chebolu—also mentioned by Venturpalli—contacted him to sponsor his visa. He paid. 'One day she emailed me saying my petition wasn't picked in the lottery and that I'd get a check for the refund money minus the attorney's fees ($1,200). I asked her to send me at least a softcopy of any document that'd prove that my petition was filed and it wasn't picked in the lottery. She said we don't provide any proofs and that I should "trust" them! Now it's been 2 months, and I'm still waiting for my refund!'[22] Srinivas Vemuri wrote, 'They take money for H-1B. You will get your salary after five week. Literally a mental torture.'[23]

Riding the dot-com wave, Y&L Consulting, headquartered in San Antonio, had opened in 1999 with three employees.[24] Two decades later, it grew to a staff strength of 450, expanding its operations across the country, establishing development centres in Costa Rica and India.[25] When its head office moved to a new address, 5750 Epsilon, the Greater San Antonio Chamber of Commerce published a glowing note, identifying USAA as its 'first client' which had 'played a key role' in establishing the firm.[26] Like its boss, Y&L claimed to support the military.[27] A forty-nine-second YouTube video thanked 'military men and women' for ensuring 'the safety of our families'.[28] Its IT Career Training programme helped 'minorities, veterans, women' and other 'historically underrepresented' groups in the field.[29] The company's co-founder John Lujan had even got elected to the Texas House of

Representatives in February 2016.[30] His motto: 'Using technology to break cycles of poverty.'[31] Irony was too small a word.

But the story of USAA's contractors didn't end—but begin—with Yash & Lujan.

48

Raghav's betrayal continued to sting Kumar. But he had a hunch that this story wasn't over. He opened a May 2016 email. His subscriber Dinesh, an IT worker in Kuwait, had wanted to move to the US. Kumar forwarded his resume to Raghav who said a company, Vectra Infogen, could help—at a cost.

The transaction shocked Kumar. He had always discouraged his subscribers from paying for the visa. Raghav said that he had just played the role of a mediator to help Dinesh, that he had nothing to do with the firm. Someone he knew owned it.

Now Kumar read Dinesh's email again. 'I applied for H-1B through Vectra Infogen and paid Rs 2,50,950 and they provided me LCA number and client letter. Now I found something fishy on DOL portal: my LCA belongs to a different company.' He had attached three PDFs: two LCAs and a client letter. His LCA's 'employer information' mentioned Vectra Infogen. But the copy on the DOL's website stated 'Tropica Tech'. Dinesh was accusing Kumar of fraud. What? He had just forwarded the resume to Raghav and nothing else. But what if Dinesh was right? Had Raghav exploited Kumar's channel to cheat more people?

Gopal! A Java professional in Hyderabad, he had wanted an H-1B visa. Raghav offered to help. When Gopal's petition didn't get approved, he requested Kumar for a refund. Kumar, in turn, emailed Raghav in May 2014. 'Gopal has to repay his bank loan it seems. Hence he messaged to return the fee.'

Kumar wrote to Gopal. 'I lost h1b fees to Raghav. Did you get your money?'

'They deducted attorney cost. I got Rs 2,17,500 from Rs 3,20,000.'

'Your lucky, got some. I didn't get single dollar. Did he show proof he paid 3rd party?'

'OMG, we were cheated by him. He didn't. I paid him as you know him and are researching these issues since long time.'

'He cheated me too. He attack Hindus and try to convert me into his converted religion.'

Kumar's ex-colleague in India, Samarth, had also contacted him for his friend, Sai. Kumar introduced him to Raghav. He paid for the H-1B filing, but it didn't clear the lottery. He got no refund or proof. Sai emailed Kumar. 'I'm sure they never filed petition. They cheated me. Could you let me know how to move legally?'

Sai got half the amount after a year. But not just these three, Kumar had forwarded other resumes, too: Shreyas D.M., Vishwanath Golla, Atulya Alladi and several more. Did they pay Raghav? Did their visas get approved?

Raghav had used Kumar's YouTube channel—exploited its fame, name and influence. Two more friends had tried something similar. After opening his consultancy, Srijan asked Kumar for the email IDs of his subscribers for 'network training'. Kumar warned him to stay away from 'crime'. He also refused the owner of an IT coaching institute. These associations could have benefited him through referral earnings, but he hadn't created Kumar Exclusive for money. He could see through them; he could not even see Raghav.

'Whatever emails you received on h1b@usa.com,' he wrote to Raghav, 'please forward to me. Because it is given to all subscribers.' Followed by: 'Stop attacking Hindus in USA. Stop religion conversions in USA.'

No reply.

Another email after five days. 'You snatched all my contacts to this email id. Did not share password though you said it is for KE channel. Second, you robbed me $2,000 in single chat. You did not reciprocate what I did to you—trust. You not only stole $2,000 from me but at least 12 of my followers. A boy said this; stop videos because you and Raghav robbed him. You not only cheated me in the name of GOD but also cheated people in the name of Kumar is unable to digest. What is the difference between you and thief? This is where you are very wrong and probably this is my last email.'

Raghav replied ten days later. 'You lack empathy and that's why I chose not to communicate with you ever again. I tried reaching you several times to return your money, but you never got back. Instead you raised false allegations on me. First, you got a job after 3 months of my work and you're not grateful. I did my best to save you, but you ruined my trust and friendship and lost my respect. I never thought you'd behave like a narcissist.'

Kumar emailed again. 'What is stopping you to return my money?'

'Q: What is stopping you to return my money? A: Your account details.'

Did Raghav not have them? Of course, he did. How did Gopi receive $2,000? Kumar had made a bank transfer.

Raghav never returned the amount.

When character is lost, everything is lost.

49

Just the negative MyVisaJobs reviews for USAA's contractors totalled 25,000 words—an eighty-page primer on employee exploitation. A pattern common to countless American clients.

'They force you to sign contract with them which have clauses like 18 month employment and 10K fine for leaving the company. Basically they try to slave you.' (PVR America.[32])

'This is the worst employer who never care of employees, without professional ethics and only caring people with same caste or same regional/racial thoughts.' (Galaxy I Technologies.[33])

'When you really want to leave them and grab a better opportunity, be ready to for go your pay for a month.' (Icloud Technologies.[34])

'The HR Ram Prasad ... replies to only a few girls. And also I have the chat screenshots that he was texted with other female employee asking for ____ favor.' (Saibersys.[35])

'I struggled hard and spend more time and energy to get payments than actual work I do at clients ... I lost my years of energy. Check bounces, wire transfers, partial payments after so much followup is common ... Due to all these and many other issues with ARCH, I had sleepless nights, health problems which indirectly effected work at client places ... I am waiting for my final settlement, i am following up on it for about 3 months now. He started blocking my numbers, whatsapp, no response to emails.' (Arch International Group.[36])

'He doesn't know have any communication or mannerse ... No consultant expects any respect but Rao should have some manners and doesn't needs to treat every of his consultants as donkey's.' (Infosmart Systems.[37])

The last few reviews, whose variants marked countless consultancies on MyVisaJobs, made the H-1B abuse baffling. Greed, deceit, crime? Easy to understand. But not cruelty. The body shop owners could pocket, on average, $25 an hour for just renting out an H-1B worker to a client. $200 a day. For doing nothing. From *one* employee. With almost no investment (or callousness). Even the most modest consultancies employed a few H-1Bs, earning several lakh dollars a year. Yet their owners perpetuated shocking psychological abuses, bordering on human rights violations, repeating a disturbing pattern. As if they were not educated elites but brainless brutes who, right after colonial enslavement, had enslaved their own.

Fifty-three third-party consultancies with certified LCAs for USAA in FY 2019 had paid back wages to their employees. Their 1,182 violations, affecting 801 H-1B workers, produced back wages worth $3.73 million.[38] The guilty parties featured reputed names: Ernst & Young US, HCL America, IBM India Private Limited and Wipro. The DOL had, in fact, fined Ernst & Young US and HCL twice. Among the remaining forty-nine companies, nine of them had coughed up multiple fines: Deemsys, Infosmart Systems, Resource Logistics, Sunrise Infotek Corp and Yasme Soft, twice; MPRSoft, Populus Group and V-Soft Consulting Group, thrice; and Compunnel Software Group, four times.[39]

Like USAA's present, its past, too, hid disconcerting secrets. On 25 February 2004, a San Antonio channel, WOAI-TV, ran a piece interviewing former USAA employees who accused the firm of replacing them with Indian workers. The broadcast showed the recording of an internal meeting, where the then CEO, Robert Davis, had praised the offshore IT talent.[40] It also quoted the IT chief, Steve Yates, who, addressing the employees' complaints, said, 'I can see where you could draw that conclusion. That wasn't the intent. If we've gotten there, we kind of backed into it.'

His IT division had spun its own success story. When he joined the insurance giant as the chief information officer in 1999, IT expenses overwhelmed the organisation's revenues. But in less than five years, he 'transformed' the IT department into 'ITCO, a subsidiary with its own profit and loss lines'.[41] Over the last three years, costs plunged and profits soared. In May 2004, a tech magazine, *CIO*, featured Yates and his team in its special issue, 'How to Run I.T. Like a Business'.[42]

But the murmurs surrounding its hiring practices had continued to intensify. In 2001, USAA fired 1,400 employees, including 'an unspecified number of IT workers'.[43] Two years later, the *San Antonio Express-News* reported that around 500 TCS techies comprised nearly '20 per cent of the jobs inside its ITCO division'.[44]

The WOAI-TV story created a huge impact. A local newspaper picked it up, and viewers 'flooded' the TV station with 'calls and emails'—even Yates. 'I wish you would report the facts. Why could you not find the positive things this company does for the San Antonio community?' Senior Vice President Bill Breslin called the piece 'outrageous, one-sided, [and] negative'.

USAA sued the reporter, Tanji Patton, and WOAI-TV's owner, Clear Channel Communications. Citing the Texas Theft Liability Act, it claimed WOAI-TV illegally got a recording and a management manual—the company's 'proprietary trade secrets'—which it 'wouldn't want' its 'competitors to see'.[45]

After two weeks, Yates was gone, with no immediate clarity on whether he had left voluntarily or been fired. Davis called an all-employee meeting, saying the firm had 'taken action—including termination and legal proceedings—against a small group of current and former employees who provided confidential information' to WOAI-TV. His message couldn't have been clearer, stated the *San Antonio Business Journal*, 'Talk to the media and it could cost you your job—or more.'[46]

But an unexpected entity, finally, settled the entire issue: Andhra-Friends folks. On 8 April 2021, a thread popped up on the forum: 'Any USAA Dallas employees/contractors here'?[47]

'A herd of desis there.'[48]

'My [useless] friend faked his interview, using someone else's face 😀😀😀😀 .. now his balls are shivering, when asked to switch on video during work.'[49]

'Put eye glasses and slightly blurr the camera. If it is a white team, they can't recognize the person.'[50]

'Only contractors desi … FT mostly white. USAA is the one of the only few big corporations that don't sponsor H1b … [It also] has great benefits (including pension) and people tended to stick to it for long time.'[51]

Another thread in January 2021: 'Anyone working for USAA? Tell me folks about work culture, about company, etc.'[52]

'For every 2 uncles working FT, 8 TCS contractors.'[53]

'USAA full time is very good bro. 95% of full timers won't leave the company till their retirement … Very comfortable to work with minimal pressure … I worked there for 1 year earlier and liked it.'[54]

'I think you can easily crack the interview … Prepare for White boarding if you are on the programming side.'[55]

'These days they grill you on white board programming for DevOps positions also. What will happen to useless IT admins like me.'[56]

'Proxxxies might have been reason why this has become a standard. Now a days even white managers dont trust a resume.'[57]

'Seeing all the desi batch white uncles might run away too …'[58]

50

After Kumar's fallout with Raghav, ByteCore Consulting replaced VersIT as his employer. Hired at a low percentage rate of 70:30, Kumar would earn $42 per hour. But over a month had passed: zero cents. He emailed the recruiter, Rocky Jones (Ramesh Arun J.), on 28 March. 'I got a call from Kiran'—another ByteCore employee—'regarding timesheets. Please share them with her. I have already put up 137 hours. Please invoice to the vendor prashanth@ohzion.com. I need advance. This is very urgent to pay room rent here.'

Another email to the ByteCore accounts team and Prashanth the next day. 'By this Friday it will be 229 hours and I end up not getting paid for one and a half month, it is impossible. Prashanth, kindly release my money to them ASAP.'

A week passed.

He emailed Prashanth. 'Sir, what will you offer if I transfer my H-1B to you? Instead of helping, guys exploiting my situation.'

'I thought you discussed percentages before joining. Why are you surprised now? Also, did they file your H1? I can transfer your visa once it is approved. While the process is on, it is risky for you to change. We can do better on rates.'

'New employer told, if you do not like the offer, you are free to go. I beg him $1,000 cash (rent and advance) to stay close to work. I am running on credit cards.'

'For now, agree to their terms and keep me posted on the H1 progress. Did they pay advance? You want me to talk to them?'

'Please wait. If you ask them, they might suspect I complained. Because if I get some cash, that solves some financial issues. Same time, I do not want to fight with anyone.'

He contacted Prashanth again after a few days. 'If I joined, would you file LCA and run paychecks for 229+ hours asap? If not paycheck, at least give advance if you apply for visa later.'

'Waiting to get approval for the filed H1 is important. One more filing and more money on it isn't advisable. Ask them for salary advance man. You have several approved timesheets, right? Priya: Did we receive any payments yet?'

'We have not,' she replied. 'I had requested ByteCore to send me the Feb invoice which I haven't got.'

'Priya, Kiran told me over the phone she sent it on March 16th. I did not get any confirmation of that email; I marked to you and her also. Sir, thanks for your kind support.'

By mid-April, Kumar had accumulated 289 hours. Cyber Techsol's Ajay said the payment got delayed because iTech raised a wrong invoice. Kumar emailed an offshore ByteCore employee, Venkat. 'I need salary to be deposited with no further delay. I am tired.' He wrote to Rocky the next day. 'I neither get email nor phone response from Deva. I badly need money to pay my auto loan and credit cards. It is too long to survive in the USA without salary. The problem is: no reply. This is humiliating.'

ByteCore had flouted H-1B rules in the past, too. A DOL investigation concluding in 2017 directed the firm to pay a hefty civil monetary penalty and back wages. Its MyVisaJobs reviews showed that Deva had also followed the other 'rituals' of desi consultancies: owning multiple body shops, charging money for visa filing, refusing to pay health insurance, extracting cash to run payroll, exploiting recent college graduates, harassing employees.

April 17: Kumar fired an email to USCIS complaining about the vendors and his employer. He also emailed the DOL officer Joe, whom he had contacted a few years ago, enclosing the spreadsheets documenting his unpaid hours. (He kept updating K as well.)

An email to the ByteCore HR, Smriti, two days later. 'I am fed up following up with India team and have no clarity if they will pay a penny. I also fedup following up with three vendors to release money. Vendors blame employer—common here. Would you give salary or advance on 289 hours approved? If not, write clearly so I would not have false hope and apply for a new credit card.'

No response.

Unpaid hours: 390.

He called Priya, saying if he didn't receive his payment, he'd stop working. She screamed: 'We will sue you if you leave in the middle of the project.'[59]

Kumar finally got paid for the first week, $1,800. But still no clarity on the rest. He had become so dejected that he'd email Rocky not to follow up but vent. 'H1B is an indentured servitude, everyone take him for a ride. No problem, I will go back to my country happily rather than facing humiliation. H1b life is not worth anymore.' He wrote to me the next day. 'Please get me a job in India brother ASAP. I hate this life.'

In mid-May, he emailed the only person who cared to reply. 'Rocky, whom do you report? I want his email id or phone. Because it is no use begging or writing emails to you, Smriti, Venkat. No response on salaries for my 466 hours. Do they not have money? Or not pay salaries? Or only to me? What is the problem?'

June 2018: still no payment for April. The long stretch of unemployment last year had drained his savings. Paying rent in both Baltimore and Webster stretched the limits of his desperation. America made no sense.

No choice anymore.

First, his wife and kids would depart, then he'd follow. He bought them one-way flight tickets to India. 'Hi everyone, I am vacating my apartment.' He recorded a video.[60] A bright day, Kumar in his car, smiling. 'I am not sure whether I will come back to America or not. So hats off to all the subscribers. Thank you one and all.' He looked tired, but smiled again. 'Haters also, I love you, raja. There is no hatred in my heart. The only problem is'—his face turned sombre—'the friend who supposed to help in making videos. He took $2,000 for H-1B, which I was supposed to send for my mum's surgery. He is involved in H-1B scams.'

But his story had found a new chapter. 'There is one journalist writing from India, Tanul. I will write his email in the next video. Those who are willing to share their experiences, they can share it to him. And Virgil, you know, right? You can share with him as well. If my project extend, then I will continue, otherwise I will leave on June 30th to India. Because I am not getting paid.' His face turned gloomy. 'Whatever it might be, it is too late … America is part of my journey. It is not a destination.'

He emailed Smriti. 'I have 43K loan on credit cards, new cards are declining and credit history is going down drastically. KINDLY DO NEEDFUL. 3 months 10 days, I lived without giving rent in Maryland by explaining my H1B plight and the landlord understood. (I still owe him.) I have no money to pay rent in NY hence I throw every stuff in the apartment and my kid cried.'

No response.

ByteCore sent him four pay cheques, detailing the amount it had not paid. Did these people have no ethics, no shame? The next day, a letter from Smriti. 'I regret to inform that effective of June 30th 2018, you are terminated from ByteCore Consulting. As your services are over before your H-1B period, the company will cover the cost of your return transportation. Let us know if you wish to accept a one-way airplane ticket.'

Kumar wrote to Ajay, enclosing a spreadsheet containing the email IDs and phone numbers, names and designations, of ByteCore employees: 'Contact who ever you want and get my money of May and June as per LCA. They are not paying medical also. I will lodge complaint about all layers if they do not take back termination letter.'

Now only one person could save his immigration status: Prashanth. His countless pleas to Ajay and iTech Infologic's Kalyan had produced nothing. But if he could transfer his visa to Ohzion, then he could stay in the US. 'I respect you sir. Under your guidance only, I can ask them for paychecks otherwise I won't get it. I called several times Deva Ram, he spoke filthy to me in Telugu. I contacted his brother Harsha who scolded me for writing emails. Please see if you can save my h1b status before June 29.'

Prashanth wasn't interested. Now Kumar didn't even want to stay till the end of the project. He bought a one-way flight ticket from Detroit, packed his bags and drove to his sister's place. He stopped at a Pennsylvania rest area, got out of the car and fixed his phone on a selfie stick. Behind him, across the road, stood a series of freight trucks, the clouds above a poetic grey. 'Friends, everyone. Probably this is my last but one video from US.'[61] He wore a cap and a faded grey t-shirt with a US flag on it. 'I vacated Maryland. I quit project one week ahead.' He walked; the sun lit his face. 'Because'—his voice beeped as he used cuss words—'are not paying salary.'

Another cut, another rest area, now in Michigan. Recording the minute details of his last road trip in the country, this unpaid H-1B worker had become the equivalent of reality TV. Kumar titled the video: 'Finally, I quit H1B life with a smile! My last video from USA.'

Before boarding his flight, he made another video.[62] 'I quit H-1B life it doesn't mean I stop fighting. Email me all the evidence—if you are not getting paid salaries or anything else related to employer—let's send them to jail.'[63]

51

WITCH firms dominated the list of contractors supplying foreign workers to USAA, mirroring their continued dominance of the H-1B programme. Cognizant secured the most visas in 2019. TCS ranked third, Infosys sixth, Wipro twelfth and HCL America eighteenth. Analysing their LCAs by salaries produced the following result:[64]

'WITCH'	Level I Wages (17th Percentile)	Level II Wages (34th Percentile)	Level III Wages (50th Percentile)	Level IV Wages (67th Percentile)	Other Wage Surveys	Total LCAs	Much Less Than Median Wages
Wipro	0	11,656	834	25	62	12,577	93%
Infosys	1	16,738	3,162	1,493	120	21,514	78%
TCS	0	14,397	1,271	16	107	15,791	91%
Cognizant	788	14,443	7,411	2,493	396	25,531	60%
HCL America	567	3,941	2,979	1,353	380	9,220	49%

Barring HCL America, none of these companies paid anywhere near the median figure. Quite far from the 'best and the brightest' metric. So yes, the 'Infosyses' exploited the H-1B programme. But what about the 'Intels'? Three spots below Cognizant, Amazon.com Services ranked fourth.[65] Google, fifth. Skip Infosys and you'd meet Microsoft at seventh. Walk past Capgemini America and you'd find Facebook at ninth, followed by Larsen & Toubro Infotech, then Apple. Unlike the WITCH firms, the Big Tech giants—the 'responsible' users of the guest worker programme—were known for lucrative pay cheques. But their LCA data[66] revealed a more layered story:

Big Tech	Level I Wages (17th Percentile)	Level II Wages (34th Percentile)	Level III Wages (50th Percentile)	Level IV Wages (67th Percentile)	Other Wage Surveys	Total LCAs	Much Less Than Median Wages
Amazon[67]	5,270	7,158	1,532	152	485	14,597	85%
Apple	558	8,279	8,432	8,838	3	26,110	34%
Facebook	1	591	1,509	994	3,023	6,118	10%
Google	13	4,944	2,752	678	698	9,085	55%
Microsoft	3,499	4,198	1,842	338	112	9,989	77%

Infosys, Cognizant and HCL dwarfed Amazon's salaries. HCL and Cognizant fared better than Microsoft. Google, poorer than HCL.

In December 2020, the U.S. Department of Justice (DOJ) sued Facebook, alleging that it 'routinely reserved jobs' for visa holders through the Permanent Labor Certification Program (PERM). As part of that process, employers had to 'test the labor market' in the job's 'geographic area' to ensure that it had 'no able, qualified, and available U.S. workers' willing to accept the job offer.[68] (The same criteria had embarrassed the immigration firm Cohen & Grigsby in 2007 when its vice president blurted out on camera, 'Our goal is clearly not to find a qualified and interested US worker.'[69]) Facebook used varied means to deter 'U.S. workers from applying to certain positions', alleged the DOJ, such as asking them to submit applications 'by mail only'. It also 'refused to consider U.S. workers who applied' to those 'positions and hired only temporary visa holders'. The Department of Labor, too, audited the firm's 'recruitment activities related to PERM applications'.

Facebook reached separate settlement agreements with the DOJ and DOL in October 2021. It agreed to pay a 'civil penalty of $4.75 million to the United States' and 'up to $9.5 million to eligible victims of Facebook's alleged discrimination'.[70] This represented the 'largest fine and monetary award', stated the DOJ, recovered under the Immigration and Nationality Act's 'anti-discrimination provision'.[71]

An H-1B critic, Professor Ron Hira, called the settlement a 'slap-on-the-wrist' for Facebook and a 'slap-on-the-face' for American workers.[72] 'The company received the 6th most PERM certifications [3,002] in FYs 2019 and 2020,' added Hira. 'How many did the [DOL] deny while

FB was discriminating? ZERO.' He considered the settlement 'too small' to 'deter future bad behaviour'. The $14 million fine appeared like 'a rounding error' when compared to Facebook's revenue, '86 billion (0.0016%)'. Its discriminatory hiring, over just one-and-a-half years, had harmed thousands of Americans. 'What will the victims receive? A few hundred dollars?'

Hira also discussed the pervasive discrimination against US workers in Silicon Valley. '[Just] see the suits against Oracle, Cisco, etc.' Facebook retained a 'leading immigration law firm' for its 'thousands of PERM applications'. The same company, Fragomen, represented 'Google, Oracle, Amazon' and countless tech giants, including Apple. 'Is DOJ examining employment practices at those firms?'[73]

This time, it did. In November 2023, Apple settled with the DOJ to resolve allegations that it had 'discriminated in hiring and recruitment against U.S. citizens and certain non-U.S. citizens' and violated the Immigration and Nationality Act's 'anti-discrimination requirements' while filling 'PERM positions'.[74]

If desi consultancies had their own playbook, then so did the Silicon Valley giants. 'Apple did not advertise [the PERM] positions on its external job website,' said the DOJ. It also directed all 'PERM position' applicants to 'mail paper applications', even though the company permitted electronic applications otherwise. In some instances, Apple did not consider electronic applications for PERM positions from its 'own employees'.[75] Almost everything about this settlement echoed the Facebook judgement—even the climax. Apple had to 'pay up to $25 million in back pay and civil penalties', the 'largest award' recovered at that time under the Immigration and Nationality Act's 'anti-discrimination provision'.[76]

Nothing satiated Big Tech though. Even after obtaining 25,000 visas[77] in 2019, it still relied on body shops. The H-1B corruption, in its most benign avatar, carried a cheeky subversive flair: workers conning corporations, powerless gaining powers, the East trumping the West. But on closer inspection, this story merely reinforced the old (colonial) order: White overlords flashing the visas to shackle Brown techies to expand their empires. Corporate America also deployed other third-world pawns, such as the WITCH firms and desi consultancies, to do its dirty work. If Big Tech solidified America's supremacy, then it had been sustained, if not built, on the backs of dehumanised workers. Consider the numbers for just one year, FY 2019, below:

Big Tech[78]	Third-Party Consultancies	H-1B Dependent Consultancies	Consultancies Paying Back Wages for H-1B Violations	Consultancies Hiring Visa Mills' Graduates	Consultancies' H-1B Workers at Client	H-1Bs Earning Much Less Than Median Salaries
Amazon[79]	33[80]	45%[81]	21%	18%	141	67%
Apple[82]	380[83]	64%[84]	16%	21%	4,358	86%[85]
Facebook[86]	86[87]	51%[88]	10%	16%	396	79%[89]
Google[90]	217[91]	62%[92]	21%	15%	1,435	75%[93]
Microsoft	246[94]	60%[95]	15%	19%	1,200	83%[96]

Seven hundred ninety-four third-party consultancies had obtained certified LCAs for 7,530 H-1Bs, offering eighty-three per cent of them much less than the median salaries.[97] Even worse, 114 companies (or 14 per cent) had paid $8.29 million in back wages to 1,403 employees for H-1B violations.[98]

Big Tech crowned the H-1B pyramid, but the 'Thought Control' ecosystem, led by the media and the academia, had played a starring role in spreading its misleading assertions via selective reporting, dubious studies and shrewd lobbying. How did they fare then? Well, let's find out.

First, the mainstream media (and other firms in the same family).

Media[99]	Third-Party Consultancies	H-1B Dependent Consultancies	Consultancies Paying Back Wages for H-1B Violations	Consultancies Hiring Visa Mills' Graduates	Consultancies' H-1B Workers at Client	H-1Bs Earning Much Less Than Median Salaries
Fox[100]	61	57%	13%	21%	160	69%
The Washington Post	6	33%	33%	17%	7	86%
The New York Times	5	80%	40%	40%	20	80%

Similar pattern: desi consultancies, H-1B violations, low salaries. The third-party players included 'WITCH' firms: Infosys (*Times*), Cognizant (Fox and *Times*), HCL America (Fox).[101] But they also comprised shady obscure entities. A *Times* contractor, Cavalier IT, had several negative MyVisaJobs reviews: 'Its a small company … run by one desi guy who treats the consultants very badly … i need to beg him for salary every month.'[102] The *Post*'s contractor, Stackit Professionals, fared no better. 'The management … don't pay as per the agreement. [It] has bad track record with Government.'[103] Of Fox's sixty-one contractors, thirty-five had negative or suspicious reviews: 'You will be forced to produce resumes with your own name and forge 6-8 years of experience. You will … be told to lie about not only your experience but your residency, including breaking the law and telling them you are a citizen or greencard holder … Oh … did I mention someone will do interview on your behalf.' (Flexon Technologies.[104])

What about academia?

Academia[105]	Third-Party Consultancies	H-1B Dependent Consultancies	Consultancies Paying Back Wages for H-1B Violations	Consultancies Hiring Visa Mills' Graduates	Consultancies' H-1B Workers at Client	H-1Bs Earning Much Less Than Median Salaries
Columbia University[106]	6[107]	83%	50%	67%	8	62.5%
Yale University[108]	19[109]	74%	32%	47%	27	89%
Stanford University[110]	45[111]	78%	20%	13%	95	71%

Made perfect sense. Drooling over cheap labour was, after all, a national obsession. But these numbers were still astounding, considering universities could hire unlimited H-1Bs at academia-level salaries. The list of third-party consultancies comprised countless body shops with awful reviews and hefty fines. But even among them, one stood out: Marlabs, a firm that had procured LCAs for 'Columbia University Information Technology'.

First, its MyVisaJobs reviews.[112]

'They will ask you [to] pay the employer tax … No bench pay.'

'INS/ IRS needs to audit this company and look into their bonus math spreadsheet which they give out to their employees quarterly.'

'This company has created fake resumes on my name without my acknowledgement and finally when I questioned them and left the company they are on my back for money. They are literally blackmailing me to pay certain amount and they warned me about legal notices.'

'To all those contemplating joining this horrible fraudster company and to all the victimized employees and ex-employees. A class action suit has been filed against Marlabs last yr.'

Sandeep R. Ramakapeta, an Indian national, had joined Marlabs as a 'programmer/analyst' on H-1B visa.[113] After his project got over, stated the lawsuit complaint, the company informed Ramakapeta it would 'not pay him' on bench. In February 2007, an employee, Mani Kurup, directed him to submit a 'false request' for a 'voluntary, unpaid leave retroactive to January 2' till March 15.[114] If he didn't, Kurup would cancel his visa. Ramakapeta obeyed. He found a project at Bausch + Lomb via the vendor System Efficiency for $100 per hour. It would take a $25 cut and, following the agreement, Marlabs would give him 75 per cent of the rest, $56.25. But his employer said the vendor had lowered the amount to $70. Marlabs told Ramakapeta to call its employee, Robert Kaufman, to crosscheck. He did; Kaufman confirmed.[115]

In May 2008, a new System Efficiency employee, Alicia Bearden, inadvertently sent an extension purchase order to Ramakapeta for … $75. Here's how the alleged wage theft worked: the vendor created a purchase order every three months stating it would pay Marlabs $75. Sending each document as an MS Word file, it knew 'Marlabs would alter' the rate from $75 to $70 before forwarding it to Ramakapeta.[116] When he confronted Marlabs about the year-long wage theft, the consultancy repaid the owed principal amount but not the interest. Besides, it only gave him—'on a monthly prorated basis'—an annual salary of $60,000.[117] It had to distribute the leftover amounts via quarterly payments. But from October 2008 to July 2009, it paid nothing. In June 2009, Ramakapeta informed Marlabs about his project's imminent expiration. Kurup demanded another unpaid leave of absence, threatening to revoke his visa. Ramakapeta quit and filed a class-action lawsuit. While the 'exact number of class members is unknown', the complaint stated, 'it is believed to be in the hundreds or thousands'.[118]

The causes of action:

Count I—Violation of the Racketeer Influenced and Corrupt Organization Act ('RICO'), 18 U.S.C. § 1962(C).
Count II—Violation of RICO, 18 USC § 1962(d) (RICO conspiracy).
Count III—Violations of 18 USC §§ 1589-1590, 1595 (forced labor and trafficking with respect to forced labor).
Count IV—Violation of 'New Jersey RICO', NJ STAT § 2C:41-2(C).
Count V—Violation of New Jersey RICO, NJ STAT § 2C:41-2(D) (RICO conspiracy).
Count VI—Violations of New Jersey statutory wage law.
Count VII—Breach of contract under New Jersey common law.

On 20 December 2010, Ramakapeta, through his lawyers, filed a notice of voluntary dismissal with the court and, ten days later, the court dismissed the case 'with prejudice, against all defendants'.[119] It set Marlabs free.[120]

The firm's sordid history, like that of many desi consultancies', included H-1B violations, too. In a two-year-long investigation, concluding in July 2010, the DOL ordered Marlabs to pay back wages worth $63,570 to three employees. Eleven years later, the federal agency struck again, finding the company had committed twenty-five H-1B violations, directing it to pay $196,150 to twenty-five employees (an amount so high it ranked eighty-ninth among the 2,321 H-1B back wages).[121]

Besides the client–contractor relationship, something else, too, connected Columbia and Marlabs: its CEO, Siby Vadakekkara, served as a mentor and digital advisor for Columbia University's Executive Master of Science in Technology Management programme.[122] In late 2013, stated the consultancy's Facebook page, Marlabs 'fondly hosted' the 'tri-city tour of the Professors from Columbia University, Pat O'Connell and Dr. Corey Hirsch', in India, who shared their 'expert opinion on the subject #TechnologyManagement for the students of Alliance University, Loyola Institute of Business Administration and Rajagiri Centre for Business Studies'.[123] They also visited Marlabs's office in Bangalore spending 'quality time' with its employees and giving them 'advice on Technology Management best practices'.[124]

After four-and-a-half years, the firm appointed Columbia's Center for Technology Management Director, Arthur Langer, as a non-executive director on the board.[125] On 17 January 2018, Marlabs sponsored a CIO Forum hosted by the Center for Technology Management at Columbia University, moderated by Langer.[126] Eleven months later, the consultancy partnered with a non-profit, Workforce Opportunity Services (founded by Langer), to enhance veterans' skills to help them find jobs.[127]

Besides Marlabs, another firm, Summitworks Technologies, had got an LCA approved for 'Columbia University Information Technology'. It had awful MyVisaJobs reviews going as far back as 2010[128] and, like Marlabs, paid back wages to its employees.[129]

To find the true extent of the H-1B abuse, I chose an illustrative example from each of these sectors: pharmaceutical, aviation, energy, insurance and non-profit.

Clients[130]	Third-Party Consultancies	H-1B Dependent Consultancies	Consultancies Paying Back Wages for H-1B Violations	Consultancies Hiring Visa Mills' Graduates	Consultancies' H-1B Workers at Client	H-1Bs Earning Much Less Than Median Salaries
Pfizer	85[131]	61%[132]	20%	24%	802	73%[133]
Boeing[134]	55	60%[135]	25%	33%	672	84%[136]
Chevron[137]	114[138]	68%[139]	20%	18%	718	86%[140]
State Farm[141]	201[142]	72%[143]	16%	28%	1,125	78%
United Nations[144]	22[145]	73%	18%	18%	90	78%

Here too, one 'contractor' stood out: the University of Washington had filed an LCA for Pfizer. None of these clients were above the shadow of 'WITCH' corporations or awful desi consultancies, not even the UN, which was associated with four companies committing H-1B violations: Compunnel Software Group, Hexaware Technologies, Infosys and Synaptein Solutions.[146]

The collective transgressions of deceitful contractors made for an alarming picture, producing back wages worth $6.54 million.[147] Like the associates of Big Tech, media and academia, they had committed egregious H-1B violations in recent years. But the companies thrived;

the workers suffered. Congress had given the best possible gift to corporate America—a present that never ran out, for a birthday that came each day.

52

Manu's office moved from Uppal to HITEC City. He didn't want to stay in the company guesthouse anymore. With a colleague's help, he found a one-bedroom flat close to the office for Rs 12,220 per month. He didn't buy a fridge or a microwave. The kitchen had no utensils or a gas stove; he stored his bags in it. The bedroom was as bare: just a portable fan near a low-lying bed. He put a table in the living room, his play and work station. To its right stood a grey washing machine with a plastic cover.

He had spiders and cockroaches for company. Cockroaches in his bathroom, cockroaches in his bed sheets, cockroaches in his suitcases. Sometimes, rats showed up. Once a centipede bit him, and he had to skip work. While walking to the office at night, he worried about street dogs biting him. He whistled and ambled, hoping his practised nonchalance would work. HITEC City was polluted; his cough had returned. He popped tablets and kept a medical kit.

Manu got his Canadian PR result the next month. 'Dear Mr Mitra, following a careful review of your application and supporting materials we are unable to nominate you under the SINP Occupations In-Demand (No Employment Offer) Category. You must have proof of $12,164 CAD in your account(s) for at least 3 months prior to your application and maintained throughout the immigration process.'

He called Bhargava to check about the bank statement. No help this time. Manu relied on MS Paint again. He emailed a bank letter to

Sagar which showed the balance on 26 November 2016 as Rs 8,21,353. He also enclosed a bank statement from July 2016 to January 2017, where his balance ranged from Rs 7 lakh to 8.21 lakh. Sagar uploaded the documents and submitted the application.

'Please inform beforehand that the application will get rejected if the documents are not as per the laws of government,' Manu wrote to Glonect Solutions's case coordinator, Prabhu. 'For example, I submitted the documents, but my bank statement was not three months old and it got rejected. You all are experienced, right? You have handled so many applications, right? If you could have warned me, I would have tried a different option. I am not blaming, some of it is also my fault that I already knew, but I thought you guys will take care, so I did not worry.'

Glonect Solutions notified him about his application a few months later. 'The SINP occupation list got revised and your occupation got removed. We are working on other alternatives and will update you ASAP.'

Manu emailed the branch head, Janhvi. 'Can you please get me the refund? If you would have properly conveyed that I needed to maintain three months' bank statement, I would have been satisfied. But I felt very bad that even after paying Rs 74,750, I did not get that information and you people just submitted the application like that. Pure negligence, which always happens in India. As you know, my mom kicked me out and my dad does not care if I am dead or alive. No friends, no cousins and at home they said they will donate the [family] property to charity. There is no reason to stay in this country since I lost everything. Please consider refunding the amount as I have to pay a loan.' Glonect returned 25 per cent.

Manu's insomnia worsened. He drank a bottle of Blender's Pride every week. He relied on it so much that he needed increasing amounts to fall asleep. His meagre salary couldn't sustain such a coping mechanism. So he began popping the old tablets again, buying sleep.

One day, he wrote a long Facebook post, copy-pasting his resume, asking a question: how could he find a good life? A friend called him, suggesting an idea: Manu had written many research papers and got a patent, why did he not consider the EB-1 green card?[148] A premium immigration category, EB-1 was reserved for 'an alien of extraordinary ability', 'an outstanding professor or researcher' or a 'multinational executive or manager'.[149]

To be eligible for 'extraordinary ability', a foreign national had to 'meet at least 3 of the 10 criteria,' stated the USCIS website, 'or provide evidence of a one-time achievement (i.e., Pulitzer, Oscar, Olympic Medal) as well as evidence showing that you will be continuing to work in the area of your expertise. No offer of employment or labor certification is required'.[150] Manu scrolled down and read all ten conditions. Three of them seemed relevant: 'Evidence of your original scientific, scholarly … contributions of major significance to the field', 'evidence of your authorship of scholarly articles in professional or major trade publications or other major media' and 'evidence of your membership in associations in the field which demand outstanding achievement of their members'.[151]

Based on his patent filing and review and research papers—ranging from material science to nanotechnology to data processing, published in obscure journals—Manu thought he cleared the first two criteria. Quantity never bothered him, quality did. Because when he had written to *IEEE*, *Nature* or *Science*, they rejected him. But he had become so desperate to leave India that hope elbowed out pragmatism. If his green card got approved and he moved to the US, then he'd contact Nitish. Maybe Infocon Logix would offer him a job? He'd work as a contractor for the first two years, then ask the client for a full-time position. His dream. As a green card holder, he wouldn't have to worry about the bench, payroll or projects. Or limited time to find employment. Or living at his employer's mercy.

Manu would be—finally—free.

53

AndhraFriends folks continued to discuss not just Appi's fortunes but also his duplicity.

'[He] is nicely rolling in money, right … but I have heard he doesn't pay anyone properly. How true is it?'

'Yes plenty of complaints on him for withholding payments from OPT students, sometimes upto 6 months …'

'So much OA [OverAction] from some guy who robs OPT students off money?'[152]

But something else, too, intrigued them.

'What was the query? Appi palyed poker with uscis?'[153]

'[S]omething about company tax returns … also DOL complaints.'[154]

'Budweiser beer + 2 pieces of chicken biryani + 15 people in Single room accomdation with no job for six months = MICROINFO Consultancy DOL twweted.'[155]

A DOL investigation—from 1 January 2018 to 30 March 2018—directed MicroInfo to pay $18,698 in back wages.[156] ICE had also raided Silicon Valley University[157] (or Appi's cash cow, according to AndhraFriends members),[158] precipitating its downfall in April 2018. The two federal agencies had zoomed in on him.

But, wait, where was he?

'I think he jusdt ran away from US after defaulting on so many people salaries etc—not sure how true but always pending salaraise etc only took care of few key people who are doing all the PR …'[159]

'Uncle went back because of potential investigation on him?'

'Before he could be imprisoned in the USCIS jail, he very cleverly escape[d] to India.'

Appi had, yes, left for India, leaving an obvious question in his trail: what next? The last two decades had proven that desi consultancy owners, drenched in affluence, coveted clout. But schmoozing with politicians, film stars and public intellectuals still meant power by proximity. Significant, sure, but still removed. Appi Anna wasn't satisfied with the shore or the splash. He craved the ocean. So, back home, he raced to conquer the final frontier: political power.

54

While investigating different American clients—or, as Virgil called them, 'H-1B junkies'—I pondered their connections with him. In 2009, he had worked for the Office of the Attorney General in San Antonio via a desi consultancy, ObjectWin Technology, which had paid $206,541 in back wages for H-1B violations in 2008.[160] But even in 2019 …

Office of the Attorney General, Texas[161]

Third-Party Consultancies	H-1B Dependent Consultancies	Consultancies Paying Back Wages for H-1B Violations	Consultancies Hiring Visa Mills' Graduates	Consultancies' H-1B Workers at Client	H-1Bs Earning Much Less Than Median Salaries
16	62.5%	6%	31%	36	61%

… nothing had changed.

'It is the worst company in USA they don't have minimum ethics to behave with employees and also they don't give salary on time.' (Nitco.[162])

'Never got encouragement from Management and abused with bad language.' (Mythri Consulting.[163])

'It is completely a fraudulent company involved in money laundering via M&A, visa fraud, tax evasion.' (Pioneer Global.[164])

Over the last decade, Virgil had written to many government agencies—telling his story, sharing his findings, asking for help—especially those instituted to protect people like him. But forget helping, their own hiring patterns raised grave concerns. Starting from:

Texas Workforce Commission[165]

Third-Party Consultancies	H-1B Dependent Consultancies	Consultancies Paying Back Wages for H-1B Violations	Consultancies Hiring Visa Mills' Graduates	Consultancies' H-1B Workers at Client	H-1Bs Earning Much Less Than Median Salaries
15	60%[166]	20%	7%	22	59%

The DOL had investigated three consultancies: Paramount Software Solutions (2008), Echelon IT (2011) and Genuine IT (thrice; 2010, 2015 and 2018—a year before it got an LCA approved for the Texas Workforce Commission). GenuineIT paid $15,766,[167] $7,156 and $11,647 in back wages,[168] while Paramount Software Solutions, $33,998, and Echelon IT, $13,749.

'I had to beg for my pay check every month. They call themselves as women owned company but … stone hearted men … controls everything.' (GenuineIT.[169])

'It is only a desi loser who … Files H1b for anyone without verifying details etc and makes money on withdrawing the application. WORST ORGANIZATION !!!!' (Synergy Global Technologies.[170])

'I am not sure how they are trapping people on h1, opt, cpt from 1997 … this company should be closed by USCIS … Be sure to sacrifise atleast 30 to 40k while leaving the company … I complained to DOL about all their misdoings.' (Paramount Software Solutions.[171])

In April 2015, Virgil had written a post on Keep America At Work. 'I now know for a fact why I can't get hired at the Veterans Administration—H-1B.'[172] Here was its record, in different states, four years later:

Department of Veterans Affairs[173]

Third-Party Consultancies	H-1B Dependent Consultancies	Consultancies Paying Back Wages for H-1B Violations	Consultancies Hiring Visa Mills' Graduates	Consultancies' H-1B Workers at Client	H-1Bs Earning Much Less Than Median Salaries
56	64%	20%	23%	79	75%[174]

Out of the seventy-nine certified LCAs—spread across thirteen states, including the VA's headquarters in Washington DC—fifty-three (or 67 per cent) of them were in Texas.[175] Out of those, at least twenty-nine[176] belonged to the IT Infrastructure Operations, the 'corporate IT center' for the 'VA's nationwide systems', which also supported other federal agencies.[177] Fifty-three positions in one year in Virgil's state—and more than half of them in his specialty. And yet, he could get nothing but a job as a janitor.

The third-party consultancies included Manu's employer, Infocon Logix; Appi Reddy's MicroInfo; and a desi consultancy, Sriven Systems Inc, coughing up back wages so huge—$421,373—that it ranked thirty-first in the history of DOL investigations.[178] One in five VA contractors had committed H-1B violations, some as recently as 2021. They even infiltrated the federal agency's headquarters, where two out of three body shops, SVK Systems and SBase Technologies, had paid back wages in 2010 and 2016. The former's fine, $257,636, figured in the ninety-eighth percentile.

The VAs, however, didn't always need body shops to underpay H-1B workers because they could do that themselves. In December 2017, the DOL had ordered the VA in Leavenworth, Kansas, to pay $66,137 to an H-1B worker. The average back wages for all H-1B violators totalled $50,188—the Leavenworth VA fared 32 per cent worse.[179]

Was that all? Nope.

Because in the late 1990s, the VA's Medical Center (DVAMC), in Dallas, had failed to pay an H-1B worker, Dr Mirza Hassan, the required prevailing wage. To 'remedy the matter', the DOL ordered DVAMC to pay $17,842 to Hassan. The case first went to the Administrative Law Judge (ALJ), then the Administrative Review Board (ARB). The VA argued that it did 'not fall within the regulatory definition' of an employer—'a person, firm, corporation, contractor, or other association'—because it was 'an executive department of [the] federal government' and so 'not subject to the [prevailing] wage requirements of the H-1B program'.[180]

The ALJ found that 'neither the statute nor the regulations' prohibited a 'government agency from being an employer'. The ARB agreed.[181] Plus, the VA had already 'secured all the benefits' of an H-1B 'employer', such as hiring H-1Bs, and even submitted an LCA 'declaring itself' an 'employer'.[182] Looking at the VA's enabling statute and DVAMC's earlier statement, the ARB found that DVAMC's 'primary mission [was] not research' but the 'provision of medical care and treatment to veterans'.[183] Which meant it was not a 'governmental research organization' and thus not exempted from the prevailing wage requirement applicable to most employers.[184] So the ARB 'affirm[ed]' the DOL investigation: that 'DVAMC violated the H-1B regulations' and Hassan was 'entitled to $17,842.18 in back wages'.[185]

Was that all? Nope.

Because an H-1B worker at the VA in Fargo, Dr Rudranath Talukdar, participated in a DOL investigation that found in February 2002 that the VA had failed to pay the prevailing wages to ten H-1B physicians, exceeding $200,000. The VA received bad publicity, including a piece in a local newspaper. But 'as the months went by', Talukdar faced 'increasing hostility' from his 'supervisors and other officials'. Then, the VA fired him. The reason: 'budget deficit'.[186]

The ARB upheld the ALJ's conclusion that the federal agency advertising a 'physician' role after terminating Talukdar showed that the VA had 'not been as concerned about the budget as it claimed'. It also agreed with the ALJ's finding that the VA had 'retaliat[ed]' and 'discriminat[ed]' against Talukdar.[187]

The VA consulted the Office of Legal Counsel (OLC) to check if it was statutorily required to pay back wages. The OLC explained that 'Sovereign immunity' shielded 'the Federal Government and its agencies from suit'.[188] (Inheriting a legal maxim from the English common law, it also meant 'the king can do no wrong'.) Sovereign immunity barred any action against the US, added the OLC, if the 'judgment sought would expend itself on the public treasury or domain'.[189]

The DOL, however, argued that 'sovereign immunity should not apply to enforcement actions between two federal agencies'. So an administrative action, arising from a clash between two federal agencies and resolved within the executive branch, did not 'constitute a suit against the United States'. The penalty then would not 'expend itself on the public treasury or domain' but merely constitute a 'transfer of money from one part of the federal Government to the other'.[190]

But the OLC stated that the DOL-VA dispute 'did not fall wholly within the executive branch' because the suit was 'brought at the behest, and on behalf, of private parties [the H-1B physicians]'. The back wages then 'would go directly' to those 'private parties', which 'clearly expend[ed] itself on the public treasury'. The federal agencies, clarified the OLC, could not 'order another federal agency to pay money judgments to private parties' unless Congress had 'waived sovereign immunity'. The H-1B statutes contained no such waiver. This 'dispute' showed that Congress did not 'consider the consequences of applying the H-1B program to federal employers'.[191] Or, maybe, even Congress failed to imagine that federal agencies would squeeze H-1Bs like 'employers'.

'The uncertainty over [the VA's back wages] question' showed that unlike 'other federal laws', Congress 'did not clearly address the impact of the H-1B program on federal pay statutes'. Still, if the VA could not 'honor' the H-1B programme's 'prevailing wage requirements', concluded the OLC, then it 'should not file a Labor Condition Application'.[192]

Nothing mattered. The VA's sovereign immunity prevailed: it could have its cake, eat it too, open a bakery. The H-1Bs received no back wages.

The king could, indeed, do no wrong.

Next, an agency supposed to protect both foreign and American workers: the U.S. Department of Labor. First, its statistical arm that researched salary levels, unemployment figures and working conditions.

Bureau of Labor Statistics[193]

Third-Party Consultancies	H-1B Dependent Consultancies	Consultancies Paying Back Wages for H-1B Violations	Consultancies Hiring Visa Mills' Graduates	Consultancies' H-1B Workers at Client	H-1Bs Earning Much Less Than Median Salaries
23	70%	13%	35%	49	78%

Irony turned in its grave and twisted a muscle.

Producing extensive statistical reports on varied wages (classified by occupations, regions and genders), the BLS itself benefitted from a vast majority of H-1Bs on suspiciously low salaries. Besides, the three consultancies[194] committing H-1B violations—Elite IT Professionals, Horizon Softech and Softech International Resources (investigated thrice)—had paid $10,931, $8,292 and $7,778 in back wages.

Finally: the DOL's second office, the gatekeeper of the H-1B programme.

U.S. Department of Labor (DOL)[195]

Third-Party Consultancies	H-1B Dependent Consultancies	Consultancies Paying Back Wages for H-1B Violations	Consultancies Hiring Visa Mills' Graduates	Consultancies' H-1B Workers at Client	H-1Bs Earning Much Less Than Median Salaries
25[196]	44%	8%	12%	67[197]	75%[198]

Wait: the DOL had hired H-1B workers from consultancies investigated for H-1B violations by ... the DOL?

Here's their record:

Firm	*H-1B Violations*	*Back Wages*	*Year*
I Q Systems	30	$320,460	2008
ILogik	3	$18,818	2020

The DOL had investigated ILogik from 1 July 2018 to 31 July 2020—in the very same period, it had approved the company's LCA for, well, itself. And even though I Q Systems had been penalised over a decade ago, it had paid a fine so huge that it ranked thirty-eighth among all H-1B violations.[199]

What about the other contractors? Desi consultancies, low salaries, awful MyVisaJobs reviews.

'Don't Join this company. Owner is Psycho.' (International Software Systems.[200])

'If you are on student visa than they will ask you to take transfer to one black listed university because they are getting commission through that university.' (Maganti IT Resources.[201])

'If you dont have a degree but have money, this company is good to get H1 and Green Card. I know many guys who got their H1 through this company and were working in motel, flipping burgurs and driving cabs ... I hope IRS and USCIS will hunt them one day.' (22nd Century Technologies.[202])

Out of the sixty-nine certified LCAs, eleven (or 16 per cent) of them offered Level I wages. The lowest slab among the four tiers, Level

I corresponded to employees who only had a 'basic understanding of the occupation', stated the DOL's policy document, performing 'routine tasks' that required 'limited, if any, exercise of judgment'. The federal agency provided examples—'a research fellow', a trainee, an intern—all far from the 'best and the brightest' workers. Yet the DOL had itself hired eleven such professionals, dismissing American techies in one clean sweep.[203]

None of it was new.

A 2016 *Politico* report had stated that the Labor Department employed 'at least three' foreign IT consultants earning 'significantly lower' than the average wage.[204] 'I'm actually surprised it's that small,' said Alexander Bastani, the president of the American Federation of Government Employees Local 12. 'I honestly still doubt it's that small. I think that's just the data you were able to get.'[205]

In April 2017, a *Computerworld* reporter, Patrick Thibodeau, shared a post on a Facebook group, 'White-Collar Workers of America.'[206] He enclosed a spreadsheet containing countless LCA rows, all pointing to the same address. 'Who can tell us what federal office is located at 200 Constitution Ave. in Washington?' The group's moderator replied, 'US Department of Labor.' Another member posted the photo of a building: 'Francis Perkins, Department of Labor Building.' One more commented: 'US DOL is the most corrupt agency in the US and the root cause of all H1B abuses in the country.'

A 2014 *Guardian* investigation had revealed that, since 2000, the federal government had 'awarded contracts and other benefits worth nearly half a billion dollars' to 'labor brokers and tech firms cited for violating' H-1B related laws.[207] Even the ones 'facing the ultimate penalty'—'debarment' from the guest worker programme—'found ways back in.'[208] Several agencies had 'looked past these violations or did not check the record', such as the Department of Homeland Security, the Department of Defense and, of course, the DOL.[209]

The Labor Department rewarded H-1B violators even after 2014. They also received contracts from other federal agencies, totalling $1.07 billion. A desi consultancy, EcomNets, which had paid $92,032 in back wages to thirteen employees in 2005,[210] obtained two DOL contracts worth $34,906 in 2014 and 2015.[211] Seven more agencies awarded it benefits amounting to $609,394, including the Department of State and Homeland Security.[212] The name should have sounded familiar because these very entities investigated EcomNets. They found in early 2016 that its owner, Raju Kosuri, had submitted fraudulent[213] LCAs and visa petitions, via shell companies, for 'more than 900' workers.[214] The span of this scam: fifteen years. Illegal earnings: $20.9 million.

The DOL's hiring associations said it all. A government beholden to corporations, behaving like a corporation, had perfected what corporations do: cut costs. Not just a regular corporation but a cannibalistic corporation, a beast so untrammelled and famished that it could only satiate its hunger by eating its own.

55

Kumar's last few videos—especially 'I quit H1B life with a smile'—had gone viral. By June 2018, his channel crossed 7,000 subscribers, 847 in a month alone. 'Overwhelming response,' he told me. 'Many sent emails.' A man named Michael McGehee wrote to him. 'We Americans are sorry to see you go. H-1b destroyed my career, made me near suicidal.' Virgil, too, left a comment on his channel: 'If I could raise the money, you would be in Texas with me fixing this problem. But nobody from America or India puts up those funds, so we both struggle—may your struggles end my friend.'

On 2 July, his first week in India, the Indian news portal *Scroll.in* published a piece: 'Watch this Indian techie with a H1B visa say goodbye to the US after not being paid.'[215] It included three Kumar Exclusive videos, hinting at his probable cause of return, the 'Donald Trump administration'. The newspaper *Andhra Jyothi* published an article on him the next day: 'America to Kakinada—via Trump's kick.'[216] NTV Telugu broadcasted a twenty-minute story on H-4s' deferred work authorisation status.[217] Castigating Trump, it also covered Kumar's trip.

'They are connecting things without understanding the root cause of the problem,' he emailed me. 'I tried to explain the exploitation of H-1Bs to Indian news channels when they come to USA but none show interest. They linked H4 EADs to h1bs returned to President Trump. But they returning because desi consultancies doing human trafficking and not paying salaries. Indian media failed to understand because most of them paid by caste groups and Indian Incs to write bad about USA government rather than the ground realities.'

Before leaving the US, he had written a LinkedIn post, saying he'd job hunt in India. Siva, a desi body shop owner, read it, contacted Kumar and arranged a client interview for him in Novi, Michigan. A few days after the phone interview, Siva informed him to join the client. The vendor also confirmed the project.

A new hope charged him.

Kumar borrowed money and flew to Detroit. 'My father almost begged me. Don't go,' he wrote to me. 'He was taking care of my hospitalized mother. May salary, deposited. June, no salary, no expectations. I am feeling greatly home sick.'

He continued to upload videos from his India trip; his channel became even more popular. Many contacted him—some from countries he hadn't even expected. 'It is not a sin to return to India and you are not a loser,' wrote a Nigerian national, Ayoka. 'Please do not listen to negative people. I could not understand what you said in a Telugu video, but you said something about $600. Please let me know how I can give some money to you. This is not a handout. It is a hand up to help you.'

An email from Virgil. 'Let me know if you don't get something through PayPal.'

He had transferred $20.

'Got it, thank you.'

'Welcome. Will try and send more.'

'Nigerian American sister gave another $170 today,' Kumar told me. 'I am shocked.'

He continued interacting with his subscribers and, now no longer under Raghav's control, unleashed. 'Earlier I thought of taking a toll-free number and receive all calls and VM,' he wrote to me. 'That way, my cell number (my privacy) will remain protected. Same time, available during my free time. What do you say?'

By mid-August, he had still not got the Michigan project. The same story again: the employer and the vendor had lied. Kumar attended two more interviews at the Novi headquarters. Still no clarity—he contemplated returning to India. He faced a three-member team for the next round. This time, the client confirmed his employment.

One afternoon, standing in the queue for the lunch buffet in the office cafeteria, Kumar met a young Indian man, Gaurav. He told Kumar that he had seen his videos. Kumar smiled and shook his hand. Gaurav also said something that wouldn't leave Kumar for a long time: 'I am meeting a YouTube celebrity for the first time in my life.' He encountered another subscriber at work who told him, 'You are very famous, sir.' Two days later, he met a young man in a grocery store. He asked, 'Can I take a selfie?'

November 2018: Kumar had worked at Siva's company, Integrisys, for over two months. No salary, no difference. One evening, he sat in his car and switched on the phone camera. Wearing a cap and a jacket and holding a collar mic, he began. 'Hi friends. If your employer, especially your Indian employer body shop, is not paying salaries, please call on my Google Voice number.[218] I am receiving volumes of emails and messages on Facebook, but I don't have time to reply. All I need from you is your employer's name. Because a decade almost I have scanned a lot of Indian [employers], [so] if they are in my list, my blacklisted list, then definitely I will need to inform the government.' (He meant K.) 'Don't worry, I am here.'

The comments section erupted.

'Excellent, sir. Thanks for helping those in trouble.'

'Very bold decision, sir. I wish you all the best.'

'You will receive many calls. Many consultancies called me with such deals. I have their details, but it will be ideal if their employees complain. I hope they get caught and punished.'

He received seventeen calls in the first three days. '1 Canada. 1 India. Rest USA,' he emailed me. 'One from IL, employer doing illegal recovery. Another one, TCS victim, filed case with DOL.' But a problem that had annoyed him for long continued to persist. 'They afraid to speak, are you going to share this information? First question they ask. Second, they have a serious problem with employer but not sharing.'

Over a month passed. Kumar kept receiving calls; he kept counselling and introducing the aggrieved H-1Bs to K. But what about the activist himself?

'Dear Tanul,' he wrote to me on 1 January 2019, 'I wish you a wonderful new year and your writings in the book.'

'Thank you, Kumar. Best wishes to you too!'

'I reached home yesterday after drove 3,000 miles.' He had returned from Florida with his family. 'Yet to get Nov salary.'

56

On Capitol Hill, H-1B abusers didn't stop at the headquarters of the Veterans Affairs and the Department of Labor. They also milked more holy cows, such as the …

Library of Congress[219]

Third-Party Consultancies	H-1B Dependent Consultancies	Consultancies Paying Back Wages for H-1B Violations	Consultancies Hiring Visa Mills' Graduates	Consultancies' H-1B Workers at Client	H-1Bs Earning Much Less Than Median Salaries
5[220]	60%	20%	20%	6	83%

The DOL had ordered a Fremont-based company, SRS Consulting, to pay back wages in 2007, and at least one more firm, Code Ace Solutions, had disconcerting MyVisaJobs reviews.[221]

And then …

House of Representatives[222]

Third-Party Consultancies	H-1B Dependent Consultancies	Consultancies Paying Back Wages for H-1B Violations	Consultancies Hiring Visa Mills' Graduates	Consultancies' H-1B Workers at Client	H-1Bs Earning Much Less Than Median Salaries
2	100%	50%	0%	2	50%

Both consultancies—Logic Planet and Integrated Resources—had committed H-1B violations, though only the latter had to pay back wages. A staggering 50 per cent rate.

Even worse?

U.S. Senate[223]

Third-Party Consultancies	H-1B Dependent Consultancies	Consultancies Paying Back Wages for H-1B Violations	Consultancies Hiring Visa Mills' Graduates	Consultancies' H-1B Workers at Client	H-1Bs Earning Much Less Than Median Salaries
1	100%	100%	100%	1	100%

One firm, one violator, four DOL investigations ($114,361). A consultancy linked to USAA, Big Tech, Yale University, Boeing and the United Nations: Compunnel Software Group.

Deceitful body shops even got LCAs approved for a state Senate whose representative ran for president in 2016 who, without even knowing the basic rules of H-1B, had championed the guest worker programme.[224]

Florida Senate (Office of Marco Rubio)[225]

Third-Party Consultancies	H-1B Dependent Consultancies	Consultancies Paying Back Wages for H-1B Violations	Consultancies Hiring Visa Mills' Graduates	Consultancies' H-1B Workers at Client	H-1Bs Earning Much Less Than Median Salaries
2	100%	50%	50%	5	100%

Both desi consultancies. One of them, System Soft Technologies, had paid hefty back wages in the last decade.

Violations	*Employees Affected*	*Back Wages*
47	45	$161,005

A fine so high it ranked 119th among all such violations. The other firm, Shubh Solutions LLC, had a Hindi name, whose MyVisaJobs reviews told a familiar story.[226]

'The owner (Mr. Keshav) ... is using Fake experience of the consultant and asking lot money for Jobs. Never prefer this San Diego's most stupid, unethical, money oriented consultant.'[227]

'Shubh solutions is my current petitioner who has got my I-797 approved and has been holding it. He is not exposing any information to me including my I-94. Now He is not having any client for me, so he is threatening me for the money to run my paystub for October. When I denied to give money, he asked me to revoke my H1.'[228]

'Such a waste company, all fake promises, And most important of all, mis behaves with women and this is a fact. Acts like a gentleman but all fake promises, Once you are under his H1, you are doomed. Very less pay … ITS "ASHUBH" [bad luck] SOLUTION FOR YOUR LIFE.'[229]

But the most precise MyVisaJobs review—ever—appeared on System Soft Technologies's page. 'They easily, proudly take 40K out of your rate. WTF. 2080 hours I work hard … what logic in the world say … just for name u get 30% commision. These bl**dy Uncle Sam created this nonsense system and who else can exploit it better … We desi …'[230]

This scam had run from one end of the East Coast to another, from the U.S. Senate to the Florida Senate, enslaving Indian workers, exiling American workers, perverting American capitalism and democracy—year after year, for the last thirty years.

This was the true Wild Wild East.

VII

ACCEPTANCE

57

A social distancing champ long before the COVID-19 lockdown, Manu didn't worry about the lack of company. Something else troubled him. Without a fridge, microwave or kitchen, he struggled for food. He ate bread-butter for breakfast, lunch and dinner. When he got sick of it, he switched to bread-jam, then bread-Nutella. He lost a lot of weight and, to combat weakness, popped B-Complex vitamin pills.

Infocon Logix reduced his salary to Rs 8,000 per month in early 2020. Wanting a part-time job, he uploaded his resume on Naukri.com. A Houston-based consultancy, Candidatez Solutions, contacted him for a full-time admin role in Bangalore for a Californian semiconductor firm, Diode Force.

Used to countless rejections, Manu was calm on the day of the interview. The panel comprised three Indians. They checked his proficiency in MS Excel and database. Manu explained the VLOOKUP function and the SQL and Oracle servers.

Candidatez's owner, Sarvesh, called a couple of days later. 'You got selected. Congratulations.' He asked Manu's expected annual salary.

'Rs 10 lakhs.'

Based on his last four pay stubs—totalling Rs 5 lakh per year—Sarvesh said he couldn't give Rs 10 lakh.

'Okay, I will drop off.'

'Don't worry. We are good guys. You can look us up online,' Sarvesh said. 'It's an excellent position. Don't let it go.'

Another call after a few days: 'The client agreed.'

Manu began working from home. But he still nursed niggling scars: was the company legit? Would it pay on time?

I had the same concern: 'Did you get paid?'

'No, I think they will pay on 10 July. They just took my void cheque.'

Manu said he had quit Infocon Logix and informed Prakash about the new job.

I followed up on 11 July. 'Did you get the salary?'

'No, they said Monday.'

Manu got paid on that date—and on time in the subsequent months. No 'layers' sat between Candidatez and Diode Force. He got his desired salary, a bump of more than 100 per cent, the most he had ever earned in India: Rs 80,000 per month. Amid a pandemic ravaging countless careers, Manu stole his piece from the universe.

He met with his father. Falling in the kitchen, he had injured himself. He looked frail and sounded sentimental; he wanted to give money to his son. Manu refused. His father insisted. Manu cleared his bank and credit card loans and paid the attorney fees for the EB-1 green card application. It relieved him.

The immigration firm, managing his application, told him that recommendation letters from college deans, professors or department heads, or CEOs or supervisors, could boost his chance. Manu wrote to many professors: no response. Sarvesh ignored his request, too. He called Prakash who kept dilly-dallying, treating him like an intern. When a phone conversation looked impossible, he emailed. 'Dear Sir, can you please approve the offer Letter (attached)? No one helps in this company except you and Nitish Sir. If you want changes, please let me know.' Printed on the Infocon Logix letterhead—and signed by Manu and Prakash—it offered him a System Analyst position at a salary of 'around $70,000'.

'This is *fraud*. How come you wrote your own letter? I will never sign this. I lost respect for you.'

'I am not doing any fraud. You can reject it. I just wanted help.'

What a hypocrite. Prakash had himself manipulated so many resumes, documents and interviews, including once telling Manu to edit an OPT EAD. He had built his entire business on deceit and now spat out a moral lecture? Manu deleted him from his Facebook and LinkedIn. He'd never contact him or Infocon Logix, or have anything to do with the body shop world, ever again.

58

Appi Reddy joined the Telangana Rashtra Samiti (TRS) party.[1] As expected, AndhraFriends exploded with comments.

'Long live Appanna ... OPTs beam of hope appanna.'[2]

'Appi anna zindabad, mla appi anna.'[3]

'Anna's seat guarantee[d].'[4]

'My ass, [he] is gonna win 😁.'[5]

Deccan Chronicle published an article on TRS's preparations for the 'full-fledged poll campaign', stating it would either field Shanampudi Saidireddy or Appi for the Huzurnagar constituency.[6] An erstwhile owner of a famous Indian restaurant in Canada, Saidireddy had returned to India in 2015 and opened a youth organisation, Sye, expanding his social work in the town.[7] Appi lost the ticket to him.

But he continued to ascend. A shining example of American capitalism, he bankrolled the biopic of a Marxist student leader. *George Reddy* released in November 2019 to mixed reviews. His next production, *Pressure Cooker*, a February 2020 release, befitted his image more. The breezy comedy told the story of a young graduate, Kishore, who is pressured by his father to move to the US. He bungles several visa attempts. His cousins in America make him feel like a loser—trapped in a pressure cooker. The film depicts NRIs as callous, greedy and narcissistic who disrespect their parents. But something else, too, makes it remarkable: Easter eggs. Around the twenty-five-minute mark, Kishore visits an educational consultancy in Hyderabad.

'You don't worry at all,' says its owner. 'You will go to America. Look there, H-1B visa.' He points to a soft board containing the pinned photos of H-1B workers.

'But sir, I don't have work experience.'

'Experience?' He laughs. 'This guy Ganesh had only one year experience. But we tweaked his resume and showed six years. These Americans are innocent. They believe whatever is written in the papers. Many went just like this.'

Later, Kishore meets another man who promises him a visa.

'Next week RITA has a dance programme in New Jersey. Royal Indian Telugu Association. You are going to America in that dance troop.' Before leaving, he tells Kishore, 'The next time you come, get Rs 25 lakh, okay?'

'TANA, ATA, NATA. Now RITA gone as well,' says Kishore's friend, Pawan. 'Hey Kishore, once you go to America, form an association called PATA.'

PATA?

'Panileni [jobless] American Telugu Association. You become its president. Receive all the respected members who come to the US. Arrange road shows, dances, gulp all the money and get into every cheap thing.'

After getting jailed for visa fraud, Kishore applies for jobs in India. One day, he stands outside a house, looking for an office where he has an interview appointment.

'Excuse me,' he interrupts a middle-aged man who is smoking.

'Yes?'

'There used to be an IT company here.'

'Which one?'

'MicroInfo.'

The man points to the top of the house. The camera lingers on the firm's board.

'Oh, is this an IT company?'

'Yes, a start-up.'

He turns out to be MicroInfo's owner, Prakash, who hires Kishore. Cut to: Kishore pitching the investors. One of them, (the real) Appi

Reddy. He occupies the centre of the frame; the scene cuts to him several times. After the presentation, Appi tells Prakash, 'See, this is the problem with the current generation. Guys, why do you want to create something new? Why don't you leave that to the US and Europe? Take a successful website from the US and replicate it here. In India, we should go online. Why don't you consider online trading? Come up with something original.'

'Original?' Kishore thunders out an impassioned monologue about the lack of homegrown firms, saying everything in the country—from 'the god in my shrine to the kites we fly'—comes from China. 'If you don't invest in product companies, when will Indian brands come up? When will India develop, sir?'

Annoyed by Kishore, Appi tells the investors to leave. A bald man stays behind, though, who seems to symbolise the real Appi Reddy. He appreciates Kishore's passion and product, promising to invest in MicroInfo. Before leaving, he says, 'By the way, I never went to IIT or IIM but still built a world class company.'

59

Kumar got a LinkedIn request from an American techie, John Chemers, in late 2018. They exchanged resumes, spoke over the phone and became friends. Around a year later, he emailed Kumar: 'John needs your help.' It contained a copy of the cease-and-desist letter sent by his company's attorney directing him to return the office laptop. John said his firm had fired him due to age discrimination. Kumar forwarded that email to me. 'My American follower from IL fired for wrong reasons, organization blaming him.'

John researched the H-1B programme, commenting on Kumar's YouTube videos and LinkedIn posts. He took immense interest in India: its H-1B workers, their specialisations, its colleges, their graduates. John sent articles on immigration fraud to Kumar; he also interacted with Indians on social media. He once wrote to Kumar about his Twitter spat with some Indians. When they turned abusive, he reported their accounts. Used to online bullying, Kumar empathised with him. He once told me over email: 'John is a great man with humanity helping Indians here.' John, like many strangers, had ensconced himself in Kumar's ever-expanding universe.

A world without people was no world for Kumar. He was an eternal maximalist, a glass filled to the brim—one nudge, and he could spill it all. He purged his H-1B trauma by 'pumping emails' to his friends, ex-colleagues, acquaintances, subscribers, reporters and anyone else willing to listen. Kumar spent many hours every month, helping and counselling H-1B workers.

Among all the strangers he befriended, though, he reserved his most empathetic side for American IT workers. Maybe he felt guilty that his dream had cost them their livelihoods. Maybe he felt helpless about the fact that the victims of a grave injustice would never get justice. Maybe his own self-loathing, his inherent 'third-world' condition kept reminding him that he deserved less, that he was less—confirmed, in some measure, by the H-1B scam.

Over the years, as more Indians gamed the H-1B programme, Kumar became an American patriot. He bemoaned the H-1B fraud destroying the American middle-class countless times on his YouTube channel. He loved Trump. Recording videos wearing a MAGA cap, he showered praises on America. His friendship with John then encapsulated his H-1B life: a stranger who had contacted him, a stranger victimised by the IT industry, a stranger requesting help. A stranger, an American. A hapless American. A jobless American.

Kumar's subscriber Saad—an engineering student in Chennai wanting to pursue his master's from the US—emailed him. 'Respected sir, your friend John Chemers is in contact with me for a long time. He said some things that I would love to confirm. 1) Are all IT jobs low-skilled and can be outsourced to India? 2) Are Data science and business analytics not highly skilled fields? 3) Are 100% of the IT positions outsourced?'

Kumar was confused: how did John know Saad?

In March 2020, Kumar received a message from John. 'Indians are too f****** stupid. Kerala calls New Delhi dumb. New Delhi calls Hyderabad Dumb. Hyderabad calls Madras dumb. Madras calls Bangalore dumb. Nobody will ever learn. They are all dumb.'

'Did you type this?' Kumar asked.

'Yes, I give up. If those students want to be cheated, let them get cheated.'

'Remember, several good Indians supporting you and me.'

'Look, I don't have to agree with you to support you. That's the beauty of the First Amendment.'

'I am against generalization which you typed above.'

John sent a five-minute video called 'The First Amendment' song. 'It's just an expression.'

'You are sending same video multiple times.'

'I give up.'

'Good for you. Because your losing time and energy on this topic.'

'Well at least I met you so that's good. But that Muslim student Saad is just so f****** dumb. He's got his finger in his ass he's so f****** lazy spends his time masturbating in his mother's bed. So f****** dumb.'

John began to message daily. Long rants, irrelevant rants—many articles, many videos.

'More people in India have a cell phone than a toilet. How can you have a refrigerator or a TV but not a toilet?'

'Sir, am not interested.'

Another message five days later. 'I don't give a s***. I would refuse to go to any place that is full of illness and India will be full of illness and coronavirus. I'd refuse.'

'The problem with you is, you hate India and Indians. Generalization a lot. If you don't like Indians and me, don't chat. I respect you that, I understand that.'

'Every day I get messages from some Indian that they want to get out of that shithole country. Hindu Brahmin treating Dalits. Dalit acting like criminals. Hindu Brahmin discriminating against Muslims. I don't hate India and I don't hate you.'

'But your messages speaking differently.'

'I hope you can refuse to go back to India because of coronavirus.'

'Please email if any questions. I welcome you to have a video interview. About advice to Indian students. Because you are a nice person and love to help people.'

Kumar introduced me to John, believing his age discrimination experience would help my research. I figured out over the call that he didn't lose his job because of age discrimination, but we still had a long pleasant chat. But he soon sent me a series of hostile texts. He didn't want a conversation, so I blocked him.

'You are an exploitist taking advantage of people.' A random email in my inbox startled me. 'You said you want to be a film critic but can't take criticism yourself.' It came from a 'Gay Yash Mittra'.

'Gay Yash Mittra,' Kumar emailed me. 'He created it to attack one YT guy.'

Yash Mittra's YouTube channel, Yash Mittra—YMGrad, counselled US-bound students. It had become popular, collecting close to one lakh subscribers. On 27 February 2020, Yash uploaded a seventeen-minute video.[8] 'It started in October 2019. Someone started calling me repeatedly from a US phone number … and told me [to] stop sending Indian students abroad. Stop sending them to America. They said we'll finish you if you don't stop doing this. Imagine getting a phone call every time you have your phone in your hands … every two minutes. At first you maybe try to hang up, you try to block them, but they still keep calling. When you block them, they try to use some other client—like Skype or something—to get a local Indian number. So you block that number, but within the … next … two minutes, you get a different phone call from a different number. He tried to contact me *everywhere* on my social media. Everywhere on my email. I checked his Twitter, that's when I came to know he's actually a racist and he hates Indians. He's some sort of a fascist.'

On 1 April 2020, the Novi client fired countless IT professionals, including Kumar. Then his employer, Integrisys, fired him. The two-month countdown began.

He got a text. 'You're a f******. Your book writer in India is cheating you. You're a f****** loser. You're a stupid f*****.'

A month passed.

Still jobless.

John kept messaging.

'Am busy applying for jobs. Talk to you later. I have no enmity. Please understand.'

'Your journalist friend Tanul is a scumbag.'

'Please ignore him sir. My need of the hour is getting a job. Rest not needed.'

A week later, his phone buzzed at 1:37 in the night. A video of an Indian YouTuber, Yudi J., and a message. 'There is your problem lady you don't want to have good English skills you don't want to speak proper English you don't want to succeed.'

'You unnecessarily fight with right people. Wrong time.'

'This is called deflecting. You have poor education because you came from India.'

Kumar blocked him.

John messaged and called from different numbers, commenting on his videos via different monikers. Kumar wrote a post on YouTube. 'John is a good follower of KE. He used to attack KE's haters but suddenly turned KE's hater and started attacking KE in emails, texts with FUCK words etc. He sent 10,000 whatsapp messages in a week that includes his fight with Indians on youtube and twitter. He is a very good friend no doubts but Truth has no friends and at each stage, am eliminating few friends whoever not with truth. Tell me, can I give hugs, kisses and roses to John?'

Saad emailed him two months later. 'Dear Sir, your friend John is troubling me a lot. 1) He is indirectly telling me not to come to America and saying nasty things about me, Indian and Muslim. 2) He opened a fake Instagram account and sending nasty messages to my friends and other girl classmates. Is anything wrong with him sir? He's putting my photo and displaying as terrorist. He's calling with different numbers.'

'Sorry for that brother. Just block him. He turned hater.'

Hounded by John, betrayed by Raghav and harassed by desi consultancies, Kumar had just one hope left: K. Because, unlike Kumar, K had access to power. His whistle-blowing lawsuit against a WITCH firm had made him a star. He had broken a shocking story about high-skilled immigration, helping the US government recoup millions of dollars. The American mainstream media adored him. Countless news outlets, including the *New York Times*, gave him glowing press coverage. K interacted with law enforcement officers, testified before Congress and knew renowned attorneys. In the H-1B world, where IT workers tottered like pawns, K towered like a king.

For H-1B victims, who barely protested and regularly lost, K's victory transcended their drunken dreams. Perhaps their stories, too, like many great stories, awaited a stirring twist. K had also urged Kumar to sue 4M and YBMyles Crown. After some reluctance, Kumar followed that fire, taking his activism to its last logical conclusion. For someone encouraging his subscribers to be courageous, Kumar found in K an even fiercer ally: an activist who prodded *him* to fight. K was where Kumar wanted to reach; K was who Kumar wanted to be.

K also embodied America's morals. Kumar had spent a decade living them, inspiring his subscribers through his own inspiration ('Are we learning anything from America or are we breaking every single rule here?'). India had only offered him dejection and deceit. Even his lawsuit against the IAS officer had failed. But he trusted America—more than many Americans.

K had continued to assure him. 'My brother, I've worked out a deal for you and me with a law firm,' read his email in April 2019. 'They'll take every Indian brother and sister and help them get their money. In return we'll help them get a Visa. If they deserve. When the cases roll you'll earn off them. And hopefully a monthly fee. We'll market your YouTube videos for the good of the people. They're actually paying for my Washington DC plane ticket. To help with your Visa.'

Relying on the Victims of Trafficking and Violence Protection Act of 2000, K had amped up his fight, creating a website to protect the victims of body shops. Since Kumar admired K's activism—someone also handling his lawsuit—he introduced his subscribers to K, including those who had contacted him through his 'hotline'. The offer was reassuring: the H-1Bs wouldn't have to pay upfront fees (or the attorney's costs), and K would take a cut only if they won the case.

But, in person, K asked for help: thousands of dollars, several times, promising to return in a week. Even asked for money for Kumar's 'whistle-blower protection U visa' in 2020, saying the attorney needed it. Kumar ignored, then paid: $1,418.

No result.

But not just Kumar.

Ganesh Yarlagadda, a Vijayawada resident, had contacted Kumar in August 2018, wanting help with his green card application. 'My GC paused as my employer deserted my petition. Can I restart the process with the same Priority Date?' When Ganesh kept emailing and calling, Kumar introduced him to K.

'Hi Mr. Parker, I need a Green Card application help using my priority date from NOV 3, 2003. I lived in USA from 1998-2015. Please help.'

'If you can pay for my travel to Washington DC, I'll gladly help. I've tried by phone, but it doesn't work. My lawyer won't charge, but I still have to travel.'

'What would be the course of action? What grounds do we have for victory? Except my resume you don't have any details so legally how to proceed?'

'My reputation and clout. I need what you've done to date. I can sponsor you via my contacts and my company.'

Ganesh wired $2,500 to K.

He followed up in July 2019. 'What are my case numbers? I request clarity. It has been a year … pls.'

'You still have to address what you'll do when you get here. Which city will you live in, where will you fly into? You must answer these questions before I can proceed.'

'North Carolina, Raleigh as a Senior software engineer/Manager for TecViser or I can work for you.'

'My friend—I have no job for you. Wish I did—I need an offer letter from TecViser.'

'Why would I need your help if I already have a job visa? Request to return my money as one year passed.'

'I am tired of trying to help fucking people that don't help themselves. You blame me for your plight while you're still in India. Wanna come to this country when you have no job, no place to live. Send me your job visa and let me make sure it's a valid cause. Enough of your nonsense.'

'What nonsense are you talking? I should send you the job visa are you ok? Do you know what is H1B? Get education sir rather than living on others money.'

Ganesh kept emailing.

March 2020: 'How close are we? Tracking number. Case numbers?'

May 13: 'I didn't get any receipt notice. Did u receive?'

June 23: 'Follow up with USCIS as neither of us got the receipt.'

August 25: 'Is this a scam for Indians who already lost their lifes coz of some idiot Indians? God is seeing, will punish everyone.'

An Indian H-1B worker awaiting several months' salaries, enduring his employer and vendors' harassment, Abhay, contacted Kumar. K said he'd aim for a $60,000 settlement, including his fees, $5,754. Abhay paid. K shared encouraging updates: 'they're really scared of me'; 'they'll settle with you, but you'll have to sign a waiver to not sue or contact them'. But then, the delays. First, one reason ('I need attorney to review, however his sister died yesterday because of a heart attack'), then another ('I'm ill, I'll try') and another ('I cannot make them do anything. I'm waiting on them'). He later told Kumar he had dropped the case, as Abhay had contacted his employer. (K didn't return the amount.)

An American woman in New Jersey, 'Adolescent Doctor' (her YouTube moniker), fell in love with an Indian man and married him. She sponsored visas for his mother and sister, but the guy turned abusive, and the marriage didn't last. She sent long texts to Kumar, sharing her plight, sometimes called him. She told Kumar that she had paid K, that she resented K, even hired an attorney to straighten him out.

K hadn't informed Kumar either about the YBMyles case or the U visa. Every query produced a story—pivoted on K's high-profile 'contacts'.

22 January 2019: 'I'm leaving for Washington DC to meet with authorities.'

11 April 2019: 'I need your YouTube channel path for U visa.'

31 March 2020 (a forwarded email): 'I can/will help Kushner and the President. I need a GC for my friend Kumar P.'

Did K ever contact them? Did he even know them? He shared nothing concrete—just promised and promised and promised. Sometimes ordered Kumar: I want the names of corrupt body shops; I want the list of H-1B victims; I want the emails of Indian journalists. He sounded less like an activist in those interactions and more like a White boss lording over a Brown employee. Even when Kumar provided all the leads, sent countless tips, introduced him to sources, K didn't even bother to thank him. But Kumar could stomach these insults if K delivered. More than four years had passed. Like Raghav, K had tainted Kumar's reputation. People were accusing him of stealing their money.

Who was K?

> Dear K, from my 12 plus years of experience in the USA, I have not seen single H-1B won cases against his/her employers. All victims told, employers fired, no justice done. Do you know anyone or read any H-1B success stories? Do you see any H-1B get any justice ever since the inception of H-1B?
>
> I read lots of stuff on U visa or GC whistle blower protection—all that looks nonsense to me, because I do not see anyone who received U visas in his/her life time. Not even a single case.
>
> Keeping the above points, is it NOT BOGUS that America is cheating Indian H-1Bs who are already victims of bad employers? Do you see any hope for any H-1B in America? If I do not get U visa and I do not get justice, what the heck I can promise to my subscribers on videos about protection from their worst employers and getting justice from USA?
>
> For me today, India = USA regarding Laws, judiciary and systems. In fact, India is much better in getting some results.
>
> In America, I lost that HOPE. Correct me if I am wrong. Finally, I feel America is protecting bad employers and crime is winning and those who confront lose everything. If show me some results or success stories, I will get some hope and speak positively to my people. Otherwise, I would tell them, do not FIGHT with your employers because you lose your H-1B and Green Card because your employer fires and none in USA can protect you. Just like me.

60

Virgil got a job offer in June 2019—a six-month programming gig for $30 an hour—from a firm owned by his ex-boss at the 2005 Arizona project. It paid much more than Lee and offered the possibility of an extension. Virgil quit Davisoft. Next: his mad dream, his old dream, his unfulfilled dream—since 2012. The 'lowest man on the totem pole' wanted to set an example and change the conversation. But he needed $5,000 to put his name on the ballot and, as usual, he had none.

'I will raise the money for your Senate run,' Gamm emailed him. 'Do you have a link where you ask for donations?'

VirgilBierschwale.com. It discussed free trade agreements, the destruction of manufacturing jobs and the unceasing wave of guest workers. 'It is time we elect a Texan Senator who will stand up for Americans and legal immigrants to help maintain the balance between our businesses' needs and our citizens' rights.' His slogan: 'American workers will NOT go quietly into the night.'

Gamm's American for Workers Coalition (AWC) donated $1,800. 'Once you're on the ballot, contact me. I will need your suit and shirt size. You will have to shave off facial hair and get a haircut and a headshot. After that, I will do your marketing materials—a logo, a brochure, etc.' Virgil received more donations on his GoFundMe campaign, but $5,000 still looked far and the deadline near, December 8.

10 September: $2,215.

The constant delayed payments at the new job had worsened his desperation. It also disappointed him that besides AWC and Sara Blackwell, no other organisation mentioned his campaign. So when he received an activist's email—who called him a 'hero' and yet didn't acknowledge his campaign and still asked for help—Virgil ignored it. He emailed Gamm: 'It seems they are just attacking India and Indians, which I can't agree with.'

24 October: $2,435.

Not a single donation over the last month. He wrote to Gamm: 'I'm thinking of returning everybody's money.' AWC's Twitter account shared his GoFundMe page and posted a tweet: 'Help #AmericaFirst candidate @VBierschwale get in US Senate race and expose the system displacing #AmericanWorkers with #H1B and #H4EAD.'[9] It also hosted a 'please donate to Virgil' Halloween fundraiser, which included an entrance to a 'haunted house with a donut'. It raised $1,145.

Gamm contacted her allies. The donations poured in the next few days.

'How much left???' she asked.

'About 950.'

More patrons came forward—many of Indian origin. One of them, Yashwant Samarth, contributing $200, often shared his frustrations about the widespread IT fraud. 'Indians forced out apparently,' he forwarded Yashwant's message to Gamm. 'Not just age but also caste.'

'Good luck for the Senate post,' Kumar wrote to him.

Blackwell's Protect US Workers sent its members the meeting agenda and added: 'As you're aware, Virgil Bierschwale is running for Congress. Please share his campaign url and LET'S PUT VIRGIL IN CONGRESS!!!!!'

19 November: over $5,000.

Finally, Bierschwale for Senate 2020.

'Hell yea. Just got the news.' An email from Lee. 'Congrats, I knew you would win.'

'5,000 poorer, but I'm in. Now comes the fun part.'

His ex-boss' firm had continued to delay the payments. Virgil quit, almost a month before the contract got over. As the polling date came closer, newspapers, organisations and regular Texans contacted Virgil. The Conservative Coalition of Harris County asked, 'What will be your top priorities?'

'Free trade, non-immigrant guest workers, homelessness.'

The Patriot Texas Conservative Activist group sent him fifteen questions. The last one asked for his voting record.

'Voted for Obama twice because he said he would fix the jobs situation, but he didn't. Voted for Trump, but he hasn't. Voting for myself because I will.'

Another asked: what about abortion?

'I am against it. BUT I do not have the right to force my belief on a woman who knows everything about her circumstances.'

The VA offered him the housekeeping aid position. He joined in early February 2020, hoping to stay for as long as possible. A week later, he battled a severe cold and fever, missing work for days. When he returned, he had a new supervisor, Maria, who told him that he needed to call the office to ask for permission before going to the bathroom.

'Ya'll need children for your employees.' Virgil handed in his badge and walked out.

John Cornyn won the Republican primary election in Texas by a huge margin, collecting 1,469,209 votes (76.31 per cent). But a nobody from a nobody town also got 20,494 votes. Someone who knew less than 150 people, couldn't afford advertisement and just relied on his website.

'Are you saying YOU got 20,000 votes???' Gamm emailed him. 'Are you kidding???? Virgil!!! We need to celebrate big time!!!! We are all so proud of you!!!!'

Kumar: 'Congratulations! OMG, great news. Right people don't have money in this world.'

Virgil applied for unemployment benefits amid the COVID-19 pandemic. The response: 'You are disqualified because you quit your job.'

He wrote to the VA, enclosing a YouTube video explaining his reason for quitting. Contacted HR, the DOL and over 400 members of

Congress. Uploaded another video: 'Die, says Texas Workforce Commission'.

Appealed to Trump.

Nothing.

61

Trump had promised to reform the H-1B programme in 2016; he hadn't. Three years later, he appointed Chad Wolf—a former *lobbyist* for the Indian IT trade group NASSCOM—as the Homeland Security chief.[10] In June 2020, Trump's top economic advisor Stephen Moore praised the guestworker programme on the radio show *Chicago's Morning Answer*. Virgil sent that link to a few friends. 'To understand why the President does not support us, you must listen to his court jester.'[11]

But then something remarkable happened. Tennessee Valley Authority, a federally owned power company, announced it would outsource more than 100 IT jobs.[12] Many American workers had already trained their replacements. On 3 August, though, Trump fired the chairperson, removed another board member and signed an executive order mandating all federal agencies to complete an internal audit proving they didn't replace Americans with foreigners.[13]

On 8 October 2020, the DOL published a policy revising the prevailing wage levels.[14] Level I had jumped to the forty-fifth percentile of all salaries in a particular occupation and area. Level II, sixty-second. Level III, seventy-eighth. Level IV, ninety-fifth. All much higher than the previous bands: seventeen, thirty-four, fifty and sixty-seven.

Norm blogged about it, calling it 'one of the most carefully-reasoned government reports' ever, which would help employ more American techies.[15] The proposed rule, however, kept the same 'age-related' four-tier system (a 'government enabler for age discrimination') and failed to 'account for the level of talent of a foreign worker'.[16] Despite these reservations, he considered the move 'very solid' and 'well-justified'—'30 years overdue'.[17]

A week later, a consortium of staffing firms, ITServe Alliance, sued the DOL's secretary, Eugene Scalia, and the assistant secretary for the Employment and Training Administration, John Pallasch.[18] The lawsuit complaint stated that the federal agency 'violated the notice and comment procedures', 'acted contrary to a relevant statute' and acted in an 'arbitrary and capricious' manner.[19] The consortium called the studies cited by the DOL, advocating increased pay slabs, either 'inadequate or unreliable'.[20] ITServe pointed to a 'large body of evidence' that showed H-1Bs often earned 'higher wages than their domestic counterparts'.[21] The guestworker programme, as a result, had a 'positive impact on the domestic labor force'.

On 3 December 2020, the Court granted a 'preliminary injunction' to ITServe and prohibited the federal agency from enforcing the regulation.[22]

But this wasn't ITServe's first—or only—win.

In January 2018, USCIS's website had a new rule that stopped STEM OPT students from working at client locations. ITServe sued in July, stating that the agency 'did not comply' with the Administrative Procedure Act's 'notice and comment requirements' before making the rule. Around a month later, the agency revised the portal and removed almost all the restrictive clauses.[23]

ITServe Alliance – 2, US government – 0.

USCIS had also issued the Neufeld Memo in 2010, whose definition of the 'employer–employee' relationship forbade firms to place H-1B workers at clients, threatening the desi consultancy ecosystem.[24] The agency implemented it with vigour during the first Trump administration; the denial rates shot up from 6 per cent in 2015 to 30 per cent in the first quarter of 2020. In February 2018, it had passed a 'Contract and Itinerary Memorandum' requiring employers to list all work agreements for the entire visa period. The duration of approved petitions shrank—some as short as a day.[25]

ITServe sued again.

On 10 March 2020, the Court ruled that the federal agency's interpretation of the 'employer–employee' relationship was 'inconsistent with its regulation' and 'applied without rulemaking.'[26]

ITServe Alliance – 3, US government – 0.

On 20 May, the Contract and Itinerary memo was adjudged 'arbitrary and capricious' and 'not supported by the statute or regulation'. USCIS settled with ITServe and rescinded both memos.[27]

ITServe Alliance – 4, US government – 0.

Several other lawsuits, filed by the lobbying group, targeted the gatekeepers of the H-1B programme. It prompted a question: which firms comprised ITServe Alliance?

Yeah, here as well, desi consultancies.

Formed in 2010 in Dallas, ITServe's popularity (or notoriety) had spread in the summer of 2016, when AndhraFriends members discovered its true intent: to enslave H-1Bs for as long as possible in the green card queue, opposing legislation that would slash their waiting time. Exacting revenge, they released footage of over a dozen closed-door meetings.[28]

One video featured the ITServe ex-president explaining the organisation's reach in Andhra Pradesh, via offshore offices, to the state's IT minister, requesting help on tax deductions and clarity on the government's IT policy.[29] Its first annual conference in November 2015—broadcast on TV9 Telugu—included encouraging messages from Telangana's IT minister, K.T. Rama Rao; the mayor of Richardson, Paul Voelker; and Senator Cornyn.[30] One clip captured a senior member gloating over the 'success and power' of their 'voice on Capitol Hill'.[31] Two more showed the founder of the Reddy Neuman law firm, Rahul Reddy, suggesting ways for consultancy owners to exploit recent graduates and sue the US government to protect their interests.[32]

In 2016, ITServe Alliance's 'About us' page listed 452[33] companies as members[34]—and at least sixty of them investigated by the DOL. Many coughed up enormous fines, many multiple times: 1,051 H-1B violations, 447 affected employees, $2.57 million in back wages. The same ITServe that had humiliated the US government multiple times.[35]

Welcome to the eternal nights of the H-1B universe, where the moon had gobbled up the sun.

62

Manu submitted his EB-1 application in January 2021. For someone itching to escape India, he estimated his chance using a famous Indianism: '50-50'. If he got the green card, he'd apply for jobs, get an offer letter and move to the US. He'd resort to desi body shops only in 'the worst case'. That too, not Infocon Logix. He had left that 'junk life' forever.

Manu continued to work from home. After clearing his loans and earning a decent salary, he no longer needed alcohol or antidepressants to fall asleep. But disturbing flashbacks still tormented him in the shower: Tanuja screaming at him, Pulkit firing him, Jack firing and laughing at him. He sweated; his heartbeat raced.

Why now? It's over.

Manu hadn't got an increment since he joined. 'You should ask for a raise,' his manager told him in early 2022. 'If you won't ask, he won't give.' Diode Force, he added, paid Candidatez $28 an hour. Manu earned Rs 80,000 a month, $7 per hour. After working for a reputed American firm for close to two years, using his original resume and skills, he fought for something always denied to him: dignity. He called Sarvesh and demanded a pay hike: Rs 15 lakh per year.

'Give me a few points why you need an increment.'

Manu explained his duties, the equivalent of three employees' work. 'You can check with my manager. You don't need to listen to one side of the story.' Sarvesh said his company gave a raise of '12 to 15 per cent'. Manu had asked for 50 per cent. He told Manu to email his increased responsibilities. Manu sent around two dozen points. Not that they'd affect Sarvesh, a typical consultancy owner. He didn't expect a raise. He didn't get a raise.

Annoyed at another parasitic body shop, Manu looked for a job, both in India and the US—but not in corporate America. It had humiliated him enough. He submitted his resume to the IT departments of American universities instead.

Manu hadn't met his mother in the last six years. He once spoke to her on the phone before the lockdown. No longer angry, she asked him to come home. He refused. In mid-2022, his father told him about her frail health. He wanted Manu to tell her that he'd send her money.

'Why don't you tell her yourself?'

'What do I do with such arrogant people?'

His father emailed later. She was feeling better; he had given her money. He added: 'Make peace with your mother.'

They spoke one Friday afternoon. Over a long chat, she reiterated, 'You are lying. I never told you to leave.'

'Ask Mamaji. He kept saying, "Your mother said."'

Manu said he needed to hang up; he had to log in at work. She didn't listen. He reminded her again and again. She kept talking.

He hung up, then cried the whole day.

I had begun talking to Manu over Google Hangouts in May 2018. We chatted every Sunday at 9 p.m. for an hour. Manu sat at the table in his living room, his back to the kitchen. Over the next many months, I figured that the traumatic circularities overwhelming his life hadn't made him bitter. He absorbed them like a sponge, withdrawing further, sharpening his Indian fatalism. But I also discovered his other sides: the sly Manu, the sarcastic Manu, the funny Manu. Sometimes he got animated, recalling a joyous moment, and his body jerked and his eyes glowed—like a blissful teenager's. Even though he had got so little from life, he still expected little from it. Joys trickled in through routine, computer games and solitude—the only things he could control, the only things that wouldn't corrode his self-worth.

Manu and I stopped chatting around May 2020, resuming our ritual in short bursts over the next two years. In June 2022, a new Manu appeared on my screen. He looked lighter and smiled more; his voice bounced. He had paid off his loans, earned a decent salary now and had applied for his green card. He had also found something eluding him for long: hope. But the background to our conversations remained the same—the same empty kitchen, the same old suitcase, the same table fan—as if the person had changed, not his world. I had wanted to ask him something for years, but I refrained because the answer was obvious. His new avatar, though, made me take a risk.

'Are you happy, Manu?'

'Yes, I am.' He dropped his vintage self-effacing smile. 'But could be better.'

63

Kumar wrote to K in January 2021. 'Any updates on U visa? Just for your information, those with 4M got EAD (Green Card) on Jan 14. It is so depressing that I chose confrontation route and lost my GC. If I get U visa or GC, there is worth for my fight in America.'

Two days passed.

'Generally, you reply instantly but do not see any replies from you. Just checking, is everything okay?'

'Kinda … working on some things … will reply later with data.'

Another email the next day.

> I have few questions. 1) 2016, 2017 we filed case. Though I am not willing to file, you promised h1B Whistle blower Protection etc and employer won't fire. But 4M fired. Is America failed in protecting h1b victims? If so, why false promises?
>
> 2) If am with bad employer (4M) I would get EAD by January 14, 2021.
>
> 3) By taking risk, broken my immigration status, I came with you. What's the result? U visa or green cards? No.
>
> 4) Regarding U visa, where is the evidence in the system that it has entered to get some confidence to me? I trust you, you are my brother but I am asking systems side.
>
> 5) We know from other YouTube subscribers no one gets justice and they run behind me for follow-up and I am bothered about my immigration status and cases. Your my last hope. I am very down due to lost GC in this fight. Please reply so it gives me confidence.

The response:

> In one email—one email again—I need everything from 4M. Attorneys want. ASAP. I need more people that 4M cheated. I need the years. You've sent it to me before, but there are thousands of emails. You might have a thousand or 2 thousand dollars pursing this, and I'm still helping and feel confident. I can't control people. With the new administration I feel it'll move faster. I've also put more than $2,500 of my own cash into this, not to mention $3,300 in travel and the thousands of dollars of my own time to help my brother and his family. Confidentially, I am actually in contact with the Biden Administration. Chin up my brother.

Kumar: 'I am NOT worried about "a thousand or 2 thousand dollars pursing". I'm worried about my family paying price for my fight. They also lose GC (especially kids). "In one email—one email again—I need everything ..." I sent several times K. I sent recorded audio files of victim in google drive. I will re-send. "I need more people that 4M cheated." You know better than me that no Indian will come forward. "My time to help my brother." I appreciate that and I am thankful to you always.'

'Please know that my heart loves my brother. Please get me 4M victims.'

'I have shared almost all 4M information between 2016-2017. Later VersIT, ByteCore (print screens of Deva Ram—you said you will file U visa in 2018).'

K: 'I need victims from any company that will let us file DOL charges.'

'I need the U visa case number. For that you misunderstood and wrote about money. Question is not money. Question is, why am I fighting? When I lost my GC with 1st employer. You should rescue people like me to get U visa or GC otherwise how can I tell in videos that K will help h-1b victims? Already I have seen blame game between you and Ganesh and you could not provide proof of USCIS filing. Abhay $1,500. The other woman from NJ also told she lost money. Do you know, outside they might tell KE is cheating by taking money?

'But you are replying in same tone when I ask for U visa receipt number. If filed, why no number? Whenever I follow up on U visa, I do not get any authentic information to cross check in USCIS site. I need proof. I am in USA because of your support. Hoping we will win against 4M, YBMyles and get U visa or GC. If this trust is breached, am almost dead.'

K emailed Kumar in the second week of April. 'Found out the delay. John Chemers. I'm working on a narrative. This ONLY strengthens your case due to harassment and injustice.'

'John is my follower but turned hater. He also attacked my Muslim Subscriber student and couple of others.'

'He's why—trying to get a copy of what he sent USCIS.'

'Thanks for all your help. What I do not understand, if a racist emails USCIS does it believe blindly? They do their own background check, correct? Even if delayed, we will get the visa, right?'

'I think the outcome is good … think this helps.'

More questions after a week. '1) When did you file my U visa? 2) When did you get receipt of my U visa? 3) When was my U visa application approved? Or when will it approve?'

'We'll file everything the old fashioned way in the next 2 days.'

'I am confused because you said you already filed, right? All I am asking, when did you file and when did you get receipt? If not filed, then I will NOT have false HOPES.'

He emailed K a link. 'Case Status Online—Case Status Search (uscis.gov). Avoid Scams | USCIS.'

'I am aware. I am working on this without exposing your case in NY.'

'Do you want me to trust? 2016-17 you said U visa. 2018: I filled forms on USCIS and sent screen shots of ByteCore scams, you said U visa. 2020 Oct: you sent an attorney picture and said DREAM and asked $1,500. You then said Corona lockdown and asked me to check mail box every day. Gave April 8, 2021 deadline. If not they will return money. April 15, 2021: "We will file everything the old fashioned way." Is it lie or story? Are you creating false hopes? I am tired. Looks like I got scammed.'

'What the fuck have you done for me Kumar? I work and work and don't see a penny.'

K returned a few days later. 'Resubmit T visa will have receipt by Thursday as I was told.'

'T visa? Because we are always talking about U visa and receipt numbers, correct? Thursday—which Thursday? Could you please show proof of submissions? Who is cheating you by taking my money and not giving receipt numbers? Or am I getting fooled? Please do not write bad words. Write email with a receipt number of U or T visas otherwise return my money.'

'My sisters cancer is back and I have been out of pocket. Please watch your words making accusations. After all I have done for u free. I told you we were waiting on information on your case.'

'I'm sorry to know and praying for God to recover soon. I asked receipt number, you are saying accusations. If you failed to show proof, what do you expect the other person to understand? If you cannot return the money, cannot give receipt numbers, cannot show proof of submission, please do not do false promises. I am NOT Ganesh or Abhay or adolescent doctor to get fooled.'

And then, John.

Calls, emails, voicemails—different names, different numbers. Now even when genuine subscribers contacted Kumar, he suspected their identities.

An email from 'Saad Sheikh Terrorist'. 'You didn't get paid until I helped you. You claim I am harassing thousands of Indian students. You are a liar.'

A flurry of images and videos. All photos of Yash Mittra. The superimposed text read:

'Fuck off.'

'Fuck you.'

'Fuck off.'

Followed by a message: 'You're a dumbass what makes you think some low-cost Indian student has taken my job you're a f****** dumbass.'

Then a picture of Yash: 'Fuck you'.

Kumar made a video, 'Haters sms', featuring screenshots of John's messages' but didn't reveal his name. The next upload: 'Truth about John Chemers & his attacks on Indians & Americans'.

John responded.

He created two YouTube channels—Kumar Exclusive Sreenivas Pandruvada and I am Saad—and released eighty-nine videos: 'Pedophile Kumar Exclusive', 'Sex rape with cow Kumar Sreenivas Pandruvada +1-585-484-7605', 'My button kicks you out of America Kumar Exclusive'.

Kumar flagged all of them for copyright violations.

John had ensured that Kumar would never get a project, as even a cursory Google search on him flung vulgar posts carrying his photos and name. He emailed Virgil and me. 'Do you think placing a sorry video for John Chemers cool him? He is sending threats.'

'I would turn them to the local police department,' Virgil said, 'or the DOJ/FBI and let them cool him down.'

'I reported to FBI Chicago. I will report to NOVI POLICE also.'

John flagged Kumar's videos for copyright violations. YouTube acted: two strikes.

'One more strike,' Kumar wrote to me, 'and I will lose channel.'

He made his channel private. But John continued to send endless emails and videos. I also got around two dozen videos with Kumar's pictures and abusive texts. He changed his number. Many YouTube and Instagram accounts popped up, attacking him and other Indians.

Even Kumar's wife. A text on WhatsApp: a screenshot from a YouTube channel, 'Kumar Exclusive News'. Under it, fifteen videos. Another message to her from a different number: 'You are a criminal. You are a bully. I am stalking you in Novi Michigan and I am going to kill you.'

John sent her over a hundred messages in a few days.

He contacted Kumar from a new ID. 'Michigan's cyberbullying law House Bill No. 5017. Posting videos, pictures, statements on YouTube, LinkedIn, Instagram, personal blog about me that intends to put me in fear of bodily harm or death and expresses an intent to commit violence against me.'

Kumar forwarded it to Virgil and me.

'Hey putz. Deal me in,' Virgil wrote to John. 'You want to threaten, threaten me. I'll make sure it reaches the proper people.'

Kumar kept a Google Alert on his name and searched its variants online (as John used different combinations). One such result stumped him. 'I'm shocked,' he shared a screenshot with me. The website, DocketBird: a repository of legal documents. The link: the YBMyles lawsuit.

'Do you know what happened?' I asked. 'Did you lose the case, is it still going on—did K give any update?'

'According to him neither lose nor win. When I say lost he didn't agree. Attorney said government dismissed it. No details. Can you find some pdf etc? Another site asked me to purchase to get the cases.'

I went to the Public Access to Court Electronic Records (PACER) website. The case history comprised seventeen documents. The last file read: 'Notice of Voluntary Dismissal'. I informed Kumar.

'I think K decided something with his attorneys without involving me. They try to convince me that USA government dismissed it. But why does it show here that I dismissed it?'

He wrote to K.

'Do you know more people who will complain? That was one of the government reasons for not going forward. It was only you.'

Kumar demanded more clarification. K said he was at the hospital; he'd call later and explain.

'I do not understand his replies,' Kumar told me. 'Always connect to sister and hospitals.'

The case popping up online still worried him. John could use it to harass him further. He emailed DocketBird's link to Virgil. 'Is it okay to request them to remove this? I lost the case.'

'No idea. But if it is a public record, then maybe nothing can be done.'

'In the USA, it is useless to fight body shops or anyone if you do NOT have a green card or citizenship. Initially I thought "LAWS AND IMMIGRATION LAWS are ultimate in the USA". It took a decade and money and family life to know it is a myth. Several subscribers told, they went to court and the judge struck out the cases by saying his employer paid salaries by looking at the fake paychecks. So the USA believes in the Employer version, not the employees. I lost a huge amount of time on social media. I lost everything because of my fight or confrontation.'

64

Confined indoors during the pandemic with no job prospects, Virgil hired himself. He created a data-crunching website in May 2020: DOLINW.com (Department of Labor I Need Work).[36]

'Can you please help me make a webpage?' An email from Kumar. 'How much does it cost?'

He wanted a portal for his H-1B experiences and investigations.

'For you I'll do it for free. I normally get 500 bucks and 10 dollars a month to host, plus an annual domain worth $15.'

'$500. OMG.'

'Not for you. What do you want your domain name to be?'

'What would you suggest? KumarExclusive.com.'

'KumarExclusive.com is available.'

'I will think. Because it costs you money, right? I do not want to be a burden and I am in a financial crisis.'

'Naw, I owe you. It's only 15 to register.'

'Please do not think like that, you are my best friend.'

'Trust me, glad to do it. You helped me when I was down. I'm returning the favor. It is an American thing.'

That time again: po. Virgil couldn't pay the car mortgage for the past two months and expected to lose it any day. He survived on food stamps (about to expire in July 2021). His renewed housing forbearance would last till March 2021. After that, his social security cheques would cover the rent. Reducing his essential monthly costs to $350 per month, he had mastered the art of frugal living, but still fell short.

The VA increased the salary for the housekeeping aid position to $12.5 an hour. Virgil applied for his 'fifth prison sentence'. He continued to scale up his activism through DOLINW, GuestWorkerVisas.com and Keep America At Work. He created another website, GlobalWorkersUnited,[37] followed by VJBTrading,[38] something he had wanted to do since 1996.

Next: DestoryingYourFuture.com.[39]

He emailed its link to Kumar and me. 'I think we can defeat the bastards.'

'I am NOT discouraging you,' Kumar replied. 'But from my 12 years experience, CRIME NEVER ENDS, and America failed to do anything. I have never ever come across a single H-1B or displaced American get justice.'

'Yep, but letting that happen is not an option.'

Virgil joined the VA in February 2021. On the first morning, he cleaned the four floors, emptied the trash carts and headed towards the canteen. He stopped by the vending room to check the trash compactor, then walked across the hallway to inspect round trash cans. His supervisor, Maria, accused him of wasting time in the hallway. He tried to explain that he was finishing work and going for lunch, but she ate him.

Two days later, on Sunday, he emailed the Medical Center director, Christopher Sandles, explaining the 'abusive environment' at the VA—a 'pattern'—forcing him to 'quit many times' since 2016. 'I'm trying for the fifth time to get back to work and came close to quitting again. I see people getting promoted to positions that are not advertised and, most times, when I visit with them, I realize they may not even have the skills for the job. Many have told me that if you are not a vet, you won't get promoted, but I am a vet and I don't get promoted. The Office of Information and Technology in Austin apparently makes the hiring decisions. While researching them, I was shocked to find an environment of negligence and a total lack of compliance as documented in VAOIG-13-01730-159[40] (attached).'

The report stated that the Austin Information Technology Center had 'failed to follow' the 'security policy and contract security requirements', approving contractors to access its 'network from China and India'.[41] The VA information security employees 'failed to quickly respond to stop the practice' and determine if it compromised 'any VA data'.[42] A desi consultancy, Zen Infotech, had sponsored an H-1B for one such contractor. A firm so callous it had once paid back wages worth $470,043—the twenty-sixth highest fine in the history of DOL investigations.[43] The US government brought a criminal case against Zen Infotech employees—Satish Gudaru, Prakash Kanyadara and Carol Nelson—in the Kansas District Court. The affidavit supporting the criminal complaint repeated the story common to countless desi consultancies: Zen Infotech imported H-1B workers when it didn't have jobs for them, failed to pay them on bench, didn't match their LCA amounts and so on.[44] On 3 July 2014, its owner, Gudaru, 'pled guilty' for his role in 'an H-1B visa fraud scheme'.[45]

Virgil went to work on the first-floor ward on Monday. Wearing a mask, a face shield and a gown, he entered each room and collected trash. Once done, he reached a sliding-door dumpster. Since he hadn't got the badge, he used the key to hold open the door. It worked, and he began dumping the trash. Maria came and yelled at him for 'breaking the law'. When he tried to clarify, she screamed again, calling him 'insubordinate' and threatening to 'report' him.

After she left, he trolleyed the cart to its original location, picked up his coat and headed towards her to return his access keys. But she and her supervisor were screaming, so he looked for the work leader on the first floor. When Virgil couldn't find him, he walked towards Maria's office and found her and a cop at the sliding door. He said Maria never listened to the workers. Virgil handed in his keys and radio and left.

Two days later, he emailed the VA retirement office. 'I'd like to retire. I am currently an employee and was trying to buy back my military time [for an increased annuity]. I believe I only owe $435 out of $960. Can you please forward this to somebody who can tell me my options and what I need to do?'

No reply.

He uploaded a video: 'Why did I quit the Department of Veterans Affairs for the fifth time'.

The comments unleashed rage.

'My daughter has been with the VA for 11yrs and has an a**hole supv.'

'I was an executive and quit.'

'I worked at the DOD & VA and they are the same. Friends and family MOVE UP FAST. Veterans Get Second Crumbs.'

'I've had two different jobs at different locations and can't work there. I desperately wanted to be of service to my fellow Vets but the culture at the VA is something I've never experienced.'

'The VA is the worst. Prayers, Brother.'

Virgil wrote to Sandles, attaching the relevant documents, for processing his buyback time.

No reply.

He submitted a help request on the OPM Retirement Services webpage. A response eight days later: 'You should contact your current personnel office'—the VA.

He emailed the Office of Resolution Management, Diversity and Inclusion. 'Nobody will help me resolve this and I believe it is an attempt to run out the clock and say he isn't an employee, so we do not have to abide by our rules.' He received a reply the next day: 'I will forward this message to the ORMDI District Management team for their awareness to give additional assistance.' Then, eight minutes later, another email, almost as an afterthought: 'Thank you for your service to our Country.'

After three weeks, he 'stirred up the pot', applying for his supervisor's position, hospital housekeeping officer. Virgil sent his latest resume; it featured eleven points detailing his battles at the VA. Eight days later, he got rejected. He rented out his house to an old couple for $1,000 who allowed him to stay in the garage. No toilet, no AC—heavy rains could flood the place. But no choice: 'that time again'.

End of April: no response about his military buyback inquiries. So, as always, he wrote a letter.

To: President Joe Biden
Honorable Denis Richard McDonough
Senator Ted Cruz
Senator John Cornyn
Senator Charles Perry
Representative Andrew S. Murr
Congressman August Pfluger
Subject: Retirement

I could not resolve this on my own. Maybe you'll have a different experience. I am 63. I have around 7 to 8 years of service in the United States Navy. At 62, you can retire with as little as 5 years of service. I won't work for supervisors who tell me I need to ask for permission to go to the bathroom or call the police on me for doing my job, and after several hundred attempts to get a computer programming or a support job with over 30 years of experience (including project management), it is evident I will never get hired, so I wish to retire.

I have 'bought back' $525 of my military time leaving a $435 balance. I want to pay that and apply for retirement. I am still an employee of the Department of Veterans Affairs based on the enclosed email message from my supervisor and her supervisor.

Respectfully,
Virgil Bierschwale
You will find 2 videos on this link describing my side of the story: www.ICanCodeJoe.com.

Epilogue
(May 2025)

Manu got his EB-1 green card and moved to California in November 2024. Free from the H-1B shackles, he felt relieved and confident. He dived headlong into the job search, applying for '200 IT positions' per day. Weeks passed, then months passed: 'Not even a single response'. He contacted over a dozen desi consultancies. They demanded $10,000 and directed him to take 'one-month training'. Manu said he had a green card and fifteen years of experience.

So?

He approached friends, acquaintances and managers from Diode Force and Infocon Logix. No one helped. He interviewed for part-time gigs. Rejected. He still worked for Diode Force, on his India salary, but Santa Clara's living expenses bled him dry. Manu owed around Rs 20 lakh. Even his gaming laptop, his only solace, had turned sluggish and old. 'That life is also coming to an end,' he told me over the phone. What would he do, I asked, if he failed to find a job? 'I will blame God.' He laughed. 'Because I tried everything.' Contemplating his despair, he laughed several times during our chat. At times, he fell quiet and sniffled. 'I will search for jobs for one more month,' he said. 'If nothing happens, I will return to India.'

After Integrisys fired Kumar, he joined another desi consultancy. He reactivated his green card application and, in August 2023, became a permanent resident. 'I suddenly felt relaxed,' he said. 'All the stress was gone.' He didn't use that freedom, though, to change his job. He continued living in Michigan, as his elder son studied in a college in the same state. 'After some time,' he added, 'your children's careers become more important than yours.'

His YouTube channel had dwindled in popularity after the lockdown. No matter how many videos he recorded, or scams he exposed, his subscriber count stagnated—for years—at 13,300. If Kumar had tired of the world, then the world, too, had tired of Kumar. Nothing dented his enthusiasm though. He kept releasing videos and posting tweets. His popularity soared again in late 2024. His tweets went viral, and his channel exceeded 17,000 subscribers. The backlash returned, too. In March 2025, X restricted his tweets' visibility for 'hateful conduct' and suspended his account. Kumar contested the decision many times. Nothing happened.

He couldn't meet Virgil, but they stayed in touch, exchanging over a dozen emails a week. Over the last few years, he had also received cease-and-desist letters from desi consultancies. Either remove your tweets and videos, they warned, or fight us in court. Kumar created a GoFundMe page to battle such threats.[1] Under it, he posted a plea. 'This is not just about me—it's about standing up for every worker who has been exploited, every person who has faced unfair treatment, and every immigrant who dreams of a fair chance at success in the U.S.' The petition received $375 and a comment. 'Honesty is often very hard. The truth is often painful. But the freedom it can bring is worth trying.'

The VA rejected Virgil's claim for the increased monthly pension, around $250, as he needed at least five years of civilian federal service. His cumulative duration at the VA totalled two years and five months. Any government employer would have sufficed (if it hired him), but he could find only one near Harper: the Kerrville VA. So he applied to it countless times. Each time, the same response: not selected. In October 2022, when the agency snubbed him again for the housekeeping aid position, he filed an age discrimination complaint with the Equal

Employment Opportunity Commission. It emailed the decision in July 2023, concluding that Virgil had 'failed to establish a causal connection between his age and non-selection' and dismissed his case.

He continued to rent out his house, but the leaking roof, rats and spiders made it impossible for him to stay in the garage. He rented two cabins: a 10-by-16, where he watched TV and slept, and an 8-by-12, where he worked. Even though he had protested the H-1B programme for over a decade, almost nothing stirred, as if he was locked in a soundproof room. But the walls collapsed, overnight, a day before the 2024 Christmas. A right-wing influencer, Laura Loomer, berated Trump for appointing an Indian-American entrepreneur, Sriram Krishnan, as the policy advisor on Artificial Intelligence. Then, Elon Musk, heading the Department of Government Efficiency, declared that he'd 'go to war to defend' the guest worker programme.[2] His comment ignited fiery backlash, and the Musk-MAGA battle foregrounded the H-1B debate in the American and Indian media for weeks.

Virgil escalated his data-driven activism. This time, after eighteen years, the dam broke. Many American techies messaged him, admiring his work, revealing their plight, giving him donations. He announced his plan to contest the Senate elections the next year. More contributions poured in, sailing him across $5,000. In May 2025, his tweet, 'By not hiring Americans to work in America, India has woken a sleeping giant', went viral. The *Times of India* spun a piece around it, calling him a 'Republican leader' (!).[3]

But his new fight also made him collide with those who distorted the H-1B issue to hurl abuses at Indians. He blocked such accounts and tweeted his frustration. 'One thing I hate about this war is all the racism. Folks, I have said it a thousand times. If you use racism instead of math, you will lose.' The last few months had resurrected his vitality and purpose, gifting him renewed hope. But something else, too, changed, a change so remarkable that it hadn't happened in the last twenty-two years, a change that looked like an end but promised a beginning: Virgil had stopped looking for a job.

Notes

PART I: DREAM

1. SAP, a famous software, stands for System Analysis Program Development (translated from the company's original German name: Systemanalyse Programmentwicklung).
2. Private engineering colleges exploded in Andhra Pradesh from the late 1990s onwards. See 'Andhra Pradesh Opens More Technical Colleges to Stem Brain Drain'. *India Today*. Amarnath Menon. 25 August 1997. https://www.indiatoday.in/magazine/states/story/19970825-andhra-pradesh-opens-more-technical-colleges-to-stem-brain-drain-831948-1997-08-24.

   'The growth of engineering colleges from 1997 to 2006 [in Andhra Pradesh] is substantial because of the boom in the software sector,' noted a 2019 research paper. 'The state government and AICTE [All India Council of Technical Education] opened the floodgates for private engineering colleges from 1997. The total number of engineering colleges in A.P. reached 281 with a total intake of 91,716 by April 2006. In 2008 the state government introduced fee reimbursement scheme for engineering students and many engineering colleges started cropping-up during this period and the total number of engineering colleges in A.P. reached 535 by the end of the year. From 2009 to 2012 … [the] total reached to 893.' See more at 'Dynamics of Technical Education in Andhra Pradesh'. *Paripex—Indian Journal of Research*. K. Krishna Veni and G.V. Chalam. November 2019. https://www.worldwidejournals.com/paripex/recent_issues_pdf/2019/

November/dynamics-of-technical-education-in-andhra-pradesh_November_2019_1574170610_0711693.pdf.

See also the U.R. Rao Committee's 2003 report on AICTE: https://www.documentcloud.org/documents/24360789-revitalizing-technical-education-ur-rao-committee-report-2003; 'Warning Bells.' *Frontline*. R. Ramachandran. 26 March 2004. https://frontline.thehindu.com/the-nation/education/article30221655.ece; 'Engineering Education in India: A Story of Contrasts.' World Education News + Reviews. 1 January 2007. https://wenr.wes.org/2007/01/wenr-january-2007-engineering-education-in-india-a-story-of-contrasts.

3. 'The faculty shortage has been a topic of discussion within the engineering education system in India for a long time … The issue in India seems to be the exceptionally large number of engineering institutions, which leads to the low numbers of students and faculty per institution,' stated a 2013 World Bank report. 'Assuming that the number of faculty is close to the true situation, the number of engineering faculty per institution is quite low. … [But] the issue of the engineering faculty in India is not only one of quantity; it is also an issue of quality. The percentage of engineering faculty with PhD degrees is low. Even at competitively selected institutions involved in the Technical Education Quality Improvement Program in Andhra Pradesh, one of the most advanced states in terms of engineering education, the share of engineering faculty with PhD degrees is merely 20 percent. This is low even among the BRIC countries.' See more at 'International Comparative Study: Engineering Education in India'. World Bank. April 2013. https://documents1.worldbank.org/curated/en/586761468044369699/pdf/781820Revised00ndia02013060100FINAL.pdf.
4. See 'Ameerpet Houses Hundreds of IT Institutes and Over One Lakh Students'. *The Economic Times*. Devina Sengupta. 22 September 2010. https://economictimes.indiatimes.com/jobs/ameerpet-houses-hundreds-of-it-institutes-and-over-one-lakh-students/articleshow/msid-6604215,curpg-4.cms?from=mdr; 'Scaling Classroom IT Skill Tutoring.' *Proceedings of the 2018 CHI Conference on Human Factors in Computing Systems*. Meghna Joshi, Tanmay Joshi and Nimmi Rangaswamy. 21 April 2018. https://doi.org/10.1145/3173574.3174204 (pp. 1–12); 'Ameerpet, India's Unofficial IT Training Hub.' *The*

Economist. 30 March 2017. https://www.economist.com/business/2017/03/30/ameerpet-indias-unofficial-it-training-hub; 'Hyderabad May Not be Silicon Valley, but it Has a SAP Street: From Quick Classes to Fake Certificates, Here's Why Ameerpet is Always on IT Students' Radar.' EdexLive. Sadaf Aman. 24 April 2017. https://www.edexlive.com/live-story/2017/apr/24/hyderabad-may-not-be-silicon-valley-but-it-has-a-sap-street-from-quick-classes-to-fake-certificate-358.html.

5. Section 214(b) of the Immigration and Nationality Act relates to visa denials on the basis that an applicant failed to establish non-immigrant intent.
6. Form I-20 is a Department of Homeland Security document signed by a foreign student and an approved American school attesting that the foreign student is eligible to study at the institution. See 'Students and the Form I-20'. Department of Homeland Security. https://studyinthestates.dhs.gov/students/prepare/students-and-the-form-i-20.
7. 'The H-1B visa category was created to enable U.S. employers to hire temporary workers as needed in specialty occupations, or those that require theoretical and practical application of a body of highly specialized knowledge,' stated the Government Accountability Office's June 2006 report (pp. 5–6). 'It also requires a bachelor's or higher degree (or its equivalent) in the specific occupation as a minimum requirement for entry into the occupation in the United States.'

   See 'Labor Could Improve Its Oversight and Increase Information Sharing With Homeland Security'. U.S. Government Accountability Office. June 2006. https://www.gao.gov/assets/gao-06-720.pdf [hereinafter 2006 GAO Report, 'Labor Could Improve Its Oversight'].
8. Between 2008 and 2012, Hyderabad globally ranked fourth—after Seoul, Beijing and Shanghai—in sending the highest number of students to American universities, 26,220 (nearly 30,000 when combined with Secunderabad). See 'The Geography of Foreign Students in U.S. Higher Education: Origins and Destinations'. Brookings. Neil Ruiz. 29 August 2014. https://www.brookings.edu/interactives/the-geography-of-foreign-students-in-u-s-higher-education-origins-and-destinations/.

   Hyderabad's obsession with America only intensified in the subsequent years. See, for instance, the following reports from 2014 and 2023 carrying near-identical headlines. 'Hyderabad Sends More Students to US than Delhi, Mumbai.' *The Times of India.* Chidanand Rajghatta. 31 August 2014. https://timesofindia.indiatimes.com/education/news/hyderabad-sends-more-students-to-us-than-delhi-mumbai/articleshow/41314839.cms; 'Hyderabad Sent More Students to US Than Mumbai, Delhi.' *Deccan Chronicle.* Sanjay Paul. 20 January 2023. https://web.archive.org/web/20230523152946/https://www.deccanchronicle.com/education/200123/hyderabad-sent-more-students-to-us-than-mumbai-delhi.html.

9. 'US Knows Only 15 of 2,000 Hyderabad Education Consultants.' *Deccan Chronicle.* 26 December 2015. https://www.deccanchronicle.com/151226/nation-current-affairs/article/us-knows-only-15-2000-hyderabad-consultants.
10. 'Students Under Scanner for Taking Part-Time Jobs in US.' *The Sunday Guardian.* 26 December 2015. http://web.archive.org/web/20160109231728/https://www.sundayguardianlive.com/news/2376-students-under-scanner-taking-part-time-jobs-us/.

    'The number of visa consultancy firms has gone up from 100 five years ago to over 400 currently,' noted the piece. 'Most charge around Rs 8,000 per student apart from the five to 10% commission on tuition fees charged by the US universities. "Lesser the reputation of a university, higher our commission," a consultant said on the condition of anonymity.'
11. 'Visa Consultant Nabbed for Forging Documents.' *The Times of India.* 24 December 2015. https://timesofindia.indiatimes.com/city/hyderabad/Visa-consultant-nabbed-for-forging-documents/articleshow/50305013.cms.
12. See '7 Arrested for Selling Fake Educational Certificates in Hyderabad.' *The Indian Express.* 28 February 2023. https://indianexpress.com/article/cities/hyderabad/7-held-selling-fake-educational-certificates-hyderabad-8471736; 'Fraud Consultants, Bogus Certificates, Gullible Students: How Hundreds of Indians are Faking the American Dream.' *ETV Bharat.* 14 April 2022. https://www.etvbharat.com/english/bharat/fake-student-us-visa-racket-busted-in-delhi-cops-crack-whip-against-consultancies/na20220414153752275/; 'Fake Educational Consultancy Raided, 2 Held in Hyderabad.' *Telangana Today.* 15 February 2022. https://telanganatoday.com/fake-educational-consultancy-raided-2-held-in-hyderabad/.

13. 'American Dream Sours, Students Cry Foul.' *Deccan Chronicle*. 25 February 2014. https://www.deccanchronicle.com/140225/news-current-affairs/article/american-dream-sours-students-cry-foul.
14. 'Recruiting Students Overseas to Fill Seats, Not to Meet Standards.' *The New York Times*. Stephanie Saul. 19 April 2016. https://www.nytimes.com/2016/04/20/us/recruiting-students-overseas-to-fill-seats-not-to-meet-standards.html/.
15. 'The Visa Temple.' *Slate*. Suman Naishadham. 3 April 2017. https://www.slate.com/news-and-politics/2017/04/at-hyderabads-visa-temple-indians-pray-to-come-to-the-u-s.html/.
16. 'These Temples Have Become Famous Among Visa-Seekers; Here's Why.' *Travel + Leisure*. Priyaja Bakshi. 2 September 2023. https://www.travelandleisureasia.com/in/destinations/india/visa-temples-in-india/.
17. Manu's anxiety wasn't unfounded. See, for instance, the following that discuss the employability of recent Indian graduates in the aughts: 'The Engineering Gap.' *The Economist*. 28 January 2010. https://www.economist.com/business/2010/01/28/the-engineering-gap; 'Employability and Skill Set of Newly Graduated Engineers in India.' Policy Research Working Paper; no. WPS 5640. © World Bank. Andreas Blom and Hiroshi Saeki. April 2011. https://doi.org/10.1596/1813-9450-5640; 'Only 25% IT Graduates Readily Employable: Nasscom.' *The Economic Times*. Harsimran Julka and Pankaj Mishra. 7 April 2011. https://economictimes.indiatimes.com/jobs/only-25-it-graduates-readily-employable-nasscom/articleshow/7894300.cms; 'India's Skills Famine.' *The New Yorker*. James Surowiecki. 9 April 2007. https://www.newyorker.com/magazine/2007/04/16/indias-skills-famine.
18. In the India Semi-Annual Fraud Update dated 13 March 2009, the Fraud Prevention Unit (FPU) had found that 'Andhra Pradesh, and in particular its capital of Hyderabad, has been identified as a large center of documentary fraud'. It also found that 'Hyderabadi applicants comprised over one-third of Chennai's total visa workload in FY-2008, but well over half of the FPU workload'. Regarding student visas, the report noted that '[m]any student applicants, even legitimate ones, are taken in by document vendors. They present fraudulent packages of bank statements and land documents in their interviews, and they are guided by advertising and news articles, such as the one in Hyderabad which declared, "Study Part-Time, Work Full-Time"

on an F-1 student visa'. Several US consulates launched 'initiatives to combat H and L [visa] fraud', including the 'actual start-up of a new consulate general in Hyderabad'. 'India Semi-Annual Fraud Update.' Public Library of US Diplomacy. WikiLeaks. 13 March 2009. https://wikileaks.org/plusd/cables/09CHENNAI77_a.html.

See also 'Inside Visa Fraud in India'. *Computerworld*. Patrick Thibodeau. 27 April 2011. https://www.computerworld.com/article/2471242/inside-visa-fraud-in-india.html.

PART II: DECEPTION

1. Link to what the front page of Keep America At Work looked like on 5 November 2007: https://web.archive.org/web/20071112092046/http://www.keepamericaatwork.com/.
2. 'Bridgeport U. Ponders Its Future.' *The New York Times*. Constance Hays. 27 April 1992. https://www.nytimes.com/1992/04/27/nyregion/bridgeport-u-ponders-its-future.html.
3. 'Strike by Professors is Settled at the University of Bridgeport.' *The New York Times*. George Judson. 29 August 1992. https://www.nytimes.com/1992/08/29/nyregion/strike-by-professors-is-settled-at-the-university-of-bridgeport.html [hereinafter Bridgeport Professors' Strike].
4. 'The Silence the Students Left Behind; In Bridgeport, a University's Decline Has a Ripple Effect.' *The New York Times*. 5 December 1992. https://www.nytimes.com/1992/12/05/nyregion/silence-students-left-behind-bridgeport-university-s-decline-has-ripple-effect.html/ [hereinafter Bridgeport Students' Silence].
5. See *supra* note 3, Part II: Deception, Bridgeport Professors' Strike.
6. See *supra* note 4, Part II: Deception, Bridgeport Students' Silence.
7. 'Bridgeport U. Approves a Pact With Unification Church Affiliate.' *The New York Times*. Steven Myers. 26 April 1992. https://www.nytimes.com/1992/04/26/nyregion/bridgeport-u-approves-a-pact-with-unification-church-affiliate.html.
8. 'Sun Myung Moon Dies at 92; Washington Times Owner Led the Unification Church.' *The Washington Post*. Emma Brown. 2 September 2012. https://www.washingtonpost.com/world/asia_pacific/sun-myung-moon-dies-at-92-washington-times-owner-

led-the-unification-church/2012/09/02/001b747a-f531-11e1-aab7-f199a16396cf_story.html.

9. 'Unification Church School on a Campus Raises Alarms.' *The New York Times*. 2 December 1997. https://www.nytimes.com/1997/12/02/nyregion/unification-church-school-on-a-campus-raises-alarms.html.
10. 'Stymied in U.S., Moon's Church Sounds a Retreat.' *The Washington Post*. Marc Fisher and Jeff Leen. 24 November 1997. https://www.washingtonpost.com/wp-srv/national/longterm/cult/unification/part2.htm.
11. 'University of Bridgeport Stands on its Own After Parting With Church.' *The Connecticut Post*. Linda Lambeck. 4 June 2019. https://www.ctpost.com/local/article/After-parting-with-church-University-of-13914570.php.
12. '2007 Annual Report.' University of Bridgeport. https://www.documentcloud.org/documents/24485738-ub-report-2007 (p. 1).
13. Ibid. at p. 9.
14. '2008 Annual Report.' University of Bridgeport. https://www.documentcloud.org/documents/24360322-ub-report-2008 (p. 10).
15. 'Radar Names America's 50 Worst Colleges.' *Radar*. Sarah Howes. 28 August 2008. https://www.manoanow.org/radar-names-americas-50-worst-colleges/article_b0ea2344-7eda-59af-9d3d-017526f44c23.html [hereinafter Radar].
16. See Bridgeport's crime rate from 2006 to 2008 here: http://web.archive.org/web/20250311095052/https://www.macrotrends.net/global-metrics/cities/us/ct/bridgeport/crime-rate-statistics.
17. See *supra* note 15, Part II: Deception, Radar.
18. 'Frequently Asked Questions: How Many International Students Attend UB?' University of Bridgeport. 22 February 2008. http://web.archive.org/web/20080222121134/http://www.bridgeport.edu/pages/3280.asp#A4.
19. 'F-1 students may not work off-campus during the first academic year,' explained the U.S. Citizenship and Immigration Services (USCIS) website, 'but may accept on-campus employment subject to certain conditions and restrictions.' See more at 'Students and Employment'. U.S. Citizenship and Immigration Services. https://www.uscis.gov/

working-in-the-united-states/students-and-exchange-visitors/students-and-employment.

So, in most cases, working off-campus in the first year, while enrolled as a full-time student, is illegal. This hasn't deterred many Indian students, though, from working in gas stations, convenience stores and restaurants. In some (rare) cases, they've been denied entry and their visas cancelled for such transgressions. See, for instance, 'F1 Student Deported at Port of Entry for Working at Gas Station'. Happy Schools. 13 September 2011. http://www.happyschools.com/f1-student-deported-at-port-of-entry/; 'Student From India on F-1 Visa Deported for Working Illegally in Restaurant.' *The American Bazaar*. 4 January 2016. https://www.americanbazaaronline.com/2016/01/04/student-from-india-on-f-1-visa-deported-for-working-illegally-in-restaurant/#google_vignette.

See also 'Working in the United States (Students and Employment)'. U.S. Citizenship and Immigration Services. https://www.uscis.gov/working-in-the-united-states/students-and-exchange-visitors/students-and-employment.

20. Virgil was referring to a widely circulated email forward that stated Obama 'refused to not only put his hand on his heart during the Pledge of Allegiance but refused to say the Pledge'. See 'Blow's My Mind'. Keep America At Work. Virgil Bierschwale. 3 January 2008. https://web.archive.org/web/20080112112848/http://keepamericaatwork.com/ [hereinafter 'Blow's My Mind'].

    See also 'Obama "Refused to Not Only Put His Hand on His Heart During the Pledge of Allegiance But Refused to Say the Pledge"'. *PolitiFact*. Bill Adair. 8 November 2007. https://www.politifact.com/factchecks/2007/nov/08/chain-email/photo-was-taken-during-anthem-not-pledge/.
21. Ibid. at 'Blow's My Mind'.
22. 'Obama Angers Midwest Voters With Guns and Religion Remark.' *The Guardian*. Ed Pilkington. 14 April 2008. https://www.theguardian.com/world/2008/apr/14/barackobama.uselections2008.
23. 'Am I Legit?' Keep America At Work. 28 October 2008. https://web.archive.org/web/20081029224316/http://www.keepamericaatwork.com/.

24. 'Here is an Interesting Article by Mitch Gurney.' Keep America At Work. 17 January 2009. http://web.archive.org/web/20090129164126/http://keepamericaatwork.com/?p=858.
25. 'This Has Really Been Bothering Me.' Keep America At Work. 19 January 2009. https://web.archive.org/web/20090129164351/http://keepamericaatwork.com/?p=872.
26. 'Who Do We Blame it On?' Keep America At Work. 17 February 2009. https://web.archive.org/web/20090221015133/http://keepamericaatwork.com/.
27. 'A Displaced Texas Programmer Analyzes the Pattern of Low Salaries and Immigration That Leads to American Job Loss.' VDare. 7 April 2009. https://www.documentcloud.org/documents/24252380-a-displaced-texas-programmer-analyzes-the-pattern-of-low-salaries-and-immigration-that-leads-to-american-job-loss-vdare.
28. 'Why We Need to Ensure That the Caste System NEVER Comes to America.' Keep America At Work. 29 June 2009. https://web.archive.org/web/20090629162419/http://keepamericaatwork.com/.
29. Wage and Hour Division (WHD), an agency within the U.S. Department of Labor (DOL), has the authority to investigate claims related to an employee's wages, hours and work conditions. The WHD may also bring enforcement action, such as pursuing back wages, liquidated damages and civil monetary penalties to remedy violations. See more here: https://www.dol.gov/sites/dolgov/files/WHD/fact-sheets/WH1030.pdf (October 2023).

    Part of the DOL's authority is to conduct investigations related to alleged H-1B violations. See 'Fact Sheet #62U: What is the Wage and Hour Division's Enforcement Authority Under the H-1B Program?' Wage and Hour Division, U.S. Department of Labor. November 2016. https://www.dol.gov/agencies/whd/fact-sheets/62u-h1b-enforcement-authority [hereinafter, DOL, 'Enforcement Authority'].
30. Ibid. The Department of Labor can initiate H-1B related investigations in the following four cases:
    - 'WH receives a complaint from an aggrieved person or organization.
    - WH receives specific credible information from a reliable source (other than a complainant) that the employer has failed to meet certain Labor Condition Application (LCA) conditions,

has engaged in a pattern or practice of failures to meet such conditions, or has committed a substantial failure to meet such conditions that affects multiple employees.

- The Secretary of Labor has found, on a case-by-case basis, that an employer (within the last five years) has committed a willful failure to meet a condition specified in the LCA or willfully misrepresented a material fact in the LCA. In such cases, a random investigation may be conducted.
- The Secretary of Labor has reasonable cause to believe that the employer is not in compliance. In such cases, the Secretary may certify that an investigation be conducted.'

See more at 'Fact Sheet #62U: What is the Wage and Hour Division's Enforcement Authority Under the H-1B Program?' Wage and Hour Division, U.S. Department of Labor. November 2016. https://www.dol.gov/agencies/whd/fact-sheets/62u-h1b-enforcement-authority.

31. WHD maintains a database of its compliance action on the DOL's Data Enforcement web page: https://enforcedata.dol.gov/views/data_catalogs.php [hereinafter WHD dataset]. 'The dataset contains all concluded WHD compliance actions since FY 2005. The dataset includes whether any violations were found and the back wage amount, number of employees due back wages, and civil money penalties assessed.'

Here's how you can access the spreadsheet for the WHD dataset: Click on the link that says 'WHD data'; then click on the CSV file named 'whd_whisard'. It contains a huge spreadsheet—comprising over 300,000 rows and 100 columns—listing firms found to have committed labour violations. This list encompasses different visa programmes and various workers' rights provisions (such as Occupational Safety and Health Administration, Family and Medical Leave Act, Fair Labor Standards Act, etc.). Columns relevant to H-1B violators are **B** (the company's name), **AF** (the number of H-1B violations), **AG** (the back wages paid to H-1B employees), **AH** (number of H-1B employees affected) and **AI** (an even rarer fine, Civil Monetary Penalty).

Searching 'Objectwin Technology' (**B**) on the spreadsheet produces the following values:

Column AF (Number of H-1B Violations) = 205

Column AG (Back Wages Owed) = 206,540.95

Column AH (Number of Affected Employees) = 43
Column AI (Civil Monetary Penalty) = 0

I've found the numbers corresponding to the H-1B back wages in the rest of the book using the above methodology. For the purpose of readability, I've rounded up the amounts in decimal to the nearest integer.

32. Ibid. at WHD dataset. This analysis considered the WHD investigations till 2023. Applying the filter H-1B back wages > 0 in the WHD spreadsheet produced the figure '2,321'.
33. *Awasthi v. Infosys Technologies Limited et al.* United States District Court, Northern District of California. 24 February 2010. https://www.courtlistener.com/docket/4176962/1/awasthi-v-infosys-technologies-limited/.
34. Ibid.
35. Ibid.
36. Faking resumes is such an integral part of the desi consultancy ecosystem that even a simple Google search, such as 'desi consultancy + fake resume', spits out hundreds of posts. For example, 'I Went to a Consultant for Training. They Offered Classes for "How to Create a Fake Resume"'. Happy Schools. 6 April 2016. http://www.happyschools.com/consultant-training-faking-resume/; 'Why Do Indian Consultancies in the US Fake Resumes and Market Candidates for IT Jobs? Why Has This Practice Continued?' Quora. 22 February 2015. https://www.quora.com/Why-do-Indian-consultancies-in-the-US-fake-resumes-and-market-candidates-for-IT-jobs-Why-has-this-practice-continued; 'Unethical Use of F1 and OPT by Desi Consulting Companies.' Murthy Law Firm. 21 October 2011. http://forum.murthy.com/index.php?/topic/27159-unethical-use-of-f1-and-opt-by-desi-consulting-companies/.
37. In desi consultancy parlance, a 'vendor' is a firm between an H-1B employer and a client. It's common for a hiring chain to have more than one vendor, where a big outsourcing firm, just below the client, is called the 'prime vendor'.
38. This piece, written by an ex-desi consultancy employee, details the ubiquity of fake resumes on his blog. See 'Flexi-Staffing in the United States: Fake Resumes for Survival'. 1 March 2013. http://crazymotts.blogspot.com/2013/03/flexi-staffing-in-united-states-fake.html [hereinafter Flexi-Staffing in the US].

Specifically, see this part: 'During the training period, the newly recruited consultants are offered a set of fake resumes … and asked to go through them to get a "feel" of how their resumes are going to be while they are being marketed to mid-clients and end-clients as experienced professionals. The consultants are given a sample position and experience domain and asked to prepare a sample fake resume that would meet the requirement. A mock interview, or a resume analysis, is done as a class so that the entire batch gets to know what to do and what not to do while fabricating resumes for requirements. This training goes to the nuts and bolts of resume writing where the specifics are discussed elaborately such as the date/time lines of each project that is included in the resume. Depending on the level of intimacy and moral surrender of the consultant to the management, a specific set of resumes are forwarded to each consultant individually.'

It further states, 'Consultants go to great lengths, trying to get a good impression in the consultancy's senior personnel so that they get a "Good Set of Fake Resumes" that others don't get. The want for a set of descriptions of interesting projects that may lure the vendor/mid-client to call for an interview grows exponentially at this stage of the training. There is a paradigm shift we need to note here. From accepting to defend[ing] fake resumes in the beginning, the consultants go to the far extreme of scrambling for good-looking fake resumes.'

39. 'Proxy interviews' have existed—and flourished—in the desi consultancy ecosystem for more than two decades (if not longer). Just a cursory Google search of 'proxy interviews + desi consultancy' throws up numerous results across the years of individuals seeking proxies for phone and web interviews and HR professionals cautioning against proxy interviewers.

For examples of people seeking information on proxy interviews, see 'Can Anybody Suggest DevOps Proxy Support in Java in Pune?' Quora. 23 May 2019. https://www.quora.com/Can-anybody-suggest-DevOps-proxy-support-in-Java-in-Pune (a brazen response by a Mohammed Unish admitting to using proxy support); 'IT Job Support & Interview Proxy.' Facebook. 16 December 2022. https://www.facebook.com/groups/jobsupportinterviewproxy (a Facebook group where consultants can solicit proxy interviews and 'job support', last accessed 29 August 2025);

'How Do I Arrange for a Proxy Interview Over Skype, so That the Interviewer Does Not Notice?' Quora. 19 February 2015. https://www.quora.com/How-do-I-arrange-for-a-proxy-interview-over-Skype-so-that-the-interviewer-does-not-notice.

See also Cassandra Podskalny, a technical recruiter, describe an 'all too common scene' while interviewing applicants. 'It starts like this … a visibly panic-stricken young man appears on my Webex computer screen for his scheduled interview. After a series of greetings and introductions, I begin to ask him technical Salesforce questions. … Suddenly I realize he is mouthing words but making mistakes and it's not matching up to his speech. Folks, we have a proxy interview. We have someone standing off camera actually answering the questions while this dishonest man tries to appear as though he is the one answering by lip-syncing on the fly. Occasionally they are receiving answers via text/instant message and trying to read them to me which is equally obvious. Every. Single. Time.' See 'DEATH to the Proxy Interview'. LinkedIn. 9 March 2018. https://www.linkedin.com/pulse/death-proxy-interview-cassandra-podskalny/.

See also Jim Holcomb, a provider of global workforce solutions, explain how video interviews are carried out: '[T]he companies that engage in this fraud got smarter and started having the individual who was faking their way through the interview on the screen, but someone else on the other side of the screen, unseen to the interviewer, actually answering the questions.' See 'When Your New Hire is Not Who You Thought They Were—AKA the Fake Resume Scam'. LinkedIn. 19 November 2015. https://www.linkedin.com/pulse/when-your-new-hire-who-you-thought-were-aka-fake-resume-jim-holcomb/.

40. 'Bashing Indians.' Keep America At Work. 29 October 2008. https://web.archive.org/web/20081029224316/http://www.keepamericaatwork.com/.

41. Virgil also wrote many posts about the Department of Labor's unemployment rates. See, for instance, 'I Don't Even Monitor the Unemployment Numbers Anymore Because They are Garbage!' Keep America At Work. 7 May 2010. https://web.archive.org/web/20100512175331/http://keepamericaatwork.com/.

In the subsequent years, many American media outlets reported on the Department of Labor's unemployment rates. See, for instance, the following: 'Jack Welch: I was Right About That Strange Jobs Report.' *The Wall Street Journal.* Jack Welch. 11 October 2012. https://www.wsj.com/articles/SB10000872396390444897304578046260406091012; 'The Chart Obama-Haters Love Most—And the Truth Behind It.' *Quartz.* Matt Phillips. 4 November 2014. https://www.documentcloud.org/documents/24356445-the-chart-obama-haters-love-most-and-the-truth-behind-it/; 'Is the Unemployment Rate Really Just a "Big Lie"?' *Fortune.* Chris Matthews. 4 February 2015. https://fortune.com/2015/02/04/unemployment-rate-gallup/; 'Unemployment Indicators Only Tell Part of the Story.' *U.S. News & World Report.* Andrew Soergel. 19 June 2015. https://www.usnews.com/news/articles/2015/06/19/the-problem-with-the-labor-departments-unemployment-indicators; 'Why America's Impressive 5% Unemployment Rate Feels Like a Lie for So Many.' *Quartz.* Sarah Kendzior. 21 April 2016. https://www.documentcloud.org/documents/24356446-why-americas-impressive-5-unemployment-rate-feels-like-a-lie-for-so-many; 'If the US Unemployment Rate Included Everyone Who Says They Want a Job, It Would be Nearly Double.' *Quartz.* Dan Kopf. 6 January 2017. https://www.documentcloud.org/documents/24356447-if-the-us-unemployment-rate-included-everyone-who-says-they-want-a-job-it-would-be-nearly-double; 'Donald Trump is Finally Floating an Idea Liberals Can Love.' *Quartz.* Dan Kopf. 20 July 2022. https://qz.com/900439/donald-trump-wants-to-change-the-official-unemployment-rate; 'What the Unemployment Rate Does—and Doesn't—Say About the Economy.' Pew Research Center. Drew Desilver. 7 March 2017. https://www.pewresearch.org/short-reads/2017/03/07/employment-vs-unemployment-different-stories-from-the-jobs-numbers/; 'Unemployment is Low, but That's Only Part of the Story.' *The New York Times.* Louis Uchitelle. 11 July 2019. https://www.nytimes.com/2019/07/11/business/low-unemployment-not-seeking-work.html.

42. 'Let Me Show You a Picture I Found of John Boehner.' Keep America At Work. 23 June 2011. https://web.archive.org/web/20110628185324/http://keepamericaatwork.com/.
43. 'So Cantor is Using Smoke and Mirrors and the Presidents Dog to Lie to the People?' Keep America At Work. 22 December 2011. https://web.archive.org/web/20111225142004/http://keepamericaatwork.com/.

44. 'So Rick Perry is Just Another Right Wing Extremist?' Keep America At Work. 29 August 2011. https://web.archive.org/web/20110902072633/http://keepamericaatwork.com/.
45. 'Your Future—Part I.' Keep America At Work. 2011. https://web.archive.org/web/20110726055701/http://keepamericaatwork.com/?page_id=72770.
46. 'I wish I Could Teach the World Humanity.' Keep America At Work. 21 June 2011. https://web.archive.org/web/20110628185324/http://keepamericaatwork.com/.
47. A green card (or a permanent resident card) allows a foreign worker the right to live and work permanently in the US. Unlike the H-1B visa, which ties a worker to their employer (so much so that if a H-1B worker loses their job they, in general, only have sixty days to find a new H-1B job), the green card imposes no such restriction. A foreign worker in the US, who entered the country as a student, usually takes the following route for permanent residency: F-1 visa (student visa) → H-1B visa (non-immigrant status/work visa) → Green card (permanent residency).

    See 'FAQs for Individuals in H-1B Nonimmigrant Status.' U.S. Citizenship and Immigration Services. https://www.uscis.gov/working-in-the-united-states/temporary-workers/h-1b-specialty-occupations/faqs-for-individuals-in-h-1b-nonimmigrant-status [hereinafter H-1B FAQs].
48. For more information about guesthouses provided by desi consulting firms, see *supra* note 38, Part II: Deception, Flexi-Staffing in the US. A guesthouse, it stated, 'is a typical two-bedroom apartment' shared by around seven to ten consultants. Within the guesthouse there is 'a hierarchy.' People in the living room are 'newbies'; people in the master bedroom are the 'Big-Daddies … who are supposed to lead the brotherhood and therefore get to lay the ground rules for the pack to follow' and the people in the guest bedroom are the 'Dukes who are eagerly waiting to become the future Big Daddies.'

    See also 'Silicon Valley's "Body Shop" Secret: Highly Educated Foreign Workers Treated Like Indentured Servants.' NBC Bay Area. Stephen Stock, Julie Putnam, Scott Pham and Jeremy Carroll. 27 October 2014. https://www.nbcbayarea.com/news/local/silicon-valleys-body-shop-secret/78781/. ('A guesthouse is a small apartment or home where as many as eight to ten workers stay at once. A dozen different interviews confirmed that the guesthouses are commonly used by body shops. One worker from India described how the body shops explained the guesthouse when he arrived: "We are placing you in the guesthouse. Until you get the job you have to stay in the guesthouse, you should not go out, even for a walk," the worker said. This worker, too, asked to remain anonymous because of fears he will jeopardize his future job prospects. He stayed in guesthouses for several months and was told not to leave.')

49. The offshore branches of desi consultancy firms in India engage in a variety of activities. See 'Offshore Marketing Team'. H-1B Abuse. https://h1b-abuse.weebly.com/marketing-team.html. 'The team in India is called the OPT-H1B Marketing Team. These employees … use services like Magic Jack to get a US phone number that they can use to make calls from India. They pretend to be someone living in the USA. They often have American names such as Mike, John, Smith, Sam and so on.' The OPT-H1B Marketing Team's work involves preparing 'fake resumes and fake H1B documents', receiving 'job descriptions from different Vendors' (basically business-to-business contract jobs), sending 'emails to vendors with the resumes of H1B/OPT consultants sitting "On the Bench"', searching for 'corp-to-corp positions in job portals, mostly in Dice.com', applying 'for jobs in job portals on behalf of the H1B/OPT consultant' and 'confirming the hourly rate with vendors'.

50. Many desi consultants work on a 'percentage basis' after the first year of their employment. '[A] 70 to 30% ratio … means you get 70% of the billing rate and 30% goes to employer,' explained a post on the website RedBus2US. 'This is a good deal because if you are working for a big company, the chance of having layers before client are less. So, your employer will have good billing rate. Again, you have to trust your employer and it is your call. Some are good and some are not trustworthy. Most of them are not trustworthy. There is at least 10% money just not showed to you.'

    See 'Negotiation Salary & Benefits With H1B Sponsoring Consulting Companies'. RedBus2Us. Satheesh Ilu. 22 July 2021. https://redbus2us.com/negotiation-salary-benefits-with-consulting-companies/.

51. Even though both the prime vendor and implementation partner directly serve the client, the latter's scope of work is wider, related to deploying, integrating and supporting software. A prime vendor, on

the other hand, primarily resolves a client's hiring needs by providing suitable consultants for a project (through either its own employees or a different vendor in the hiring chain).

52. 'Optional Practical Training (OPT) is temporary employment that is directly related to an F-1 student's major area of study.' See more at 'Optional Practical Training (OPT) for F-1 Students'. U.S. Citizenship and Immigration Services. 25 November 2024. https://www.uscis.gov/working-in-the-united-states/students-and-exchange-visitors/optional-practical-training-opt-for-f-1-students.

    In 2008, USCIS increased the OPT duration from twelve months to twenty-nine months for graduates with STEM degrees (which was in place in 2011 when Manu began working for Infocon Logix, see more at *infra* note 114, Part III: Thought Control). In 2016, the Obama administration increased the OPT duration to three years for graduates with STEM degrees. An international student usually first works on OPT, then applies for an H-1B visa.

53. 'Job Brokers Steal Wages and Entrap Indian Tech Workers in US.' *The Guardian*. Matt Smith, Jennifer Gollan and Adithya Sambamurthy. 28 October 2014. https://www.theguardian.com/us-news/2014/oct/28/-sp-jobs-brokers-entrap-indian-tech-workers/ [hereinafter The Guardian, 'Job Brokers Steal Wages'].

54. See more at *supra* note 47, Part II: Deception, H-1B FAQs (listing various scenarios, duration of authorised stay and whether an H-1B employee may request to change status).

55. The green card backlog continued to increase for Indian H-1B workers in the subsequent years—as some wait times grew to 195 years by 2023. 'Lawmakers Write to President Biden to Make Green Card Priority Dates for Indians to Current as Wait Time Grows to 195-yrs.' *Hindustan Times*. Paurush Omar. 29 July 2023. https://www.hindustantimes.com/world-news/joe-biden-urged-clear-backlog-green-card-wait-time-indians-grows-195-years-bipartisan-56-lawmakers-raja-krishnamoorthi-101690643588364.html/.

56. To read the official complaint filed by the US government against Infosys, click on the link 'court documents' in the ICE press release here: 'Indian Corporation Pays Record $34 Million Fine to Settle Allegations of Systemic Visa Fraud and Abuse of Immigration Processes'. U.S. Immigration and Customs Enforcement. 29 October

2013. https://www.ice.gov/news/releases/indian-corporation-pays-record-34-million-fine-settle-allegations-systemic-visa-fraud/.

57. 'Deal Reached in Inquiry Into Visa Fraud at Tech Giant.' *The New York Times*. Julia Preston. 29 October 2013. https://www.nytimes.com/2013/10/30/us/indian-tech-giant-infosys-said-to-reach-settlement-on-us-visa-fraud-claims.html/.

58. 'As reflected in the settlement, Infosys denies and disputes any claims of systemic visa fraud, misuse of visas for competitive advantage, or immigration abuse,' stated the firm's press release. 'Those claims are untrue and are assertions that remain unproven. The Company's use of B-1 visas was for legitimate business purposes and not in any way intended to circumvent the requirements of the H-1B program.' See more at 'Infosys Completes Civil Settlement With U.S. Government'. Infosys. 2013. https://www.infosys.com/newsroom/press-releases/2013/company-statement-official.html.

59. '8 Biggest H-1B Employers in 2015.' *InformationWeek*. Dawn Kawamoto. 24 March 2016. https://www.informationweek.com/it-sectors/8-biggest-h-1b-employers-in-2015.

60. 'Outsourcers Corner Market for U.S. Skilled Worker Visas.' *The New York Times*. Anand Giridharadas. 12 April 2007. https://www.nytimes.com/2007/04/12/business/worldbusiness/12iht-visa.4.5257621.html.

61. 'Offshore Firms Took 50% of H-1B Visas in 2013.' *Computerworld*. Sharon Machlis and Patrick Thibodeau. 1 April 2014. https://www.computerworld.com/article/1511471/technology-law-regulation-offshore-firms-took-50-of-h-1b-visas-in-2013.html.

62. 'Despite H-1B Lottery, Offshore Firms Dominate Visa Use.' *Computerworld*. Patrick Thibodeau and Sharon Machlis. 30 July 2015. https://www.computerworld.com/article/2954612/despite-h-1b-lottery-offshore-firms-dominate-visa-use.html.

63. 'The Fix is In: Proof That H-1B Visa Abuse is Rampant.' *InfoWorld*. Bill Snyder. 12 November 2015. https://www.infoworld.com/article/3004501/proof-that-h-1b-visa-abuse-is-rampant-in-tech.html.

64. The table on p. 81 only documented H-1B violations and back wages resulting from the federal Department of Labor's investigations (see *supra* note 31, Part II: Deception, WHD dataset, on how to view their results). That dataset also includes non-H-1B violations and back wages, such as the Family and Medical Leave Act (FMLA), the Fair Labor Standards Act (FLSA), the Service Contract Act (SCA)

and so on. The 'WITCH' firms have been found guilty of violating some of these Acts as well, besides a host of other transgressions.

Washington-DC-based non-profit Good Jobs First has been tracking corporate crime and misconduct in the US since 1998 via its Violation Tracker database that records 'WITCH' firms' other offenses, too. '[Our website] covers banking, consumer protection, false claims, environmental, wage & hour, safety, discrimination, price-fixing, and other cases resolved by federal regulatory agencies and all parts of the Justice Department since 2000—plus cases from state attorneys general and selected state and local regulatory agencies,' says Good Jobs First's webpage. 'We also cover selected types of class action lawsuits.' The database contains granular information on, among others, the investigation case ID, primary offense type, agency name and links to the source of data.

Entering the names of 'WITCH' firms in Violation Tracker produced many penalties not documented in Chapter 16. They run below:

Company	*Primary Offense Type*	*Year*	*Penalty*
Wipro	Accounting Fraud or Deficiencies	2016	$5,000,000
	Wage and Hour Violation	2017	$38,061
	Wage and Hour Violation	2018	$128,777
	Wage and Hour Violation	2018	$18,050
	Wage and Hour Violation	2019	$5,794
	Wage and Hour Violation	2022	$9,225
	Wage and Hour Violation	2023	$6,883
Infosys	Wage and Hour Violation	2018	$5,500
	Wage and Hour Violation	2022	$18,000
	Wage and Hour Violation	2022	$16,660
	Wage and Hour Violation	2022	$15,576
	Wage and Hour Violation	2022	$14,501
TCS	Wage and Hour Violation	2013	$23,186
	Wage and Hour Violation	2015	$11,543
	Wage and Hour Violation	2015	$7,812

Company	*Primary Offense Type*	*Year*	*Penalty*
	Wage and Hour Violation	2015	$5,130
	Wage and Hour Violation	2016	$10,912
	Wage and Hour Violation	2020	$6,000
	Wage and Hour Violation	2022	$40,910
Cognizant	Wage and Hour Violation	2010	$29,203
	Wage and Hour Violation	2010	$17,119
	Wage and Hour Violation	2020	$120,581
HCL America	Benefit Plan Administrator Violation	2012	$10,001
	Wage and Hour Violation	2012	$46,400
	Wage and Hour Violation	2013	$14,847
	Wage and Hour Violation	2015	$19,138
	Wage and Hour Violation	2015	$32,102
	Family and Medical Leave Act	2018	$24,531
	Wage and Hour Violation	2020	$13,500
	Workplace Safety or Health Violation	2022	$32,400
	Benefit Plan Administrator Violation	2022	$50,001
	Wage and Hour Violation	2023	$29,126
	Wage and Hour Violation	2023	$6,981
	Workplace Safety or Health Violation	2023	$6,600

See more at 'Wipro'. Good Jobs First. https://violationtracker.goodjobsfirst.org/?company_op=starts&company=wipro; 'Infosys.' Good Jobs First. https://violationtracker.goodjobsfirst.org/?company_op=starts&company=infosys; 'Tata Consultancy Services (TCS).' Good Jobs First. https://violationtracker.goodjobsfirst.org/?company_op=starts&company=tata+consultancy+services; 'Cognizant.' Good Jobs First. https://violationtracker.goodjobsfirst.org/?company_op=starts&company=cognizant; 'HCL America.' Good Jobs First. https://violationtracker.goodjobsfirst.org/?company_op=starts&company=hcl+america.

65. See *supra* note 31, Part II: Deception, WHD dataset. The '2,708' figure also comprised cases where the DOL found labour violations but

imposed no back wages. Out of the 2,708 cases, though, 2,321 of them resulted in back wages greater than 0.

66. See *supra* note 31, Part II: Deception, WHD dataset.
67. See *supra* note 31, Part II: Deception, WHD dataset. The WHD investigation also looks into whether violations are subject to civil monetary penalty (CMP) such as 'a violation pertaining to strike/lockout or displacement of US workers'; 'a substantial violation pertaining to notification, labor condition application specificity, or recruitment of US workers'; 'a misrepresentation of material fact on the labor condition application' and a few others.

    To see the complete list of violations qualifying under CMP in the H-1B context, see here: https://www.dol.gov/agencies/whd/resources/penalties.
68. See, for instance, the following posts on 'WITCH' firms: 'WITCH Style Fraud H1B Company Penalized.' Trackitt. 2 May 2018. http://web.archive.org/web/20180506154632/http://www.trackitt.com:80/usa-discussion-forums/i140/1838892907/witch-style-fraud-h1b-company-penalized/page/last_page; 'Why Do WITCH Companies Treating Employees Like Labours?' Reddit. Neo_The_bluepuill_One. 19 November 2022. https://www.reddit.com/r/india/comments/yz7xyc/why_do_witch_companies_treating_employees_like/; 'Fraud WITCH Companies Find Another Loophole—No Bonus.' Trackitt. 14 August 2018. https://www.documentcloud.org/documents/26360042-fraud-witch-companies-find-another-loophole-no-bonus/.
69. To read more about the EB-1 green card's eligibility criteria, see 'Employment-Based Immigration: First Preference EB-1.' U.S. Citizenship and Immigration Services. 24 January 2025. https://www.uscis.gov/working-in-the-united-states/permanent-workers/employment-based-immigration-first-preference-eb-1. There's no green card category called 'EB-1C' though; it's a colloquial way to refer to the third category in the EB-1 green card reserved for 'Certain Multinational manager or executive' (as can be seen in the link in this endnote).
70. 'How Can I Sue CTS for EB1C Fraud? CTS is Filing EB1Cs for Testers and Support Folks in the US who were SA Even for a Day Before They Landed in the US.' Quora. 30 June 2017. https://www.

quora.com/How-can-I-sue-CTS-for-EB1C-fraud-CTS-is-filing-EB1Cs-for-testers-and-support-folks-in-the-US-who-were-SA-even-for-a-day-before-they-landed-in-the-US/.

71. 'How Can We Stop Rampant Abuse of EB1C India by TCS, CTS? Visa Meant for Executive Managers is Being Abused for All.' Quora. 1 September 2017. https://www.quora.com/How-can-we-stop-rampant-abuse-of-EB1C-India-by-TCS-CTS-Visa-meant-for-executive-managers-is-being-abused-for-all/.
72. 'Why Does the USCIS Not Punish the EB1C India Green Card Scam?' Quora. 21 June 2017. https://www.quora.com/Why-does-the-USCIS-not-punish-the-EB1C-India-green-card-scam/.
73. 'Stop EB1C Abuse and Fraudulent Filing.' Petition2Congress. 2012. http://web.archive.org/web/20250812162715/https://www.petition2congress.com/ctas/stop-eb1-c-abuse-fraudulent-filing/
74. 'TCS Fined $940m in US for "Stealing" Healthcare Software.' *The Times of India*. Chidanand Rajghatta. 17 April 2016. https://timesofindia.indiatimes.com/business/india-business/tcs-fined-940m-in-us-for-stealing-healthcare-software/articleshow/51853815.cms.
75. 'TCS Faces $210 Million Penalty in DXC Lawsuit.' *The Economic Times*. Romita Majumdar. 27 November 2023. https://economictimes.indiatimes.com/tech/information-tech/tcs-faces-210-million-penalty-in-dxc-lawsuit/articleshow/105527977.cms

    Two years after the Texas federal court found the company guilty, a 'US appeals court upheld $194.2 million in damages against Tata Consultancy Services (TCS)' regarding its 'trade secrets battle with Computer Sciences Corporation'. See more at 'Setback for TCS—US Court Upholds $194 Million Penalty in CSC Trade Secrets Case'. *Financial Express*. 23 November 2025. https://www.financialexpress.com/business/setback-for-tcs-us-court-upholds-194-million-penalty-in-csc-trade-secrets-case-4053609/.
76. 'Firm Sues TCS for IP Infringement in US.' *Livemint*. Varun Sood. 20 August 2018. https://web.archive.org/web/20180821114329/https://www.livemint.com/Companies/M69mYgHfDoU1YaJiB1JlmJ/Firm-sues-TCS-for-IP-infringement-in-US.html/.
77. 'Whistleblower Complaints: Five US Law Firms Launch Class-Action Suit Against Infosys.' CNBC TV18. 29 October 2019. https://www.cnbctv18.com/legal/whistleblower-complaints-us-law-firm-begins-preparing-class-action-suit-against-infosys-4571111.htm.

78. 'SEC Charges Cognizant and Two Former Executives With FCPA [Foreign Corrupt Practices Act] Violations.' U.S. Securities and Exchange Commission. 15 February 2019. https://www.sec.gov/news/press-release/2019-12.
79. 'Infosys Faces Lawsuit in US Over Non-Payment of 1,000 Hours of Overtime.' *Business Standard*. 10 September 2018. https://www.business-standard.com/article/companies/infosys-faces-lawsuit-in-us-over-non-payment-of-1-000-hours-of-overtime-118091000578_1.html/.
80. 'Infosys Technologies Limited—Financial Release December 31, 2007.' https://www.infosys.com/investors/reports-filings/quarterly-results/2007-2008/q3/documents/indiangaap-press-release.pdf (p. 2).
81. 'India's TCS Pays $29.75 Million to Settle Class Action Suit.' *Reuters*. 1 March 2013. https://www.reuters.com/article/tataconsultancy-lawsuit-us/indias-tcs-pays-29-75-million-to-settle-class-action-suit-idUKL4N0BT1ZZ20130301/.
82. 'Cognizant to Pay $5.7m in Class-Action Suit.' *The Times of India*. Shilpa Phadnis. 3 June 2020. https://timesofindia.indiatimes.com/business/india-business/cognizant-to-pay-5-7m-in-class-action-suit/articleshow/76167302.cms.
83. 'A.G. Schneiderman Announces Settlement With Infosys for Failing to Follow U.S. Visa Requirements for Foreign Workers in New York State.' New York State Office of the Attorney General. 23 June 2017. https://web.archive.org/web/20180929124508/https://ag.ny.gov/press-release/ag-schneiderman-announces-settlement-infosys-failing-follow-us-visa-requirements.
84. 'Infosys to Pay $1 Million to Settle Case of Visa Violations in New York.' *The Economic Times*. Jochelle Mendonca. 23 June 2017. https://economictimes.indiatimes.com/tech/ites/infosys-to-pay-1-million-to-settle-case-of-visa-violations-in-new-york/articleshow/59290650.cms?from=mdr.

    See Infosys's statement from the same piece: "'Infosys' agreement concludes the State of New York's investigation relating to the amount of taxes the Company paid in 2010-2011 without any criminal or civil charges being filed. While this investigation centered on alleged paperwork errors, the company committed no wrongdoing and denies all allegations made in this regard," Infosys told ET in an emailed statement. "This settlement relates to legal issues already resolved under the 2013 settlement with the US Department of Justice, and was reached by both parties to avoid protracted litigation. Infosys maintains robust policies and procedures to ensure adherence with all applicable regulations and laws. Infosys will continue to focus on boosting American innovation, hiring American workers and better serving our valued customers across the United States," the company added.'

85. 'Infosys to Pay California $8,00,000 Over Foreign Workers' Visas, Tax Fraud.' *The Economic Times*. 18 December 2019. https://economictimes.indiatimes.com/tech/ites/infosys-to-pay-california-800000-over-foreign-workers-visas-tax-fraud/articleshow/72862074.cms.
86. *Green v. Infosys, Ltd.* United States District Court, Eastern District of Texas. 19 June 2017. https://www.documentcloud.org/documents/24251555-2-erin-green-vs-infosys.
87. On 22 February 2021, Green filed a 'stipulation of dismissal' and, a week later, the court dismissed the case, 'including the claims of Plaintiff asserted in this action against Defendant, with prejudice'. See more at *Green v. Infosys, Ltd.* United States District Court, Eastern District of Texas. https://www.pacermonitor.com/public/case/21737062/Green_v_Infosys%2C_Ltd.
88. That reference appears in p. 2 (and point 6) of Erin Green's lawsuit complaint.
89. *Jonathan Beasley v. Cognizant Technology Solutions US Corporation.* United States District Court, Central District of California. 10 June 2011. https://storage.courtlistener.com/recap/gov.uscourts.cacd.504501.1.0.pdf.
90. On 20 September 2011, a few months after the lawsuit, Molina Healthcare filed a breach of contract complaint against the plaintiffs, alleging they had violated the confidentiality clauses by disclosing the settlement agreements in electronic media and providing information beyond the agreed short response ('the matter has been resolved'). Molina sought damages and contractual attorney fees. (In July 2010, the plaintiffs' attorney had sent a demand letter to Molina, asserting discrimination based on national origin. The parties mediated and consequently, signed a settlement agreement containing a confidentiality clause that required the parties to keep the settlement and negotiations confidential. Breaching that agreement would have resulted in liquidated damages worth 20 per cent of the settlement sum.) Responding to Molina's complaint, the appellants (originally plaintiffs in Molina lawsuit) moved to strike

it under California's anti-SLAPP (Strategic Lawsuits Against Public Participation) statute, arguing that the complaint arose from a protected activity and lacked 'minimal merit'. The trial court denied the motion, stating Molina's complaint didn't arise from protected activity because it was neither connected to ongoing litigation nor to an issue of public interest. The appellants appealed the motion.

The appellate court found that a *Computerworld* article, published on 16 August 2011, had indeed disclosed the settlement's existence. Molina's declarants denied disclosing settlement information to the reporter, stating Molina handled media communications via a third party that didn't know the details of the settlement, supporting an inference that the disclosure came from either the two appellants or their attorney interviewed for the piece. After considering all the arguments and evidence, the Court of Appeal found that Molina had presented sufficient evidence to establish a prima facie breach-of-contract claim, so appellants' anti-SLAPP motion failed. It also affirmed the trial court's order denying the appellants' motion to strike the firm's breach of contract complaint under Code of Civil Procedure section 425.16. Since the anti-SLAPP motion was properly denied, the appellants weren't entitled to attorneys' fees, and Molina was entitled to costs on appeal.

See more at *Molina Healthcare, Inc. v. Beasley et al.* United States Court of Appeal, California, Second Appellate District, Division Eight. 22 October 2013. https://www.casemine.com/judgement/us/5914ae0 dadd7b04934745a7e.

The initial lawsuit, however, was far from resolved as, in August 2011, Desai filed a cross-complaint against the plaintiffs and appellants. He alleged that, in January and February 2010, 'each of the Group 1 plaintiffs' entered into 'severance agreements and written releases' with Molina, agreeing to 'compromise, fully settle and fully release all claims which [the Group 1 plaintiffs] may have or claim to have against Company arising out of or in any way relating to … employment with and separation of employment from Company'. Here, the 'Company' was defined to include Molina, as well as its 'agents, officers, directors, employees, and owners'. When the Group 1 plaintiff had signed the releases, Desai was a Molina employee. His cross-complaint alleged that, by filing the initial complaint, the 'Group

1 plaintiffs breached the terms of the releases, and that Desai was entitled to an award of attorney fees in connection with this breach'.

Desai also filed the operative First Amended Cross-Complaint (FACC). It made the same broad allegations as his first complaint but also added new cross-defendants ('the Group 2 plaintiffs'). The FACC alleged that 'Molina participated in mediation with the Group 2 plaintiffs and thereafter entered into written release agreements' with them. According to the FACC, when the Group 2 releases were executed, Desai was not a Molina employee. The Group 1 and Group 2 plaintiffs filed separate anti-SLAPP motions. The trial court denied the Group 1 plaintiff's motion, stating that Desai made a 'prima facie showing of breach of contract'. But the court granted the Group 2 plaintiffs' motions, concluding that 'Desai was no longer employed by Molina when the Group 2 releases were executed', and that he 'failed to show he was an intended third party beneficiary of the releases'. The Group 1 plaintiffs appealed the order 'denying their anti-SLAPP motion', and Desai 'appealed the order granting the Group 2 plaintiffs' anti-SLAPP motion'.

The appellate court affirmed both the orders, stating that Desai had shown prima facie evidence of a valid contract and breach (for the Group 1 plaintiffs) but, for the Group 2 plaintiffs, the release language only applied to current Molina employees, not former ones, and Desai was not a third-party beneficiary. Besides, a non-disparagement clause referencing 'past employees' did not extend the release to Desai. 'Desai shall recover his costs associated with responding to the Group 1 plaintiffs' appeal,' concluded the appellate court, '[and] the Group 2 plaintiffs shall recover their costs on appeal from Desai.'

See more at *Desai v. Choudhury CA2/2*. United States Court of Appeal, California, Second Appellate District, Division Two. 14 October 2015. https://www.courtlistener.com/opinion/3062685/desai-v-choudhury-ca22/pdf/.

91. 'Infosys Faces Racial Discrimination Suit Amid "Black Lives Matter" Protests in US.' *Business Today*. June 13 2020. https://www.businesstoday.in/latest/corporate/story/infosys-faces-race-discrimination-suit-black-lives-matter-movement-us-261151-2020-06-13.

92. *Linguist v. Infosys Limited.* United States District Court, Eastern District of Texas. 11 June 2020. https://www.documentcloud.org/documents/24251557-4-davina-linguist-vs-infosys.
93. *Koehler v. Infosys Technologies Limited Incorporated.* United States District Court, Eastern District of Wisconsin. 1 August 2013. https://www.courtlistener.com/docket/4537990/koehler-v-infosys-technologies-limited-incorporated/.
94. On 16 October 2020, Linguist filed a 'notice of voluntary dismissal' and closed the case. See more at *Linguist v. Infosys Limited.* United States District Court, Eastern District of Texas. https://www.pacermonitor.com/public/case/34667341/Linguist_v_Infosys_Limited.
95. *Thayyullathil v. Infosys Limited.* United States District Court, Eastern District of Missouri. 1 May 2018. https://www.pacermonitor.com/public/case/24376809/Thayyullathil_v_Infosys_Limited.

    See also 'Infosys Engaging in Visa Fraud, Again, Former Employee Says'. *Bloomberg.* Laura Francis. 20 September 2018. https://news.bloomberglaw.com/daily-labor-report/infosys-engaging-in-visa-fraud-again-former-employee-says.
96. On 30 July 2019, the court 'granted' Thayyullathil's 'motion for leave to voluntarily dismiss with prejudice'. 'This case between Plaintiff and Defendant Infosys, Limited,' added the Court, 'shall be dismissed with prejudice, each party to bear its own costs.' See more at *Thayyullathil v. Infosys Limited.* United States District Court, Eastern District of Missouri. https://www.pacermonitor.com/public/case/24376809/Thayyullathil_v_Infosys_Limited.
97. Many more American workers, of different ethnic origins, had sued the WITCH firms in the 2010s for racial and employment discrimination. See, for instance, the following lawsuits:
    - *MacLean v. Wipro Limited.* United States District Court, District of New Jersey. 30 March 2020. https://www.documentcloud.org/documents/24360744-gregory-maclean-rick-valles-ardeshir-pezeshki-james-gibbs-and-ronald-hemenway-v-wipro.
    - *Phillips v. Wipro, Ltd.* United States District Court, Northern District of California. 15 March 2018. https://www.documentcloud.org/documents/24360745-james-phillips-and-robert-saemian-v-wipro.

- *Clark v. Wipro USA, LLC.* United States District Court, District of New Jersey. 23 December 2019. https://www.documentcloud.org/documents/24360738-kevin-clark-v-wipro.
- *Trewin v. Wipro Enterprises Limited.* United States District Court, District of Colorado. 16 March 2018. https://www.documentcloud.org/documents/24360739-rex-trewin-v-wipro.
- *Watkins v. Infosys Ltd.* United States District Court, Western District of Washington. 13 December 2017. https://www.documentcloud.org/documents/24360734-marilyn-watkins-vs-infosys.
- *Degaonkar v. Infosys Limited et al.* United States District Court, Northern District of Texas. 6 January 2020. https://www.documentcloud.org/documents/24360735-nitin-degaonkar-vs-infosys-toyota.
- *Buchanan v. Tata Consultancy Services, Ltd.* United States District Court, Northern District of California. 15 May 2015. https://www.documentcloud.org/documents/24360729-brian-buchanan-v-tcs/.
- *Slaight v. Tata Consultancy Servs. Ltd.* United States District Court, Northern District of California. 10 September 2018. https://www.documentcloud.org/documents/24360730-christopher-slaight-seyed-masoudi-nobel-mandali-vs-tcs.
- *Stacy v. Tata Consultancy Services, Ltd.* United States District Court, District of New Jersey. 14 March 2019. https://www.documentcloud.org/documents/24360731-darryl-stacy-donald-bradley-hesham-hafez-vs-tcs.
- *Heldt v. Tata Consultancy Services, Ltd.* United States District Court, Northern District of California. 28 September 2015. https://www.documentcloud.org/documents/24360732-steven-heldt-brian-buchanan-christopher-slaight-vs-tcs/.
- *Palmer et al v. Cognizant Technology Solutions Corporation et al.* United States District Court, Central District of California. 18 September 2017. https://www.documentcloud.org/documents/24360723-christy-palmer-vartan-piroumian-ed-cox-v-cognizant.
- *Weaver v. Cognizant.* United States District Court, Southern District of New York. 11 February 2019. https://www.documentcloud.org/documents/24360724-jeremy-weaver-v-cognizant.

- *Garrett v. HCL America, Inc.* United States Superior Court, California, Santa Clara. 12 July 2018. https://www.documentcloud.org/documents/24360728-william-garrett-vs-hcl/
- *Claytor v. HCL America, Inc.* United States District Court, Eastern District of North Carolina. 12 September 2019. https://www.documentcloud.org/documents/24360727-sierra-claytor-vs-hcl/
- *Voll v. HCL Technologies Limited et al.* United States District Court, Northern District of California. 15 August 2018. https://www.documentcloud.org/documents/24360726-reese-voll-vs-hcl.
- *Handloser v. HCL America, Inc. et al.* United States District Court, Northern District of California. 7 March 2019. https://www.documentcloud.org/documents/24360725-gregory-handloser-vs-hcl.

In fact, the 'WITCH' lawsuits overlapped so much that several of them were represented by one firm: Kotchen & Low. Read more about its owner, Daniel Kotchen, here: 'Daniel Kotchen: Man Behind Legal Threats to Indian IT Firewall'. *The Economic Times.* Jochelle Mendonca. 24 October 2018. https://economictimes.indiatimes.com/tech/ites/daniel-kotchen-man-behind-legal-threats-to-indian-it-firewall/articleshow/66036399.cms.

98. 'Outsourced Staff to Show Council Their "True Feelings"'. *The Sydney Morning Herald.* Tony Moore. 22 February 2013. https://www.smh.com.au/technology/outsourced-staff-to-show-council-their-true-feelings-20130221-2eu7r.html/.
99. The Services Union [@servicesunion]. 23 August 2018. https://twitter.com/servicesunion/status/1032415133161553921.
100. Ibid.

PART III: THOUGHT CONTROL

1. 'The Scourge of Silicon Valley.' *Salon.* Ed Frauenheim. 19 October 2000. https://www.salon.com/2000/10/19/matloff/.
2. 'The Immigration Guru.' *Science.* Beryl Benderly. 9 July 2010. https://www.science.org/content/article/immigration-guru.
3. 'Three Win Public Service Awards.' UC Davis. Andy Fell. 6 May 2002. https://www.ucdavis.edu/news/three-win-public-service-awards.

4. Science, Technology, Engineering and Mathematics.
5. The ITAA study hinged on a non-public survey questionnaire sent to 1,000 employers in the IT sector and 1,000 companies outside the sector. See the full report here: 'Help Wanted: The IT Workforce Gap at the Dawn of a New Century'. Information Technology Association of America. 1997. https://files.eric.ed.gov/fulltext/ED407491.pdf.
6. 'America's New Deficit: The Shortage of Information Technology Workers.' Office of Technology Policy, U.S. Department of Commerce. 29 September 1997. https://files.eric.ed.gov/fulltext/ED412360.pdf.
7. 'Vacant Cubicles: A Special Report: Software Jobs Go Begging, Threatening Technology Boom.' *The New York Times*. Amy Harmon. 13 January 1998. https://www.nytimes.com/1998/01/13/business/vacant-cubicles-special-report-software-jobs-go-begging-threatening-technology.html/.
8. 'We consider a 14-percent response rate to be unacceptably low as a basis for any generalizations about the population being surveyed,' read a part of the 1998 GAO report (p. 7). 'In order to make sound generalizations, the effective response rate should usually be at least 75 percent for each variable measured—a goal used by many practitioners. Furthermore, ITAA's estimate of the number of unfilled IT jobs is based on reported vacancies and adequate information about those vacancies is not provided, such as how long positions have been vacant, whether wages offered are sufficient to attract qualified applicants and whether companies consider jobs filled by contractors as vacancies.'

   Read the full report here: 'Assessment of the Department of Commerce's Report on Workforce Demand and Supply'. Government Accountability Office. 1 March 1998. https://www.gao.gov/assets/hehs-98-106.pdf/.
9. Matloff said that the Intel lobbyist Eva Jack had admitted to *Computerworld* magazine in an interview that the company focused on hiring new graduates. It had also been a defendant in several age-discrimination lawsuits. The firm was so intent on hiring young graduates that its recruitment brochures often classified them by acronyms: 'NCG' (New College Graduates) and 'RCG' (Recent College Graduates). See more here: 'Matloff's Congressional Testimony'. United States House of Representatives. 21 April 1998. https://commdocs.house.gov/committees/judiciary/hju58001.000/hju58001_0f.htm

[hereinafter Matloff, '1998 Congressional Testimony'] at p. 160 and p. 168.

10. Ibid. at p. 160. 'An official statement by Sun Microsystems, one of the major industry voices claiming a desperate labor shortage, classifies anyone with six years of experience—typically only of age 28—as the "Senior" level,' said Matloff. 'This is common in the field.'
11. Ibid. 'Cypress Semiconductor,' added Matloff, 'once advertised a "Senior" position for engineers with only three years of experience.'
12. Ibid. at p. 166.
13. 'The Age Factor.' *InformationWeek*. Bob Violino. 5 July 1999. https://web.archive.org/web/20000423061556/https://www.informationweek.com/742/agefact.htm/.
14. Matloff continued to update his Congressional testimony on his website in the subsequent years. See 'Debunking the Myth of a Desperate Software Labor Shortage.' U.S. House Judiciary Committee, Subcommittee on Immigration. 24 June 2000. https://www.documentcloud.org/documents/24360790-debunking-the-myth-of-a-desperate-software-labor-shortage-norm-matloff/ [hereinafter Matloff Updated Congressional Testimony, 'Debunking the Myth'] at p. 9.
15. Ibid.
16. Here's the list of more firms that labelled a professional 'Senior' with just few years of work experience.

Firm	*Designation*	*Work Experience (Senior)*
Best Buy	Senior Programmer Analyst	2 years
Compaq	Senior Software Engineer	3–5 years
Geoworks	Senior Software Engineer	5 years
Lotus	Senior Software Engineer	5 years
Oracle	Senior Software QA	4 years

See *supra* note 14, Part III: Thought Control, Matloff Updated Congressional Testimony, 'Debunking the Myth' at p. 40.

17. *Inside Intel: Andy Grove and the Rise of the World's Most Powerful Chip Company*. Tim Jackson. Dutton Books. 1998.
18. Matloff provided a more detailed account of the conversation with Intel's Coetta Chambers on his blog. 'We're Desperate to Hire—Unless You Refer Applicants to Us.' Upon Closer Inspection. 8 April 2015.

https://normsaysno.wordpress.com/2015/04/08/were-desperate-to-hire-unless-you-refer-applicants-to-us/.

(Matloff's piece pivoted on his interaction with Virgil. In 2015, during a Senate testimony, a German-origin entrepreneur, Bjorn Billhardt, spoke about help signs all over Austin and that he'd be happy to introduce anyone looking for a job. Virgil reached out to him asking for help, then followed up. Billhardt ignored him. Virgil wrote to Matloff, recounting the snub.)

19. See *supra* note 9, Part III: Thought Control, Matloff, '1998 Congressional Testimony' at p. 172.
20. Ibid. at p. 172.
21. Ibid. at p. 168.
22. Ibid. at p. 163.
23. Ibid. at p. 165.
24. Ibid. at p. 180
25. Ibid. at p. 180.
26. Ibid. at p. 188.
27. Ibid. at pp. 185–186.
28. See *supra* note 14, Part III: Thought Control, Matloff Updated Congressional Testimony, 'Debunking the Myth' at p. 66.
29. Ibid. at p. 7.
30. See *supra* note 7, Part I: Dream, 2006 GAO Report, 'Labor Could Improve Its Oversight' at pp. 6–7. It also explains how to file a Labor Condition Application (LCA): 'Filing an application with Labor's Employment and Training Administration is the employer's first step in hiring an H-1B worker, and Labor is responsible for either certifying or denying the employer's application within 7 days. By law, it may *only review applications for omissions and obvious inaccuracies. Labor has no authority to verify the authenticity of the information* [emphasis mine]. Employers must include on the application information such as their name, address, rate of pay and work location for the H-1B worker and employer identification number. All employers are also required to make four attestations on the application as to:
    - Wages: The employer will pay nonimmigrants at least the local prevailing wage or the employer's actual wage, whichever is higher, and pay for non-productive time caused by a decision

made by the employer; and offer nonimmigrants benefits on the same basis as U.S. workers.

- Working conditions: The employment of H-1B nonimmigrants will not adversely affect the working conditions of U.S. workers similarly employed.
- Strike, lockout, or work stoppage: No strike or lockout exists in the occupational classification at the place of employment.
- Notification: The employer has notified employees at the place of employment of the intent to employ H-1B workers.'

31. *Balancing Interests: Rethinking U.S. Selection of Skilled Immigrants.* Demetrios Papademetriou and Stephen Yale-Loehr. Carnegie Endowment for International Peace. 1996.
32. 'The System is Broken and Needs to be Fixed.' Office of Inspector General, U.S. Department of Labor. 22 May 1996. https://www.oig.dol.gov/public/reports/oa/pre_1998/06-96-002-03-321.pdf (p. 3).
33. See *supra* note 14, Part III: Thought Control, Matloff Updated Congressional Testimony, 'Debunking the Myth' at p. 62.

    'This obsession with specific skills is unwarranted,' Matloff added, 'akin [to] what would happen if Chevy dealers refused to hire seasoned mechanics with experience on Fords.'
34. Ibid. at p. 11.
35. Senior Research Associate at Harvard Law School Michael Teitelbaum charted the fascinating history of America's STEM crisis in his 2014 book, *Falling Behind?: Boom, Bust, and the Global Race for Scientific Talent*, published by Princeton University Press [hereinafter Teitelbaum, *Falling Behind?*].
36. The narrative of NSF's flawed 'STEM crisis' study is largely constructed from the following two sources: Teitelbaum's book *Falling Behind?* and the 1992 Congressional hearing interrogating the federal agency, which is compiled in a 1,332-page book, *Projecting Science and Engineering Personnel Requirements for the 1990s: How Good are the Numbers?* U.S. House of Representatives, Subcommittee on Investigations and Oversight of the Committee on Science, Space, and Technology, 102 Cong. 8 April 1992 [hereinafter Congressional Probe Book]. The Congressional Probe Book is available at https://books.google.co.in/books?id=HbBWXaO5cDsC&printsec=frontcover&source=gbs_ge_summary_r&cad=0#v=onepage&q&f=false/.

'April 1987' recurs throughout the Congressional Probe book (see, for example, p. 18, 39, 151, 152 and 155). Ditto the '675,000' figure (see p. 2, 3 and 5). For '2006', see, among others, p. 417, 537 and 1,065.

37. Ibid. at Congressional Probe Book, p. 7. The opening statement of Sherwood Boehlert (R-New York).
38. 'Scientist Shortfall a Myth.' *The Washington Post.* Boyce Rensberger. 8 April 1992. https://www.washingtonpost.com/archive/politics/1992/04/09/scientist-shortfall-a-myth/f4f88e0e-921e-48c3-9cae-8bb894de2588/.
39. See *supra* note 36, Part III: Thought Control, Congressional Probe Book, p. 387. Statement of Eric Bloch, NSF Director, at the hearing before the committee on Labor and Human Resources. U.S. Senate. 26 March 1986.
40. See *supra* note 35, Part III: Thought Control, Teitelbaum, *Falling Behind?* at Chapter 2: No Shortage of Shortages.
41. See *supra* note 36, Part III: Thought Control, Congressional Probe Book, p. 445. Robert White's speech on 2 October 1990.
42. Ibid. at p. 336. A small portion of the revealing conversation between Wolpe and House unfolded as follows:

    House: 'No, not for demand. I called that a target year; I called it a proxy demand, but when you read that.'

    Wolpe: 'You did call it proxy demand?'

    House: 'But what it was described as is proxy demand was clearly meant to say that if you need this number of people, then you will have. It was not a demand in the sense of a market demand. Will you state that clearly?'

    Wolpe: 'I'm quoting from your own study here. It says instead, and I'm quoting you at this point, "Instead the average production during 1984 to 1986 has been taken as a proxy for future demand. This proxy is conservative".'
43. Ibid. at p. 1,237. When Alan Fechter considered the years 1945–88 for 'proxy demand', he found out it was 37 per cent less compared to the PRA study.
44. Ibid. at p. 2. Rep. Howard Wolpe's opening statement. (Bloch had used the '692,000' figure in his 1986 written testimony.)
45. Ibid. at p. 152.
46. Ibid. at p. 405.
47. Ibid. at p. 406.

48. Ibid. at p. 25.
49. Ibid. at p. 477.
50. Ibid. at p. 477.
51. Bloch had used the word 'shortfall' and the '675,000' figure in the May 1990 Senate hearing. See more at 'Shortage of Engineers and Scientists. Hearing Before the Subcommittee on Science, Technology, and Space of the Committee on Commerce, Science, and Transportation'. U.S. Senate. 8 May 1990. https://files.eric.ed.gov/fulltext/ED328428.pdf (pp. 25-26).
52. See *supra* note 36, Part III: Thought Control, Congressional Probe Book, p. 551. A part of Wolpe's exchange with House reads as follows:

    Wolpe: '*Science* Magazine, I'm told, refused actually to publish it when it was offered it. There is a February 21, 1991 memo from Alan Levitt to Ray Bye that says quote, "The editor of *Science* called me this afternoon, and he was quite negative about the piece that we submitted to him. He called it garbage, a puff piece, and old stuff"'.
53. Ibid. at p. 551.
54. Ibid. at pp. 557–558.
55. See *supra* note 9, Part III: Thought Control, Matloff, '1998 Congressional Testimony' at p. 155.
56. 'How and Why Government, Universities, and Industry Create Domestic Labor Shortages of Scientists and High-Tech Workers.' Working Draft, National Bureau of Economic Research. Eric Weinstein. 2003. https://users.nber.org/~sewp/references/archive/weinsteinhowandwhygovernment.pdf.
57. Ibid. at p. 12.
58. Ibid. at p. 13.
59. Ibid. at p. 14.
60. Ibid. at p. 14.
61. Ibid. at p. 13.
62. 'Significant Milestones.' Keep America At Work. https://web.archive.org/web/20130321163945/http://keepamericaatwork.com/significant-milestones.
63. *Who Stole the American Dream?* Hedrick Smith. Random House. 2012 [hereinafter Smith, *Who Stole the American Dream?*].
64. 'Powell Memorandum: Attack On American Free Enterprise System.' Lewis F. Powell Jr. 1971. https://scholarlycommons.law.wlu.edu/powellmemo/1/.

65. See *supra* note 63, Part III: Thought Control, Smith, *Who Stole the American Dream?* at Chapter 1: The Business Rebellion.
66. Ibid.
67. Ibid. at Chapter 5: The New Economy of the 1990s.
68. Virgil wrote a post on FWD.us's first anniversary. 'FWD.us is Celebrating its First Birthday Today Made Possible by Enormous Sums of Technology Founder Cash While American Programmers Go Hungry.' Keep America At Work. 10 April 2014. https://web.archive.org/web/20140423101525/http://keepamericaatwork.com/
69. 'Opinion|Facebook's Mark Zuckerberg: Immigration and the Knowledge Economy.' *The Washington Post*. 10 April 2013. https://www.washingtonpost.com/opinions/mark-zuckerberg-immigrants-are-the-key-to-a-knowledge-economy/2013/04/10/aba05554-a20b-11e2-82bc-511538ae90a4_story.html
70. See the year-wise database of Labor Condition Application (LCA) files on the DOL's website, under the section 'LCA Programs (H-1B, H-1B1, E-3)' here: 'Performance Data.' U.S. Department of Labor. https://www.dol.gov/agencies/eta/foreign-labor/performance.
71. See the diagrammatic representation of how to obtain an H-1B visa at 'Reforms Are Needed to Minimize the Risks and Costs of Current Program.' United States Government Accountability Office. January 2011. https://www.gao.gov/assets/gao-11-26.pdf [hereinafter 2011 GAO Report, 'Reforms Are Needed'] at p. 10.
72. Virgil would make many data-driven comparisons on his website in the next few years. See, for instance, one of his first such findings here: 'Why Did the U.S. Government Throw So Many Veterans That Served Under the Bus in the #STEM Industry?' Keep America At Work. 14 May 2014. https://web.archive.org/web/20140517210005/http://keepamericaatwork.com/.
73. Matching the timeline in Kumar's story, these rates correspond to 2011. But even in the subsequent years, when the rates somewhat increased, the proportion of an H-1B worker's pay didn't change by much.
74. American Competitiveness in the Twenty-First Century Act. Senate Report No. 106-260. 2000. https://www.govinfo.gov/content/pkg/CRPT-106srpt260/html/CRPT-106srpt260.htm. Specifically, see the section that reads: 'Detailed below are key enforcement provisions of the 1998 legislation related to H-1B visas.'

75. 'Fact Sheet #62C: Who is an H-1B-Dependent Employer?' Wage and Hour Division, U.S. Department of Labor. https://www.dol.gov/sites/dolgov/files/WHD/legacy/files/whdfs62C.pdf.
76. See *supra* note 71, Part III: Thought Control, 2011 GAO Report, 'Reforms Are Needed' at p. 9. H-1B dependent employers 'need *only attest, rather than demonstrate*, that they took good faith steps to hire a U.S. worker'. [Emphasis mine.]
77. See *supra* note 14, Part III: Thought Control, Matloff Updated Congressional Testimony, 'Debunking the Myth'.
78. 'On the Need for Reform of the H-1B Non-Immigrant Work Visa in Computer-Related Occupations.' *University of Michigan Journal of Law Reform*, 36:4, 815–913. Norman Matloff. 2003. https://repository.law.umich.edu/cgi/viewcontent.cgi?article=1424&context=mjlr [hereinafter Matloff, 'Need for Reform'].
79. See *supra* note 14, Part III: Thought Control, Matloff Updated Congressional Testimony, 'Debunking the Myth' at p. 85.
80. See *supra* note 78, Part III: Thought Control, Matloff, 'Need for Reform' at p. 825.

    'It took the DOL two years to issue regulations regarding the provisions,' wrote Matloff, 'and in the end only 50 out of 50,000 H-1B employers were declared to be H-1B dependent' (internal citation omitted).
81. 'Creating High-Tech Sweatshops: U.S. Computer Firms Find Skilled—and Cheap—Programmers Abroad. Some Say the Workers Are Exploited and American Jobs Are Threatened.' *Los Angeles Times.* Leslie Helm. 15 November 1993. https://www.latimes.com/archives/la-xpm-1993-11-15-mn-57210-story.html.
82. See *supra* note 14, Part III: Thought Control, Matloff Updated Congressional Testimony, 'Debunking the Myth' at p. 13.
83. Ibid. at p. 15.
84. Ibid. at p. 77.
85. 'Visa Program, High-Tech Workers Exploited, Critics Say.' *The Washington Post.* William Branigin. 26 July 1998. https://www.washingtonpost.com/archive/politics/1998/07/26/visa-program-high-tech-workers-exploited-critics-say/bcbf950a-e890-4879-9853-2d8bb2ab00bd/.
86. See *supra* note 78, Part III: Thought Control, Matloff, 'Need for Reform' at p. 865.

87. 'Can Occupational Labor Shortages be Identified Using Available Data?' *Monthly Labor Review*. Carolyn Veneri. March 1999. https://www.bls.gov/opub/mlr/1999/03/art2full.pdf.
88. Ibid. at p. 18: 'A major drawback in using detailed occupational unemployment rates in analyses of shortages is that the unemployment rate is calculated based on a person's last job, rather than the longest job held or occupation in which he or she trained and is actually looking for work. This means an individual with experience as a computer programmer who is seeking a programming job, but who last worked as a cashier, is classified as an unemployed cashier, not an unemployed programmer' (internal citation omitted).

    Matloff elaborated that point in his 2015 blog post, writing, 'I've said before, unemployment rates in this field aren't very useful, since tech workers find it necessary to bail from the field after encountering major obstacles in finding work; the former engineer now working as a sales clerk at Radio Shack counts as employed, even though he/she is UNDERemployed.' See 'Yet Another Pro-H-1B Study, Seemingly Tied to Industry Money'. Upon Closer Inspection. 9 April 2015. https://normsaysno.wordpress.com/2015/04/09/yet-another-pro-h-1b-study-seemingly-tied-to-industry-money/.
89. 'The Digital Work Force: Building Infotech Skills at the Speed of Innovation.' Office of Technology Policy. Carol Meares and John Sargent, Jr. June 1999. https://files.eric.ed.gov/fulltext/ED441150.pdf.
90. 'Assessing the Demand for Information Technology Workers.' IT Workforce Data Project. Richard Ellis and Lindsay Lowell. November 1999. https://web.archive.org/web/20031204084920/http://www.cpst.org/it-4.pdf.

    '[O]n the whole,' noted the report, 'there is no compelling evidence to suggest a national shortage of IT workers, either now or in the near future.'
91. 'Bill to Boost Tech Visas Sails Through Congress: Clinton Expected to Sign Popular Measure.' *SFGate*. Carolyn Lochhead. 4 October 2000. https://www.sfgate.com/news/article/Bill-to-Boost-Tech-Visas-Sails-Through-Congress-2735682.php.
92. See *supra* note 78, Part III: Thought Control, Matloff, 'Need for Reform' at p. 827.
93. Ibid. at p. 823.

94. 106 Cong. Rec. H8699, statement of Rep. Llyod Doggett. 3 October 2000. https://www.congress.gov/congressional-record/volume-146/issue-121/house-section/article/H8699-1?s=1&r=3410. ('I am here not because I think this is a good bill, but because it is the only bill that the House leadership will permit us to consider on this issue. To schedule this debate 3 hours after Members were told they could leave the Capitol because there would be no further votes, to schedule it in a way that limits the debate time to a few minutes, to deny all perfecting amendments, is all too typical of the way this House has operated this year under the Republican leadership.')
95. In September 2000, a month before the congressional debate, the GAO released a scathing study on the H-1B program. Yet the 19,000-word Senate discussion only praised the bill; the GAO's detailed criticism didn't get a word. See 'Better Controls Needed to Help Employers Protect Workers'. U.S. General Accounting Office. September 2000. https://www.govinfo.gov/content/pkg/GAOREPORTS-HEHS-00-157/pdf/GAOREPORTS-HEHS-00-157.pdf [hereinafter 2000 GAO Report, 'Better Controls Needed'].
96. 'H-1B Visas Jump in 2001.' *CNET News*. Rachel Konrad. 22 January 2002. https://www.cnet.com/tech/tech-industry/h-1b-visas-jump-in-2001/.
97. 'The Reverse Brain Drain.' *Fortune*. Eryn Brown and David Kirkpatrick. 11 November 2002. http://web.archive.org/web/ 20120118024849/ https://money.cnn.com/magazines/fortune/fortune_archive/2002/11/11/331802/index.htm.
98. 'Dun Workers Fear Layoffs.' *Daily Record*. Douglass Krouse. 3 June 2000.
99. 'U.S. Workers Taking H-1B Issues to Court.' *San Jose Mercury News*. Jennifer Bjorhus. 26 September 2002 [hereinafter Bjorhus, 'H-1B Issues to Court'].
100. 'L1s Slip Past H-1B Curbs.' *EWeek*. Lisa Vaas. 6 January 2003.
101. See *supra* note 99, Part III: Thought Control, Bjorhus, 'H-1B Issues to Court'.
102. *The Betrayal of the American Dream* at Chapter 4—Phantom Jobs. Donald Barlett and James Steele. PublicAffairs. 2013.
103. Ibid.
104. Ibid.

105. For more information on prevailing wage, see 'Prevailing Wage Information and Resources'. U.S. Department of Labor. https://www.dol.gov/agencies/eta/foreign-labor/wages.
106. See 'Fact Sheet #62G: Must an H-1B Worker Be Paid a Guaranteed Wage?' Wage and Hour Division, U.S. Department of Labor. July 2008. https://www.dol.gov/agencies/whd/fact-sheets/62g-h1b-required-wage. ('The actual wage is the wage rate paid by the employer to all individuals with experience and qualifications similar to the H-1B nonimmigrant's experience and qualifications for the specific employment in question at the place of employment.')
107. 'Fact Sheet #62A: Changes Made by the H-1B Visa Reform Act of 2004.' Wage and Hour Division, U.S. Department of Labor. July 2008. https://www.dol.gov/agencies/whd/fact-sheets/62a-h1b-visa-reform-act.
108. 'L-1 and H-1B Visa Provisions in the FY 2005 Budget Bill.' IEEE-USA. 22 November 2004. https://web.archive.org/web/20041124053408/www.ieeeusa.org/policy/features/h-1b-update.asp.
109. See *supra* note 78, Part III: Thought Control, Matloff, 'Need for Reform' at pp. 902–904.
110. John Miano, a leading expert on the effect of foreign labour on technology workers, wrote a long, data-driven report in December 2005, examining the 'effectiveness of the prevailing wage requirements in the H-1B program and to determine whether there is a difference between wages paid to H-1B workers in computer programming fields and wages for U.S. workers in the same fields'. See 'The Bottom of the Pay Scale Wages for H-1B Computer Programmers'. Center for Immigration Studies. https://cis.org/sites/cis.org/files/articles/2005/back1305.pdf.
111. 'H1B Changes 2004.' Matloff's H-1B/L-1/Offshoring E-newsletter. 4 December 2004 (updated later). https://web.cs.ucdavis.edu/~matloff/Archive/H1BChanges2004.txt.
112. See Jack Krumholtz's letter to Michael Chertoff, Secretary of U.S. Department of Homeland Security, here (15 November 2007): https://www.bloomberg.com/graphics/2021-opinion-optional-practical-training-problems-stem-graduates-deserve-better-jobs-opportunities/documents/krumholtz.pdf.
113. Ibid. See also 'The STEM Graduate System is Broken. Here's How to Fix It'. *Bloomberg*. Rachel Rosenthal. 11 March 2021. https://www.

bloomberg.com/graphics/2021-opinion-optional-practical-training-problems-stem-graduates-deserve-better-jobs-opportunities/ [hereinafter Rosenthal, 'STEM Graduate System is Broken'].

114. In 2016, the Obama administration extended the OPT extension duration from seventeen months to twenty-four months (for a total of three years) and added the requirement that the employer attest that an OPT employee would not replace a US worker and that their duties, hours and compensation were 'commensurate' with 'similarly situated' US workers at the job location. But '[a]s straightforward as these parameters sound ... they raise some fundamental questions,' wrote Rosenthal. 'Because the 2008 rule had no minimum wage provision, the "commensurate" guidance introduced in 2016 marked a step forward. Yet the concept of a commensurate wage is vague: How would an employer determine that level, and could DHS even verify it? The department doesn't have the staff or resources to regularly conduct such analysis, and its collection of wage data is spotty. (For non-STEM OPT, identifying an employer isn't even required to obtain work authorization, which makes wage verification a guessing game.) Most critically, there's little to prevent OPT workers from being hired as unpaid interns—and though data are scarce, this isn't uncommon.' See more at *supra* note 113, Part III: Thought Control, Rosenthal, 'STEM Graduate System is Broken.'

115. To know more about the OPT tax breaks, see the answer to the following question on USCIS's website: '[As an employer] Am I required to pay FICA taxes (payroll taxes for Social Security and Medicare contributions)?'

'It depends. Under current tax laws, if your STEM OPT participant is exempt from payroll taxes, you save an amount equal to 6.2 percent of the STEM OPT participant's salary up to the taxable wage base and an additional 1.45 percent of the total salary that would have been your contribution to the Social Security and Medicare trust funds. STEM OPT participants generally are not subject to FICA taxes or Social Security and Medicare contributions until after the first five calendar years that they hold an F-1 non-immigrant status, but many STEM OPT participants will already have accrued such physical presence and thus will be subject to FICA taxes.'

See more at 'STEM OPT Frequently Asked Questions'. Department of Homeland Security. https://studyinthestates.dhs.gov/stem-opt-hub/additional-resources/stem-opt-frequently-asked-questions.

116. 'Feds Provide Almost $2 Billion in Subsidies to Hire Alien Grads Rather Than U.S. Grads.' Center for Immigration Studies. David North. 27 February 2018. https://cis.org/North/Feds-Provide-Almost-2-Billion-Subsidies-Hire-Alien-Grads-Rather-US-Grads.
117. 'Lawsuit Filed Against OPT Extension.' Matloff's H-1B/L-1/Offshoring E-newsletter. 6 June 2008. https://web.cs.ucdavis.edu/~matloff/Archive/OPTLawsuit.txt.
118. Ibid.
119. Ibid.
120. 'Chapter 6—Permanent Labor Certification.' U.S. Citizenship and Immigration Services. https://www.uscis.gov/policy-manual/volume-6-part-e-chapter-6 [hereinafter Green Card Approval].
121. See *supra* note 14, Part III: Thought Control, Matloff Updated Congressional Testimony, 'Debunking the Myth' at p. 19.

In January 2012, the Department of Homeland Security - Office of Inspector General released an audit report—titled 'The Effects of USCIS Adjudication Procedures and Policies on Fraud Detection by Immigration Services Officers'—where, among others, it expressed concerns about the 'level of outside influence on the adjudication process'. It contained several revealing insights. Some of them run below:

- 'The DOJ OIG wrote that adjudicators "perceived a perpetuation of the historical favoritism shown to certain organizations". According to interviewees and survey respondents, a culture of "get to yes" continues to exist at USCIS.'
- 'A survey respondent wrote of a sense that private immigration attorneys are "running our offices".'

And of course, the most important and relevant:

- 'An Immigration Services Officer said that the American Immigration Lawyers Association "owns" USCIS. USCIS is aware of this perception and has taken some steps to treat this organization less uniquely.' [Emphasis mine.]

Read the full report here: https://www.govinfo.gov/content/pkg/GOVPUB-HS-PURL-gpo33508/pdf/GOVPUB-HS-PURL-gpo33508.pdf (pp. 25–27).

122. 'PERM Fake Job Ads Defraud Americans to Secure Green Cards.' Programmers' Guild. 17 June 2007. https://www.youtube.com/watch?v=TCbFEgFajGU [hereinafter Programmers' Guild, 'PERM Fake Job Ads Defraud Americans'].
123. 'Immigration Law Seminar Generates Unwanted Publicity for Firm.' *The Legal Intelligencer*. Gina Passarella. 25 June 2007. https://web.archive.org/web/20070627203604/https://www.law.com/jsp/article.jsp?id=1182503156967.
124. See Senator Chuck Grassley and Representative Lamar Smith's letter to the Department of Labor, including an attached letter to Cohen & Grigsby (21 June 2007), here: http://heather.cs.ucdavis.edu/GrassleySmith.pdf.

    See also 'Sen. Grassley and Rep. Smith Take Action on YouTube Videos.' Matloff's H-1B/L-1/Offshoring E-newsletter. 21 June 2007. https://web.cs.ucdavis.edu/~matloff/Archive/GrassleySmithLtrs.txt.
125. 'Legal Rejection of U.S. Workers.' *Immigration Daily*. Joel Stewart. 24 April 2000. https://www.ilw.com/articles/2000,0424-Stewart.shtm.
126. 'Pittsburgh Local Angle About YouTube-Gate.' Matloff's H-1B/L-1/Offshoring E-newsletter. 22 June 2007. https://web.cs.ucdavis.edu/~matloff/Archive/PittsburghYouTube.txt.
127. Ibid.
128. 'Cohen & Grigsby and the Prevailing-Wage Scam.' Matloff's H-1B/L-1/Offshoring E-newsletter. 23 June 2007. https://web.cs.ucdavis.edu/~matloff/Archive/CohenAndGrigsbyPrevailingWage.txt.
129. 'YouTube Video Puts Sharp Focus on Tech Job Ads.' *Network World*. Patrick Thibodeau. 28 June 2007. https://www.networkworld.com/article/822009/infrastructure-management-youtube-video-puts-sharp-focus-on-tech-job-ads.html.
130. 'DOL to Audit Permanent Labor Certifications Filed by Fragomen Firm.' Ogletree Deakins (originally published in the June 2008 issue of *Immigration eAuthority*). 24 June 2008. https://ogletree.com/insights-resources/blog-posts/dol-to-audit-permanent-labor-certifications-filed-by-fragomen-firm/. See also 'Fragomen and DOL Agree to Return to Normal Processing for Newly Filed PERM Cases.' Thomson Reuters Westlaw. 1 August 2008. https://content.next.westlaw.com/Document/I45a4274fd2b611de9b8c850332338889/View/FullText.html?contextData=(sc.Default)&transitionType=Default.

131. 'A "Eureka" Moment Regarding the Fragomen Case.' Matloff's H-1B/L-1/Offshoring E-newsletter. 6 July 2008. https://web.cs.ucdavis.edu/~matloff/Archive/Fragomen4.txt.
132. 'Texas Woman Confronts Obama on H-1B issue—Sea Change?' Matloff's H-1B/L-1/Offshoring E-newsletter. 30 January 2012. https://web.cs.ucdavis.edu/~matloff/Archive/JenniferWeddelVsObama.txt.
133. See the whole exchange between Obama and Jennifer Wedel at 'Obama Comments on the H-1B Visa Program During Google+ Hangout'. Michael Hill. 31 January 2012. https://www.youtube.com/watch?v=K_CMXLBd17k.
134. 'Texas Engineer, Whose Wife Sent Obama His Résumé, Still Unemployed.' *The Fort Worth Star-Telegram*. Anna Tinsley. 9 April 2012. https://www.modbee.com/latest-news/article3142880.html.
135. 'Why Did the U.S. Government Throw So Many Veterans That Served Under the Bus in the #STEM Industry?' Keep America At Work. 14 May 2014. https://web.archive.org/web/20140517210005/http://keepamericaatwork.com/.
136. 'About H1B, H-1B My Experiences.' Kumar Exclusive. 18 June 2013. https://www.youtube.com/watch?v=-63W6OLSeCw.
137. 'H-1B—Epi 2 FAQs.' Kumar Exclusive. 18 June 2013. https://www.youtube.com/watch?v=pBBxTYa9gAQ.
138. See videos uploaded by Kumar on his YouTube channel, Kumar Exclusive: 'F1 Visa Preparation Complete Check List'. 13 September 2013. https://www.youtube.com/watch?v=LRNQ03R_sN4; 'Experience About Life in India & USA.' 25 September 2013. https://www.youtube.com/watch?v=bBwqpYoTMx4; 'Political Analysis of Indian Democracy.' 12 October 2013. https://www.youtube.com/watch?v=dH8WwwS9_7U.
139. 'The Dark Side of H1B Life in America.' Kumar Exclusive. 22 November 2013. https://www.youtube.com/watch?v=q1vnpxQEkQ8.
140. 'H-1B Helpless and Hopeless Life in America.' Kumar Exclusive. 25 March 2014. https://www.youtube.com/watch?v=zhr2lyQaxto.
141. See more at 'About the Suicide Project—Read This First'. The Suicide Project. https://suicideproject.org/about/.
142. 'H-1B Visas and the STEM shortage: A Research Brief.' Brookings. Jonathan Rothwell and Neil Ruiz. 11 May 2013. https://papers.ssrn.com/sol3/papers.cfm?abstract_id=2262872 (p. 11).

143. 'Immigration and the Tech Industry: As a Labor Shortage Remedy, for Innovation, or for Cost Savings?' *Migration Letters*. Norman Matloff. 2013. https://migrationletters.com/index.php/ml/article/view/144.
144. 'Brookings's Flawed Study.' Matloff's H-1B/L-1/Offshoring E-newsletter. 12 May 2013. https://web.cs.ucdavis.edu/~matloff/Archive/Brookings Flawed Study.txt [hereinafter Matloff, 'Brookings's Flawed Study'].
145. Ibid.
146. Ibid.
147. Ibid.
148. Ibid.
149. 'Are Foreign Students the "Best and Brightest"?' Economic Policy Institute. Norman Matloff. 28 February 2013. https://files.epi.org/2013/outstanding-talent-high-skilled-immigration.pdf (p. 9).
150. See *supra* note 144, Part III: Thought Control, Matloff, 'Brookings's Flawed Study'.
151. Ibid.
152. 'Brookings H-1B Report's Flawed Analysis & Flawed Process.' Economic Policy Institute. Ron Hira. 13 May 2013. https://www.epi.org/blog/brookings-1b-reports-flawed-analysis-flawed/.
153. Ibid.
154. 'At Fast-Growing Brookings, Donors May Have an Impact on Research Agenda.' *The Washington Post*. Tom Hamburger and Alexander Becker. 30 October 2014. https://www.washingtonpost.com/politics/at-fast-growing-brookings-donors-help-set-agenda/2014/10/30/a4ba4e8e-48ef-11e4-891d-713f052086a0_story.html/.
155. Ibid.
156. Ibid.
157. Ibid.
158. Ibid.
159. Ibid.
160. Ibid.
161. 'TCS, Other High-Tech Leaders Launch America's First "Software Industry Center" at Carnegie Mellon University.' Tata Consultancy Services. 21 June 2001. http://web.archive.org/web/20021024100541/http://www.tcs.com/0_media_room/releases/200106june/20010621_carnegie.htm.
162. 'Carnegie Mellon and Tata Consultancy Services Break Ground on Global Research Facility in the U.S.' Carnegie Mellon University.

8 November 2019. http://web.archive.org/web/20200330212514/https://makepossible.cmu.edu/tata-groundbreaking/.

163. Tata Group's $50 million donation to Harvard Business School was the largest gift by a foreign donor in the college's 102-year history. It built a 161,000-square-foot building—comprising two classrooms, 179 bedrooms and three gathering spaces for the students of the Executive Education programme—naming it Tata Hall (after then chairperson, Ratan Tata). Seven years later, an Indian parliamentary committee pressed for a probe into Tata Trusts's 'blatant tax violations' regarding the tax-exempted donation. The Income Tax department demanded a tax levy of over Rs 100 crore, but the Income Tax Appellate Tribunal ruled in the multinational's favour.

    See more at 'Harvard Business School to Dedicate Tata Hall, a New Executive Education Building'. Harvard Business School. 4 December 2013. https://www.hbs.edu/news/releases/Pages/hbs-to-dedicate-tata-hall.aspx; 'Parliamentary Panel Recommends Probe Into "Blatant Tax Violations" by Tata Trusts.' NDTV. 9 April 2018. https://www.ndtv.com/india-news/parliamentary-panel-recommends-probe-into-blatant-tax-violations-by-tata-trusts-1834976; 'Donations for Cornell/Harvard: ITAT Rules in Favour of Tata Trust.' *The Hindu BusinessLine*. 24 July 2020. https://www.thehindubusinessline.com/news/education/endowment-funds-itat-rules-in-favour-of-tata-education-trust/article32182553.ece.

164. 'Carnegie Mellon Receives $20 Million From Bill & Melinda Gates Foundation to Build a New Home for the Study of Computer Science.' *Carnegie Mellon Today*. Teresa Thomas and Anne Watzman. 14 September 2004. https://web.archive.org/web/20231121072414/https://www.cmu.edu/cmnews/extra/040914_gates.html.

165. 'Wright State University Agrees to Pay Government $1 Million for Visa Fraud.' U.S. Attorney's Office, Southern District of Ohio. 16 November 2018. https://www.justice.gov/usao-sdoh/pr/wright-state-university-agrees-pay-government-1-million-visa-fraud.

166. The Wright State University (WSU) scandal revealed at least two key, hitherto unknown, facets of the H-1B programme: a) that just like the corporate world, even in academia, a well-known entity exploited the loopholes and breached legal bounds (as opposed to the obviously maligned figures, such as the visa mills) and b) an American

university had functioned as a body shop or, since it supplied workers to contracting firms, a body-shop-within-a-body-shop.

In the summer of 2010, a WSU official approached a Dayton-based desi consultancy, Web Yoga, with a proposal: the university would hire H-1B workers on the firm's behalf and subcontract them to it, which could further farm them out to different US clients. Web Yoga could of course hire these workers directly—and it had indeed submitted more than two dozen LCAs over the last few years—but this collaboration would be even more profitable. Since WSU, as an educational institution, was exempted from the H-1B cap, it didn't have to worry about the annual lottery and, more importantly, could hire foreign workers at (much lower) academia-level salaries. The firm, in turn, would pay the university a fee for this 'service'.

In 2007, Sundaram Narayanan co-founded the Wright State Research Institute (WSRI), the university's applied research arm, with president Dave Hopkins. Narayanan became WSRI's executive director and later the dean of the engineering and computer science college. In October 2010, Web Yoga awarded WSU $413,463 for 'Web Yoga System Development'. In the same month, the university was approved to hire a pair of software developers on employment visas for $40,000 per year. Their work address? Web Yoga's office. Two months later, the Web Yoga president, Vijay Vallabhaneni, signed a contract with WSRI to develop SpiderXchange. The project intended to employ sixty people; eight of them were named in the contract and hired by WSU—seven on work visas. Phani Kidambi—a PhD graduate from WSU working at WSRI as an associate researcher under director Ryan Fendley who reported to Narayanan—was listed as the project manager.

In the same month, the firm awarded WSRI $1.5 million for 'Web Yoga SpiderXchange System'. From October 2010 to early 2012, Wright State hired at least nineteen H-1B workers for Web Yoga. But the college didn't disclose in the LCAs that they would be actually working for Web Yoga, serving clients across the country, including New York, Atlanta and Orlando. Over the years, WSU charged Web Yoga a total of $1.8 million for 'employees' visas, salaries, benefits' and the university's 'administrative costs'.

In March 2013, Narayanan was promoted to the university provost, who made Fendley his senior advisor. Kidambi became the director of Wright State International Gateway, a department recruiting international students. The university had signed similar contracts with several firms, including Lexis Nexis; Universal Technology Corporation; and a Dayton defence contractor, UES. Turns out, UES's CEO was Nina Joshi, a former WSU trustee. WSU hired at least twenty-eight H-1B workers for its business partners, but the charade didn't continue forever. A joint probe by the Homeland Security Investigations and the Defense Criminal Investigative Service found Wright State and Web Yoga guilty of visa fraud. The U.S. Attorney's Office didn't pursue civil or criminal prosecution of the university, as it agreed to pay $1 million in three instalments and agreed to cooperate in any additional investigations. The university fired Narayanan and Fendley, and Kidambi resigned. Web Yoga was ordered to pay a fine of around $566,000.

To know more about the case, see below:

- 'Suspended WSU Employees Tied to IT Contract.' *Dayton Daily News.* Josh Sweigart. 11 September 2015. http://web.archive.org/web/20190320135032/https://www.daytondailynews.com/news/crime--law/suspended-wsu-employees-tied-contract/hLMEABtJYhBi8F9RsZVFdJ/.
- 'Wright State U. Played Much the Same H-1B Role as an Indian Body Shop.' Center for Immigration Studies. David North. 15 September 2015. https://cis.org/North/Wright-State-U-Played-Much-Same-H1B-Role-Indian-Body-Shop.
- 'Some Interesting Details on the Wright State Case.' Upon Closer Inspection. Norman Matloff. 15 September 2015. https://normsaysno.wordpress.com/2015/09/15/some-interesting-details-on-the-wright-state-case/.
- 'LexisNexis One of 4 Area Companies Linked to WSU Visa Misuse Probe.' *Dayton Daily News.* Josh Sweigart. 7 April 2017. http://web.archive.org/web/20170411153603/https://www.daytondailynews.com/news/lexisnexis-one-area-companies-linked-wsu-visa-misuse-probe/gYyKeAaPYp2lO7HAmsMqUI/.
- 'Wright State Firing Long-Suspended Provost; Researcher Resigns.' Wright State University Newsroom. 26 September 2017. https://webapp2.wright.edu/web1/newsroom/2017/09/26/

whio-com-story-wright-state-firing-long-suspended-provost-researcher-resigns/.

- 'Wright State Provost Fired for Visa Scandal Could Get Faculty Job Back.' *Dayton Daily News.* Max Filby. 21 March 2019. https://www.daytondailynews.com/news/wright-state-provost-fired-for-visa-scandal-could-get-faculty-job-back/fiMfqfG8Pbw7K0WlUtYecL/.
- 'Dayton Technology Staffing Company Pleads Guilty in Connection to University Visa Fraud.' U.S. Attorney's Office, Southern District of Ohio. 28 August 2019. https://www.justice.gov/usao-sdoh/pr/dayton-technology-staffing-company-pleads-guilty-connection-university-visa-fraud.
- 'Area Company Sentenced in Wright State Visa Fraud Case.' *Dayton Daily News.* Parker Perry. 5 December 2019. https://www.daytondailynews.com/news/local/area-company-sentenced-wright-state-visa-fraud-case/oksj4hKgYycAImbzpFyHJP/.

167. 'The Myth of Postgraduate Degrees.' Matloff's H-1B/L-1/Offshoring E-newsletter. 7 August 2004. http://heather.cs.ucdavis.edu/Archive/ForeignGradStudents.txt.
168. 'Cartoons, the NIH and H-1B.' Matloff's H-1B/L-1/Offshoring E-newsletter. 5 July 2012. https://www.cs.ucdavis.edu/~matloff/Archive/ NIH.txt.
169. 'Immigration and American Jobs.' American Enterprise Institute and the Partnership for a New American Economy. Madeline Zavodny. 2011. https://www.newamericaneconomy.org/sites/all/themes/pnae/img/NAE_Im-AmerJobs.pdf [hereinafter Zavodny, 'Immigration and American Jobs'].
170. In September 2014, Zuckerberg's FWD.us posted a YouTube video detailing a series of myths and facts about the guestworker programme. 'Myth: H-1B visas hurt local economies,' stated the video, followed by, 'Fact: Every foreign-born worker with a STEM degree creates an average of 2.6 jobs for native-born Americans.' *The New York Times*'s columnist David Brooks used the Zavodny study to write that the evidence supporting the benefits of increased immigration of foreign workers was 'overwhelming.'
171. 'The Easy Problem.' *The New York Times.* David Brooks. 31 January 2013. https://www.nytimes.com/2013/02/01/opinion/brooks-the-easy-problem.html?fbclid=IwAR20Sk4opqqKrhuYI887AODWS0YOGMX4oBer_Ya6qz1bfbg1SHroOSYdiHg.

172. 'Detroit Homestead Act.' *The Wall Street Journal.* 12 March 2014. https://www.wsj.com/articles/SB10001424052702303795904579431523594192390.
173. 'Donald Trump's Undefined Stance an Opportunity to Reform H-1B Visa System: Alan Fleischmann.' *The Indian Express.* 14 November 2016. https://indianexpress.com/article/world/world-news/donald-trump-us-immigration-urged-to-reform-h1b-visa-system-4374434/.
174. 'The Benefits of the H-1B Visa.' *The Boston Globe.* John Hailer. 2 April 2013. https://www.bostonglobe.com/opinion/2013/04/02/the-benefits-visa/WPOr4ET4gZnTKGDhopQ0AL/story.html.
175. 'Facebook Founder Mark Zuckerberg Slams Donald Trump's Anti-H1-B Visa Policy.' *The Economic Times.* 21 August 2015. https://web.archive.org/web/20150826222137/https://articles.economictimes.indiatimes.com/2015-08-21/news/65706119_1_h-1b-visas-facebook-founder-immigration-policy.
176. 'H-1B Visa Reform: Issa Bill Worth Considering.' *San Francisco Examiner.* Jaya Padmanabhan. 11 January 2018. https://web.archive.org/web/20190204112000/http://www.sfexaminer.com/h-1b-visa-reform-issa-bill-worth-considering/.
177. 'America Needs to Tap the High-Tech Skills of Ready and Willing Immigrants.' *New York Daily News.* 7 December 2012. https://www.nydailynews.com/2012/12/07/america-needs-to-tap-the-high-tech-skills-of-ready-and-willing-immigrants/.
178. 'Immigration Cap Drags on US Manufacturing.' *Financial Times.* 11 February 2013. https://www.ft.com/content/12ce6d3c-740e-11e2-a27c-00144feabdc0#axzz3RqVCIAGD.
179. 'Tech Demands More H-1B Visas as Critics Cry Foul.' *NBC News.* 11 April 2014. https://www.nbcnews.com/business/business-news/tech-demands-more-h-1b-visas-critics-cry-foul-n77161.
180. 'H-1B Visa Lowers Wages, Has Negligible Impact on Patents: Study.' *Business Standard.* 7 May 2015. https://www.business-standard.com/article/pti-stories/h1b-visa-lowers-wages-has-negligible-impact-on-patents-study-115050700066_1.html.
181. 'Immigration Reform for Foreign STEM Graduate Students.' *The Hill.* Rajib Al Mamun. 8 February 2015. https://thehill.com/blogs/congress-blog/education/232021-immigration-reform-for-foreign-stem-graduate-students/.

182. 'Keeping America's Doors Open.' *Bloomberg*. 22 February 2017. https://www.bloomberg.com/view/articles/2017-02-22/u-s-should-keep-door-open-to-high-skilled-immigrants.
183. 'Tech Executives: Immigration Reform a Top Priority.' *Forbes*. Gary Shapiro. 27 March 2013. https://www.forbes.com/sites/garyshapiro/2013/03/27/tech-executives-immigration-reform-a-top-priority/.
184. 'How President-Elect Trump Can Spur More Growth Through Tech.' *Fortune*. Alan Fleischmann. 14 November 2016. https://web.archive.org/web/20161115123322/https://fortune.com/2016/11/13/donald-trump-immigration-wall-2/.
185. 'Bill Seeking H-1B Limits Exemption for Foreigners With US PhD Re-Introduced.' *DNA*. 27 May 2017. https://www.dnaindia.com/world/report-bill-seeking-h-1b-limits-exemption-for-foreigners-with-us-phd-re-introduced-2452820.
186. United States, Congress, Senate, Border Security, Economic Opportunity, and Immigration Modernization Act. 113 Congress, S. 744. 11 June 2013. https://www.govinfo.gov/content/pkg/CREC-2013-06-11/pdf/CREC-2013-06-11-pt1-PgS4086.pdf#page=5.
187. Congressional Record—Senate. 29 January 2013. https://www.govinfo.gov/content/pkg/CREC-2013-01-29/pdf/CREC-2013-01-29-pt1-PgS358-3.pdf#page=3 (p. 3). Specifically, see this: 'We cannot continue to simply hope American companies do not move operations to countries where they have greater access to individuals trained in these STEM fields,' said Senator Hatch. 'We cannot continue to ignore this problem; it is that simple. Continued inaction causes us to miss out on an important opportunity, especially since, as the American Enterprise Institute has confirmed, *100 foreign-born workers with STEM degrees create an average of 262 additional jobs for native-born workers*. Those countries would love to have their American-educated Ph.D.s and other highly educated individuals return and boost their economy—not only from their acquired skills but also by creating these new jobs as well. An updated, high-skilled immigration system is directly tied to creating jobs and spurring growth across all sectors of our economy. We cannot afford any further inaction on this issue.' [Emphasis mine.]
188. 'Blumenthal Defends Bill to Increase Guestworkers.' *The Day*. Lee Howard. 19 January 2015. https://www.theday.com/local-news/20150118/blumenthal-defends-bill-to-increase-guestworkers/.

189. 'Quigley, Paulsen Introduce Bipartisan Immigration Bill Encouraging American Innovation.' Congressman Mike Quigley. 30 April 2015. https://quigley.house.gov/media-center/press-releases/quigley-paulsen-introduce-bipartisan-immigration-bill-encouraging.
190. Ibid.
191. 'International Students are US Business' Best Hope for Growth.' Chicago Council on Global Affairs. 12 July 2016.
192. 'Low H-1B Visa Caps Don't Reflect Market Reality.' The American Action Forum. Laura Collins. 1 April 2014. https://www.americanactionforum.org/insight/low-h-1b-visa-caps-dont-reflect-market-reality/.
193. 'Has America Run Out of Room for Immigrants?' American Freedom Institute. Dallin Overstreet. 31 December 2019. http://web.archive.org/web/20200811122744/https://americanfreedominstitute.com/2019/12/31/has-america-run-out-of-room/.
194. 'Help Wanted: The Role of Foreign Workers in the Innovation Economy.' U.S. Chamber of Commerce, Information Technology Industry Council and Partnership for a New American Economy. December 2012. https://web.archive.org/web/20140725233446/http://www.renewoureconomy.org/wp-content/uploads/2013/07/stem-report.pdf.
195. 'Debunking the Myth That Immigration Destroys America.' American Immigration Lawyers Association. 6 April 2015. https://www.aila.org/aila-files/BCC90E71-6621-4BB5-A5AF-79978B4EE3FA/15040665.pdf?1697589923.
196. 'Immigrants as Economic Contributors: Immigrants Fill the Temporary Needs of American Employers.' National Immigration Forum. Dan Kosten. 16 January 2019. https://immigrationforum.org/article/immigrants-as-economic-contributors-immigrants-fill-the-temporary-needs-of-american-employers/.
197. 'The U.S. Economy Still Needs High-Skilled Immigrant Workers.' American Immigration Council. Walter Ewing. 7 December 2012. https://immigrationimpact.com/2012/12/07/the-u-s-economy-still-needs-high-skilled-immigrant-workers/.
198. David Brooks's *New York Times* column ('The Easy Problem', linked in *supra* note 171, Part III: Thought Control). Compete America. 2 February 2013. https://www.facebook.com/competeamericaorg/posts/138846439610188.

199. 'Contributing to American Growth.' Business Roundtable. June 2014. https://s3.amazonaws.com/brt.org/archive/0_immigration_report/2014.06.06%20BRT%20Immigration%20Report.Contributing%20to%20American%20Growth.pdf.
200. On 16 March 2015—a day before the Senate hearing on the H-1B visa programme—over a dozen advocacy groups, including FWD.us, submitted a long document to the Senate Judiciary Committee's chairman, Charles Grassley, 'rebutting some of the flawed studies and non-representative anecdotes used to create myths that suggest immigration harms America and American workers'. The letter also referenced Zavodny's '2.62' and '1.83' figures. See the 'Letter From Immigrant Advocate Groups to the Committee on the Judiciary' here: http://web.archive.org/web/20240517235227/https://www.uschamber.com/assets/archived/images/multi-association_myths_facts_letter_for_sjc_hearing.pdf.
201. 'The Economic Benefits of Fixing Our Broken Immigration System.' Executive Office of the President of the United States. July 2013. https://obamawhitehouse.archives.gov/sites/default/files/docs/report.pdf.
202. 'The Urgency of Immigration Reform: Attracting the World's Best and Brightest.' The White House Blog. Todd Park. 16 June 2014. https://obamawhitehouse.archives.gov/blog/2014/06/16/urgency-immigration-reform-attracting-world-s-best-and-brightest.
203. 'The Trouble With State-By-State Analyses of H-1B.' Upon Closer Inspection. Norman Matloff. 19 November 2014. https://normsaysno.wordpress.com/2014/11/19/the-trouble-with-state-by-state-analyses-of-h-1b/ [hereinafter Matloff, 'Trouble With State-By-State Analyses'].
204. Ibid.
205. 'Do Foreign STEM Workers With Advanced Degrees Create More Jobs Than They Take? (Part 1).' R. Davis. November 2014. https://econdataus.com/amjobs1.htm [hereinafter Davis, 'Foreign STEM Workers'].
206. Ibid.
207. See *supra* note 169, Part III: Thought Control, Zavodny, 'Immigration and American Jobs' at p. 9.
208. Ibid. at p. 4. (The emphasis in this quote is mine.)
209. Ibid. at p. 10. (The emphasis in this quote is mine.)

210. Ibid. at p. 13. (The emphasis in this quote is mine.)
211. Ibid. at p. 8.
212. Ibid. at p. 8. (The emphasis in this quote is mine.)
213. Ibid. at p. 13. (The emphasis in this quote is mine.)
214. See *supra* note 205, Part III: Thought Control, Davis, 'Foreign STEM Workers'.
215. 'The Paradox of Job Creation.' *Science*. Beryl Benderly. 5 February 2015. https://www.science.org/content/article/paradox-job-creation.
216. See *supra* note 203, Part III: Thought Control, Matloff, 'Trouble With State-By-State Analyses'.
217. See *supra* note 169, Part III: Thought Control, Zavodny, 'Immigration and American Jobs' at p. 16.
218. *Sold Out: How High-Tech Billionaires & Bipartisan Beltway Crapweasels Are Screwing America's Best & Brightest Workers* at Chapter 3—Marketing, Media, and Myths. John Miano and Michelle Malkin. Simon & Schuster. 2015.
219. 'Foreign STEM Workers and Native Wages and Employment in U.S. Cities.' Working Paper, the National Bureau of Economic Research. Giovanni Peri, Kevin Shih and Chad Sparber. May 2014. https://doi.org/10.3386/w20093.
220. Ibid at p. 24.
221. 'Skilled Foreign Workers a Boon to Pay, Study Finds.' *The Wall Street Journal*. Josh Zumbrun and Matt Stiles. 22 May 2014. https://www.wsj.com/articles/SB100014240527023037499045795784617272571 36/ [hereinafter *WSJ*, 'Skilled Foreign Workers'].
222. 'Analysis of "Foreign STEM Workers and Native Wages and Employment in U.S. Cities".' R. Davis. https://econdataus.com/wsjstem.htm [hereinafter Davis, 'Analysis Foreign STEM'].
223. Ibid.
224. Ibid.
225. See *supra* note 221, Part III: Thought Control, *WSJ*, 'Skilled Foreign Workers'.
226. See *supra* note 222, Part III: Thought Control, Davis, 'Analysis Foreign STEM'.
227. Ibid.
228. 'STEM Workers, H-1B Visas, and Productivity in US Cities.' *Journal of Labor Economics*, *33*(S1), S225–S255. Giovanni Peri, Kevin Shih

and Chad Sparber. July 2015. https://www.journals.uchicago.edu/doi/abs/10.1086/679061.

229. Matloff's H-1B/L-1/Offshoring E-newsletter. 1 July 2013. https://web.cs.ucdavis.edu/~matloff/Archive/KerrKerrLincoln.txt [hereinafter Matloff, 1 July 2013 E-newsletter].
230. Ibid. See also a 1973 study conducted at the University of California, Berkley that found that its graduate school was 1.8 times more likely to admit men than women. The granular rejection rates, however, told a more layered story: women applied to more competitive departments with a lower rate of admission, while men applied to less competitive ones with a higher rate of acceptance. The combined data revealed 'a small but statistically significant bias in *favor* of women'. See 'Sex Bias in Graduate Admissions: Data from Berkeley'. *Science*. Peter Bickel, Eugene Hammel and JW O'Connell. 7 February 1975. https://web.archive.org/web/20160604220121/http://homepage.stat.uiowa.edu/~mbognar/1030/Bickel-Berkeley.pdf.
231. 'Is an Economist Qualified to Solve Puzzle of Autism?' *The Wall Street Journal*. Mark Whitehouse. 27 February 2007. https://www.wsj.com/articles/SB117131554110006323/.
232. See *supra* note 229, Part III: Thought Control, Matloff, 1 July 2013 E-newsletter.
233. 'Food Industry Enlisted Academics in G.M.O. Lobbying War, Emails Show.' *The New York Times*. Eric Lipton. 5 September 2015. https://www.nytimes.com/2015/09/06/us/food-industry-enlisted-academics-in-gmo-lobbying-war-emails-show.html/.
234. 'Debunking the Myth of the Job-Stealing Immigrant.' *The New York Times*. Adam Davidson. 24 March 2015. https://www.nytimes.com/2015/03/29/magazine/debunking-the-myth-of-the-job-stealing-immigrant.html/.
235. 'How the Democrats Lost Their Way on Immigration.' *The Atlantic*. Peter Beinart. 10 July 2017. https://www.theatlantic.com/magazine/archive/2017/07/the-democrats-immigration-mistake/528678/.
236. Ibid. Peri clarified that such grants were 'neither large nor crucial' to his work, and that they did not 'determine … the direction of' his 'academic research'.

    But it wasn't just Peri or Zavodny, producing results championing the H-1B visa programme, who had received money from the industry.

Matloff wrote a fascinating piece on his blog that showed a vast network of such connections. See 'Researchers as Hired Guns.' Upon Closer Inspection. 21 March 2015. https://normsaysno.wordpress.com/2015/03/21/researchers-as-hired-guns/.

237. 'The Great Immigration Debate—Now the Great Peri-Borjas Debate.' Upon Closer Inspection. Norman Matloff. 21 January 2016. https://normsaysno.wordpress.com/2016/01/21/the-great-immigration-debate-now-the-great-peri-borjas-debate/.
238. 'The Economic Effects of Administrative Action on Immigration.' Executive Office of the President of the United States. November 2014. https://web.archive.org/web/20150225211546/https://www.whitehouse.gov/sites/default/files/docs/cea_2014_economic_effects_of_immigration_executive_action.pdf.
239. 'Egregiously One-Sided White House Report on Obama Executive Action.' Upon Closer Inspection. Norman Matloff. 24 November 2014. https://normsaysno.wordpress.com/2014/11/24/egregiously-one-sided-white-house-report-on-obama-executive-action/ [hereinafter Matloff, 'Egregiously One-Sided'].
240. 'The Economic Effects of the Obama Immigration Order.' *Financial Times.* 22 November 2014. https://www.ft.com/content/1e028cd1-a8f3-3b0f-9cdf-f5c4580b4beb/.
241. See *supra* note 239, Part III: Thought Control, Matloff, 'Egregiously One-Sided.'

PART IV: FIGHT

1. 'Confrontational Book—H-1B is Indians Immigration Boat.' Kumar Exclusive. 20 December 2014. https://www.youtube.com/watch?v=zxGmRkCQ0CQ.
2. '#Telugu Video #Donate $50 Hour Billing to Virgil 57 Badly Displaced by H1B.' Kumar Exclusive. 26 February 2015. https://www.youtube.com/watch?v=ry5966N2fgE.
3. 'Ten Thousand Dollars Worth of Software Development for $2,500.' Keep America At Work. 4 February 2015. https://web.archive.org/web/20150214024844/http://keepamericaatwork.com/ten-thousand-dollars-worth-of-software-development-for-2500-dollars/.

4. 'Southern California Edison IT Workers "Beyond Furious" Over H-1B Replacements.' *Computerworld*. Patrick Thibodeau. 4 February 2015. https://www.computerworld.com/article/2879083/southern-california-edison-it-workers-beyond-furious-over-h-1b-replacements.html.
5. 'Southern California Edison Layoffs Get U.S. Senate Attention.' *Computerworld*. Patrick Thibodeau. 7 February 2015. https://www.computerworld.com/article/2881315/southern-california-edison-layoffs-gets-us-senate-attention.html.
6. '10 U.S. Senators Seek Investigation Into H-1B-Driven Layoffs.' *Computerworld*. Patrick Thibodeau. 10 April 2015. https://www.computerworld.com/article/2908124/10-us-senators-seek-investigation-into-h-1b-driven-layoffs.html. See the letter here: https://files.epi.org/2014/h1b_letter_10_senators.pdf.
7. 'Thank You Dept of Labor and Veterans Administration for Making Me Realize You Have No Honor.' Keep America At Work. 18 February 2015. https://web.archive.org/web/20150520124637/http://keepamericaatwork.com/thank-you-dept-of-labor-and-veterans-administration-for-making-me-realize-you-have-no-honor/.
8. 'A Beautiful Day to Die.' Keep America At Work. 20 February 2015. https://web.archive.org/web/20150302101722/http://keepamericaatwork.com/a-beautiful-day-to-die/.
9. Virgil was right. In FY 2015 alone, twenty-five firms with the address '5 Independence Way' in Princeton, New Jersey, had applied for 588 LCAs. Out of the LCAs filed, fourteen companies claimed to be from the same address and even the same suite: '5 Independence Way, Suite #300'.
10. 'Two Indian-Americans Arrested for H-1B Visa Fraud in US.' *DNA*. 13 May 2015. https://www.dnaindia.com/world/report-two-indian-americans-arrested-for-h-1b-visa-fraud-in-us-2085599/.

    See also 'Human Resources Manager for Information Technology Companies Admits Obstruction of Justice'. United States Attorney's Office. 14 February 2017. https://www.justice.gov/usao-nj/pr/human-resources-manager-information-technology-companies-admits-obstruction-justice.
11. Kumar would make many videos referencing Virgil's plight, research and website in the subsequent years. See, for instance, a small sample here: 'Is H-1B Program NOT Working?' Kumar Exclusive. 25 May

2016. https://www.youtube.com/watch?v=ssEKIS_TZEk; 'Do You Know This?' Kumar Exclusive. 28 September 2016. https://www.youtube.com/watch?v=FADlf5WRTqY; 'Caste Reservations, My Questions to You & Solutions.' Kumar Exclusive. 9 September 2017. https://www.youtube.com/watch?v=nSI7V6v55XI.

12. 'Truth vs Hype—H1B Life in America.' Kumar Exclusive. 18 January 2015. https://www.youtube.com/watch?v=192fnhVsXSw.

13. By the 2010s, 'proxy calls' had become so famous that techies began advertising such services online. See, for instance, the screenshot of one such website (now defunct) whose owner used to call himself 'The One: King of Proxy' accompanied by an image from an Indian mythological film, *Baahubali* (2015). Under the section 'what I have done', it stated: '5,000 video calls. 3,000 audio calls. 1,000 coding rounds.' https://www.documentcloud.org/documents/24360256-bahubali-proxy-call-bookings.

    Another Facebook group, 'Devops Proxy Support From USA and India [phone number]', advertises similar services: https://www.facebook.com/Devopsproxycall/.

14. Kumar's initial feelings about America could be best summarised by a post he wrote on his Facebook page on 5 August 2013: 'Before I describe what is life in America, let me describe WHAT IS AMERICA first. And here is my description about AMERICA: If you miss to see America, here is my imagination of America explaining to you from poor English with rich thoughts in mind with pure heart after extensive travel here during past.

    'If you stand on the rock which is above 10,000 feet from sea level under the full moon just after the beautiful sun set and while you are looking down stairs into a ocean where 10,000 rivers are flowing and merge into the ocean. You can feel the cold breeze, sound of the roaring water falls with your ears and naked eye and by watching whole night till the full moon vanishes slowly and sun start rises and the rays are falling on the waters. America is that beautiful and the rivers are like people comes from various nations on this globe and the great ocean is America, a great melting pot where it absorbs multiple people enters here as immigrant or non immigrant with their rich thoughts and races, religions, cultures, languages and love towards the building of a great nation. It does not matter whether they carry single dollar or thousand dollars but for sure

America makes them super rich after test their patience, passion and persistence and offer them a Green Card and later a local citizenship as American i.e. America. This is one of the major reasons; people outside America thrive to come into America. America Rocks and God Bless AMERICA.'

15. 'How to Avoid Illegal Layers?' Kumar Exclusive. 5 February 2015. https://www.youtube.com/watch?v=Ih4noTS3Si8; 'Lie, Fraud, King H1B Life in America.' Kumar Exclusive. 14 February 2015. https://www.youtube.com/watch?v=jLV7g3VKu5I; 'H1B Episode 39, H1B SCAM.' Kumar Exclusive. 21 February 2015. https://www.youtube.com/watch?v=gXMDfq51WPk.
16. "EDU-Episode 53, Students FAQs—BTECH, MS In US.' Kumar Exclusive. 6 April 2015. https://www.youtube.com/watch?v= XoSiZ2C5PSc.
17. 'The Student and Exchange Visitor Program (SEVP) collects, maintains, analyzes and provides information so only legitimate foreign students or exchange visitors gain entry to the United States,' stated ICE's website. 'SEVP also ensures that the institutions accepting nonimmigrant students are certified and follow the federal rules and regulations that govern them.' See more at 'Student and Exchange Visitor Program.' U.S. Immigration and Customs Enforcement. 14 July 2025. https://www.ice.gov/sevis.
18. On 19 January 2011, the United States Attorney's Office for the Northern District of California filed a civil forfeiture complaint against the property of TVU's president and founder, Susan Xiao-Ping Su. See the complaint, which details TVU's history and modus operandi, here: *United States v. Real Property Located at 405 Boulder Court, Suite 800, Pleasanton, California*. United States District Court, Northern District of California. https://www.documentcloud.org/documents/24354908-tri-valley-court-case [hereinafter 'TVU, Civil Forfeiture Complaint'].
19. 'Immigration Officials: Tri-Valley U. and Students Involved in Visa Scam.' *ABC News*. 23 February 2011. https://abcnews.go.com/US/immigration-officials-tri-valley-university-sham-selling-student/story?id=12974636/.
20. 'Duped Indian Students Ignored Red Flags.' *The Times of India*. Chidanand Rajghatta. 31 January 2011. https://timesofindia.indiatimes.com/world/us/duped-indian-students-ignored-red-flags/articleshow/7393658.cms [hereinafter Rajghatta, 'Duped Indian Students Ignored Red Flags'].

21. 'Little-Known Colleges Exploit Visa Loopholes to Make Millions off Foreign Students.' *The Chronicle of Higher Education.* Tom Bartlett, Karin Fischer and Josh Keller. 20 March 2011. https://www.chronicle.com/article/little-known-colleges-exploit-visa-loopholes-to-make-millions-off-foreign-students/ [hereinafter Bartlett, 'Little-Known Colleges Exploit Visa Loopholes'].
22. The Department of Homeland Security's website states that an international student is eligible for CPT if she '[h]as been lawfully enrolled on a full-time basis for at least a full academic year'. It also notes, however, that '[a]n exception exists for students in graduate studies whose programs require earlier training'—which isn't typically the case for STEM students. See 'F-1 Curricular Practical Training (CPT)'. U.S. Department of Homeland Security. 28 April 2025. https://studyinthestates.dhs.gov/sevis-help-hub/student-records/fm-student-employment/f-1-curricular-practical-training-cpt.
23. See *supra* note 21, Part IV: Fight, Bartlett, 'Little-Known Colleges Exploit Visa Loopholes'.
24. See *supra* note 18, Part IV: Fight, 'TVU, Civil Forfeiture Complaint' at p. 8.
25. 'Tri-Valley Was Promoted by City "Brokers".' *Deccan Chronicle.* 4 February 2011. https://web.archive.org/web/20110206021826/www.deccanchronicle.com/hyderabad/tri-valley-was-promoted-city-'brokers'-932.
26. 'Immigration Officials: Tri-Valley U. and Students Involved in Visa Scam.' *ABC News.* 23 February 2011. https://abcnews.go.com/US/immigration-officials-tri-valley-university-sham-selling-student/story?id=12974636.
27. Ibid. https://www.immigration.com/sites/default/files/tri-valley_ABCNews.pdf.
28. 'Indian Students of "Sham" US Varsity Launch Petition Campaign.' *Hindustan Times.* 28 January 2011. https://www.hindustantimes.com/india/indian-students-of-sham-us-varsity-launch-petition-campaign/story-MNNcIUUVbMu7WFFJETjtZL.html.
29. 'Petition Filed by the Victims of Tri-Valley University.' NDTV. 29 January 2011. https://www.ndtv.com/india-news/petition-filed-by-the-victims-of-tri-valley-university-446308/.

The petition stated that the students believed they had enrolled in a 'bona fide and legitimate University' registered in the SEVIS database. If it took ICE 'several months or longer to unearth' the TVU fraud, then it was 'patently unfair and unrealistic to expect foreign students' unfamiliar with the 'American way of life' and its 'system and culture' to find out TVU's 'potential irregularities'. Many students had 'invested a substantial portion' of their 'parents' lifetime savings and taken a huge leap of faith' to travel to the US to study in a SEVP-approved college. 'Honestly, it is a dream come true for most of us to be able to study in the U.S.,' it added. 'For many people all over the world, the U.S. is still viewed as the land of milk and honey, the land of opportunity where one's dreams can come true!'

The students 'relied on the government to do its job'. They just wanted to 'live in the U.S. for a few years or return' to their 'home countries with a good education and then obtain good jobs' there. They requested DHS and ICE to help them pursue their 'lifelong dream to study in the U.S.' by allowing them to transfer to another university or file a change of status, such as an H-1B or an F-2 visa. 'We respectfully plead with you not to penalize us or our families and bring shame to our entire family and the village/towns we come from, by deporting (removing) us from the U.S.,' stated the petition. This would also cause them 'loss of name, reputation, money, resulting in devastation to us and our families and crashing all of our dreams'.

See the full petition here: https://www.documentcloud.org/documents/24538576-petition-by-tvu-students-1 and https://www.documentcloud.org/documents/24538577-petition-by-tvu-students-2.

30. 'Frustration Over Pleasanton University's Closure Spreads to India.' *The Mercury News*. Robert Jordan. 28 January 2011. https://www.mercurynews.com/2011/01/28/frustration-over-pleasanton-universitys-closure-spreads-to-india.
31. The ATA Community Services Chair, Bangar Reddy, said, 'The students are from the respectable families in India; never committed any crime and they have high respect and dream to study in USA.' A.V.N. Reddy from the North American Telugu Association (NATA) also organised a conference call for affected students to address their legal troubles.

See more at 'Update on Assistance to Tri-Valley Students'. American Telugu Association. 27 January 2011. https://americanteluguassociation.org/news/update-on-assistance-to-tri-valley-students.php.

32. 'Tags Unwarranted, Should be Removed: MEA.' *The Hindu*. Sandeep Dikshit. 13 October 2016. https://www.thehindu.com/news/national/Tags-unwarranted-should-be-removed-MEA/article15538398.ece/.

33. 'Justice Will be Done to Tri-Valley Students, Says Hillary.' *The Hindu.* 17 November 2021. https://www.thehindu.com/news/national/Justice-will-be-done-to-Tri-Valley-students-says-Hillary/article15443185.ece.

34. 'TVU President Indicted on Visa Fraud Allegations.' *The Economic Times.* 5 May 2011. https://economictimes.indiatimes.com/nri/visa-and-immigration/tvu-president-indicted-on-visa-fraud-allegations/articleshow/8160762.cms?from=mdr.

See also 'President of Bay Area University Convicted in Student Visa Fraud Scheme'. U.S. Immigration and Customs Enforcement. 24 March 2014. https://www.ice.gov/news/releases/president-bay-area-university-convicted-student-visa-fraud-scheme; 'CEO and President of East Bay University Sentenced to 198 Months for Fraud Scheme.' United States Attorney's Office. 3 November 2014. https://www.justice.gov/usao-ndca/pr/ceo-and-president-east-bay-university-sentenced-198-months-fraud-scheme.

35. *United States v. Dasa.* United States District Court, Northern District of California. 27 November 2012. https://www.casemine.com/judgement/us/5914d73aadd7b0493486cf8b.

36. A *Rediff* article noted impressions from attorneys and affected students. 'This is a significant development,' said attorney Kalpana V. Peddibhotla, 'as prior to this new indictment, the Department of Justice had not officially recognised the fraud by Susan Su against the students.' A former TVU student, Raj Kumar, said, 'This is a ray of light in the darkness. If TVU students are considered to have been cheated, [then] they should re-instate us back to F1 status without delay. Every passing day is important to us. I hope the United States Citizenship and Immigration Services considers this development.'

See 'Tri-Valley Students Victims of Fraud: US Court'. *Rediff*. Ritu Jha. 22 November 2011. https://m.rediff.com/news/report/tri-valley-students-victims-of-fraud-us-court/20111122.htm/.

37. See *supra* note 20, Part IV: Fight, Rajghatta, 'Duped Indian Students Ignored Red Flags'.

38. Ibid.
39. See *supra* note 18, Part IV: Fight, 'TVU, Civil Forfeiture Complaint' at p. 14.
40. 'Tri-Valley University—CPT, OPT.' Trackitt. 5 April 2010. https://www.trackitt.com/usa-discussion-forums/h1b/512950847/tri-valley-university-cpt-opt/ [hereinafter Trackitt, 'TVU CPT']. Last accessed 5 September 2025.
41. Ibid. at comment #72. Anngan. 16 May 2010.
42. 'Student and Exchange Visitor Program—DHS Needs to Assess Risks and Strengthen Oversight Functions.' United States Government Accountability Office. June 2012. https://www.gao.gov/assets/gao-12-572.pdf [hereinafter 2012 GAO Report, 'DHS Needs to Assess Risks'] at p. 9.
43. See *supra* note 40, Part IV: Fight, Trackitt, 'TVU CPT'. Guggi (comment #412). 12 January 2011.
44. Ibid. at comment #6. Sathishkvvsm. 7 April 2010.
45. Ibid. at comment #400. Life2010. 7 January 2011.
46. 'Was Tri-Valley Used to Run an Immigration Racket?' *The Times of India*. Nikhila Henry. 4 February 2011. https://timesofindia.indiatimes.com/city/hyderabad/was-tri-valley-used-to-run-an-immigration-racket/articleshow/7422555.cms.
47. See *supra* note 40, Part IV: Fight, Trackitt, 'TVU CPT'. Khushboo143 (comment #19). 13 April 2010.
48. Ibid. at comment #90. Saimallipeddi. 18 May 2010.
49. Ibid. at comment #172. Priyakg. 26 July 2010.
50. Ibid. at comment #411. Cscms. 12 January 2011.
51. Ibid. at comment #399. Vinibisht. 6 January 2011.
52. Ibid. at comment #98. RisingSun. 21 May 2010.
53. Ibid. at comment #194. RisingSun. 27 July 2010.
54. Ibid. at comment #32. RisingSun. 4 May 2010.
55. Ibid. at comment #174. RisingSun. 27 July 2010.
56. Ibid.
57. 'Tri-Valley Gave its Students a 20% Cut to Lure Buddies: Report.' *The Economic Times*. 3 February 2011. https://economictimes.indiatimes.com/tri-valley-gave-its-students-a-20-cut-to-lure-buddies-report/articleshow/7415809.cms.

58. See *supra* note 40, Part IV: Fight, Trackitt, 'TVU CPT'. Member2010 (comment #119). 11 June 2010.
59. Ibid. at comment #269. Pannochka. 19 August 2010.
60. 'Varsity Blues | Did They Make an Educated Choice?' *Livemint*. Yogendra Kalavalapalli and Malia Politzer. 15 September 2011. https://web.archive.org/web/20140803044316/https://www.livemint.com/Politics/jUiOQwKT1alKEl4ABGQOSM/Varsity-Blues--Did-they-make-an-educated-choice.html/.
61. See *supra* note 40, Part IV: Fight, Trackitt, 'TVU CPT'. Priyakg (comment #173). 27 July 2010.
62. Ibid. at comment #437. Peterp88. 20 January 2011.
63. '[UNVA's] chancellor, David V. Lee … concedes that there had been trouble in the past,' noted a *Chronicle of Higher Education* piece in March 2011, four months before the ICE raid. 'A recruiter working for the college in India was "throwing I-20's up into the air and letting the wind blow them around," Mr. Lee tells the students. He clarifies later that the recruiter was encouraging applicants to falsify the I-20 immigration documents so they could come to the United States. That recruiter, he says, was let go.' See more at *supra* note 21, Part IV: Fight, Bartlett, 'Little-Known Colleges Exploit Visa Loopholes'.
64. 'Another Varsity Being Probed for Fraud.' *Hindustan Times.* 29 July 2011. https://web.archive.org/web/20110927185110/http://www.hindustantimes.com/Another-varsity-being-probed-for-fraud/H1-Article1-726881.aspx.
65. 'ICE Raid Targets University of Northern Virginia.' *The Washington Post*. Justin Jouvenal. 29 July 2011. https://www.washingtonpost.com/blogs/post_now/post/ice-raid-targets-university-of-northern-virginia/2011/07/29/gIQAblKzgI_blog.html.
66. See *supra* note 40, Part IV: Fight, Trackitt, 'TVU CPT'. Watchdogg (comment #202). 28 July 2010.
67. Ibid. at comment #342. 4Indians. 9 October 2010.
68. Ibid. at comment #572. Usher. 1 February 2011.
69. Ibid. at comment #590. Nishant1981. 1 February 2011.
70. Ibid. at comment #594. Nishant1981. 1 February 2011.

71. Besides Herguan, two more colleges raided by ICE—TVU and UNVA—and three under suspicion (SVU, NPU and ITU) were SEVP-approved as well. But … *how*?

The answer to that was closely related to how SEVIS was conceived. At the heart of the SEVIS programme lay not institutions or students, but terrorists. It had happened twice before: terrorists had entered the country on F-1 visas and, in the absence of an electronic system that monitored international students and visitors, slipped in and out of the schools undetected. Eyad Ismoil, a convict in the 1993 World Trade Center bombing, entered the US in 1989 on a student visa to study engineering at Wichita State University. He overstayed his visa, moved to New York City and began preparing for the attack. 'Falsifying documents to get student visas was simple, and INS [Immigration and Naturalization Service] processing used an antiquated paper system and hand entry of data. It could take two years to detect fraud, plenty of time for a new entrant to disappear into the population and cause mayhem,' wrote Daniel Benjamin and Steve Simon, former staff members of the counter terrorism office of the National Security Council, in their book *The Age of Sacred Terror* (2002). Similarly, after the 9/11 attacks, it was found that one of the terrorists, Hani Hanjour, entered the country on a student visa but never showed up on campus.

In response to the terror attacks, the Congress passed the USA Patriot Act, and SEVIS was implemented to monitor international students. In creating SEVIS though (see *supra* note 21, Part IV: Fight, Bartlett, 'Little-Known Colleges Exploit Visa Loopholes'), 'lawmakers adopted existing language in which accreditation had never been required for a school or college to admit foreign students, even though it is necessary to participate in other programs, like federal financial aid. The focus was—and still is—on keeping terrorists, not questionable colleges, out of the higher-education system.' See more at *The Age of Sacred Terror*. Daniel Benjamin and Steven Simon. Random House. 2002.

See also *supra* note 42, Part IV: Fight, 2012 GAO Report, 'DHS Needs to Assess Risks' at p. 13, pp. 15–16 and 22–24. The GAO report found many faults and oversights by SEVP and ICE's officials, who failed to discharge their basic duties, creating an environment where visa mills not just existed but also thrived. Some of these findings read:

- 'SEVP adjudicators have not consistently verified all evidence submitted in lieu of accreditation, specifically "in lieu of" letters that support non-accredited schools' petitions for SEVP certification because, according to SEVP officials, the program has not historically focused enough attention on fraud prevention until the Tri-Valley University case demonstrated the program's vulnerabilities.
- '[A]ccording to SEVP officials, SEVP has not looked across previous cases of school fraud and school withdrawals to identify lessons learned on program vulnerabilities and opportunities to strengthen internal controls.
- 'SEVP has maintained a compliance case log since 2005—a list of approximately 172 schools as of December 2011—that officials have determined to be potentially noncompliant with program requirements. The compliance case log represents those schools that SEVP, based on tips and leads and out-of-cycle reviews, is monitoring for potential noncompliance ... [B]ut, according to SEVP officials, it has not looked across schools on this list to identify and evaluate possible trends in schools' noncompliance, which could provide useful insights to SEVP to assess programwide risks.
- 'ICE has not consistently maintained certain evidence of selected schools' eligibility for the program. Based on our review of a stratified random sample of 50 SEVP-certified school case files, 30 files lacked at least one piece of evidence required by the program's policies and procedures. In addition, ICE was unable to produce two schools' case files that we requested as part of our randomly selected sample. The results of our analysis of the 48 remaining case files are not generalisable, but the following summarises these results.

'*7 of the 48 school case files did not include reports of the required initial site visit;

'*22 of the 48 school case files did not include proof of the designated school officials' U.S. citizenship or lawful permanent residency;

'*7 of the 34 case files for non-flight schools and non-accredited schools lacked adequate evidence in lieu of accreditation (e.g. "in lieu of" letters).' (Internal citations omitted.)

- 'Further, according to investigators at three of the eight field offices we interviewed, SEVP allowed designated school officials to maintain SEVIS access and the ability to modify records in the system while being the subject of an ongoing criminal investigation, despite requests from CTCEU [Counterterrorism and Criminal Exploitation Unit] to terminate SEVIS access for these officials.
- 'Without verification of evidence and complete case files, ICE cannot provide reasonable assurance that schools were initially and continue to be eligible for certification.'

A 2014 GAO report—titled 'DHS Needs to Assess Risks and Strengthen Oversight of Foreign Students with Employment Authorization'—found that a) ICE did not adequately identify or assess risks relating to students' OPT; b) ICE was unable to completely ensure that students working on OPT were maintaining legal status in the United States; c) ICE did not have consistent procedures to collect information relating to OPT requirements and d) ICE did not monitor whether student employment complied with ICE regulations.

Read the full report here: https://www.gao.gov/assets/gao-14-356.pdf.

72. 'Another US University in Visa Fraud Row; Fate of 450 Students, Mostly Indians, Uncertain.' *The Times of India*. 4 August 2012. https://timesofindia.indiatimes.com/nri/us-canada-news/another-us-university-in-visa-fraud-row-fate-of-450-students-mostly-indians-uncertain/articleshow/15350846.cms.
73. 'Indians Again Enmeshed in U.S. University Visa Scam.' *The Hindu*. Narayan Lakshman. 17 November 2021. https://www.thehindu.com/news/international/Indians-again-enmeshed-in-U.S.-university-visa-scam/article12680736.ece.
74. See *supra* note 21, Part IV: Fight, Bartlett, 'Little-Known Colleges Exploit Visa Loopholes'.
75. 'Visa Scam: Telugu Students May Lose an Academic Year.' *The Hindu*. 5 August 2012. https://www.thehindu.com/news/cities/Hyderabad/visa-scam-telugu-students-may-lose-an-academic-year/article3730597.ece.

76. See *supra* note 21, Part IV: Fight, Bartlett, 'Little-Known Colleges Exploit Visa Loopholes'.
77. Ibid.
78. Ibid.
79. Ibid.
80. You can read Concepcion Saenz-Cambra's amended complaint under case information here: 'International Technological University Will Pay $1.17 Million to Settle Whistleblower's Allegations of Visa Fraud'. The Employment Law Group. 15 August 2016. https://www.employmentlawgroup.com/wp-content/uploads/2016-08-15-us-ex-rel-saenz-cambra-v-itu-amended-complaint.pdf.
81. Ibid.
82. 'International Technological University Pay $1.17 Million to Settle False Claims Act Allegations Related to Student Visa Fraud.' Office of Inspector General. 27 January 2021. https://www.oig.dhs.gov/news/press-releases/2021/01272021/international-technological-university-pay-117-million-settle-false-claims-act-allegations-related-student-visa.
83. 'List of CPT Giving Universities Pros/Cons.' AndhraFriends. Heartlavender. 24 April 2015. https://www.andhrafriends.com/topic/601117-list-of-cpt-giving-universities-proscons/.
84. Indian students discussed 'Day-1 CPT' colleges on not just AndhraFriends but also several other forums, such as the appropriately named DesiOpt.com. See the following examples: 'Colleges That Don't Require GRE and Offer CPT from Day 1'. 21 December 2014. https://forum.desiopt.com/forum/desiopt/cpt-topics/3283-; 'Harrisburg University—Day1 CPT?' 3 August 2017. https://forum.desiopt.com/forum/desiopt/cpt-topics/9282-; 'Day 1 CPT—How Does it Work?' 10 November 2015. https://forum.desiopt.com/forum/desiopt/cpt-topics/4854-; 'Inquiry About Day 1 CPT Universities.' 3 October 2017. https://forum.desiopt.com/forum/desiopt/f1-visa-topics/9467-.

    Some inquires hinged on Day-1 CPT colleges in specific states, such as in the following links: 'Universities Offering CPT from Day 1 in Los Angeles Area'. 16 May 2015. https://forum.desiopt.com/forum/desiopt/cpt-topics/4069-; 'Day 1 CPT Colleges in Michigan.' 25 August 2016. https://forum.desiopt.com/forum/desiopt/cpt-topics/5873-/page2; 'University in Florida for Day 1 CPT?' 10 July 2014. https://forum.desiopt.com/forum/desiopt/cpt-topics/2451-.

85. 'List of CPT Giving Universities Pros/Cons.' AndhraFriends. Heartlavender. 24 April 2015. https://www.andhrafriends.com/topic/601117-list-of-cpt-giving-universities-proscons/#findComment-1306840776.
86. Ibid. at Srin. 24 April 2015. https://www.andhrafriends.com/topic/601117-list-of-cpt-giving-universities-proscons/#findComment-1306838183.
87. Ibid. at Srin. 24 April 2015. https://www.andhrafriends.com/topic/601117-list-of-cpt-giving-universities-proscons/#findComment-1306838178.
88. Ibid. at Heartlavender. 24 April 2015. https://www.andhrafriends.com/topic/601117-list-of-cpt-giving-universities-proscons/#findComment-1306838220.
89. Ibid. at Kal. 26 April 2015. https://www.andhrafriends.com/topic/601117-list-of-cpt-giving-universities-proscons/page/2/#findComment-1306849530.
90. Ibid. at Heartlavender. 28 April 2015. https://www.andhrafriends.com/topic/601117-list-of-cpt-giving-universities-proscons/page/3/#findComment-1306859744.
91. Ibid. at Bobby12345. 24 April 2015. https://www.andhrafriends.com/topic/601117-list-of-cpt-giving-universities-proscons/#findComment-1306838172.
92. Ibid. at Dr_sheldoncooper2. 29 April 2015. https://www.andhrafriends.com/topic/601117-list-of-cpt-giving-universities-proscons/page/4/#find Comment-1306862117.
93. 'Indian Incs & Fake Resumes, Americans Must Watch.' Kumar Exclusive. 28 July 2015. https://www.youtube.com/watch?v=U8Um5tYHMZQ.
94. 'Kumar Srinivas Pandruvada About MS and Life in USA.' Andhra Friends. Fake_Bezawada. 15 September 2015. https://www.andhrafriends.com/topic/631475-kumar-srinivas-pandruvada-about-ms-and-life-in-usa/.
95. Ibid. at Fake_Bewazada. 15 September 2015. https://www.andhrafriends.com/topic/631475-kumar-srinivas-pandruvada-about-ms-and-life-in-usa/#findComment-1307444699.
96. Ibid. at JammichettuPandu. 16 September 2015. https://www.andhrafriends.com/topic/631475-kumar-srinivas-pandruvada-about-ms-and-life-in-usa/page/2/#findComment-1307449928.

97. Ibid. at Dotnetrockz. 17 September 2015. https://www.andhrafriends.com/topic/631475-kumar-srinivas-pandruvada-about-ms-and-life-in-usa/page/2/#findComment-1307450608.
98. Ibid. at Vasu123. 17 September 2015. https://www.andhrafriends.com/topic/631475-kumar-srinivas-pandruvada-about-ms-and-life-in-usa/page/5/#findComment-1307451347.
99. Ibid. at DaleSteyn1. 17 September 2015. https://www.andhrafriends.com/topic/631475-kumar-srinivas-pandruvada-about-ms-and-life-in-usa/page/4/#findComment-1307451126.

    In the subsequent years, Kumar made a few videos confronting his 'haters'. See, for instance, 'Kevin Sama'. Kumar Exclusive. 7 February 2019. https://www.youtube.com/watch?v=nJ6Bd1YHbM0; 'Andhra Friends NOT Secure Website, an Asylum Center for Criminals.' Kumar Exclusive. 23 February 2021. https://www.youtube.com/watch?v=FTtABxQB4bM; AndhraFriends and Chalanachithram Websites Trolling Kumar Exclusive.' Kumar Exclusive. 9 September 2022. https://www.youtube.com/watch?v=syXDXKb1Lhk.
100. '19 US-Bound Students Stopped From Boarding Air India Flight in Hyderabad.' *The Times of India.* 21 December 2015. https://timesofindia.indiatimes.com/india/19-us-bound-students-stopped-from-boarding-air-india-flight-in-hyderabad/articleshow/50273784.cms.

    One of the detained students, Deepak, asked, 'If the universities were blacklisted, why did they issue us the visa?' Another said, 'We were treated like criminals and sent back.'
101. 'We Are Not Blacklisted, Says US University After Indian Students' Deportation Issue.' India.Com. Abhijeet Kar. 23 December 2015. https://www.india.com/news/india/we-are-not-blacklisted-says-us-university-after-indian-students-deportation-issue-807459/.
102. 'US Varsity Slams [Air India's] "Tortious" Conduct.' *The Times of India.* Sudipta Sengupta. 31 December 2015. https://timesofindia.indiatimes.com/city/hyderabad/us-varsity-slams-ais-tortious-conduct/articleshow/50388528.cms.
103. '20 More Students Stopped From Going to US.' *The Times of India.* Preeti Biswas and Sudipta Sengupta. 24 December 2015. https://timesofindia.indiatimes.com/india/20-more-students-stopped-from-going-to-us/articleshow/50305154.cms.

104. 'MEA Advises Students to Defer Travel to US for Admission to 2 Varsities Under "Scrutiny"'. *International Business Times*. 23 December 2015. https://www.ibtimes.co.in/mha-advises-students-defer-travel-us-admission-2-varsities-under-scrutiny-660656.
105. Sushma Swaraj [@SushmaSwaraj]. 23 December 2015. https://twitter.com/SushmaSwaraj/status/679511495005212672.
106. '18 More Andhra Students Sent Back to Hyderabad From New York Airport.' *Firstpost*. 3 January 2016. https://www.firstpost.com/world/18-more-andhra-students-sent-back-to-hyderabad-from-new-york-airport-2568678.html/.
107. 'Now, 20 Indian Students Deported From Chicago Airport.' *Deccan Herald*. 29 December 2015. https://www.deccanherald.com/india/now-20-indian-students-deported-2168283.
108. An SVU-bound student said, 'Apart from saying that they are looking into the matter, the external affairs ministry has done nothing else … [T]hey have jeopardized the careers of hundreds of students like me.' See '30 Students Sent Back From US'. *The Times of India*. 3 January 2016. https://timesofindia.indiatimes.com/india/30-students-sent-back-from-us/articleshow/50422515.cms.

    An AndhraFriends user pinned the blame on something else. 'The Indian electronic media spread bull s h i t news about these two Universities … They doesn't telicast actual matter … So frds we have to fight against the Indian government and US government … Y because the US government cheated to us … Please frds we have valid visa also don't get Fear we have to inform modi sir.' See 'Regarding SVU and NPU'. AndhraFriends. Ronitreddy. 24 December 2015. https://www.andhrafriends.com/topic/651223-regarding-npu-and-svu/page/4/#comment-1307777134.
109. 'Chinese-Run U.S. School for Indian Foreign Students Reaps Profits of $30 Million a Year.' Center for Immigration Studies. David North. 28 December 2015. https://cis.org/North/ChineseRun-US-School-Indian-Foreign-Students-Reaps-Profits-30-Million-Year/.
110. Ibid.
111. Northwestern Polytechnic University changed its name to San Francisco Bay University in 2021. See 'San Francisco Bay University's Tax Filings Summary'. *ProPublica*. https://projects.propublica.org/nonprofits/organizations/942933165/.

For FY 2014, the figures on the *ProPublica* page didn't match the original tax filings. In such cases, the analysis recorded the numbers from the original tax filings. In FY 2014, for instance, the *ProPublica* page stated NPU's revenue as $40,109,184, while the college's tax filing stated $38,776,089. See NPU's original tax filing for FY 2014 (from the *ProPublica* page) here: https://projects.propublica.org/nonprofits/display_990/942933165/2016_10_EO%2F94-2933165_990_201412 (p. 1 and p. 9).

112. Silicon Valley University changed its name to American Innovation University in 2024. See 'American Innovation University's Tax Filings Summary'. *ProPublica*. https://projects.propublica.org/nonprofits/organizations/770495439/.

For FY 2011, the figures on the *ProPublica* page didn't match the original tax filings. In such cases, the analysis recorded the numbers from the original tax filings. In FY 2011, for instance, the *ProPublica* page stated SVU's revenue as $3,735,361, while the college's tax filing stated $1,843,371. See SVU's original tax filing for FY 2011 (from the *ProPublica* page) here: https://projects.propublica.org/nonprofits/display_990/770495439/2013_09_EO%2F77-0495439_990_201209 (p. 1 and p. 9).

113. The entire portion on NPU in the rest of this chapter owes a huge debt to the incredible reporting by journalists Molly Hensley-Clancy and Brendan Klinkenberg in the following two pieces:
    - 'These Obscure Colleges Sign up Thousands of Foreign Students With Little Oversight'. *BuzzFeed News*. Molly Hensley-Clancy and Brendan Klinkenberg. 22 January 2016. https://www.buzzfeednews.com/article/mollyhensleyclancy/these-obscure-colleges-sign-up-thousands-of-foreign-students/ [hereinafter Hensley-Clancy, 'These Obscure Colleges'].
    - 'Inside the College That Abolished the F and Raked in the Cash.' *BuzzFeed News*. Molly Hensley-Clancy. 26 May 2016. https://www.buzzfeednews.com/article/mollyhensleyclancy/inside-the-school-that-abolished-the-f-and-raked-in-the-cash [hereinafter Hensley-Clancy, 'Inside the College That Abolished the F'].

114. Ibid at Hensley-Clancy, 'Inside the College That Abolished the F'. In December 2013, NPU bought a $2.2 million six-bedroom, five-

and-a-half-bathroom home—all paid in cash—in a suburban street, Harvard Common: the new home of Peter Hsieh's family.

115. Ibid.
116. See *supra* note 113, Part IV: Fight, Hensley-Clancy, 'These Obscure Colleges'.
117. Ibid.
118. See *supra* note 113, Part IV: Fight, Hensley-Clancy, 'Inside the College That Abolished the F'.
119. Ibid. NPU had stated, in its online catalogues, that it'd terminate the visas of those students who had scored GPAs of less than 3.0 for three semesters.
120. Ibid.
121. Ibid.
122. Ibid.
123. Ibid.
124. See the following memorandum of understanding between NPU and Indian educational consultancies that lists a 15 per cent cut to them and the college talking about its ACICS accreditation: 'Guide to Prospective PRSP's'—Northwestern Polytechnic University. Molly Hensley-Clancy. https://www.documentcloud.org/documents/2842816-MOU-PRSP-2.html; 'MOU Between NPU and PRSP'. Molly Hensley-Clancy. https://www.documentcloud.org/documents/2842815-MOU-PRSP-1.html#document/p1/a297815.
125. See *supra* note 113, Part IV: Fight, Hensley-Clancy, 'These Obscure Colleges'.
126. See 'NPU Whistleblower Letter'. https://www.documentcloud.org/documents/2842811-ACICS-Letter-1.html.
127. See *supra* note 113, Part IV: Fight, Hensley-Clancy, 'Inside the College That Abolished the F.'
128. Ibid.
129. Ibid.
130. 'Rubber Stamps: ACICS and the Troubled Oversight of College Accreditors.' The Office of Senator Elizabeth Warren. 10 June 2016. https://www.warren.senate.gov/files/documents/2016-6-10_ACICS_Report.pdf [hereinafter Warren, 'Rubber Stamps: ACICS'].

    See also 'Getting Tough With a Gatekeeper'. *Inside Higher Ed.* Paul Fain. 15 June 2016. https://www.insidehighered.com/news/2016/06/16/education-department-recommends-eliminating-national-accreditor-many-profit-colleges (finding that the Department of Education had been suspicious about the ACICS's laxity for long. In July 2015, the Secretary of Education Arne Duncan compared them to 'watchdogs that don't bark').

131. Ibid. at Warren, 'Rubber Stamps: ACICS'. The session on how to evade attorney general lawsuits 'was led by two lawyers for Daymar College, an ACICS-accredited for-profit school that recently reached a $12 million settlement with the Kentucky attorney general over alleged violations of the state's consumer protection laws, including lying to students about the transferability of credits, improperly denying students access to financial aid … and hiring unqualified faculty'.

132. Ibid.

133. Ibid.

134. Ibid. '73% of undergraduates at ACICS institutions borrow using federal student loans … This figure is … significantly higher than the national average of 47% for all colleges [table reference omitted]. Students at ACICS-accredited schools also borrow more to attend these schools than their peers at institutions accredited by other agencies, leaving students to grapple with higher debt loads.' Warren's report continued to cite the *ProPublica* findings that '22% of students at ACICS-accredited schools defaulted on their loans within three years … higher than the national average of 14% for all colleges'. And '[a] staggering 60% of students at ACICS-accredited schools had not paid back a single dollar of their loan principal within three years of leaving'. This wasn't necessarily surprising as students from ACICS-accredited schools earned significantly less than peers with '62% of ACICS-approved schools rank[ing] in the bottom third nationally for student earnings post-graduation'.

    On 19 August 2022, the Department of Education terminated ACICS's status as a recognised accrediting agency. See 'Termination of the Accrediting Council for Independent Colleges and Schools as an ED Recognized Accrediting Agency'. U.S. Department of Education. https://www.ed.gov/laws-and-policy/higher-education-laws-and-policy/college-accreditation/termination.

135. Ibid. In December 2017, the U.S. Government Accountability Office (GAO) released an eighty-two-page report highlighting the challenges with the accreditation system's oversight of academic quality. See the

whole report (which also includes insightful pointers on the accreditation process) at 'Higher Education—Expert Views of U.S. Accreditation'. United States Government Accountability Office. December 2017. https://www.gao.gov/assets/gao-18-5.pdf (pp. 9–10).

136. See *supra* note 130, Part IV: Fight, Warren, 'Rubber Stamps: ACICS'.
137. Besides Appi Reddy, NPU maintained close contacts with other 'Telugu community leaders' as well. On 24 March 2016, the college invited Jayaram Komati, the erstwhile president of TANA who had defended Tri-Valley students in 2011 (p. 159), to its campus. See its announcement (from NPU's website) here: https://www.documentcloud.org/documents/24356416-jayaram-komati.

    On 12 April 2016, NPU co-sponsored an event of the Bay Area Telugu Association (BATA). Among the dozen other sponsors was Swagat Restaurants, owned by Komati who also sat on the BATA Advisory Board. 'More than 40+ student volunteers from NPU,' noted the piece below, 'helped throughout the day.' See 'BATA Ugadi Celebrations 2016'. IdleBrain. 12 April 2016. https://www.idlebrain.com/nricommunity/bata-ugadi2016.html.
138. 'Round Table Conference in Northwestern Polytechnic University in California Bay Area.' NTV Telugu. 4 March 2016. https://www.youtube.com/watch?v=q8sSfmVt08U (Appi Reddy's portion appears from 5:40 to 6:30.) Last accessed 29 April 2024.
139. 'Who the Hell is Appi Reddy?' AndhraFriends. Pinnigaaru. 29 August 2016. https://www.andhrafriends.com/topic/689053-who-the-hell-is-appi-reddy/.
140. Ibid. at Nurse. 29 August 2016. https://www.andhrafriends.com/topic/689053-who-the-hell-is-appi-reddy/#findComment- 1308369579.
141. '******* Bay Area Chillar Naa Kodukulu/ Beggers.' AndhraFriends. Rrc_2015. 14 May 2016. https://www.andhrafriends.com/topic/672485-bay-area-chillar-naa-kodukulu-beggers/#comment-1308161363.
142. 'Who is Appi Reddy?' AndhraFriends. Tennisluvr. 21 December 2017. https://www.andhrafriends.com/topic/743087-who-is-appi-reddy/#comment-1309248728.
143. 'Wow ee Appi Reddy Keka Kada.' AndhraFriends. Nissan. 15 August 2016. https://www.andhrafriends.com/topic/687003-wow-ee-appi-reddy-keka-kada/page/2/#comment-1308344233.

144. 'Appi Reddy is Balayya of California?' AndhraFriends. Kalajamoon. 9 August 2017. https://www.andhrafriends.com/topic/672594-appi-reddy-is-balayya-of-california/#comment-1309016908.
145. 'Appi Reddy India Trip.' AndhraFriends. 1500. 30 December 2017. https://www.andhrafriends.com/topic/743618-appi-reddy-india-trip/page/2/#comment-1309259249.
146. 'Most Rich Consultancy Owners in US.' AndhraFriends. CH_Desi. 2 November 2019. https://www.andhrafriends.com/topic/834628-most-rich-consultancy-owners-in-us/.
147. See 'APPI Birthday 2014__Created by Well Wishers'. Appi Reddy. 3 August 2014. https://www.youtube.com/watch?v=aFyrcHkrYcE; 'Microinfo Appi B'day.' Gorrala Sandeep. 13 August 2014. https://www.youtube.com/watch?v=FyvjtNjV9ws.
148. See 'MicroInfo 5th Anniversary Celebrations'. Appi Reddy. 10 June 2014. https://www.youtube.com/watch?v=aGrcnH2uCFU; 'MicroInfo, Inc 6th Anniversary Highlights.' MicroInfo, Inc. 3 July 2015. https://www.youtube.com/watch?v=oN0H6qOQTxg.
149. 'Microinfo Company Inc. Sixth Anniversary Celebrations—USA.' V6 News Telugu. 13 May 2015. https://www.youtube.com/watch?v=v_HGJljXcjY.
150. 'Life Journey Memories of Appi Reddy.' Appi Reddy. 3 December 2014. https://www.youtube.com/watch?v=bQequzHRxVI.
151. 'Appi Reddy India Trip.' AndhraFriends. Ranku_mogudu. 30 December 2017. https://www.andhrafriends.com/topic/743618-appi-reddy-india-trip/page/4/#comment-1309259414.
152. 'Sanders and Trump on Immigration.' Upon Closer Inspection. Norman Matloff. 16 August 2015. https://normsaysno.wordpress.com/2015/08/16/sanders-and-trump-on-immigration/.
153. '¡Ay, Caramba! It Took Only a Few Days for Trump to Reverse His Stance.' Upon Closer Inspection. Norman Matloff. 18 August 2015. https://normsaysno.wordpress.com/2015/08/18/ay-caramba-it-took-only-a-few-days-for-trump-to-reverse-his-stance/.
154. Kumar also made several videos pondering the DOL's laxity and negligence, asking why there wasn't more communication between USCIS, the IRS and the DOL. See, for instance, 'Biscuits'. Kumar Exclusive. 26 November 2015. https://www.youtube.com/watch?v=p_1kF5zu1h4 ('I really don't know what USCIS or Department of Labor is doing');

'Do You Know This?' Kumar Exclusive. 28 September 2016. https://www.youtube.com/watch?v=FADlf5WRTqY ('Department of Labor also not questioning why hours not mentioned on Indian employers' paychecks?'); 'IRS Tax Fraud Indian Incs.' Kumar Exclusive. 12 February 2016. https://www.youtube.com/watch?v=qs4o-hauK6s&t=1s ('I don't understand why there is a communication gap between USCIS, IRS and Department of Labor?').

The last question didn't just bother Kumar. In June 2006, GAO released a report, where it stated (p. 4): 'Labor, Homeland Security, and Justice all have responsibilities under the H-1B program, but Labor and Homeland Security could better address the challenges they face in sharing information. Homeland Security reviews Labor's certified application but cannot easily verify whether employers submitted petitions for more workers than originally requested on the application because USCIS's database cannot match each petition to Labor's application case number. Also, during the process of reviewing petitions, staff may find evidence that employers are not meeting their H-1B obligations. For example, Homeland Security may find that a worker's income on the W-2 is less than the wage quoted on the original application. Homeland Security may deny the petition if an employer is unable to explain the discrepancy, but it does not have a formal process for reporting the discrepancy to Labor. Additionally, current law precludes the Wage and Hour Division from using this information to initiate an investigation of the employer.'

See the full report at *supra* note 7, Part I: Dream, 2006 GAO Report, 'Labor Could Improve Its Oversight'.

155. Ibid. at p. 3.
156. See *supra* note 95, Part III: Thought Control, 2000 GAO Report, 'Better Controls Needed'.
157. Ibid. at p. 5.
158. Ibid. at p. 19.
159. Ibid. at p. 21.
160. Ibid. '[A]ccording to a Labor official, H-1B workers may be vulnerable to abuse,' it stated, 'since their dependency upon their employers may lead to reluctance to complain.'

To read more about the 'four exceptional conditions' under which the DOL can initiate H-1B-related investigations, see *supra* note 29, Part II: Deception, DOL, 'Enforcement Authority'.

161. 'Understanding Requests for Evidence (RFEs).' U.S. Citizenship and Immigration Services. 2018. https://www.uscis.gov/sites/default/files/document/data/understanding-requests-for-evidence-h-1b-petitions-in-fiscal-year-2018.pdf.
162. By 2015, when Manu returned to India, the Indian engineering bubble had burst. Many colleges had proliferated in Andhra Pradesh, producing engineers of such dubious quality that they struggled to find jobs, resulting in tens of thousands of vacant seats, compelling many colleges to shut. Manu's alma mater, P. Indra Reddy Memorial Engineering College, too, had shut in 2013. See 'No Takers for Engineering Courses: Andhra Pradesh's Problem of Plenty'. NDTV. Uma Sudhir. 19 September 2013. https://www.ndtv.com/south/no-takers-for-engineering-courses-andhra-pradeshs-problem-of-plenty-535137; 'Future Unclear for Andhra Engineering Colleges.' *LiveMint*. Yogendra Kalavalapalli and Anirban Sen. 6 October 2013. https://www.livemint.com/Politics/ZXOMt6WjXcdphTs27QR96L/Future-unclear-for-Andhra-engineering-colleges.html; 'Just What is Wrong With India's Engineering Graduates?' *Rediff*. Divya Nair. 12 September 2012. https://www.rediff.com/getahead/report/slide-show-1-career-whats-ailing-indias-engineering-education/20120912.htm.
163. India's engineering crisis only continued to worsen. See, for instance, 'AICTE to Cut Number of Engineering College Seats by 600,000'. *LiveMint*. Prashant Nanda. 25 September 2015. https://www.livemint.com/Politics/BphkOxYuir6OaYcTrBtldJ/AICTE-to-cut-number-of-engineering-college-seats-by-600000.html; 'Indian Engineers Are So Unemployable That a Tech Giant Will Train High-School Graduates Itself.' *Quartz*. Ananya Bhattacharya. 21 July 2022. https://qz.com/india/941399/indian-engineers-are-so-bad-that-hcl-technologies-wants-to-hire-high-school-graduates; 'Even the IIT Heads Are Now Worried About the Quality of India's Engineers.' *Quartz*. Maria Thomas. 3 May 2017. https://qz.com/india/973435/even-the-iit-heads-are-now-worried-about-the-quality-of-indias-engineers; 'BTech and Bust: Why Indians Rush to be Engineers When There Are No Jobs.' *Hindustan Times*. Samarth Bansal. 23 August 2017. https://www.hindustantimes.com/india-news/is-the-engineering-dream-over-after-iit-students-now-prefer-mba-and-govt-jobs/story-

skQp6FdebWG7o1qSnnDUKO.html; 'India is in the Middle of an Engineering Education Crisis.' *The Economic Times*. 9 April 2018. https://economictimes.indiatimes.com/industry/services/education/india-is-in-the-middle-of-an-engineering-education-crisis/articleshow/63680625.cms?from=mdr.

India's engineering crisis, noted many experts, also arose from the All India Council for Technical Education's (AICTE) lax regulations and corruption, approving many dubious colleges, contributing to the sustained decline in the country's technical education. See, for instance, 'Anti-Corruption Nudge in Higher Education'. *The Telegraph*. Charu Kasturi. 22 August 2009. https://www.telegraphindia.com/india/anti-corruption-nudge-in-higher-education/cid/600482; 'CBI Raids Expose Why Technical Education is Sub-Standard.' *The Times of India*. D. Suresh Kumar. 7 September 2009. https://timesofindia.indiatimes.com/city/chennai/cbi-raids-expose-why-technical-education-is-sub-standard/articleshow/4979741.cms; 'CBI Registers Cases Against Several AICTE Officials, Others.' *The Hindu*. Devesh Pandey. 18 November 2009. https://www.thehindu.com/news/cities/Delhi/CBI-registers-cases-against-several-AICTE-officials-others/article16892811.ece; 'IIT, NIT Profs Involved in AICTE Scam: CBI.' *Hindustan Times*. Manish Tewari. 6 May 2010. https://www.hindustantimes.com/india/iit-nit-profs-involved-in-aicte-scam-cbi/story-mC1OKTdJiccLqd2565epvM.html; 'India's Tech-Education Woes: Is AICTE the Problem Itself?' *The Financial Express*. 4 January 2019. https://www.financialexpress.com/opinion/indias-tech-education-woes-is-aicte-the-problem-itself/1432806/.

164. Numerous desi consultancy recruiters created public groups for 'bench sales and recruiting' on Facebook and LinkedIn which, besides functioning as networking platforms, also posted jobs for IT workers and recruiters (and, at times, the names and qualifications of their benched employees). A simple search of 'bench sales recruiting' revealed many groups on Facebook and LinkedIn. See, for instance, 'Bench Sales and US IT Recruiter (Staffing)'. LinkedIn (19.3K+ members). https://www.linkedin.com/groups/10536594/; 'C2C Group By -Corp-2-Corp.com.' LinkedIn (33.7K+ members). https://www.linkedin.com/groups/10504157/; 'Bench Sales/IT Recruiting.' LinkedIn (6.7K+ members). https://www.linkedin.com/groups/1907652/; 'US IT Recruiters/Bench Sales.' Facebook (9.2K+ members).

https://www.facebook.com/groups/1738130739837456/; 'US IT Staffing Specialist, Bench Marketing, Technical Recruiting.' Facebook (4.2K+ members). https://www.facebook.com/groups/418561144873834/; 'US IT Staffing (IT Recruiter & Sales).' Facebook (27.9K+ members). https://www.facebook.com/groups/usaitstaffing/.

165. Kumar had made many videos on 'bench sales and recruiting', even interviewing many recruiters in India. See, for instance, 'Exposing Fake Bench Sales Recruiters—1/3 video || Behind the Scene Facts'. Kumar Exclusive. 18 February 2019. https://www.youtube.com/watch?v=43_tlXRx88k; 'KE Discussion With US IT Recruiters.' Kumar Exclusive. 24 June 2019. https://www.youtube.com/watch?v=GLkh5jwisN0&list=PL8sGqsTkHee5o8M4t8xtoXrJpsbfnaxxJ (Kumar's playlist on the topic, including an interview with a bench sales recruiter).

166. For a more blatant (and disconcerting) example of discrimination in the desi consultancy ecosystem, see Kumar's video on a desi consultancy, which had once emailed, 'Please do not submit Muslim candidates for below position'. See 'Nityo Infotech: Please Do Not Submit Muslim Candidates Recruiting Message'. Kumar Exclusive. 24 November 2020. https://www.youtube.com/watch?v=ym7ZyNBnuhM&list=PL8sGqsTkHee5o8M4t8xtoXrJpsbfnaxxJ&index=13.

PART V: HOPE

1. 'Disney Sued for Replacing American Workers With Indian Immigrants.' *Hindustan Times*. January 2016. https://www.hindustantimes.com/world/disney-sued-for-replacing-american-workers-with-cheaper-indian-immigrants/story-5xuSFamvFEQD6hqCOBRwGP.html.
2. 'April 2016–April 2017: Ohio Project Experiences.' Kumar Exclusive. 2 November 2017. https://www.youtube.com/watch?v=GbmDM1tRbtw.
3. 'AHR Foundation Documentary.' Appi Reddy. 9 January 2016. https://www.youtube.com/watch?v=Oj5mkJSaT5I.
4. 'Empowering Villagers With Digital Literacy.' *The Hindu*. R. Ravikanth Reddy. 20 February 2018. https://www.thehindu.com/news/national/telangana/empowering-villagers-with-digital-literacy/article22794146.ece/.

5. 'Slamma Jamma Unit Celebrate Success in California—USA.' TV9 Telugu Live. 28 March 2017. https://www.youtube.com/watch?v=B11di_KuI3k.
6. '"Slamma Jamma": Film Review.' *The Hollywood Reporter*. Frank Scheck. 24 March 2017. https://www.hollywoodreporter.com/movies/movie-reviews/slamma-jamma-988632/.
7. '*Slamma Jamma* is a Basketball Movie by Way of Ed Wood.' *The A.V. Club*. Ignatiy Vishnevetsky. 24 March 2017. https://www.avclub.com/slamma-jamma-is-a-basketball-movie-by-way-of-ed-wood-1798190785/.
8. 'US Technology Software Professionals Celebrates Telangana State Formation Day in Bay Area, CA.' Idlebrain. 10 June 2015. https://www.idlebrain.com/nricommunity/tformationday-ustechbayarea.html.
9. 'TATA Meet & Greet With Deshapathi Srinivas.' Mission Telangana. 16 November 2015. https://missiontelangana.com/tata-meet-greet-with-deshapathi-srinivas/.
10. 'TATA 2nd Telangana Formation Day Celebrations in Bay Area.' GreatAndhra. Venkat Arikatla. 5 June 2016. https://www.greatandhra.com/politics/news/tata-2nd-telangana-formation-day-celebrations-in-bay-area-75003?fbclid=IwAR1ZGDHJvc_C_sE36EzawOypuVPSdFXJykZfG9fJmY0AUg7Qb7XXfxIPj1A.
11. Telugu associations, too, interested many AndhraFriends members. See this comment, for instance, 'NATA.' AndhraFriends. Jawaani_jaaneman. 18 March 2021. https://www.andhrafriends.com/topic/901988-nata/page/3/#comment-1311815580.
12. 'Giving Back: Diaspora Philanthropy and the Transnationalisation of Caste in Guntur (India).' Amsterdam Institute for Social Science Research, University of Amsterdam, PhD thesis. Sanam Roohi. 6 December 2016. https://dare.uva.nl/search?identifier=23cdd13a-3784-4b68-ba97-efecf53bf010 (p. 143).
13. Ibid.
14. Ibid.
15. 'Kamma lore nurtures the image of a once-proud warrior clan reduced by Reddi chicanery to its present peasant status,' wrote Selig Harrison in his research paper 'Caste and the Andhra Communists.' 'Reddi duplicity, recounted by Kamma historian K.

Bhavaiah Choudary, was first apparent in 1323 A.D. at the downfall of Andhra's Kakatiya dynasty. Reciting voluminous records to prove that Kammas dominated the Kakatiya court, Choudary suggests that the Reddis, also influential militarists at the time, struck a deal at Kamma expense with the Moslem conquerors of the Kakatiya regime. The Kammas lost their noble rank and were forced into farming. In his research Choudary frankly has an axe to grind: he seeks to establish Kamma claims to Kshatriya (warrior) rank, second in the traditional Hindu caste hierarchy, rather than their present Sat-Sudra status. His main outline of Kamma and Reddi history, however, does not differ essentially from the consensus of more disinterested scholars.'

See 'Caste and the Andhra Communists'. *The American Political Science Review* (pp. 378–404). Selig Harrison. June 1956. https://doi.org/10.2307/1951675 [hereinafter, Harrison, 'Caste and the Andhra Communists']. See also *A Brief History of the Kammas*. K.B. Choudary. 1954. https://archive.org/details/brief-history-of-the-kammas/page/n1/mode/2up.

16. To read the fascinating origins of the Kammas and Reddis' caste-based associations in pre-independent India and how they commissioned caste histories—to mainly counter Brahmanical supremacy—see 'The Belief System of the Non-Brahmin Movement in India: the Andhra Case'. *Asian Survey*, 18(3), 290–300. Uma Ramaswamy. March 1978. https://doi.org/10.1525/as.1978.18.3.01p0398i. 'An important activity of [the caste] associations [in pre-independent India] was to commission caste histories,' wrote Ramaswamy. 'Even before prominent leaders such as T. Ramaswamy Choudary and G.B. Saraswathy came on to the scene, there had been claims by Kammas to Kshatriya status. The history of Kammas written by K.B. Choudary was one of the first systematic attempts to trace their ancestry. He claimed that the Kammas were the direct descendants of king Durjaya of Suryavamsam, and that the Chola kings who ruled Telugu country in the third century A.D. were their ancestors. According to him the Kammas and allied castes performed the Upanayanam ritual and donned the sacred thread till the third century B.C. when they were converted to Jainism and Buddhism. With reconversion back to the Hindu fold they lost their high status. The Reddis were equally emphatic about their claims to Kshatriya status.

P. Venkatakrishna, quoting Bhagavatham and Markandeya Puranam, argued that their ancestors were the royal caste of Rattus. They later came to be known as Rattas and Rathods and ruled over Western India. The Reddis are a branch of this caste which migrated to Andhra. The thrust of these exercises was to claim Kshatriya status for these castes.'

17. See *supra* note 15, Part V: Hope, Harrison, 'Caste and the Andhra Communists'.
18. 'Caste Dominance and Territory in South India: Understanding Kammas' Socio-Spatial Mobility.' *Modern Asian Studies*, Volume 52, Issue 6. Dalel Benbabaali. November 2018. https://www.cambridge.org/core/journals/modern-asian-studies/article/abs/caste-dominance-and-territory-in-south-india-understanding-kammas-sociospatial-mobility/3C335457E34C75BEE1A06B0BD578A7E3 (pp. 1938–1976).
19. 'Engineering Equality? Education and Im/mobility in Coastal Andhra Pradesh, India.' *Contemporary South Asia, 24*(3), 242–256. Carol Upadhya. 22 August 2016. https://doi.org/10.1080/09584935.2016.1203863.
20. 'Engineering Mobility? The "IT Craze", Transnational Migration and the Commercialisation of Education in Coastal Andhra, Provincial Globalisation.' Working Paper No. 7, Institute of Advanced Studies and Amsterdam Institute of Social Science Research, Bangalore. Carol Upadhyay. 2014. http://eprints.nias.res.in/868/ [hereinafter Upadhyay, 'Engineering Mobility?'].

    For the list of 'Kammavari' colleges on a caste-based website, see 'Kammavari Medical Colleges in AP and Tamil Nadu'. Kammas World. 4 January 2011. https://kammasworld.blogspot.com/2011/01/kammavari-medical-collges-in-ap-and.html.
21. Ibid. at Upadhyay, 'Engineering Mobility?'
22. 'Higher Education Policy in Andhra Pradesh Exploring the Dynamics of Caste and Party Affiliations.' National Institute of Educational Planning and Administration, Occasional Paper 52. Anthony Mathew. 2018. https://www.niepa.ac.in/download/Publications/Occassional_Paper_52_A.%20Mathew-Press_%20NIEPA.pdf.
23. See 'Truth, Indian Caste Groups USA, Canada'. Kumar Exclusive. 6 July 2015. https://www.youtube.com/watch?v=Y6OzZTM4lzw; 'USA Must Ban All Indian Caste Groups: TANA, ATA, NATA, NATS, TDF, etc.' Kumar Exclusive. 18 March 2023. https://www.youtube.com/

watch?v=0ZRQXGRKgKM; 'Telugu Video Truth About Reddy Caste #h1b H-1B Bodyshops Owners and ATA/NATA.' Kumar Exclusive. 22 July 2023. https://www.youtube.com/watch?v=DoDiYiSeSa8.

24. The other dignitaries included Supreme Court Judge N.V. Ramana, writer and former MP Yarlagadda Lakshmi Prasad, TDP leader and MLA Kodela Siva Prasada Rao, TDP MLA (and the chairman of PVKK Institute of Technology and Sri Balaji Educational Society) Palle Raghunatha Reddy and such film personalities as, among other notables, Venkatesh, Suresh Babu, Srikanth, Allari Naresh and a pan-Indian actress, Taapsee Pannu.

    See 'TANA Stars Meet and Greet Event Photos'. CineJosh. 14 July 2015. https://www.cinejosh.com/gallery-thumbs/22905/5/0/1/tana-stars-meet-and-greet-event-photos.html.

25. Held on a massive scale, TANA's 20th convention was made possible in large part due to a record $1.6 million fundraiser in October 2014, which 'drew more than 600 people'.

    See 'Telugu Association of North America Raised $1.6 Million at Kick-Off Meet for 2015 Conference in Detroit'. *The American Bazaar*. 29 October 2014. https://www.americanbazaaronline.com/2014/10/29/telugu-association-north-america-raised-1-6-million-kick-meet-2015-conference-detroit/.

26. 'Telugu Association of North America's Tax Filings Summary.' *ProPublica*. https://projects.propublica.org/nonprofits/organizations/363060732/.

27. 'American Telugu Association's Tax Filings Summary.' *ProPublica*. https://projects.propublica.org/nonprofits/organizations/363723725/.

28. 'North American Telugu Association's Tax Filings Summary.' *ProPublica*. https://projects.propublica.org/nonprofits/organizations/271119753/.

29. 'North America Telugu Society's Tax Filings Summary.' *ProPublica*. https://projects.propublica.org/nonprofits/organizations/264194139/.

30. Kumar, too, called the desi consulting ecosystem a 'cartel', believing it could only be stopped by something that had nailed the mafia: the Racketeer Influenced and Corrupt Organizations (RICO) Act. See, for instance, the following videos where he referenced RICO: 'Most (99.99%) Indian Bodyshops are Corrupted'. Kumar Exclusive. 24 June 2016. https://www.youtube.com/watch?v=0LZOgD-qykE; 'My Analysis: IT Group Sues USCIS Over Shorter Duration of H-1B Visas.' Kumar

Exclusive. 17 October 2018. https://www.youtube.com/watch?v=X-0sWL-H3jY.

In May 2017, the now Co-Director of the University of San Francisco's Work Law and Justice Program, Maria Ontiveros wrote an excellent research paper on the H-1B programme, flagging numerous problems in it. In a section titled 'Current Avenues for Challenging Exploitation', she referenced the RICO Act (pp. 39–40). See 'H-1B Visas, Outsourcing and Body Shops: A Continuum of Exploitation for High Tech Workers'. *Berkeley Journal of Employment and Labor Law* Vol. 38, No. 1 (2017), pp. 1–47. https://www.jstor.org/stable/26356920.

31. *USA v. Modugumudi et al.* United States District Court, Northern District of Ilinois. 30 April 2018. https://www.courtlistener.com/docket/6923862/united-states-v-modugumudi/.
32. A 2024 article on the Telugu website GreatAndhra stated that the 'matching grants fraud'—a collusion, in essence, between the members of a Telugu organisation and the professionals at an American firm—was not an exception but the norm, so much so that the IRS and the FBI had begun investigating such cases.

'The fraud committed by a single Telugu association is resulting in serious focus and investigations by IRS and FBI authorities on all the Telugu Associations in the USA,' read the GreatAndhra piece. 'Shocked by the scale of financial crime in one organization, the authorities have selected ten more Telugu organizations to scrutinize their financials. This revolves around exploiting the Matching Grants Program, a system that operates in corporate companies. When an employee donates to an NGO, their employer matches the amount, releasing it as a grant for the same NGO, aiming to encourage philanthropy. The authorities received information that taking advantage of this, a key person in a Telugu Association has been committing fraud for many years. The operation unfolds as follows:

Step 1: A Telugu Association member named XYZ contacts a Telugu individual named PQR working in a US company, through mutual friends or acquaintances.

Step 2: XYZ sends $1,000 in cash to PQR and instructs him to transfer the amount from his account to the Telugu Association's account.

Step 3: Once done, PQR's employer matches the amount, donating $1,000 to the same Telugu Association on the company's behalf.

Step 4: XYZ repeats this process with hundreds or thousands of contacts, misleading companies and pooling funds.

This leaked crime caught the attention of authorities, prompting them to investigate all Telugu Associations that have exploited the loophole over the past decade.'

See 'IRS and FBI on American Telugu Associations?' GreatAndhra. Venkat. 17 October 2024. https://www.greatandhra.com/articles/special-articles/irs-and-fbi-on-american-telugu-associations-135715.

33. 'I Hope You Will Understand Should I Pursue This Path.' Keep America At Work. 20 July 2018. https://web.archive.org/web/20180729143335/http://keepamericaatwork.com/.

PART VI: SECRETS

1. In the late 1980s, the daughter of Krishna Rao, Madhu fell in love with a man from a marginalised caste. Her father, a Brahmin, opposed the relationship. Her partner? Deva. Unable to convince their families, they eloped. She hadn't even turned eighteen. Krishna planned to inform the cops that Deva had abducted his daughter. The Ram brothers thrashed and warned him against it. And who was Krishna? Kumar's grandmother's sister's son. Kumar had met with them in their New Jersey house a few years ago. He asked Madhu: How did she come to the US? On Wizsys's H-1B, she said. Her husband accompanied her on an H-4 visa. In fact, Deva's brother, Harsha—who claimed to be an attorney—had worked as a manager for … 4M.
2. *Billions Lost: The American Tech Crisis and the Road Map to Change.* Hilarie Gamm. CreateSpace Independent Publishing Platform. 2018.
3. 'November 8, 2018. OMB Approval of Revisions to the ETA Form 9035/9035E and WH-4.' U.S. Department of Labor. https://www.dol.gov/agencies/eta/foreign-labor/news.

   See also 'Labor Condition Application: Changes to the Form ETA-9035 and Form ETA-9035E'. Office of Foreign Labor Certification Employment and Training Administration, U.S. Department of Labor. November 2018. https://www.dol.gov/sites/dolgov/files/ETA/oflc/pdfs/LCA_Webinar_November_2018.pdf.

4. 'Labor Condition Application for Nonimmigrant Workers, Form ETA-9035 & 9035E.' U.S. Department of Labor. https://flag.dol.gov/sites/default/files/2019-09/ETA_Form_9035.pdf.
5. The DOL's LCA dataset contains four kinds of LCAs (Certified, Denied, Withdrawn and Certified-Withdrawn) and four kinds of visas (H-1B, E-3 Australian, H-1B1 Singapore and H-1B1 Chile). This analysis of USAA—and all the subsequent clients in the book—considered only Certified LCAs (excluding the Denied, Withdrawn and Certified-Withdrawn) for H-1B visas (excluding E-3 Australian, H-1B1 Singapore and H-1B1 Chile visas) for FY 2019. This analysis of USAA—and all the subsequent clients in the book—also considered LCAs for, besides new applications, renewed and amended applications.

   See the DOL's LCA dataset for every financial year, which contains the list of all LCAs filed by employers (which has information on third-party consultancies' names, H-1B dependency statuses, number of H-1B workers (and their salaries) and so on) at the 'Performance Data' page: https://www.dol.gov/agencies/eta/foreign-labor/performance. On this page, under the section 'LCA Programs (H-1B, H-1B1, E-3)' and beside the year 2019, is the LCA dataset named 'H-1B FY2019.xlsx'.

   The 'H-1B FY2019.xlsx' is a huge dataset containing different hiring scenarios (represented via different LCAs): that is, H-1B workers both directly hired by clients and via third-party consultancies. Since this analysis of USAA—and all the subsequent analyses in the book—concentrates on hiring scenarios through third-party consultancies, let's see how to construct that specific dataset from the 'H-1B FY2019.xlsx' file.

   - First, download the 'H-1B FY2019.xlsx' spreadsheet from the DOL's Performance Data page.
   - The AU column of the 'H-1B FY2019.xlsx' file contains the list of American clients (or 'Secondary_Entity_Business_Name_1'). Then, apply the relevant filter to that column, so it only shows LCA entries for a particular client (such as, in this case, USAA). Then, go to column B of the same spreadsheet that shows the 'Case_Status' of different LCAs (whether Certified, Denied, Withdrawn or Certified-Withdrawn). Then, apply the relevant

filter, so it only shows Certified LCAs for a particular client (such as, in this case, USAA). Ditto column F, showing 'Visa_Class' (H-1B, E-3 Australian, H-1B1 Chile and H-1B1 Singapore), which, after the relevant filter, only shows the entries for H-1B visa. So this step ensures that the H-1B FY2019.xlsx spreadsheet only contains certified LCAs for H-1B visas, obtained by third-party consultancies, for a particular client (such as, in this case, USAA). For all the subsequent clients in the book, this spreadsheet is called the client's 'FY 2019 LCA dataset'. This is how you can obtain the FY 2019 LCA dataset for any client in the subsequent analyses.

6. To know more about H-1B Dependent firms, see the first four paragraphs of Chapter 21: 'The American Competitiveness and Workforce Improvement Act created an "H-1B Dependent" employer. The category needed one of the following three conditions: a company with twenty-five or fewer full-time equivalent employees and at least eight H-1Bs; or twenty-six to fifty full-time equivalent employees and at least thirteen H-1Bs; or fifty-one or more full-time equivalent employees and 15 per cent or more H-1Bs. Such a company had to submit three specific attestations on the LCA. It pledged to not fire an American worker ninety days before and after filing the visa petition, place its employee(s) at a firm that hadn't fired (or intended to fire) an American worker ninety days before and after the placement and ensure good-faith steps to hire an American worker before applying for the visa. But these requirements vanished if an employer paid an annual wage of over $60,000, or if the foreign professional had a master's degree or equivalent ... [The] LCA conditions tucked a key provision: "total [employees]". Most companies sought H-1B visas for computer programmers. A company's workforce also included non-tech professionals, such as HR, accounts and marketing. An employer, as a result, could hire much more than 15 per cent of its technical personnel as H-1Bs and still evade the restrictive label.'

   The 'H-1B dependent' yardstick, then, was a conservative estimate. 'It took the DOL two years to issue regulations regarding the provisions,' wrote Matloff in his 2003 research paper, 'and in the end only 50 out of 50,000 H-1B employers were declared to be H-1B dependent'. See *supra* note 78, Part III: Thought Control, Matloff, 'Need for Reform' at p. 825.

7. Some third-party consultancies in the FY 2019 LCA dataset had H-1B Dependent fields as both 'Y' and 'N' across their different LCAs. For a conservative estimate, this (and all the subsequent) analysis considered such firms 'N'.
8. This analysis considered DOL investigations from 2005, when the federal agency began publishing information on back wages, H-1B violations, employers' names and so on in a public dataset. The firms in the DOL's WHD dataset that had H-1B violations greater than zero but didn't have to pay back wages weren't included in this analysis. The firms that had to pay civil monetary penalties (CMP) but no back wage weren't considered in this analysis either. This analysis also didn't include the back wages arising from state-level Department of Labor investigations.

   To know more about how to use the DOL's WHD dataset, see *supra* note 31, Part II: Deception, WHD dataset.
9. The FY 2019 LCA dataset, like the datasets for other years, didn't contain colleges of H-1B workers, so this analysis used the PERM (or the green card) dataset for FY 2019 for this calculation, which did contain H-1B workers' colleges. Besides, since this metric measured, in essence, the percentage of third-party consultancies hiring visa mills' graduates—via the 2019 green card petitions—this analysis considered all the green card petitions: Certified, Certified-Expired, Withdrawn and Denied. This also meant that this metric measured whether a consultancy hired a visa mill graduate in not just FY 2019 but also recent years.

   To access the PERM dataset for FY 2019, see the section under 'Historical Case Disclosure Data—PERM Program' at https://www.dol.gov/agencies/eta/foreign-labor/performance. Beside the Fiscal Year 2019 is the file relevant for our calculation: 'PERM FY2019.xlsx'. For the list of visa mills (or 'Day 1 CPT' colleges), see *infra* note 12, Part VI: Secrets. The phrase 'intending to sponsor green cards' implied that this analysis included all kinds of green card petitions (Certified, Certified-Expired, Withdrawn and Denied) to find out if a company had hired alum(s) of visa mill(s).
10. Since this analysis of USAA—and all the subsequent clients in the book—considered LCAs for new, renewed and amended applications only for FY 2019, it didn't capture the actual number of all certified

LCAs for H-1B workers for a client through third-party consultancies. That's so because a third-party consultancy could have obtained an H-1B visa for a foreign worker for a client in FY 2018, which typically remained valid for three years. In such a case, it didn't have to apply for an LCA in FY 2019, so it wouldn't appear in the FY 2019 LCA dataset, even though the consultancy's H-1B worker would be working at the client.

11. To know more about the four prevailing wage levels—and how they have 'gaping loopholes' that allow law-codified underpayment of H-1B workers—see p. 115.
12. The list of fifteen dubious colleges considered in this analysis came from different immigrations forums, such as AndhraFriends, DesiOpt, Trackitt and others, where students discussed 'Day-1 CPT' schools, intending to subvert immigration laws.

    Here are their names:

    1) Tri-Valley University
    2) Herguan University
    3) University of Northern Virginia
    4) Northwestern Polytechnic University
    5) Silicon Valley University
    6) International Technological University
    7) Stratford University
    8) Wilmington University
    9) Sullivan University
    10) Harrisburg University of Science and Technology
    11) Knowledge Systems Institute
    12) Goldey-Beacom College
    13) Virginia International University
    14) University of the Cumberlands
    15) Campbellsville University

    This, too, is a conservative estimate, as this analysis only included the most famous schools that appeared again and again on immigration forums and websites. The demand for 'Day-1 CPT' colleges had reached such a high that it spawned entire websites instructing students on how to choose suitable colleges, such as, among others, day1cpt.com, day1cpt.org and day1cptuniversities.com.

13. To find the percentage of H-1B Dependent employers and employers paying back wages, we first need to calculate the total number of H-1B employers. Because the percentage of H-1B Dependent employers = (number of H-1B Dependent employers/total number of H-1B employers)*100 and percentage of employers paying back wages = (number of employers paying back wages/total number of H-1B employers)*100.

    USCIS maintains the year-wise annual dataset of employers securing H-1B visas here (starting from FY 2009): https://www.uscis.gov/tools/reports-and-studies/h-1b-employer-data-hub. To find the total number of H-1B employers from 2009 to 2023, I took the following steps:

    - I downloaded the dataset for each year. For each year's dataset, there were four columns related to visa petition numbers named 'New Employment Approval', 'New Employment Denial', 'Continuation Approval' and 'Continuation Denial'. I deleted all the rows whose 'New Employment Approval' and 'Continuation Approval' were zero but 'New Employment Denial' and/or 'Continuation Denial' greater than zero. This step ensured that every year's dataset only contained employers for approved visa petitions (for either new or renewed visas).
    - Then I removed the duplicate entries from the 'Employer (Petitioner) Name' column.
    - Then, to find out more duplicates, I removed all the spaces and special characters from each employer's name (such as commas, spaces and periods). So 'ABC, Inc' and 'ABC Inc' became 'ABCINC' and were recognised as, and reduced to, one entity. This completed the list for unique employers obtaining visa petitions for one year (say, FY 2009).
    - Then, I repeated the above three steps for every year from FY 2010 to FY 2023.
    - Finally, I clubbed all the employers in one sheet—from FY 2009 to FY 2023 (where all of them contained no spaces or special characters)—and removed the final duplicate entries to arrive at 312,120.

14. Since 2015, the DOL had asked employers to list if they were H-1B Dependent or not on their LCAs ('Y' or 'N'). After clubbing all the firms and their H-1B dependency statuses ('Y') from FY 2015 to FY 2023, then removing the duplicate entries produced the number of

unique H-1B Dependent firms. Then, dividing that number by the total number of H-1B employers (312,120) produced the probability of an average H-1B firm to be H-1B Dependent as around 5 per cent.

Another estimate could be found from the website MyVisaJobs, which had its own figures for H-1B Dependent employers (3,685) and total H-1B employers (818,308). That made the probability of an average H-1B firm to be H-1B Dependent as (3,685/818,308)*100 = 0.45 per cent. See the number of H-1B Dependent employers for 'All Years' on MyVisaJobs here: https://www.documentcloud.org/documents/24402824-no-of-h-1b-employers-mvj. See the number of total H-1B employers for 'All Years' on MyVisaJobs here: https://www.documentcloud.org/documents/24402823-no-of-h-1b-employers-mvj.

For a conservative estimate, this analysis considered the higher probability for a firm to be H-1B Dependent: 5 per cent.

15. The names of H-1B employers paying back wages for H-1B violations could be found in the WHD dataset. To access it, see *supra* note 31, Part II: Deception, WHD dataset.

    From 2005 to 2023, the DOL found that 2,125 employers owed back wages. This made the average percentage of a firm paying back wages for H-1B violations as—[(2,125/312,120)*100]%—0.68 per cent (or '<1%'). (The '2,125' figure came from the DOL's WHD dataset, from 2005 to 2023, with H-1B back wages greater than $0 and removing the duplicate companies from the list.)

16. A foreign professional needed at a minimum a bachelor's degree to qualify for an H-1B visa. Let's assume the conservative scenario of a firm hiring a foreign professional only from a SEVP-certified American school (even though countless H-1B workers, like Kumar, got their bachelor's degrees from colleges outside the US). The number of such schools total 7,683, according to a 2022 ICE report on SEVIS. That made the probability of a firm hiring a visa mill graduate = 15/7,683 = 0.19 per cent (or '<1%'), as probability = favourable cases/possible cases [(favourable cases = number of 'Day-1 CPT Schools', see *supra* note 12, Part VI: Secrets) and (possible cases = total number of SEVP-certified schools)].

    For the '7,683' figure, see 'Student and Exchange Visitor Program (SEVP) 2022 SEVIS by the Numbers Report'. U.S. Immigration and Customs Enforcement. http://web.archive.org/web/20230505063614/https://www.ice.gov/doclib/sevis/pdf/sevisBTN2022.pdf (p. 3).

But since our analysis primarily considers IT workers, let's make our calculation even more conversative and consider only those American colleges that provide a degree in 'engineering technologies & engineering-related fields'. That number, from the *U.S. News & World Report's* website, is 1,789. That makes the probability of an H-1B firm hiring a visa mill graduate = 15/1,789 = 0.83 per cent, still less than 1 per cent. See the '1,789' figure at the *U.S. News and World Report's* website: https://tinyurl.com/4c5hxce8.

17. To find the true number of USAA's third-party consultancies, this analysis counted the following pairs as one: IBM Corporation and IBM India Private Limited and Tata Consultancy Services Limited and TCS E-Serve America (as they are part of the same group of companies).

    This analysis of USAA also considered, besides certified LCAs for USAA, the following Secondary Entity Business Names: USAA Real Estate Company, USAA Federal Savings Bank, USAA Life Insurance Company and USAA Acceptance.

18. Five firms in USAA's FY 2019 LCA dataset—Binary Computer International Corp, Mastech Inc, Cod Cores, Skilltune Technologies and Solware IT Technologies—had different H-1B Dependent values ('Y' and 'N') across their LCAs. They were all considered 'N' for a conservative estimate.

19. This figure included the certified LCAs for both IBM Corporation and IBM India Private Limited.

20. Even though DesiCrunch and Goolti have been defunct for quite some time, you can read their archived pages here. 'DesiCrunch.' https://web.archive.org/web/20080715094732/http://www.desicrunch.com/; 'Goolti.' https://web.archive.org/web/20080715144916/http://www.goolti.com/.

21. Yash & Lujan Consulting. MyVisaJobs. Venturpalli. 7 June 2018. http://web.archive.org/web/20200218131933/https://www.myvisajobs.com/Visa-Sponsor/Yash/607208_Review.htm/.

    'State and local government agencies, more so than even private sector companies, have to get more done with less,' stated Y&L Consulting's web page. 'Sistema Technologies, Inc., a sister-company of Y&L Consulting, Inc., focuses on local and state government IT development opportunities. Founded in 2002, … Sistema has worked for many state agencies and municipalities, including TX Education Agency, CoSA, HHSC, OCCC,

SAWS, TX DMV, ESC 20, TX Dept. of Family & Protective Services, TX Water Development Board, TX General Land Office, TX DOT, TX Attorney General's Office and the Comptroller of Public Accounts (CPA).' See 'Y&L Consulting—Government'. http://web.archive.org/web/20201021093331/https://ylconsulting.com/industries/government/.

22. Yash & Lujan Consulting. MyVisaJobs. 29 July 2016. http://web.archive.org/web/20200218131933/https:/www.myvisajobs.com/Visa-Sponsor/Yash/607208_Review.htm/.
23. Reply to a comment at Ibid. Srinivas Vemuri. 29 March 2018.
24. 'Y&L Consulting Has a New Place to Call Home!' The Greater San Antonio Chamber. https://www.sachamber.org/news/2018/09/12/chamber-news/y-l-consulting-has-a-new-place-to-call-home/.
25. Ibid.
26. Ibid.
27. 'Y&L Consulting appreciates every member of the military and their families for the sacrifices you are willing to make on behalf of all of us and our nation,' stated the firm's website. 'If, while you were in the military, you gained skills in the Information Technology realm, we would like to hear from you.' See 'Giving Back'. 2020. http://web.archive.org/web/20200922210725/https://www.ylconsulting.com/about/giving-back/.
28. Ibid. See the video at 'Y&L Consulting—Heroes Day'. YLConsulting. 15 August 2017. https://www.youtube.com/watch?v=M81q-sHTM3w.
29. 'Y&L Consulting—Our Current Initiatives' (fifth slide, under 'Our Current Initiatives', titled 'IT Career Training'). https://web.archive.org/web/20201201090146/https://ylconsulting.com/about/giving-back/.
30. Page of Rep. John Lujan—District 118. Texas House of Representatives. https://www.house.texas.gov/members/member-page/?district=118.
31. 'Y&L Consulting—Our Current Initiatives' (fourth slide, under 'Our Current Initiatives', titled 'Public Service'). https://web.archive.org/web/20201201090146/https://ylconsulting.com/about/giving-back/.
32. PVR America. MyVisaJobs. 20 July 2017. https://www.myvisajobs.com/employer/pvr-america/#reviews.
33. Galaxy I Technologies. MyVisaJobs. 27 December 2017. https://www.myvisajobs.com/Visa-Sponsor/Galaxy-Technologies/1110151_Review.htm/.

34. Icloud Technologies Corporation. MyVisaJobs. 7 January 2019. https://www.myvisajobs.com/Visa-Sponsor/Icloud-Technologies/1299273_Review.htm/.
35. Saibersys. MyVisaJobs. 17 July 2018. https://www.myvisajobs.com/Visa-Sponsor/Saibersys/1157466_Review.htm/.
36. Arch International Group. MyVisaJobs. 18 January 2018. https://www.myvisajobs.com/employer/arch-international-group/#reviews.
37. Infosmartsystems. MyVisaJobs. 9 July 2013. https://www.myvisajobs.com/employer/infosmartsystems/#reviews.
38. I followed the steps below to find out the total number of H-1B violations, affected H-1B workers and back wages for USAA's third-party consultancies:
    - I first went to the DOL's Performance Data page at the link: https://www.dol.gov/agencies/eta/foreign-labor/performance.
    - On the Performance Data page, I went to the section named 'LCA Programs (H-1B, H-1B1, E-3)'. Under that section, beside Fiscal Year 2019 is a file named 'H-1B FY2019.xlsx'. I downloaded that spreadsheet.
    - The AU column of the 'H-1B FY2019.xlsx' file had the list of American clients (or 'Secondary_Entity_Business_Name_1'). I applied the relevant filter to that column, so it only showed the LCA entries for USAA as the client. I then went to column B that showed the 'Case_Status' of different LCAs (whether Certified, Denied, Withdrawn or Certified-Withdrawn). I applied the relevant filter, so it only showed Certified LCAs for USAA as the client. Ditto column F, showing 'Visa_Class' (H-1B, E-3 Australian, H-1B1 Chile and H-1B1 Singapore), which, after the relevant filter, only showed the entries for H-1B visa. So this step ensured that the H-1B FY2019.xlsx spreadsheet only had certified LCAs for H-1B visas, obtained by third-party consultancies, for USAA as the client. Let's call this spreadsheet USAA_FY_2019.
    - Then, I went to column T ('Employer_Name'), which had the list of third-party consultancies that had obtained certified LCAs for USAA. That number was 295 (also the number under the 'Third-Party Consultancies' for the USAA table on p. 248).
    - Then, to find out how many consultancies had paid back wages to their H-1B workers, I turned to the DOL's WHD dataset.

(See *supra* note 31, Part II: Deception, WHD dataset, to find out how to use that dataset.) On the Back Wages column in the WHD dataset (column AG, 'h1b_bw_atp_amt'), I applied the filter Back Wages > 0.

- I then compared how many companies in the T column of the USAA_FY_2019 spreadsheet matched with the companies paying back wages more than zero in the WHD dataset. That figure was fifty-three.
- Now for each company paying back wages, I recorded their back wages amount, number of H-1B violations (column AF, 'h1b_violtn_cnt') and the number of employees affected (column AH, 'h1b_ee_atp_cnt').
- Then, for all the contractors of USAA paying back wages greater than zero, I totalled the back wages amount, the number of H-1B violations and the number of affected employees to arrive at the figure $3.73 million, 1,182 H-1B violations and 801 affected employees.

This is how I've found the back wages, the number of H-1B violations and the number of affected H-1B workers corresponding to each client in the book.

39. These figures came from the DOL's WHD dataset. See *supra* note 31, Part II: Deception, WHD dataset, on how to access it.
40. 'We do [outsourcing], because it helps us get our projects done, and because the level of expertise of this technology, these technology companies and individuals is incredible,' said USAA's then CEO, Robert Davis. 'I mean, if we could get this same thing in the United States, we'd do it. [But] [i]t's not available. It's not here. It just doesn't exist.' See 'I.T. Management—USAA IT Chief Exits'. *CIO*. Ben Worthen and Stephanie Overby. 15 June 2004. https://www.cio.com/article/272445/offshoring-i-t-management-usaa-it-chief-exits.html/.
41. Ibid.
42. Ibid.
43. Ibid.
44. 'U.S. Jobs: Next Stop, India?' *San Antonio Express-News*. Sanford Nowlin and Travis Poling. 21 September 2003. https://web.archive.org/web/20031130012310/http://news.mysanantonio.com/story.cfm?xla=saen&xlb=110&xlc=1057140.

45. 'USAA spokeswoman Katie Spring says,' reported the *San Antonio Business Journal*, 'the purpose of the lawsuit is to determine what information WOAI and Clear Channel actually have, to force the media organization to return it and to force them to disclose how they obtained the information.' Spring also emphasised that this was 'not about the news story' or the 'First Amendment'. 'They have our stuff,' she said, 'and we want it back.' See 'USAA Files Lawsuit Against WOAI-TV Over Confidential Information'. *San Antonio Business Journal.* James Aldridge. 26 April 2004. https://www.bizjournals.com/sanantonio/stories/2004/04/26/daily8.html.
46. 'War of Words Between USAA and WOAI-TV Continues.' *San Antonio Business Journal.* Scott Bailey. 23 June 2004. https://www.bizjournals.com/sanantonio/stories/2004/06/21/daily22.html/.
47. 'Any USAA Dallas Employees/Contractors Here.' AndhraFriends. Pandubabu. 8 April 2021. https://www.andhrafriends.com/topic/904776-any-usaa-dallas-employeescontractors-here/.
48. Ibid. at Zarathustra. 9 April 2021. https://www.andhrafriends.com/topic/904776-any-usaa-dallas-employeescontractors-here/#findComment-1311856933.
49. Ibid. at Pandubabu. 9 April 2021. https://www.andhrafriends.com/topic/904776-any-usaa-dallas-employeescontractors-here/#findComment-1311856883.
50. Ibid. at Tellugodu. 9 April 2021. https://www.andhrafriends.com/topic/904776-any-usaa-dallas-employeescontractors-here/#comment-1311856891.
51. Ibid. at Tellugodu. 9 April 2021. https://www.andhrafriends.com/topic/904776-any-usaa-dallas-employeescontractors-here/#findComment-1311857046.
52. 'Anyone Working for USAA?' AndhraFriends. Tellugodu. 8 January 2021. https://www.andhrafriends.com/topic/892906-anyone-working-for-usaa/.
53. Ibid. at Zarathustra. 8 January 2021. https://www.andhrafriends.com/topic/892906-anyone-working-for-usaa/#findComment-1311672788.
54. Ibid. at Spidie. 12 January 2021. https://www.andhrafriends.com/topic/892906-anyone-working-for-usaa/page/4/#findComment-1311681468.
55. Ibid. at Amrita. 8 January 2021. https://www.andhrafriends.com/topic/892906-anyone-working-for-usaa/#findComment-1311672783.

56. Ibid. at Zarathustra. 8 January 2021. https://www.andhrafriends.com/topic/892906-anyone-working-for-usaa/#findComment-1311672791.
57. Ibid. at Amrita. 8 January 2021. https://www.andhrafriends.com/topic/892906-anyone-working-for-usaa/page/2/#findComment-1311672812.
58. Ibid. at Amrita. 8 January 2021. https://www.andhrafriends.com/topic/892906-anyone-working-for-usaa/page/2/#findComment-1311672807.
59. Desi consultancies often threatened to sue (and many times actually sued) their employees. See, for instance, *supra* note 53, Part II: Deception, The Guardian, 'Job Brokers Steal Wages'; 'Desi Consultant Wants to Sue—Urgent Help Please.' Immihelp. Aceraspire. 6 June 2009. https://www.immihelp.com/forum/usa-h1b-h4-visa/60804-desi-consultant-wants-to-sue-urgent-help-please; 'Desi Consultancy Threatening Legal Action.' Immihelp. Kumar1987. 7 January 2017. http://www.immihelp.com/forum/showthread.php/212088-Desi-Consultancy-Threatening-Legal-Action; 'H1B Employer (Desi Consultant) Harassing and Threatening.' RedBus2US. H1B0201. February 2014. https://redbus2us.com/qa/20162/h1b-employer-desi-consultant-harrassing-and-threatening; 'Employer Filed a Lawsuit for Joining End Client.' Murthy Law Firm H1B Forum. Sairam4114. 26 April 2017. http://forum.murthy.com/topic/107626-employer-filed-a-law-suit-on-me-for-joining-end-client/; 'Urgent Help Needed. Desi Consultancy Harassing Friend.' Trackitt. CleanSock. 27 August 2015. http://www.trackitt.com/usa-discussion-forums/i485-eb/1587108237/urgent-help-needed-desi-consultancy-harassing-friend/page/1.
60. 'Vacating Northponds, Webster, New York USA.' Kumar Exclusive. 9 June 2018. https://www.youtube.com/watch?v=itZvMdLg7ZU.
61. 'Finally, I Quit H1B Life With a Smile! My Last Video From USA (Until I Come Back!).' Kumar Exclusive. 25 June 2018. https://www.youtube.com/watch?v=46eAMJTbXm4.
62. 'Take Off USA.' Kumar Exclusive. 25 June 2018. https://www.youtube.com/watch?v=gGX_ExojqOA.
63. Given the huge extent of desi consultancies' crimes, only a few of their owners were arrested. Here are some news reports about those who couldn't evade the law: 'Indian National Arrested in $21 Million H-1B Visa Fraud Conspiracy in US'. *The Economic Times.* Priyanka

Sangani. 21 August 2020. https://economictimes.indiatimes.com/news/international/business/indian-national-arrested-in-21-million-h-1b-visa-fraud-conspiracy-in-us/articleshow/77670682.cms?from=mdr; 'Telugu NRI Duo Among Four Arrested for H1B Fraud in the U.S.' *The Hindu*. Tharun Boda. 3 July 2019. https://www.thehindu.com/news/national/andhra-pradesh/telugu-nri-duo-among-four-arrested-for-h1b-fraud-in-the-us/article28274089.ece; '3 Telugu Businessmen Face H-1B Fraud Case in US.' *The Times of India*. Ch Sushil Rao. 3 April 2019. https://timesofindia.indiatimes.com/city/hyderabad/3-telugu-businessmen-face-h-1b-fraud-case-in-us/articleshow/68697281.cms; 'Brothers Sentenced on Visa Fraud Convictions.' United States Attorney's Office. 3 June 2016. https://www.justice.gov/usao-ndtx/pr/brothers-sentenced-visa-fraud-convictions.

64. 'H-1B Visas and Prevailing Wage Levels.' Economic Policy Institute. Ron Hira and Daniel Costa. 4 May 2020. https://www.epi.org/publication/h-1b-visas-and-prevailing-wage-levels/ (Table 5).
65. Ibid. at Table 3.
66. Ibid. at Table 5.
67. In the chart, Amazon included both Amazon.com and Amazon Web Services.
68. See *supra* note 120, Part III: Thought Control, Green Card Approval.
69. See *supra* note 122, Part III: Thought Control, Programmers' Guild, 'PERM Fake Job Ads Defraud Americans'.
70. 'Justice, Labor Departments Reach Settlements With Facebook Resolving Claims of Discrimination Against U.S. Workers and Potential Regulatory Recruitment Violations.' U.S. Department of Justice. 19 October 2021. https://www.justice.gov/archives/opa/pr/justice-labor-departments-reach-settlements-facebook-resolving-claims-discrimination-against.
71. Ibid.
72. 'Slap-On-Wrist Settlement With Facebook's Discrimination Against US Workers.' LinkedIn. Ron Hira. 20 October 2021. https://www.linkedin.com/pulse/slap-on-wrist-settlement-facebooks-discrimination-against-ron-hira/.
73. Ibid.
74. 'Justice Department Secures $25 Million Landmark Agreement With Apple to Resolve Employment Discrimination Allegations Based on Citizenship Status.' U.S. Department of Justice. 9 November 2023.

https://www.justice.gov/archives/opa/pr/justice-department-secures-25-million-landmark-agreement-apple-resolve-employment.

75. Ibid.
76. Ibid.
77. Even though the Big Tech giants had 65,899 certified LCAs in FY 2019, they had in total 26,970 approved H-1B visa petitions. That's so because not every certified LCA resulted in an approved H-1B visa, as the petitions also needed to be approved by the Department of Homeland Security and the Department of State, which could result in rejections. Sometimes, the employer, too, withdrew the petitions after obtaining certified LCAs.
78. See *supra* notes 5-16, Part VI: Secrets, for the methodology behind this table and how to create the FY 2019 LCA dataset for any Big Tech firm. See also p. 248 for the probabilities of an 'average' H-1B firm to be H-1B Dependent, paying back wages for H-1B violations and hiring a visa mill's graduate.
79. This analysis of Amazon also considered, besides certified LCAs for Amazon, the following Secondary Entity Business Names: Amazon Robotics, Amazon Game Studios and Amazon Web Services Data Center.
80. Amazon's FY 2019 LCA dataset contained ten certified LCAs where Amazon.com Services was both the Employer and the Secondary Entity Business. Those LCAs weren't included in this analysis.
81. One firm in Amazon's FY 2019 LCA dataset, MakeUrCareer, had different H-1B Dependent values ('Y' and 'N') across its LCAs. This analysis considered it 'N' for a conservative estimate.
82. Apple's FY 2019 LCA dataset contained two certified LCAs where Apple Inc was both the Employer and the Secondary Entity Business. Those LCAs weren't included in this analysis.
83. To find the true number of Apple's third-party consultancies, this analysis counted the following pairs as one: Cognizant Technology Solutions US and Cognizant Worldwide, Infosys and Infosys BPM, Larsen & Toubro Infotech and L&T Technology Services, Tata Consultancy Services and Tata America International, and First Tek and First Tek Dos (as they had the same addresses in the LCAs or are part of the same group of companies).
84. Five firms in Apple's FY 2019 LCA dataset—Federal Soft Systems, Orange Information Technology Solutions, OSO Ventures, Red Oak

Tech and VMC Soft Technologies—had different H-1B Dependent values ('Y' and 'N') across their LCAs. This analysis considered them 'N' for a conservative estimate.

85. Seventeen certified LCAs in Apple's FY 2019 LCA dataset, corresponding to 115 H-1B workers, didn't contain the prevailing wage levels. Those LCAs weren't included in this analysis.
86. This analysis of Facebook also considered, besides certified LCAs for Facebook, the following Secondary Entity Business Names: Facebook Technologies and Facebook Reality Labs.
87. Facebook's FY 2019 LCA dataset contained seventy-seven certified LCAs where Facebook, Inc was both the Employer and the Secondary Entity Business. Those LCAs weren't included in this analysis. Besides, to find the true number of Facebook's third-party consultancies, this analysis counted Deloitte Consulting and Deloitte Financial Advisory as one.
88. One firm in Facebook's FY 2019 LCA dataset, VBridgeIT, had different H-1B Dependent values ('Y' and 'N') across its LCAs. This analysis considered it 'N' for a conservative estimate.
89. Two certified LCAs in Facebook's FY 2019 LCA dataset, corresponding to sixteen H-1B workers, didn't contain the prevailing wage levels. Those LCAs weren't included in this analysis.
90. This analysis of Google also considered, besides certified LCAs for Google, the following Secondary Entity Business Names: Google Fiber, Google International, Google Cloud and Google Nest.
91. Google's FY 2019 LCA dataset contained 267 certified LCAs where Google LLC was both the Employer and the Secondary Entity Business. Those LCAs weren't included in this analysis.

    To find the true number of Google's third-party consultancies, this analysis counted the following pairs as one: Infosys BPM and Infosys and IBase Consulting of Fairfield County and IBase of Fairfield County (as they had the same addresses in the LCAs or are part of the same group of companies).

    Among all third-party contractors, one stood out: Howard University. It had gotten two certified LCAs for Google LLC.
92. Ten firms in Google's FY 2019 LCA dataset—Ab Ovo, Bristlecone, Indus Group, Intuites, Intellipro Group, Metrix IT Solutions, Platinum Infosys, Sar Tech, Vings Technologies and World IP Phone—had

different H-1B Dependent values ('Y' and 'N') across their LCAs. This analysis considered them 'N' for a conservative estimate.

93. Fifteen certified LCAs in Google's FY 2019 LCA dataset, corresponding to twenty-one workers, didn't contain the prevailing wage levels. Those LCAs weren't included in this analysis.

94. To find the true number of Microsoft's third-party consultancies, this analysis counted the following pairs as one: Tech Mahindra (Americas) and Tech Mahindra Technologies and Artech Information Systems and Artech (as they had the same addresses in the LCAs or are part of the same group of companies).

95. Six firms in Microsoft's FY 2019 LCA dataset—Biblioso Corporation, Cirquetech Group, Couloir Technology Group, Namitus Technologies, Averon Solutions and Data Glove—had different H-1B Dependent values ('Y' and 'N') across their LCAs. This analysis considered them 'N' for a conservative estimate.

96. Six certified LCAs in Microsoft's FY 2019 LCA dataset, corresponding to six H-1B workers, didn't contain the prevailing wage levels. Those LCAs weren't included in this analysis.

97. Here's the breakdown of Big Tech's cumulative third-party consultancies:

Third-Party Consultancies	H-1B Dependent Consultancies	Consultancies Paying Back Wages for H-1B Violations	Consultancies Hiring Visa Mills' Graduates	Consultancies' H-1B Workers at Client	H-1Bs Earning Much Less Than Median Salaries
794	58%	14%	16%	7,530	83%

98. Here's the breakdown of Big Tech's third-party consultancies paying back wages to their employees:

Third-Party Consultancies	*H-1B Violations*	*Affected Employees*	*Back Wages*
114	2,166	1,403	$8.29 million

99. See *supra* notes 5-16, Part VI: Secrets, for the methodology behind this table and how to create the FY 2019 LCA dataset for any media firm. See also p. 248 for the probabilities of an 'average' H-1B firm to be H-1B Dependent, paying back wages for H-1B violations and hiring a visa mill's graduate.

100. This analysis of Fox also considered, besides certified LCAs for Fox, the following Secondary Entity Business Names: Fox News, Fox Entertainment Group, 20th Century Fox Television, Fox Corporation,

Fox Networks Group, Foxcorp Holdings, FoxNext, Fox Sports, Fox Interactive Media, Fox Studios, Fox Broadcasting Company and Fox Cable Network Services.

101. The list of third-party consultancies for the media firms (and all the other) analyses in the book came from the steps below:
    - I first went to the DOL's Performance Data page at the link: https://www.dol.gov/agencies/eta/foreign-labor/performance.
    - On the Performance Data page, I went to the section named 'LCA Programs (H-1B, H-1B1, E-3)'. In that section, corresponding to Fiscal Year 2019 contained a file named 'H-1B FY2019.xlsx'. I downloaded that spreadsheet.
    - The list of American clients (or 'Secondary_Entity_Business_Name_1') is in the AU column of the H-1B FY2019.xlsx spreadsheet. I first applied the relevant filter to that column, so it only showed the LCA entries for the *New York Times*. Then, I went to column B that showed the 'Case_Status' of different LCAs (whether Certified, Denied, Withdrawn or Certified-Withdrawn) and applied the relevant filter, so it only showed the Certified LCAs. Ditto column F, showing 'Visa_Class' (H-1B, E-3 Australian, H-1B1 Chile and H-1B1 Singapore), which, after the relevant filter, only showed entries for the H-1B visa. So this step ensured that the H-1B FY2019.xlsx spreadsheet only had certified LCAs for H-1B visas for the *Times* (or the *Times*'s 'FY 2019 LCA dataset').
    - I then went to column T, which listed all the companies under 'Employer_Name' (or, in essence, third-party consultancies supplying H-1B workers to the end client, in this case, the *Times*). Under the 'Employer_Name' column for the *Times*, I found Infosys and Cognizant.
    - I then repeated the above four steps for Fox (and its subsidiaries) and, under the 'Employer_Name' column in its spreadsheet, found Cognizant and HCL America.
102. Cavalier IT. MyVisaJobs. 11 July 2012. https://www.myvisajobs.com/Visa-Sponsor/Cavalier-Inc/843237_Review.htm/
103. Stackit Professionals. MyVisaJobs. 24 December 2020. https://www.myvisajobs.com/Visa-Sponsor/Stackit-Professionals-Inc/1366292_Review.htm/.

104. Flexon Technologies. MyVisaJobs. 17 June 2019. https://www.myvisajobs.com/Visa-Sponsor/Flexon-Technologies/1327651_Review.htm/.
105. See *supra* notes 5-16, Part VI: Secrets, for the methodology behind this table and how to create the FY 2019 LCA dataset for any university. See also p. 248 for the probabilities of an 'average' H-1B firm to be H-1B Dependent, paying back wages for H-1B violations and hiring a visa mill's graduate.
106. This analysis of Columbia University also considered, besides certified LCAs for Columbia University, the following Secondary Entity Business Names: Columbia University Information Technology and Columbia University Investment Management Company.
107. Columbia University's FY 2019 LCA dataset contained ten certified LCAs where Columbia University and Teachers College, Columbia University was both the Employer and the Secondary Entity Business. Those LCAs weren't included in this analysis.
108. This analysis of Yale University also considered, besides certified LCAs for Yale University, the following Secondary Entity Business Names: University of Yale and Yale (as their address—'25 Science Park, New Haven'—corresponded to a building inside the college campus).
109. Yale University's FY 2019 LCA dataset contained one certified LCA where Yale University was an Employer and Yale University Dept of Slavic Languages the Secondary Entity Business. That LCA wasn't included in this analysis.
110. This analysis of Stanford University also considered, besides certified LCAs for Stanford University, the following Secondary Entity Business Names: Stanford Health Care, Stanford Department of Radiology and Stanford Institute for Economic Policy Research.
111. Stanford University's FY 2019 LCA dataset contained three certified LCAs where Stanford Health Care was an Employer and Stanford University the Secondary Entity Business. Those LCAs weren't included in this analysis.
112. Marlabs. MyVisaJobs. https://www.myvisajobs.com/Visa-Sponsor/Marlabs/339830_Review.htm/.
113. *Ramakapeta v. Marlabs Inc.* United States District Court, District of New Jersey. 10 September 2010. https://www.documentcloud.org/documents/24251562-marlabs-lawsuit.
114. Ibid.
115. Ibid.

116. Ibid.
117. Ibid.
118. Ibid.
119. *Ramakapeta v. Marlabs Inc.* United States District Court, District of New Jersey. 20 December 2010. https://storage.courtlistener.com/recap/gov.uscourts.njd.246389.7.0.pdf.
120. Marlabs's controversies didn't end there though. On 29 October 2008, a senior Fannie Mae engineer in Urbana, Maryland, stumbled on a script hiding in a routine program. Set to execute on 31 January 2009, it'd disable all logins and delete all logs—including the 'footprints' revealing its creator—on production, backup and contingency servers. It'd then kill the backup software and ripple to 4,000 servers, destroying all data, causing 'millions of dollars of damage' and reducing, if not shutting, 'the operations for at least a week'. The engineer noticed the username accessing the development server: an IT contractor, Rajendrasinh Babubhai Makwana, fired five days ago for creating a script without his supervisor's approval. A federal jury convicted him of 'computer intrusion' in October 2010. Two months later, he got a forty-one-month prison sentence, followed by three years of supervised release. The FBI affidavit identified him as an employee of a Washington-based firm, OmniTech Systems. But its CEO said another company, IonIdea, had employed him. IonIdea's vice president refused, too. Makwana's actual employer? Marlabs.

    See more at 'Indian Convicted of Planting Virus in Fannie Mae Servers'. *The Economic Times.* 6 October 2010. https://economictimes.indiatimes.com/news/international/indian-convicted-of-planting-virus-in-fannie-mae-servers/articleshow/6697016.cms?from=mdr; 'Fannie Mae Corporate Intruder Sentenced to Over Three Years in Prison for Attempting to Wipe Out Fannie Mae Financial Data.' The Federal Bureau of Investigation. 17 December 2010. https://archives.fbi.gov/archives/baltimore/press-releases/2010/ba121710.htm; 'Ex-Engineer Pleads Innocent to Server Bomb Charge.' *Computerworld.* Gregg Keizer. 2 February 2009. https://www.computerworld.com/article/1478596/ex-engineer-pleads-innocent-to-server-bomb-charge.html; 'Jury Convicts Programmer of Planting Fannie Mae Server Bomb.' *Computerworld.* Gregg Keizer. 8 October 2010. https://www.computerworld.com/article/2749987/jury-convicts-programmer-of-planting-fannie-mae-server-bomb.html/.

121. This rank came from the DOL's WHD dataset, from 2005 to 2023. See *supra* note 31, Part II: Deception, WHD dataset, to know how to access it.
122. Siby Vadakekkara's Bio. *Forbes.* https://councils.forbes.com/profile/Siby-Vadakekkara-Chairman-CEO-Marlabs-LLC/8bb6451c-d03b-4d7f-b23f-b004d626a845.
123. Marlabs Inc's Post. Facebook. 30 September 2013. https://www.facebook.com/marlabsinc/posts/10151723526236985.
124. 'Professors From Columbia University at Marlabs Bangalore.' Marlabs Inc's Album. Facebook. 8 October 2013. https://www.facebook.com/media/set/?set=a.10151738559771985&type=3.
125. 'Art Langer Joins Marlabs Board.' *The SME Times*. 9 February 2018. https://thesmetimes.com/art-langer-joins-marlabs-board/.
126. '"Seeking the Edge—Driving Breakthrough Innovation" by Robert B. (Rob) Carter, CIO of FedEx.' Columbia Center for Technology Management. 17 January 2018. https://web.archive.org/web/ 20180620150414/https://www.ctm.columbia.edu/news/seeking-edge-driving-breakthrough-innovation-robert-b-rob-carter-cio-fedex.
127. 'Marlabs Partners With Workforce Opportunity Services to Bring Veterans Into the Digital Economy.' PR Newswire. 4 December 2018. https://www.prnewswire.com/news-releases/marlabs-partners-with-workforce-opportunity-services-to-bring-veterans-into-the-digital-economy-881504720.html.
128. Summitworks Technologies. MyVisaJobs. https://www.myvisajobs.com/Visa-Sponsor/Summitworks-Technologies/516335_Review.htm.
129. Summitworks Technologies, found guilty in a 2011 DOL investigation, had to pay back wages worth $5,000. The $5,000 figure came from the DOL's WHD dataset. To find out how to access it, see *supra* note 31, Part II: Deception, WHD dataset.
130. See *supra* notes 5-16, Part VI: Secrets, for the methodology behind this table and how to create the FY 2019 LCA dataset for any American firm. See also p. 248 for the probabilities of an 'average' H-1B firm to be H-1B Dependent, paying back wages for H-1B violations and hiring a visa mill's graduate.
131. To find the true number of Pfizer's third-party consultancies, this analysis counted the following pairs as one: IBM Corporation and IBM India Private Limited, Deloitte & Touche and Deloitte Consulting,

Cognizant Technology US Solutions and Cognizant Worldwide, Advansoft International and Advansoft Worldwide, and Avventis and Avventis Tech (as they had the same addresses in the LCAs or are part of the same group of companies).

132. Two firms in Pfizer's FY 2019 LCA dataset, Advansoft International and Advansoft Worldwide, had different H-1B Dependent values ('Y' and 'N') across their LCAs. This analysis considered them 'N' for a conservative estimate.
133. Three certified LCAs in Pfizer's FY 2019 LCA dataset didn't contain the prevailing wage levels. Those LCAs weren't included in this analysis.
134. This analysis of Boeing also considered, besides certified LCAs for Boeing, the following Secondary Entity Business Names: Boeing Employees Credit Union, Boeing Distribution Services, Boeing Global Services, Boeing Commercial Airplanes, Boeing Shared Services Group and Aviation Partners Boeing.
135. One firm in Boeing's FY 2019 LCA dataset, Aroha Technologies, had different H-1B Dependent values ('Y' and 'N') across its LCAs. This analysis considered it 'N' for a conservative estimate.
136. Eight certified LCAs in Boeing's FY 2019 LCA dataset didn't contain the prevailing wage levels. Those LCAs weren't included in this analysis.
137. This analysis of Chevron also considered, besides certified LCAs for Chevron, the following Secondary Entity Business Names: Chevron Business Real Estate Commission, Chevron Global Services Corp, Chevron Philips Chemical, Chevron Information Technological Company, Chevron USA, Chevron Shipping Company, Chevron SJV Business Unit, Chevron Federal Credit Union, Chevron Oil Corporation, Chevron Oil & Gas, Chevron Corporation, Chevron Petroleum, Chevron Marine Products and Chevron Products Company.
138. To find the true number of Chevron's third-party consultancies, this analysis counted Larsen & Toubro Infotech and L&T Technology Services as one.
139. Two firms in Chevron's FY 2019 LCA dataset, HSK Technologies and Superlogix, had different H-1B Dependent values ('Y' and 'N') across their LCAs. This analysis considered them 'N' for a conservative estimate.

140. Two certified LCAs in Chevron's FY 2019 LCA dataset didn't contain the prevailing wage levels. Those LCAs weren't included in this analysis.
141. State Farm's FY 2019 LCA dataset contained four certified LCAs where State Farm Mutual Mobile Insurance Company was both the Employer and the Secondary Entity Business. Those LCAs weren't included in this analysis.
142. To find the true number of State Farm's third-party consultancies, this analysis counted the following pairs as one: NTT Data and NTT Data Services and Teksystems and Teksystems Global Services (as they had the same addresses in the LCAs or are part of the same group of companies).
143. Three firms in State Farm's FY 2019 LCA dataset—ARV Systems, Fidelis Software Solutions and Singular Analysts—had different H-1B Dependent values ('Y' and 'N') across their LCAs. This analysis considered them 'N' for a conservative estimate.
144. This analysis of the United Nations also considered, besides certified LCAs for the United Nations, the following Secondary Entity Business Names: The United Nations Development Programme; United Nations International Computer Centre; United Nations, Department of Management; United Nations Federal Credit Union; United Nations Children's Fund (UNICEF) and United Nations—Office of ICT.
145. The United Nations's FY 2019 LCA dataset contained one certified LCA where the United Nations Foundation was both the Employer and the Secondary Entity Business. That LCA wasn't included in this analysis.
146. I followed the steps below to arrive at the names of the United Nations's contractors paying back wages to their H-1B employees (Compunnel Software Group, Hexaware Technologies, Infosys and Synaptein Solutions):
    - I first went to the DOL's Performance Data page at the link: https://www.dol.gov/agencies/eta/foreign-labor/performance.
    - On the Performance Data page, I went to the section named 'LCA Programs (H-1B, H-1B1, E-3)'. Under that section, beside Fiscal Year 2019 is a file named 'H-1B FY2019.xlsx'. I downloaded that spreadsheet.
    - The AU column of the 'H-1B FY2019.xlsx' file had the list of American clients (or 'Secondary_Entity_Business_Name_1'). I

applied the relevant filter to that column, so it only showed the LCA entries for United Nations as the client. I then went to column B that showed the 'Case_Status' of different LCAs (whether Certified, Denied, Withdrawn or Certified-Withdrawn). I applied the relevant filter, so it only showed Certified LCAs for the United Nations as the client. Ditto column F, showing 'Visa_Class' (H-1B, E-3 Australian, H-1B1 Chile and H-1B1 Singapore), which, after the relevant filter, only showed the entries for H-1B visa. So this step ensured that the H-1B FY2019.xlsx spreadsheet only had certified LCAs for H-1B visas for the United Nations as the client. Let's call this spreadsheet UN_FY_2019 (or the UN's 'FY 2019 LCA dataset').

- Then, I went to column T ('Employer_Name'), which had the list of third-party consultancies that had obtained certified LCAs for the United Nations. That number was 22 (also the number under the 'Third-Party Consultancies' for the United Nations table on p. 272).
- Then, to find out how many consultancies had paid back wages to their H-1B workers, I turned to the DOL's WHD dataset. (See *supra* note 31, Part II: Deception, WHD dataset, to find out how to use that dataset.) On the Back Wages column in the WHD dataset (column AG, 'h1b_bw_atp_amt'), I applied the filter Back Wages > 0.
- I then compared the names of the companies in the T column of the UN_FY_2019 spreadsheet with the companies paying back wages more than zero in the WHD dataset. Doing so gave me four companies: Compunnel Software Group, Hexaware Technologies, Infosys and Synaptein Solutions.

147. See *supra* note 38, Part VI: Secrets, to know the methodology behind calculating the back wages paid by third-party consultancies obtaining certified LCAs for a particular client. In that case, the client was USAA. Here, I repeated that process across five clients—Pfizer, Boeing, Chevron, State Farm and United Nations—and then totalled the back wages for all the third-party consultancies to arrive at the $6.54 million figure.
148. See Manu's patent applications here: https://patents.google.com/?inventor=Manu+Mitra.

149. 'Employment-Based Immigration: First Preference EB-1.' U.S. Citizenship and Immigration Services. 24 January 2025. https://www.uscis.gov/working-in-the-united-states/permanent-workers/employment-based-immigration-first-preference-eb-1.
150. Ibid.
151. Ibid.
152. 'Appi Reddy India Trip.' AndhraFriends. Tennisluvr. 30 December 2017. https://www.andhrafriends.com/topic/743618-appi-reddy-india-trip/page/4/#comment-1309259399.
153. 'Wow Ee Appi Reddy Keka Kada.' AndhraFriends. Nissan. 16 August 2016. https://www.andhrafriends.com/topic/687003-wow-ee-appi-reddy-keka-kada/page/2/#comment-1308344728.
154. Ibid. at Kalam_Youtheman. 16 August 2016. https://www.andhrafriends.com/topic/687003-wow-ee-appi-reddy-keka-kada/page/2/#comment-1308344729.
155. 'Budweiser Beer + 2 Pieces of Chicken Biryani + 15 People in Single Room Accomdation With No Job for Six Months = MICROINFO Consultancy ani DOL Twweted.' AndhraFriends. Lovemeagain. 23 January 2017. https://www.andhrafriends.com/topic/708867-budweiser-beer-2-pieces-of-chicken-biryani-15-people-in-single-room-accomdation-with-no-job-for-six-months-microinfo-consultancy-ani-dol-twweted/.
156. In July 2021, the Department of Labor again directed MicroInfo to pay back wages worth $72,413 to one H-1B worker for H-1B violations. The '$72,413' figure came from the DOL's WHD dataset. To find out how to access it, see *supra* note 31, Part II: Deception, WHD dataset.
157. 'Silicon Valley College, Called "Visa Mill", Shut Down With Millions Missing.' *San Francisco Chronicle*. Kathleen Pender and Nanette Asimov. 20 April 2018. https://www.sfchronicle.com/business/article/Silicon-Valley-college-called-visa-mill-12849677.php.
158. Countless AndhraFriends posts, spread over several years, alleged that Appi Reddy had massively profited from Silicon Valley University's graduates. See, for one instance, one such post: 'NavyaKanth-SVU is the Inspiration for the American Dream Movie'. AndhraFriends. RPG_Reloaded. 16 January 2022. https://www.andhrafriends.com/topic/934580-navyakanth-svu-is-the-inspiration-for-the-american-dream-movie/.

159. 'Http://www.appireddy.com/.' AndhraFriends. Basha786. 31 January 2019. https://www.andhrafriends.com/topic/789010-httpwww appireddycom/page/2/#comment-1310088673.
160. See *supra* note 31, Part II: Deception, WHD dataset to read about ObjectWin Technology's back wages.
161. See *supra* notes 5-16, Part VI: Secrets, for the methodology behind this table and how to create the FY 2019 LCA dataset for the Office of the Attorney General, Texas. See also p. 248 for the probabilities of an 'average' H-1B firm to be H-1B Dependent, paying back wages for H-1B violations and hiring a visa mill's graduate.
162. Nitco. MyVisaJobs. 22 October 2020. https://www.myvisajobs.com/Visa-Sponsor/Nitco/1094923_Review.htm/.
163. Mythri Consulting. MyVisaJobs. 29 March 2017. https://www.myvisajobs.com/Visa-Sponsor/Mythri-Consulting-LLC/1210282_Review.htm/.
164. Pioneer Global. MyVisaJobs. 1 September 2021. https://www.my visajobs.com/Visa-Sponsor/Pioneer-Global/1305868_Review.htm.
165. See *supra* notes 5-16, Part VI: Secrets, for the methodology behind this table and how to create the FY 2019 LCA dataset for the Texas Workforce Commission. See also p. 248 for the probabilities of an 'average' H-1B firm to be H-1B Dependent, paying back wages for H-1B violations and hiring a visa mill's graduate.
166. One firm in the Texas Workforce Commission's FY 2019 LCA dataset, Echelon IT, had different H-1B Dependent values ('Y' and 'N') across its LCAs. This analysis considered it 'N' for a conservative estimate.
167. In the same DOL investigation, GenuineIT paid a civil monetary penalty (CMP) of $1,000.
168. In the same DOL investigation, GenuineIT paid a CMP of $927.
169. GenuineIT. MyVisaJobs. 18 October 2012. https://www.myvisajobs.com/Visa-Sponsor/GENUINEIT-LLC/215391_Review.htm/.
170. Synergy Global Technologies. MyVisaJobs. 19 January 2015. https://www.myvisajobs.com/Visa-Sponsor/Synergy-Global-Technologies/644085_Review.htm/.
171. Paramount Software Solutions. MyVisaJobs. 17 May 2017. https://web.archive.org/web/20170526170004/https://www.myvisajobs.com/Visa-Sponsor/Paramount-Software-Solutions/412162_Review.htm/.

172. 'I Now Know for a Fact Why I Can't Get Hired at the Veterans Administration—H-1B.' Keep America At Work. 16 April 2015. https://web.archive.org/web/20150507214537/http://keepamericaatwork.com/i-now-know-for-a-fact-why-i-cant-get-hired-at-the-veterans-administration-h-1b/.
173. See *supra* notes 5-16, Part VI: Secrets, for the methodology behind this table and how to create the FY 2019 LCA dataset for the Department of Veterans Affairs. See also p. 248 for the probabilities of an 'average' H-1B firm to be H-1B Dependent, paying back wages for H-1B violations and hiring a visa mill's graduate.
174. Six certified LCAs in the Department of Veterans Affairs's FY 2019 LCA dataset didn't contain the prevailing wage levels. Those LCAs weren't included in this analysis.
175. The number of certified LCAs obtained by third-party consultancies in Texas for the Department of Veterans Affairs came from the steps below:
    - I first went to the DOL's Performance Data page at the link: https://www.dol.gov/agencies/eta/foreign-labor/performance.
    - On the Performance Data page, I went to the section named 'LCA Programs (H-1B, H-1B1, E-3)'. In that section, corresponding to Fiscal Year 2019 contained a file named 'H-1B FY2019.xlsx'. I downloaded that spreadsheet.
    - The list of American clients (or 'Secondary_Entity_Business_Name_1') was in the AU column of the H-1B FY2019.xlsx spreadsheet. I applied the relevant filter to that column, so it only showed the LCA entries for the Department of Veterans Affairs spread across different states. I then went to column B that showed the 'Case_Status' of different LCAs (whether Certified, Denied, Withdrawn or Certified-Withdrawn). I applied the relevant filter, so it only showed Certified LCAs for the VAs in different states. Ditto column F, showing 'Visa_Class' (H-1B, E-3 Australian, H-1B1 Chile and H-1B1 Singapore), which, after the relevant filter, only showed entries for H-1B visa. So this step ensured that the H-1B FY2019.xlsx spreadsheet only had certified LCAs for H-1B visas for the Department of Veterans Affairs in different states (or the Department of Veterans Affairs's 'FY 2019 LCA dataset'). This showed that fifty-six third-party

consultancies had gotten seventy-nine certified LCAs for the Department of Veterans Affairs in thirteen states.

- I then went to column AZ ('Worksite_State_1') and only selected the LCA entries corresponding to Texas. The number of certified LCAs corresponding to the VA in Texas as the end client was fifty-three.

Let's call this spreadsheet VA_Texas_FY2019.

176. On the spreadsheet VA_Texas_FY2019, I went to column AV ('Worksite_Address1_1'). In the AV column, I chose the LCA entries corresponding to 1615 Woodward Street, the address of the VA's IT Infrastructure Operations. That number was twenty-nine. (For a conservative estimate, I didn't include the LCAs corresponding to the address '1563 Woodward St'.)
177. To read more about the VA's IT Infrastructure Operations (ITIO) Business Service, see 'Franchise Fund Information Technology Segment'. U.S. Department of Veterans Affairs. 2 February 2023. https://www.va.gov/FUND/Information_Technology.asp.
178. The back wages for Sriven Systems Inc, $421,373, came from the DOL's WHD dataset. See *supra* note 31, Part II: Deception, WHD dataset, on how to access the dataset.
179. The back wages for the VA in Leavenworth, Kansas, $66,137, came from the DOL's WHD dataset. See *supra* note 31, Part II: Deception, WHD dataset, on how to access the dataset.
180. *USDOL v. Dallas VA Medical Center*. ARB Nos. 01-077 and 01-081, ALJ No. 98-LCA-3. 30 October 2003. https://www.oalj.dol.gov/PUBLIC/ARB/DECISIONS/ARB_DECISIONS/LCA/01_077.LCAP.PDF [hereinafter ARB, 'DOL-VA'].
181. Ibid.
182. Ibid.
183. Ibid.
184. The American Competitiveness in the 21st Century Act of 2000 made higher educational institutions, nonprofit research organisations and government research organisations exempt from the annual H-1B cap. It also made these three entities exempt from the usual prevailing wage determination applicable to most employers (which meant they could, in essence, set their own pay scales). So if the DVAMC technically qualified to be a 'government research organization', then it wasn't entitled to pay $17,842.18 to Dr Mirza Hassan.

185. See *supra* note 180, Part VI: Secrets, ARB, 'DOL-VA'.
186. *Talukdar and Virdee v. U.S. Dept. of Veterans Affairs, Fargo, North Dakota*. ARB No. 04-100, ALJ No. 02-LCA-25. 31 January 2007. https://www.oalj.dol.gov/PUBLIC/ARB/DECISIONS/ARB_DECISIONS/LCA/04_100.LCAP.PDF.
187. Ibid.
188. 'Payment of Back Wages to Alien Physicians Hired Under H-1B Visa Program.' Memorandum Opinion for the General Counsel, Department of Veterans Affairs and Solicitor, Department of Labor. Steven A. Engel, Deputy Assistant Attorney General Office of Legal Counsel. 11 February 2008. https://www.justice.gov/sites/default/files/olc/opinions/2008/02/31/payment-alien-physicians-h1b-visa.pdf.
189. Ibid.
190. Ibid.
191. Ibid.
192. Ibid.
193. See *supra* notes 5-16, Part VI: Secrets, for the methodology behind this table and how to create the FY 2019 LCA dataset for the Bureau of Labor Statistics. See also p. 248 for the probabilities of an 'average' H-1B firm to be H-1B Dependent, paying back wages for H-1B violations and hiring a visa mill's graduate.
194. The Bureau of Labor Statistics's contractors, too, had many awful reviews on MyVisaJobs. See a small sample here: Horizon Softech. MyVisaJobs. 9 October 2019. https://www.myvisajobs.com/Visa-Sponsor/Horizon-Softech/1111885_Review.htm/ (an anonymous commenter left a one star review, calling Horizon Softech the 'WORST Employer'); Strategic Resources International. MyVisaJobs. Naren. 5 September 2020. https://www.myvisajobs.com/Visa-Sponsor/Strategic-Resources-International/513624_Review.htm/ (a commenter called the company 'Cold Blooded' with 'Negligent Management'); RJT Compuquest. MyVisaJobs. 19 November 2015. https://www.myvisajobs.com/Visa-Sponsor/Rjt-Compuquest/443580_Review.htm/ (an anonymous commenter called the company 'the worst ... ever seen on earth. They are a big time liers and bassturds').

    But even the overall positive reviews of some desi consultancies didn't make them above suspicion. That was so because even positive reviews could be rigged on MyVisaJobs. H-1B workers knew that game and spoke about it. I sleuthed around more and found out the four main ways in which reviews could be manipulated on the website:

- Many H-1B workers accused the consultancies of fraudulent or coercive practices regarding MyVisaJobs reviews. A contractor of USAA, for instance, had the following review: 'The HR Manager from offshore making sales team to write good reviews with fake email account.' (Reliable Software Resources, Inc.) See Reliable Software Resources. MyVisaJobs. 4 May 2018. https://www.myvisajobs.com/employer/reliable-software-resources/#reviews.

  Ditto Horizon Softech: 'The owner forced others to write positive comments to cover up the first negative comment.' See Horizon Softech. MyVisaJobs. 9 October 2019. https://www.myvisajobs.com/employer/horizon-softech/#reviews.
- H-1B workers flagged another pattern. A review of a USAA contractor, SmartWorks, LLC, read: 'I strongly doubt the authenticity of the reviews ... some ... are given on the same day. Like the most recent have 2 reviews on the same day and the next 3 reviews etc. Moreover, they don't sound like reviews (looks more like an advertisement). I have neither worked with nor planning to work with Smartworks Llc just to show that I don't have anything against them. I just wanted to show that you can't fool people who are looking for jobs to review yourself and give a higher rating.' See SmartWorks. MyVisaJobs. 15 May 2014. https://www.myvisajobs.com/employer/smartworks/#reviews.

  A contractor of the *New York Times*, I2uSystems, had more than a dozen five-star reviews. Again, the same trick: the dates mattered. Seven reviews were posted in a span of less than two weeks. For another example of such manipulation, see Maganti IT Resources's MyVisaJobs review at *infra* note 201, Part VI: Secrets.
- Some reviews sounded suspicious because they praised the consultancies for doing the bare minimum. The positive reviews of I2uSystems, for example, highlighted this pattern: 'they have a good salary structure and they pay on time'; 'they pay you great and it is been credited to my account on the fixed date'. Besides, if H-1B workers were indeed the 'best and

the brightest', then why were these reviews talking about the following? 'They have good *training* facilities in all of the areas in IT'; 'we got *training* in Big Data for about 1 month and placed within two weeks after *training*' (all emphasis are mine). See I2U Systems. MyVisaJobs. https://www.myvisajobs.com/employer/i2usystems/#reviews.

- Finally, MyVisaJobs revamped its review section after 2023. Before that, it allowed employees to write reviews in the way they wanted. But the new change made writing the review optional and instead added two options—'Things I like [about the company]' and 'things I don't like [about the company]', with a list of twenty checkboxes for each provided by MyVisaJobs—making even negative reviews seem better than what they could have originally been.

A five star review of Horizon Softech, for instance, listed the following in the 'Things I don't like' section: 'Unsupportive or Toxic Management, Workplace Discrimination or Lack of Diversity, Low Salary Raises'. Besides, it had seven five-star reviews posted within a span of five days: five on 16 March 2023, out of which three reviews had the same text; and two on 20 March 2023. There was more: two five star reviews on 29 July 2014 and one five star review on 31 July 2014; one five star review on 30 November 2021 and another five star review on 1 December 2021. What was even worse? The five-star review on 31 July 2014 was an *exact* match with another five-star review posted on 16 March 2023, right down to random capitalisations and grammatical mistakes: 'I have been with them over couple of years with them now. The recruiters (Especially the Owner of the Company) I worked with were friendly, listened to what I was looking for, and really matched my skill set with positions that I could apply my skills to as well as learn from ...'

Which is why Horizon Softech's MyVisaJobs rating, 4.2/5, painted a less flattering picture of the company than it should have otherwise done.

195. See *supra* notes 5-16, Part VI: Secrets, for the methodology behind this table and how to create the FY 2019 LCA dataset for the U.S. Department of Labor. See also p. 248 for the probabilities of an

'average' H-1B firm to be H-1B Dependent, paying back wages for H-1B violations and hiring a visa mill's graduate.

196. Eight certified LCAs with the correct addresses—'200 Constitution Avenue NW', 'Patriots Plaza II' and '375 E Street SW' in Washington, DC—didn't mention the client's name. Those LCAs have been included in this analysis.
197. Three certified LCAs with the correct address—'200 Constitution Avenue NW'—didn't list the number of workers. Those LCAs have not been included in the number of H-1Bs.
198. One certified LCA in the DOL's FY 2019 LCA dataset didn't contain the prevailing wage level. That LCA wasn't included in this analysis.
199. The 'thirty-eighth' rank for I Q Systems came from the DOL's WHD dataset. See *supra* note 31, Part II: Deception, WHD dataset, on how to access the dataset.
200. International Software Systems. MyVisaJobs. 7 March 2013. https://www.myvisajobs.com/Visa-Sponsor/International-Software-Systems/271170_Review.htm.
201. This review of Maganti IT Resources appeared on 12 June 2012. After that, a flurry of positive reviews inundated its MyVisaJobs page (several around the same dates). See Maganti IT Resources. MyVisaJobs. 12 June 2012. https://www.myvisajobs.com/Visa-Sponsor/Maganti-Resources/851730_Review.htm.
202. 22nd Century Technologies. MyVisaJobs. 18 March 2010. https://web.archive.org/web/20101210050946/https://www.myvisajobs.com/Visa-Sponsor/22nd-Century-Technologies/1549_Review.htm.
203. 'Employment and Training Administration Prevailing Wage Determination Policy Guidance.' U.S. Department of Labor. November 2009. https://www.dol.gov/sites/dolgov/files/ETA/oflc/pdfs/NPWHC_Guidance_Revised_11_2009.pdf (p. 7).
204. 'Guest Workers Toil ... at the Labor Department?' *Politico*. Brian Mahoney. 11 March 2016. https://www.politico.com/story/2016/03/guest-workers-employed-at-labor-department-headquarters-220647/.
205. Ibid. 'The BLS, which is housed within the Labor Department, may also be making use of the program,' noted the *Politico* piece. '[Geoff] Rhodes [who crunched the DOL LCA data] says there were at least 13 LCAs for visas there. Rhodes's data also show that companies have sought visas for workers at the U.S. Patent and Trademark

Office, Securities and Exchange Commission, the Department of Transportation, the Department of Agriculture and the U.S. courts.'

206. 'What Federal Office is Located at 200 Constitution Ave. in Washington?' White-Collar Workers of America's Facebook page. Patrick Thibodeau. 24 April 2017. https://www.facebook.com/groups/HireAmerican/posts/1627852417255521/.
207. See *supra* note 53, Part II: Deception, The Guardian, 'Job Brokers Steal Wages'.
208. Ibid.
209. Ibid.
210. The back wages for EcomNets, $92,302, came from the DOL's WHD dataset. See *supra* note 31, Part II: Deception, WHD dataset, on how to access the dataset. After the joint investigation by the DOL, Homeland Security and the Diplomatic Security Service—which resulted in EcomNets's owner, Raju Kosuri, pleading guilty to visa fraud—EcomNets shut down.
211. See the details of the contracts awarded by the DOL to EcomNets here: https://www.usaspending.gov/search?hash=ef5e01dc5dee86e1d83167d78dbe0f34.
212. Ibid.
213. 'Couple Indicted for $20 Million Visa Fraud Scheme Involving Indian Workers.' U.S. Immigration and Customs Enforcement. 27 April 2016. https://www.ice.gov/news/releases/couple-indicted-20-million-visa-fraud-scheme-involving-indian-workers.
214. 'Couple Pleads Guilty to $20 Million Visa Fraud Involving Indian Workers.' United States Attorney's Office Eastern District of Virginia. 25 August 2016. https://www.justice.gov/usao-edva/pr/couple-pleads-guilty-20-million-visa-fraud-involving-indian-workers.
215. 'Watch This Indian Techie With a H1B Visa Say Goodbye to the US After Not Being Paid for his Work.' *Scroll*. 2 July 2018. https://scroll.in/video/884842/watch-this-indian-techie-with-a-h1b-visa-say-goodbye-to-the-us-after-not-being-paid-for-his-work/.
216. *Andhra Jyothi* published that piece on 3 July 2018. See Kumar's response to it here: 'Telugu Video: #ABN, #AndhraJyothi … Fake News'. Kumar Exclusive. 2 November 2020. https://www.youtube.com/watch?v=KtRfvTu6Q8w/. (In this video, the article on the screen is the one published by *Andhra Jyothi*.)

217. 'Trump Leaves H-4 Visa Work Permit Dangle Again | H1B Workers Spouse Life at Crossroads.' NTV Telugu. 4 July 2018. https://www.youtube.com/watch?v=FewKFvZ-AwE/.
218. 'Victims: KE Helping Indian Victims.' Kumar Exclusive. 16 November 2018. https://www.youtube.com/watch?v=gNryjMbNttY.
219. See *supra* notes 5-16, Part VI: Secrets, for the methodology behind this table and how to create the FY 2019 LCA dataset for the Library of Congress. See also p. 248 for the probabilities of an 'average' H-1B firm to be H-1B Dependent, paying back wages for H-1B violations and hiring a visa mill's graduate.
220. A certified LCA with the client name 'Liberty of Congress', though with the correct address ('101 Independence Ave SE, Washington, DC'), was included in this analysis.
221. Code Ace Solutions. MyVisaJobs. https://www.myvisajobs.com/Visa-Sponsor/Code-Ace-Solutions/1181167_Review.htm/.
222. See *supra* notes 5-16, Part VI: Secrets, for the methodology behind this table and how to create the FY 2019 LCA dataset for the House of Representatives. See also p. 248 for the probabilities of an 'average' H-1B firm to be H-1B Dependent, paying back wages for H-1B violations and hiring a visa mill's graduate.
223. See *supra* notes 5-16, Part VI: Secrets, for the methodology behind this table and how to create the FY 2019 LCA dataset for the U.S. Senate. See also p. 248 for the probabilities of an 'average' H-1B firm to be H-1B Dependent, paying back wages for H-1B violations and hiring a visa mill's graduate.
224. See 'Marco Rubio's Claim That it's "Illegal" to Replace American Workers Using H-1B Visas'. *The Washington Post.* Michelle Lee. 17 March 2016. https://www.washingtonpost.com/news/fact-checker/wp/2016/03/17/marco-rubios-claim-that-its-illegal-to-replace-american-workers-using-h-1b-visas/; 'Fired Disney Workers Support Trump, Slam H-1B Visa Programme.' *The Economic Times.* 1 March 2016. https://economictimes.indiatimes.com/nri/visa-and-immigration/fired-disney-workers-support-trump-slam-h-1b-visa-programme/articleshow/51204577.cms?from=mdr.
225. See *supra* notes 5-16, Part VI: Secrets, for the methodology behind this table and how to create the FY 2019 LCA dataset for the Florida Senate. See also p. 248 for the probabilities of an 'average' H-1B firm

to be H-1B Dependent, paying back wages for H-1B violations and hiring a visa mill's graduate.

226. Shubh Solutions. MyVisaJobs. https://www.myvisajobs.com/Visa-Sponsor/Shubh-Solutions/487924_Review.htm/.
227. Ibid., 12 April 2010.
228. Ibid., 25 September 2009.
229. Ibid., 4 May 2013.
230. System Soft Technologies. MyVisaJobs. 19 May 2011. https://www.myvisajobs.com/Visa-Sponsor/System-Soft-Technologies/523762_Review.htm/.

PART VII: ACCEPTANCE

1. In October 2022, the Telangana Rashtra Samiti changed its name to Bharat Rashtra Samiti. See 'Telangana Rashtra Samiti renames itself to Bharat Rashtra Samiti'. *The Hindu.* 5 October 2022. https://www.thehindu.com/news/national/telangana/trs-renames-itself-to-bharat-rashtra-samiti-forays-into-national-politics/article65971610.ece.
2. 'Appi Reddy Back With Back Fire...' AndhraFriends. Tennisluvr. 2 October 2018. https://www.andhrafriends.com/topic/773836-appi-reddy-back-with-back-fire/page/2/#comment-1309826965.
3. Ibid. at Tom Bhayya. 2 October 2018. https://www.andhrafriends.com/topic/773836-appi-reddy-back-with-back-fire/#comment-1309826808.
4. Ibid. at Boeing747. 2 October 2018. https://www.andhrafriends.com/topic/773836-appi-reddy-back-with-back-fire/#comment-1309826857.
5. Ibid. at Solman. 2 October 2018. https://www.andhrafriends.com/topic/773836-appi-reddy-back-with-back-fire/#comment-1309826697.
6. 'Assembly Elections: TRS Gears up to Go With Full Force Against Congress.' *Deccan Chronicle.* L. Venkat Ram Reddy. 29 October 2018. https://web.archive.org/web/20181115211945/https://www.deccanchronicle.com/nation/current-affairs/291018/trs-gears-up-to-go-with-full-force-against-congress.html/.
7. 'Ex-BRS Leader Shanampudi Saidireddy, BJP Candidate From Nalgonda Constituency.' *Timeline.* 20 April 2024. https://timelinedaily.com/elections/ex-brs-leader-shanampudi-saidireddy-bjp-candidate-from-nalgonda-constituency.

8. 'I Was Mentally Harassed by This US Citizen || US Resident Who Harasses Indians, Chinese, Iranians.' Yash Mittra—YMGrad. 27 February 2020. https://www.youtube.com/watch?v=eeAexxbWzDw.
9. American Workers Coalition [@AmWorkCo]. 26 October 2019. https://x.com/AmWorkCo/status/1187807013893484544.
10. 'New Head of US Homeland Security is Ex-Lobbyist of Indian Trade Body Nasscom.' *Hindustan Times*. Yashwant Raj. 15 November 2019. https://www.hindustantimes.com/world-news/new-head-of-us-homeland-security-is-ex-lobbyist-of-indian-trade-body-nasscom/story-BHiCEs31t1HJZmpgIweE9I.html.
11. 'Economist Stephen Moore Talks Infrastructure With Dan & Amy.' *Chicago's Morning Answer*. 17 June 2020. https://www.youtube.com/watch?v=L4FKEUVBgWU.
12. 'TVA Cutting 120 Jobs in IT as it Outsources Software Work; Chattanooga Employees to be Hit Hardest.' *Chattanooga Times Free Press*. Dave Flessner. 28 January 2020. http://web.archive.org/web/20231202194019/https://www.timesfreepress.com/news/2020/jan/28/tvcuts-120-jobs-it-it-outsources-software-wor/.
13. See 'Trump Dismisses 2 T.V.A. Board Members After Outsourcing Dispute'. *The New York Times*. Michael Shear. 3 August 2020. https://www.nytimes.com/2020/08/03/us/politics/trump-tennessee-valley-authority.html; 'Trump Fires Tennessee Valley Authority Chair Over Compensation, Outsourcing.' *NBC News*. 3 August 2020. https://www.nbcnews.com/politics/white-house/trump-takes-disciplinary-action-against-tva-leadership-n1235653.
14. 'Strengthening Wage Protections for the Temporary and Permanent Employment of Certain Aliens in the United States.' *Federal Register*. 8 October 2020. https://www.federalregister.gov/documents/2020/10/08/2020-22132/strengthening-wage-protections-for-the-temporary-and-permanent-employment-of-certain-aliens-in-the/.
15. 'Trump Administration Makes Major H-1B Reform.' Upon Closer Inspection. Norman Matloff. 10 October 2020. https://normsaysno.wordpress.com/2020/10/10/trump-administration-makes-major-h-1b-reform/.
16. Ibid.
17. Ibid.

18. *ITServe Alliance, Inc. et al v. Scalia et al.* United States District Court, District of New Jersey. 3 December 2020. https://www.documentcloud.org/documents/24563988-itserve-all-inc-v-scalia.
19. Ibid.
20. Ibid.
21. Ibid.
22. *ITServe Alliance, Inc. et al v. Scalia et al.* United States District Court, District of New Jersey. 3 December 2020. https://www.govinfo.gov/content/pkg/USCOURTS-njd-2_20-cv-14604/pdf/USCOURTS-njd-2_20-cv-14604-0.pdf.
23. 'USCIS Changes Website, Backtracks on Foreign Student Rules.' *Forbes*. Stuart Anderson. 20 August 2018. https://www.forbes.com/sites/stuartanderson/2018/08/20/uscis-changes-website-backtracks-on-foreign-student-rules/?sh=151082e84aa4/.
24. 'Determining Employer-Employee Relationship for Adjudication of H-1B Petitions, Including Third-Party Site Placements.' Memorandum From Donald Neufeld to Service Center Directors. 8 January 2010. https://assets.aila.org/files/27708198-f9ec-407d-888c-e7bf8e04c07c/10011363.pdf?1697590761.
25. 'USCIS-ITServe Settlement Overturns 10 Years of H-1B Visa Policies.' *Forbes*. Stuart Anderson. 21 May 2020. https://www.forbes.com/sites/stuartanderson/2020/05/21/uscis-itserve-settlement-overturns-10-years-of-h-1b-visa-policies/?sh=3e0475de5bf4/.
26. *ITServe Alliance, INC. v. United States Citizenship and Immigration Services*. United States District Court, District of Columbia. 10 March 2020. https://law.justia.com/cases/federal/district-courts/district-of-columbia/dcdce/1:2018cv02350/200810/24/.

    See also 'Court Invalidates Key Trump Administration H-1B Visa Policies'. *Forbes*. Stuart Anderson. 11 March 2020. https://www.forbes.com/sites/stuartanderson/2020/03/11/court-invalidates-key-trump-administration-h-1b-visa-policies/?sh=7c779b831f52/.
27. 'Rescission of Policy Memoranda.' U.S. Citizenship and Immigration Services. 17 June 2020. https://www.uscis.gov/sites/default/files/document/memos/PM-602-0114_ITServeMemo.pdf.
28. 'IT Serve Full Details, Find in Below Links. This is After Long Hard Work and Research!' AndhraFriends. Rusky. 19 July 2016. https://www.andhrafriends.com/topic/682885-it-serve-full-details-find-in-

below-links-this-is-after-long-hard-work-and-research/. The videos in *infra* notes 29-32, Part VII: Acceptance and 35, Part VII: Acceptance have been taken from this link, with their original titles.

29. 'Mr. Sudhakar Peram, IT Serve Describing the Services of ITServe at the Meeting.' https://www.youtube.com/watch?v=4fVNdYTRMX8.
30. 'IT Bigwigs Conference in Dallas a Roaring success—USA—TV9.' https://www.youtube.com/watch?v=QwBnKN3Pwg4.
31. 'How I140EAD Was Watered Down … Made Pres Obama EO Useless.' https://www.youtube.com/watch?v=Jqh-76ZyN9Y.
32. See 'Immigration Updates Rahul Reddy at ITServe June 2016 Monthly Meeting'. https://www.youtube.com/watch?v=1so_UadHjPM&t=1s; 'Rahul Reddy, Attorney Speaking in Monthly Meeting in Sep in Dallas'. https://www.youtube.com/watch?v=n7yvWWa94es.
33. ITServe Alliance no longer publishes the list of its member companies—you need to be a member to see it. But it once did, before AndhraFriends folks released over a dozen videos and the names of its member companies by accessing a snapshot of the member directory's page on 5 July 2016. See that page here: https://www.documentcloud.org/documents/24253431-itserve_member_directory_texthtm.

    That list contains the names of 455 companies. After removing the duplicate names, the list produces 452 unique firms, the number in chapter 61. See also ITServe Alliance member directory's page through Internet Wayback Machine (dated 10 June 2016), which has 438 companies: https://web.archive.org/web/20160608083720/http://itserve.org/memberdirectory.
34. ITServe Alliance's member companies increased to around 2,000 by late 2020. See 'ITServe Alliance—About Us'. https://itserve.org/about-us/.
35. Watch the rest of the ITServe Alliance videos, released online by AndhraFriends members (with their original titles), here: 'USA IT Frauds Trying to Stop GC 140 EAD'. https://www.youtube.com/watch?v=HgIRUxZFv54; 'Sheela_Murthy_ITServe.' https://www.youtube.com/watch?v=g7GGxKKs1yw; 'Immigration Updates Rahul Reddy at ITServe June 2016 Monthly Meeting.' https://www.youtube.com/watch?v=1so_UadHjPM&t=1s; 'IT Serve Alliance Grand Kickoff Meeting in Detroit.' https://www.youtube.com/watch?v=TBTyFNRLo3E; 'Part 1 _ Immigration Seminar @ University

of Arlington.' https://www.youtube.com/watch?v=1oT0aeMklU0; 'Part 4 _ Immigration Seminar @ University of Arlington.' https://www.youtube.com/watch?v=KyOSUhRkxnI&t=2s; 'Q&A With Sheela Murthy.' https://www.youtube.com/watch?v=Quz5an2MCiM; 'Attny 1-1.' https://www.youtube.com/watch?v=6PL7E1xaE58.

36. DOLINW.com. June 2020. https://web.archive.org/web/20200621050104/https://dolinw.com/.
37. GlobalWorkersUnited.com. November 2020. https://web.archive.org/web/20201128002225/https://www.globalworkersunited.com/.
38. VJBTrading.com. December 2020. https://web.archive.org/web/20201214153233/http://vjbtrading.com/.
39. DestroyingYourFuture.com. March 2021. https://web.archive.org/web/20210302080455/https://destroyingyourfuture.com/.
40. 'Administrative Investigation Improper Access to the VA Network by VA Contractors From Foreign Countries.' Office of Information and Technology, Austin, TX. Department of Veterans Affairs—Office of Inspector General. 13 April 2015. https://www.documentcloud.org/documents/24563984-the-va-report-april-2015.
41. Ibid.
42. Ibid.
43. The back wages for Zen Infotech, $470,043, and the fact that it was the twenty-sixth highest amount in the history of DOL investigations came from the DOL's WHD dataset. See *supra* note 31, Part II: Deception, WHD dataset, on how to access the dataset.
44. *USA v. Gudaru*. United States District Court, District of Kansas. 18 April 2014. https://www.courtlistener.com/docket/6120631/united-states-v-gudaru/.
45. 'Semiannual Report to Congress.' Office of Inspector General for the U.S. Department of Labor. 2014. https://www.oig.dol.gov/public/semiannuals/72.pdf (p. 12).

EPILOGUE

1. 'Support Kumar's Fight Against Legal Threats.' GoFundMe. 7 March 2025. https://www.gofundme.com/f/support-kumars-fight-against-legal-threats.

2. 'Elon Musk Vows to "Go to War" to Defend H-1B Visa Programme; Trump Sides with Him.' *The Hindu.* 29 December 2024. https://www.thehindu.com/news/international/elon-musk-vows-to-go-to-war-to-defend-h-1b-visa-programme-trump-sides-with-him/article69039563.ece.
3. '"This Will Devastate the Economy of India": Republican Leader's Dire Warning Amid H-1B Row.' *The Times of India.* 30 May 2025. https://timesofindia.indiatimes.com/world/us/this-will-devastate-the-economy-of-india-republican-leaders-dire-warning-amid-h-1b-row/articleshow/121445998.cms.

Author's Note

I could never meet Virgil, Kumar or Manu, as much as I wished or tried. First, the visa restrictions, then the lockdown. Still, *Wild Wild East* remains a work of pure narrative non-fiction. It contains no composite characters, no fabricated scenes, no altered timelines—or any other fictional element. The texts in quotes come from emails, interviews, videos, lawsuit complaints, Congressional hearings, blog posts, immigration forums, newspaper articles, magazine pieces, research papers, books, websites, newsletters and Freedom of Information Act requests. To create a novelistic narrative, I read more than a million emails of my protagonists, watched thousands of their videos and interviewed them for five years.

Since they worked in the same industry they sought to expose, they requested me to change the names of some firms and individuals. But they also volunteered proof—such as emails, videos, photos, chats, documents and audio files—to back their accounts. Recognising the fallibility of memory, I asked them the same questions about the same events at different points to verify their versions' consistency.

Investigating the H-1B programme over the last nine years has both thrilled and disoriented me. Because my reporting and research almost always contradicted the American and Indian media. If the liberal outlets deified H-1B workers, then the right-wing ones demonised them. The actual story, as this book reveals, is much more layered and nuanced.

We crave convenient facts that echo our ideologies. It's simple; it's comforting. The H-1B programme, however, doesn't play as straight, not even close. Trump 2.0 and other right-wing regimes have also sullied any sincere discussions about immigration. Yet fair reporting—fixated on unearthing a story, not creating it—challenges both charitable and bigoted preconceptions, unveiling varied truths. Journalism is fact-facing, not wish-making. As an H-1B worker, I had discovered a mind-bending reality, so I relayed it raw. Because if I didn't disclose the whole story, then someone else would, and I would be helpless about possible distortions and deceits.

The batty H-1B world also aligns two divergent views. Yes, many entities have abused the guest worker programme, including H-1Bs themselves; and no, Trump's draconian measures, meant to isolate and humiliate them, won't resolve anything. True to his wont, he's using brawn, not brain. A systemic problem demands a systemic overhaul. If he can reform the prevailing wage rule to ensure that no H-1B worker earns less than the local median salary, then that alone would snuff countless scams.

My book has no xenophobic bone. I only intended to probe a hidden ecosystem to spotlight the human condition, the Indian condition. My own life, in fact, should make me defend the H-1B programme. My elder brother, a doctor, is an H-1B worker—so are my relatives and friends. True empathy, though, transcends tribes: my heart beats for both honest H-1Bs and displaced Americans, with no confusion or contradiction.

Even though Virgil, Kumar and Manu propel *Wild Wild East*, they don't represent anyone—or anything. Virgil is not a stand-in for all American techies; Manu and Kumar don't encapsulate all H-1B workers. They're themselves: frustrated, defiant, flawed. I felt honoured to earn their trust, but I never wanted to write their hagiographies. While interviewing them, or reading their emails, I sometimes disagreed with them. That didn't bother me because their motivations intrigued me more. So I removed the authorial scaffoldings to 'support' them. As complex and intense individuals, they could stand on their own, gaining in prose what they had lost in life: freedom. They aren't 'perfect victims' either. Think of their journeys as a trauma response. Who has always been rational while tackling something traumatic for decades?

The H-1B scam is so cruel that it doesn't just ravage lives but also slaps the 'racist' tag on anyone criticising it. It works both ways: keep blaming the immigrants, so you won't question the corporations. That's how the elites have won. In such a mad, mad world, though, I was lucky to find three people who fought with all their might and heart. One day, I'll tell them how their lives perturbed me, moved me, transformed me. But even more, I wish Virgil and Kumar meet someday: two individuals primed to be enemies by the neoliberal establishment who, squashing all its propaganda, found in each other nothing but compassion and love.

Tanul Thakur
22 August 2025

Acknowledgments

Kumar, Manu and Virgil for their courage, candour and fight. Knowing them over the last eight years has been more than a pleasure and an honour; it's felt like coming home. Because in each one of them I saw qualities that I once cherished but, over time, risked losing: innocence, honesty and grit.

Ajitha G.S., my editor, for believing in the idea; for making me a better writer; for enduring my jokes, pretensions and tantrums. Karthika V.K., my publisher, for her encouragement and generosity when the book needed it the most. Pallavi Mohan, at Westland, for her meticulous copy-editing and legal vetting. This was a tricky book to typeset, but Jojy Philip, diligent and brilliant, did a superb job.

Lauren Shapiro's legal edits—incisive, thorough and exacting (sometimes too exacting!)—made the book not only more accurate but also more honest.

Vikas Thakur created a memorable illustration for the cover, encapsulating the book's stories and themes in a bullet-like image.

This project sprawled in so many directions, sneaking into several unfamiliar realms, that I literally needed a village to finish it. Najeeb Mohammed and Ramya Maddali's Telugu-to-English translations helped complete a major part of the story; Ashutosh Anand and Aarohan Pratap Singh's legal research added a new dimension to the reporting; and Yash Kumar's data science magic saved me weeks, if not months, of work.

N. Kalyan Raman has been, in the truest sense, a friend of the book. He read an early draft, understood its intent and gave nuanced tips on how to improve it. I was also lucky to find other kind readers whose remarkable editorial feedback made me see the manuscript in a new light: Amitabha Bagchi, Arjit Sharma, M.S. Sriram, Richa Nigam, Srinivasan Murali and Tanuj Solanki.

I'm grateful to McKenzie Funk, at the excellent South Asia Speaks fellowship, for his journalistic brilliance and Yoda-like mentorship; Chetkar Jha and R. Davis for their statistical ingenuity; and Ron Hira and John Miano for their insights on the H-1B programme.

Over a decade ago, Anand Kadam encouraged an engineer to become a writer. I'll never ever forget his support and trust. Nothing saddens me more to know that I can't gift the book to him, as he passed away—way too early—last year.

Unlike many Indian fathers, my old man, Binod Kumar Thakur, allowed me to breathe and dream. I could not have done this without him.

Finally, Isha Sharma, for everything. My best friend, my oasis, my cheat code. I feel about her the same way a reporter feels about his subject: without you there is no me.

Index